MW00782650

Procreation, Parenthood, and Educational Rights

This volume explores important issues at the nexus of two burgeoning areas within moral and social philosophy: procreative ethics and parental rights. Surprisingly, there has been comparatively little scholarly engagement across these subdisciplinary boundaries, despite the fact that parental rights are paradigmatically ascribed to individuals responsible for procreating particular children. This collection thus brings expert scholars from these literatures into fruitful and innovative dialogue around questions at the intersection of procreation and parenthood. Among these questions are: Must individuals be found competent in order to have the right to procreate or to parent? What, if anything, can justify parents' special authority over, or special obligations toward, their children, particularly children they biologically procreate? How is the relationship between the right to procreate and the right to parent best understood? How ought liberal societies understand the parent–child relationship and the rights and claims it gives rise to? A distinguishing feature of the collection is that several of its chapters address these issues by drawing on philosophical work in the realm of education, one of the most controversial areas in the ethics of parenthood. This book represents a distinctive synthesis of topics and literatures likely to appeal to scholars and advanced students working across a wide range of disciplines.

Jaime Ahlberg is an Assistant Professor of Philosophy at the University of Florida. Her main areas of interest are ethics and political philosophy, with emphases in bioethics, education, and feminism. Recent publications include "Educational Justice for Students with Cognitive Disabilities" in *Social Philosophy & Policy* and "An Argument Against Cloning" (with Harry Brighouse) in *Canadian Journal of Philosophy*.

Michael Cholbi is Professor of Philosophy at California State Polytechnic University, Pomona. He has published widely in theoretical and practical ethics. His most recent work addresses paternalism, grief, and the ethics of suicide. His books include *Suicide: The Philosophical Dimensions* (2011) and *Understanding Kant's Ethics* (2016).

Routledge Research in Applied Ethics

Procreation, Parenthood, and Educational Rights

Ethical and Philosophical Issues

Edited by Jaime Ahlberg and
Michael Chobli

Routledge
Taylor & Francis Group

NEW YORK AND LONDON

First published 2017
by Routledge
711 Third Avenue, New York, NY 10017

and by Routledge
2 Park Square, Milton Park, Abingdon, Oxon OX14 4RN

Routledge is an imprint of the Taylor & Francis Group, an informa business

© 2017 Taylor & Francis

Library of Congress Cataloging in Publication Data
Names: Ahlberg, Jaime, editor.
Title: Procreation, parenthood, and educational rights : ethical and
    philosophical issues / edited by Jaime Ahlberg and Michael Chobli.
Description: 1 [edition]. | New York : Routledge, 2016. | Series:
    Routledge research in applied ethics ; 3 | Includes bibliographical
    references and index.
Identifiers: LCCN 2016038392 | ISBN 9781138206229 (hardback :
    alk. paper)
Subjects: LCSH: Family planning—Moral and ethical aspects. |
    Parenthood—Moral and ethical aspects. | Education—Moral
    and ethical aspects.
Classification: LCC HQ766.15 .P76 2016 | DDC 363.9/6—dc23
LC record available at https://lccn.loc.gov/2016038392

ISBN: 978-1-138-20622-9 (hbk)
ISBN: 978-1-315-46553-1 (ebk)

Typeset in Sabon
by Apex CoVantage, LLC

Contents

Introduction

Jaime Ahlberg and Michael Cholbi

Historically, the vast majority of human societies have been strongly 'pro-natalist.' These societies socially validate and materially incentivize biological reproduction, while their legal systems accord procreation the status of a basic right, a liberty that authorities could only infringe or deny under very limited circumstances. Such societies have by and large taken procreation to raise few, if any, ethical challenges. In recent decades, however, several sociological undercurrents have begun to exert pressure on this pro-natalist consensus. For one, procreation is less 'natural' than in the past, inasmuch as birth control measures and artificial reproductive technologies enable far greater control over the circumstances of pregnancy and procreation. Moreover, threats to the natural environment and to natural resources have raised concerns about the planet's ability to absorb additional human beings. And as the societal roles of women have changed, the assumption that women do or should prioritize childbearing and motherhood over other goods is less widespread.

Academic philosophers have also begun to subject procreation to greater scrutiny, resulting in a now lively literature on *procreative ethics*. The central questions within this field include whether procreation is a right; whether procreation ever harms children; whether prospective parents may aim at creating children with specific characteristics; whether procreation is permissible only within the context of a certain kind of relationship; the conditions under which the use of alternative reproductive technologies such as surrogacy, gamete donation, pre-implantation genetic diagnosis, etc., are morally justified; etc. A diverse range of views are represented within this literature. Some procreative ethicists affirm a largely pro-natalist position, holding that reproduction is a basic moral right on the part of would-be parents the pursuit of which should be subject to few if any limitations. Conversely, this literature also contains *anti*-natalist voices, who maintain that procreation is a serious wrong or harm to children (or to others) and should thereby be avoided or discouraged. Between these lie a range of moderate, or qualified positions: that only some instances of procreation (knowingly bringing into existence a child with disadvantageous traits, for instance) are wrong, that procreation beyond one child is morally impermissible; etc.

Simultaneous to the emergence of procreative ethics has been a growth in interest in the ethics of parenthood, and in particular, in the nature and extent of *parental rights*. To become another person's parent is to undergo a significant moral, political, and legal transformation. For parenthood is a relationship defined in no small measure by the rights (and obligations) that a parent has toward their child. Some of these rights correspond to children's needs. Children need nutrition, shelter, and the like, and parents are presumed to have the right to act so as to meet such needs. Other parental rights seem grounded at least in part in parental interests. Legally and socially, parents are accorded a broad liberty to establish intimate relations with their children and to shape their children's attitudes and character. While the exercise of such liberty may benefit children, its rationale seems in part to be that parents have reasons to want such relations with, or authority over, their children.

This rough sketch of parental rights nevertheless obscures several ethical questions about such rights. One such question is how to justify the apparent *particularity* of such rights: An individual with a parental right to do X with respect to a particular child can rightfully preclude others doing X with respect to that child. But why should parents alone have these rights? Parents have an interest in their children and their welfare, but so too (arguably) do other individuals and the community at large. In virtue of what facts, then does a person (or set of persons) come to have such rights over a particular child? One possibility is that the particularity of parental rights stems from the particularity of procreation: Adoption excepted, only a child's parents are responsible for its existence, either through their own procreative activities. But why should such *biological* facts be the basis for the various *moral* claims and relations that ground parental rights? Whatever the general normative rationale for parents enjoying the particular rights they have with respect to their own children (parents' interests, children's interests, etc.), the relationship between this rationale and the procreative facts that actually generate particular parental rights claims is not transparent. Indeed, the introduction of new reproductive technologies helps to reveal the opacity of this relationship. For example, legal and social controversy has arisen in cases in which many more than two persons have a biological connection with one child, and in which different procreative parties wish to claim exclusive parental rights.

A second question raised about this sketch of parental rights concerns the content and scope of parental rights. Such rights must at the very least be constrained in some way by the rights of children themselves, including their basic rights to healthcare, education, and a non-abusive environment. But some go further to argue that, since parental rights are themselves only made possible by the fiduciary responsibilities parents have to their children, their content is circumscribed by the interests of children. Of course, there is a diverse range of the positions articulating the way and extent to which children's interests ought to constrain parental freedom in child-rearing. One arena in which the tensions between parents' and children's rights run deep is education. Children have a right to be educated. From the standpoint of children and the overall trajectory of their lives, they benefit from an education that provides them various goods: basic literacy and numeracy; vocational skills; socialization into group norms; cultural, historical, and esthetic literacy; and more broadly, personal autonomy, decision-making capacity, and a sense of self. Clearly, children's interests in these goods can collide with presumed parental rights and interests. A parent whose religious faith maintains that women are suited only for roles as mothers and homemakers may contend that her interest in raising a child in that faith should take precedence over any putative interest the child may have in being educated so as to question the tenets of that faith. A parent with strong patriotic sentiments may argue that parents' right to raise children whose values mirror their own should permit her to remove her children from public school activities that question those sentiments. Such examples make vivid the difficulty of circumscribing the boundaries of parental discretion in providing educational goods. At what point do parents' shaping of their children's lives begin to threaten children's' well-being and autonomy-related interests? What do parents gain from the experiences of sharing their values, passions, and general orientation to the world with their children, and should those experiences be accorded moral weight? Because education is a central tool of social formation, conflicts between parental rights and children's rights are especially acute in the educational domain. Add to this (again) the apparent interest communities have in the education of their future members, and the potential for conflicting claims regarding the proper aims of education grows larger still.

To date, contact between procreative ethics and the ethics of parenthood has been sporadic (with questions relating to educational rights in particular receiving sparse attention). This is surprising, inasmuch there may well be logical and justificatory relations, admittedly very complex, between claims about the morality of procreation and about parental rights. As we have noted, parental rights are paradigmatically acquired via procreation. This suggests that parental rights may well turn on procreative facts. An obvious example is procreation resulting from nonconsensual sexual activity. An individual who compels another to engage in sex acts that result in conception may not have the same parental rights with the child so conceived (including rights to shape the child's education and upbringing) that an individual who engages in consensual sex would have. (Of course, in the former case, the individual may still have many of the same obligations with respect to that child.) Conversely, moral claims about procreation may well be predicated upon what rights parents are presumed to have over shaping their children's lives. Consider, for instance, the desire of some deaf parents to use genetic selection technologies to identify and gestate embryos predisposed to deafness. These parents may claim they have a right to procreate so as to parent children who will participate in, and thereby serve to perpetuate, their Deaf culture. But note that if parental rights do not include the right to fashion children with the attributes necessary to participate in or perpetuate their parents' culture, especially if those attributes may otherwise be detrimental to children's overall welfare, then that implies a *pro tanto* rejection of genetic selection technologies for such procreative purposes.

These are merely two examples of ways in which procreative acts and parental rights interact conceptually and morally. The essays collected in this volume explore that terrain even further. A central aim of this volume is thus to invite engagement with, and between, philosophers working in procreative ethics and philosophers working on the ethics of parenthood (especially parental rights regarding education) in the hope of illuminating issues that reside at the nexus of these two bodies of inquiry. The distinguished international roster of scholars whose work appears here bring divergent philosophical commitments and methodologies to that task, so readers should not expect unanimity in the conclusions these scholars reach, and nor should readers expect a complete accounting of all of the relevant issues. Rather, these essays make clear that the nexus of procreative ethics and the ethics of parenthood remains a fruitful, if relatively underexplored, domain of philosophical inquiry.

The essays are thematically organized into four main areas: Procreation and the Sources of Parental Rights and Obligations; Choosing Our Children; Parental Rights in a Liberal Society; The Aims and Limits in Parenting. The remainder of this introduction briefly explains and motivates each of these themes, and familiarizes the reader with each of the essay's central arguments.

Procreation and the Sources of Parental Rights and Obligations

The essays in the first section take up the question of how (if at all) procreation generates the rights and obligations standardly associated with parenthood. As noted above, most societies assume that being procreatively responsible for a child (i.e., being responsible for that child's coming into existence) makes one that child's parent, with all the customary rights and obligations associated with role. But again, it is far from obvious why such biological facts should give rise to these moral claims, and in particular, how the interests of children or parents are well served by grounding these rights and obligations in procreative acts. What Sarah Hannan and Richard Vernon term the 'Plato worry' illustrates the puzzles that such a grounding raises. Hannan and Vernon note that if the rights and obligations of parenthood are rooted in children's interests, there seems to be no *prima facie* reason why their procreative parents should be assigned these rights and obligations.

> If children's interests would be better served in being raised by people other than their biological or adoptive parents—say by those who work

within state-run institutions—then according to the child-centered view it would be not only permissible, but required, that they be taken from their current parents. . . . Moreover, this redistribution would not constitute a violation of the original parent's rights because under the child-centered account their rights are predicated solely on the interests of the child . . .[1]

Conversely, if the rights and obligations of parenthood are rooted in parent's interests, there remains a logical gap here: For why should parents who have an interest in (say) establishing the *kind* of intimate or nurturing relationship parents typically have with children be assigned rights and obligations with respect to the specific children they procreate?

The challenges here are thus multifaceted: To provide a justification of the right to procreate, yes, but also to account for how acts of procreation give rise to the specific rights and obligations parents putatively have with regard to *their* children. An adequate response to these challenges would apparently have to invoke something about which many philosophers would be skeptical, namely, some sort of principle that bridges fact and value, i.e., a principle that links specific procreative facts with specific evaluate claims that parents supposedly have with respect to the children they procreate. The essays in this section each consider different ways to bridge these domains.

In "The Compensatory Basis of Procreative Parental Rights," Michael Cholbi proposes that the bridge between procreation on the one hand and parental rights and obligations on the other is compensatory. Procreation inevitably encumbers the wills of children in ways akin to the wrongful encumbrances of the will that occurs via arranged marriage: Procreation, Cholbi argues, places a child in initial conditions determined by her genotype, familial relationships, cultural expectations, etc., conditions not of the child's choosing but which greatly shape the life she will have and the options available to her. By procreating, parents thereby incur obligations to compensate their children for these encumbrances of their wills, as well as acquiring parental rights circumscribed by these obligations. Cholbi's account of the source of parental rights and obligations is distinctive in that these rights and obligations turn out not to rest on parents' generic interest in being parents nor in children's interests in there being someone especially accountable for their welfare. Rather, they are rooted in *pro tanto* morally objectionable features of procreative acts themselves.

Russell DiSilvestro ("Teach Your Children Well") is similarly concerned with how it is that a child is someone's child, that is, a distinct individual who is the proper object of a given parent's attention and care, as opposed to the attention and care of others. DiSilvestro explores one popular answer to these questions, appealing to a child's origins. A child is yours because that child originated with you in the sense that the child is constituted by physical parts of you, and because you own your own physical parts, there is a sense in which a child so constituted is "owned" by you as well. While sympathetic to this answer, DiSilvestro has reservations about the moral implications of the parent–child relation being modeled on ownership of physical stuff, since among these would appear to be that parents have 'despotic' rights over their children to do whatever they wish to their children. He then proposes that, if this "origin essentialism" is true, children should be taught this, and furthermore, to marvel at the "radical contingency" of their own existence.

Choosing Our Children's Genes

The essays in the second part of this volume explore the ethics of parental decision-making, specifically when parents' decisions aim to shape the traits, activities, values, and beliefs of children. Legally and socially, parents are afforded a great deal of freedom in their parenting activities and practices. Most assume a parental prerogative to share with children religious and cultural beliefs and practices, hobbies, and passions. In support of these positions, some philosophers have worked to articulate the moral basis of such parental freedoms and prerogatives. Some point to the parents' right to choose how their own lives unfold, and argue that parenting according to one's own values and beliefs falls under this more general right. Different sorts of arguments point to the added value to parents' lives that is made possible by having the freedom to share their passions and pursuits with their children in intimate ways. Some claim that the most gratifying moments in parenthood are those in which one's children successfully follow in one's footsteps.

But how do such parental liberties affect children? Philosophers have argued that children's welfare and autonomy-related rights and interests can be seriously threatened by unfettered parental freedom. In certain kinds of cases, nearly everyone agrees that it is acceptable to constrain parental liberty. No one objects to (at least) minimal humanitarian standards being used to inform constraints on parenting behavior, such as those that protect children from the evils of malnutrition, a substandard education, violence, and abuse. Widespread disagreement exists, however, on how far children's rights and interests should direct and/or restrain parental freedom beyond this minimum threshold. Usually pointing to the fact that children are brought into the world as nonconsenting, innocent parties with independent moral standing, some liberal theorists have argued that parenting ought to be entirely directed by the interests of children, and in particular their future interests in self-determination. Not only is the indoctrination of children seriously morally wrong on such a view, but any activities that would strongly encourage the unreflective adoption of any one set of beliefs, values, and practices become problematic. Plausibly, this limits the extent to which parents can legitimately encourage their children into religious or political affiliation, or even the adoption of life-organizing hobbies or habits like playing a sport or musical instrument. Decisions regarding children's educations are particularly fraught.

Not only are decisions regarding education sometimes determinative of the substantive views children come to adopt, but they also often shape children's capacities for critical reflection of their views, as well as their willingness to consider alternative views.

Debates regarding the freedoms of prospective parents have followed a similar course. *Whether* to procreate and/or rear children, *with whom*, and *how many* children to create and/or rear have always been procreative decisions that are intimately tied with the ethics of parental decision-making. In this sense, the rights of prospective parents to make these sorts of procreative decisions have always been subject to moral scrutiny. But w*hat genes* to select for in one's children is a new choice made possible by ever expanding developments in reproductive technologies. One might think that these are particularly troubling cases, because the autonomy-related interests of children are particularly threatened by parents' attempts to shape children's identities through genetic selection. The three essays in this section explore the ethics of prospective parents engaging in genetic selection in particular, addressing the ways in which children, parents, and society are implicated in the practices of genetic selection. They interrogate this issue by drawing on arguments regarding parental liberty, each in a different way.

The first two essays investigate the ways in which parents selecting for children's genes is harmful to the children created, or otherwise wrong for parents to engage in. In "A Chip Off the Old Block: The Ethics of Shaping Children to Be Like Their Parents", Robert Noggle uses the case of genetic selection to shine a critical light on one type of resolution to the tension between parents' autonomy-related interest in shaping their children, and children's interest in self-determination: The approach that these two interests must be balanced against each other. Noggle argues that this 'balancing model' ought to be rejected because of its implications for what has been called the 'non-identity problem.' According to the non-identity problem, the very existence of the child in question must coincide with her suffering some kind of harm or flaw: In this case, an autonomy diminished by their parents' having chosen their genetic code. While it might be plausible to claim that children with selected genes have their autonomy constrained, it is also true that these particular children would not exist had the genetic shaping not occurred. After all, without genetic intervention, a child with a different genotype, and hence a *different* child, would have resulted. Especially if she owes her existence (in part) to her particular genotype, and she has a life worth living, it is difficult to claim that her parents acted wrongly even given the diminished possibility of self-determination. Parental rights to shape their children as they desire thus look like they can be given free rein. Since Noggle is wary of the position that parents ought to have such unlimited freedom to genetically shape their children, he argues that we adopt a different, non-balancing conception of parental rights. A variety of possibilities exist, and he favors versions that conceive of parental rights as a sort of stewardship right over children.

Where Noggle explores the harmfulness to the child resulting from genetic selection, in "The Problem of Choosing (For) Our Children", K. Lindsey Chambers argues that it can be wrong to engage in genetic selection even if one does not harm the resultant child. She does this by focusing on the ethical requirements of assuming the parental role, which she argues must be constrained by "the moral end of parenting": the development of one's child into an autonomous adult. Anyone who intentionally sets out to create a child in order to parent that child adopts the parental role. Genetic selection is morally problematic to the extent that it threatens a child's development into an autonomous adult with 'agential independence.' In cases in which children's capacities to become autonomous are directly threatened (as when they are shaped by a parent's image of a desirable child), or even in which the genetic selection is neutral between views of the good, Chambers argues that parents disrespect their children because they treat them instrumentally. But, as she puts it, "a child isn't *for* anything. A child is valuable as a person in her own right."

In "Children of Choice and Educational Responsibility", Jaime Ahlberg investigates the ways in which genetic selection highlights a tension between what are usually considered private parenting practices and society's collective interest in how parents rear their children. She is particularly interested in cases in which parental decisions seem to place additional demands on society, and uses the realm of education to focus the discussion. Children have a right to at least a minimally decent educational background, and society collectively has an obligation to provide this. But what about when parents make genetic decisions that affect how easy or difficult it is to provide that education, especially when parents select for capacities in their children while knowing the educational implications? Perhaps the most controversial cases of this are those in which deaf parents have selected for deafness, in an environment in which it costs approximately three times as much to educate a child who is deaf than a child without deafness (other things equal). Ahlberg attempts to illuminate the ways in which the social construction of talent and disability, as well as the way in which educational costs are contingent on social values, complicate answering this question. Nevertheless, she argues that when parents privately select for traits that impose additional social costs, *and* they intentionally do so for reasons stemming from their idiosyncratic value judgments regarding what kind of children they want to rear, those parents bear responsibility for the additional strain that their choices place on society.

Parental Rights in a Liberal Society

Liberals of all stripes are united in their commitment to the view that personal freedom is normatively basic; any interference in an individual's liberty stands in need of justification.

They diverge on how, and to what extent, interference in personal liberty is justifiable, and the extent to which liberty is reconcilable with the value of equality, as well as social and communal interests. They also diverge on what justifies their commitment to individual liberty. Some see the commitment as justified *politically*, in virtue of the support that it generates from the perspective of a variety of "comprehensive" conceptions of the good. Others consider individual liberty to be justified in virtue of its connection with deeper moral values: Most germane here, for example, is the value that many liberals place on individual self-determination, or autonomy.

Because all liberals accept that both parents and children have independent moral status, and agree that the state has an interest in perpetuating itself over time, the family is a battleground of sorts in the context of liberalism. While it has traditionally be conceived as a space in which individuals ought to live out their private conceptions of the good, it is clear that the ways in which parents rear their children in the 'private' sphere has implications for children as well as society at large. Which individuals will constitute the future citizenry, and what those individuals will value and how they will be oriented toward their wider community, are all of interest to the state. How, then, should family making be conceptualized in a liberal framework and what sort of status should it enjoy? How much exclusive authority ought parents to possess in the guiding of their children into adulthood? These are the questions that animate the essays in this section.

Mianna Lotz ("Liberalism and the Status of Family Making") observes that liberal states, despite their commitments to neutrality, adopt a decidedly non-neutral stance to procreation and the making and sustaining of family life. In contrast with citizens who do not have children, liberal states tend to, for instance, provide disproportionate support to families in the costs of bearing and rearing children, including the provision of a state-funded education. What could the justification for this non-neutrality for family making be, given that the same states do not subsidize other important projects and activities that people undergo in their lives? Lotz considers two forms of justification for the special status granted to family making within a liberal framework: that family making is a special kind of project, and that children are 'public' or 'socialized' goods. She finds each type of account problematic, internally and as a justification for the liberal state's privileging of families and children. Instead, she develops a liberal-minded justification on the basis of the *political* value of procreation and parenting to the state. She argues that, as proto-persons and future citizens, the state has an interest in the creation and development of children that can legitimate its non-neutral stance. Children amount to, as Lotz puts it, pre-conditions of the state's preservation and reproduction. As such, the state is thus entitled to use its resources to secure children's development into productive liberal citizens.

In his paper "Parents' Rights and the Control of Children's Education", Roger Marples provides a detailed examination of the popular position that parental rights are grounded in parental interests. As noted above, several versions of this view are in circulation: parents have an interest in the intimacy that the parent–child relationship provides; parents have an interest in playing the fiduciary role with children they help to usher into adulthood; parents have an 'expressive' interest in rearing children according to their values and commitments.[2] Marples finds that none of these accounts can support parental rights strong enough to outweigh the interests of children in becoming autonomous agents, if indeed they can support parental rights at all. Further, like Lotz, he observes that society itself has an interest in critically reflective, politically engaged, and compassionate citizens motivated by social justice. Children's interest in autonomy, together with these social interests, imply limitations on parents' child-rearing activities. Specifically, closed-minded, autonomy-foreclosing parental practices are legitimately restricted. When it comes to the sharing of religious values, for example, parents thus do not have the right to *initiate* their children into particular religions if they are even somewhat likely to uncritically adopt the associated beliefs and values. What are specific implications of this view for parental discretion over their children's education? Marples addresses several contentious areas of education: faith schools, parental input on the curriculum, home-schooling, and private schooling. Each of these practices is found to be problematic on the grounds that they frustrate either children's autonomy-related interests or social interests in diversity, solidarity, and justice (or both).

Lotz and Marples's contributions are good illustrations of how state involvement in children's education is a significant arena in which questions of parental authority, children's interests, and the commitments of liberalism come to a head. The desirability and justifiability of the content and aims of civic education, in particular, is a focal point. Undergirding the value of civic education, however, must be an account of its role in liberal society. In his essay "Liberalism, Parental Rights, and Moral Education," Marc Ramsay employs the influential *Mozert v Hawkins* case to expose important distinctions across rival conceptions of liberalism, and their different implications for the necessary shape of a properly civic education. In *Mozert*, Christian fundamentalist parents objected to a positive portrayal of alternate religions and gender equality in elementary school reading materials, known as the Holt reading program. Parents argued that they had a right to direct their children toward their reasonable, comprehensive conceptions of the good (here, fundamentalist Christianity). While Ramsay is sympathetic to the predicament of sincere fundamentalist parents and grants that there are some plausible concerns about the aims of Holt-style reading programs, he argues that in most cases parents do not have a right to object to curricula aiming at diversity and tolerance. In particular, parental objections to curricular promotion of gender equality, the protection of vulnerable youth (e.g. gay and transgender children), and even comprehensive sex education, cannot justify curricular exemptions for the children of those parents. Children's interests in the capacities for autonomy-formation, and the state's interest in promoting a political culture characterized by the values of mutual respect and tolerance, block such exemptions.

Ashli Anda draws upon the work of one liberalism's best known critics, Hegel, to challenge some of the central assumptions contemporary liberals make regarding procreation and the family. In "An Interest, Not a Project: Hegel on Love and Procreation," she argues that, contrary to the liberal inclination to view family making as a private and personal 'project,' Hegel provides a model on which procreation and child-rearing are fundamentally communal activities. As such, the justification for procreation *and* for parenting practices must be referenced to the unity and security of the family unit, as well as to the family's contribution to civil society as a whole. It is incorrect, on the Hegelian model, to think of the interests of parents, children, and society as fundamentally at odds and in need of being balanced. Rather, individual and social interests are best conceptualized as harmonious. With regard to their educational interests, Anda draws on Hegel's claim that children have a right to a 'proper upbringing' to develop an account on which a 'proper' Hegelian upbringing is one in which children are developed into participating members of political society. Integral to being developed in such a way is the provision of financial resources, but also a loving and trusting relationship with parents. Parents' duties to their children thus derive from the state's interest in rational, independent, and productive citizens, but the discharging of these duties requires intimate and loving relationships between parents and their children. Grounding the rights and responsibilities of parents in societal interests poses a number of problems that Anda considers, including: Can there procreative *duties*, were society to need different numbers of future members? And what about the status of families that do not include children? While challenging to address, she argues that these are not insurmountable problems.

The Aims and Limits of Parenting

On what grounds should we conclude that a person is qualified to be a parent? One might argue that one is qualified when one is able to discharge the duties associated with parenting, at least according to minimal standards. What amounts to minimal standards is fairly uncontroversial: Usually it includes the ability (individually, or jointly with society) to provide the goods associated with good health and a basic education, recreational opportunities, and a childhood environment relatively free from mental, emotional, and physical abuse. Because of the gravity of the stakes for children in ending up with parents that will meet at least these minimum qualifications, some have argued[3] that all prospective parents should be screened and licensed precisely because children have so much at stake in whether their parents satisfy these minimal qualifications. In cases in which people procreate "naturally" and in those in which they make use of assisted reproductive technology, there are no procedures for assessing parental ability to provide for these needs. In cases of adoption, prospective parents are often required to undergo rigorous instruction and screening. But whether would-be parents plan to acquire legal rights over children through biological procreation (assisted or otherwise) or adoption, we can ask a deeper moral questions about what ought to be expected of parents, in virtue of what experiences one might come to have the qualifications of a parent, and what social practices (if any) can or should ensure that parents have those qualifications.

In his essay "Parenthood and Transformative Experiences," Michael Austin begins exploration of these questions by asking what parents should be *aiming* for when they rear their children. In particular, he focuses on the relevance of 'personal transformative experiences' to the aims of parenting. Drawing on the work of L. A. Paul, he understands such experiences as those by way of which persons find their points of view substantially altered, their core preferences revised, or find their experience of themselves *as themselves*, changed.[4] Examples of such experiences include those people voluntarily undergo—as when having children or committing to a life partner—or those that happen involuntarily—as when a loved one dies or one loses a job. Given their ability to contribute to, and to radically compromise, well-being over the course of a life, Austin argues that parents have an obligation to prepare their children for personally transformative experiences by cultivating within them certain cognitive abilities, open-mindedness, and resilience. Various practical implications follow from his argument, and he discusses how involvement in youth sports and in certain other kinds of educational experiences are among them. With respect to education specifically, he argues that parents must allow their children to experience different sorts of challenges to the values that shape their lives. Doing so inoculates children against the potentially disruptive and dangerous effects of personally transformative experiences.

Samantha Brennan and Colin Macleod, in their contribution "Fundamentally Incompetent: Homophobia, Religion, and the Right to Parent," argue that strongly homophobic adults lack a moral right to parent because they fail to meet a minimum competency threshold of parenthood. By 'strongly homophobic,' Brennan and Macleod mean those adults who adopt and seek to express extreme anti-gay beliefs that "give rise to attitudes of contempt, disgust, and disrespect towards gay people". The possession of such beliefs and their attendant dispositions towards gay persons threaten the right children have to be loved, emotionally supported, and to the provisions of affection from their parents: In short, their right to "affective caring." In support of their argument, Brennan and Macleod detail empirical evidence showing that gay teens who experience rejection from strongly homophobic parents through forms of indifference, hatred, and disgust are at unacceptable risk for homelessness and suicide, for example. Because there is a non-trivial chance that strongly homophobic persons will become the parents of gay children, and such persons will not be able to reliably discharge their responsibilities to these children, they lack the minimum requirements necessary to be prepared to parent in general.

In "Parental Licensing and Pregnancy as a Form of Education," Christine Overall explores the general position that all prospective parents should be licensed. Screening and licensing of adoptive parents is standard practice, whereas non-adoptive parents who are biologically connected to their children have widespread freedom to parent without seeking a license. What explanation could there be for distinguishing between the two cases, when both are responsible for the well-being of nonconsenting, dependent, and vulnerable children? Overall is amenable to the idea that prospective parents (and other adults heavily involved in the rearing of the child) require preparation for parenthood through education, and in many cases, she supports the practice of licensing. However, in this essay she argues that women who have gestated the infants they come to parent and their (supportive and involved) partners should be exempt from licensing requirements. Through the process of pregnancy the gestating mother enters into a relationship with her fetus, which is the basis of her preparation for being *that fetus's* parent once it is born. Overall examines the ways in which pregnancy is often an active process by which women engage in thoughtful, deliberative learning about their fetus and about themselves in a way that is highly significant to the challenges she will face as a parent. So long as the pregnant woman's partner actively supports her and participates in the process of preparing for the arrival of the infant, that partner has a derivative right not to undergo licensing.

Notes

1   "Parental Rights: A Role-based Approach," *Theory and Research in Education* 6 (2008): 112.
2   For example, see Ferdinand Schoeman "Rights of Children, Rights of Parents, and the Moral Basis of the Family" *Ethics* 91 (1980): 6-19; Harry Brighouse and Adam Swift *Family Values: The Ethics of Parent-Child Relationships* (Princeton: Princeton University Press, 2014); Shelley Burtt "The Proper Scope of Parental Authority: Why We Don't Owe Children an "Open Future"" in *Child, Family, and State*, ed. by Stephen Macedo and Iris Marion Young, (New York: New York University Press, 2002): 243–272; William Galston "Parents, Government, and Children: Authority over Education in a Pluralist Liberal Democracy" *Law and Ethics of Human Rights* 5 (2011): 285–305.

3   For the most influential statements of this view see Hugh LaFollette "Licensing Parents," *Philosophy & Public Affairs* 9 (1980): 182–97 and Hugh LaFollette "Licensing Parents Revisited," *Journal of Applied Philosophy* 27 (2010): 327–43.

4   L. A. Paul, *Transformative Experience* (New York: Oxford University Press, 2016).

1 How Procreation Generates Parental Rights and Obligations

Michael Cholbi

> *Did I request thee, Maker, from my clay to mould me man? Did I solicit thee from darkness to promote me?*—
>
> (Milton, *Paradise Lost*)[1]

While there is more than one way to become a child's parent, *procreating* a child is typically sufficient to achieve that status. But whether a person has procreated a child and thereby become her parent requires that her acts have some causal role in bringing that child into existence. To procreate is to create, not simply to bring into being, so as we shall understand this term, 'procreating' is an action type, not merely a causal relation. The precise causal role that a parent plays in procreation may vary: Most often, a parent is genetically related to a child, but he or she may participate in procreation by fulfilling a different biological role (e.g., gestating a genetically unrelated fetus). Beyond a causal contribution to the child's existence, procreation requires that the child's existence be a fact that can be attributed to her and her choices. A person procreates a child, on this view, either by (a) acting so as to contribute to bringing into existence a child for whom one intends to serve as a parent, or (b) by engaging knowingly and willfully in acts that contribute to bringing a child into existence (for example, 'accidentally' conceiving a child via sexual acts), irrespective of whether one intends to serve as that child's parent. On this understanding, an incompetent minor, ignorant of the mechanics of biological reproduction, cannot procreate. Nor does a gestational surrogate who has relinquished any claims to serve as the child's parent.[2] As a way of becoming a child's parent, procreation thus contrasts with paths through which an individual becomes a child's parent with no causal role in bringing the child into existence, e.g. the adoption of a child who already exists.

My aim in this article is to evaluate some common ethical convictions about procreation and its relationship to both parental rights and parental obligations. In particular, I will consider the following claims, which together we may call the *procreative model*:

1 Competent adults have a right to procreate. This right is negative, entailing that others may not interfere with procreative acts or choices (except in extreme cases), and perhaps positive, entailing that individuals may be entitled to medical or other assistance to enable procreation.

2 Parents acquire a set of *rights* with respect to their children due to their being responsible for the existence of their children. These rights include the right to control a child's physical location, to guide the child's personal relationships, to exercise proxy judgment on the child's behalf, and (more controversially) to shape a child's education and to raise the child in the parent's particular religious or cultural traditions.

3 These parental rights are *exclusive*, in that only a child's parents have these rights with respect to that child (or have them to anywhere near the same extent as others may).

4 These parental rights are accompanied by a set of parental *obligations*, including providing for a child's material welfare, stimulating the child's emotional and cognitive development, not abandoning, abusing, or neglecting a child, and protecting the child from abuse, attack, and other dangers.

5 These parental obligations interact with parental rights in that flagrant or repeated violations of these obligations can result in parents losing one or more of their rights *vis-à-vis* their children, including in the most extreme cases forfeiture of parental custody and cessation of the parent–child relationship.

Obviously, the procreative model does not provide a complete account of the ethics of parent–child relations. It is silent, for instance, on the obligations children bear toward their parents. Nevertheless, the procreative model incorporates what I take to be a widely shared understanding regarding the ethical relations between parents and children with respect to the most common way in which these relations are established, namely, via procreative acts. And it is my contention that extant attempts to account for how procreation generates parental rights have serious shortcomings. Here I hope to demonstrate why this is so and develop a stronger defense of the procreative model.

Our concern, then, is with how procreative acts might serve as the *source* of parental rights and obligations. Suppose that the answer to the question 'how can parents have the rights and obligations they have toward their children?' is along the lines of 'often enough, by virtue of having procreated those children.' My purpose is to identify the best defense of this answer. In this respect, there are two important dimensions of the procreative model about which I will say little. First, aside from parental rights and obligations regarding education, I will leave much of the *content* of parental rights and obligations aside. Again, the aim here is to consider whether the procreative model can account for parents having rights and obligations vis-à-vis their children, not with precisely which rights and obligations parents have

Second, I contribute little to the issue of the procreative model's *limits*. In procreating, parents create beings with claims on other individuals and on their societies. Furthermore, those beings consume environmental and societal resources. Hence, any defense of the procreative model as a source of parental rights and obligations is incomplete absent an engagement with issues pertaining to how many times or how often parents may exercise their procreative rights. I do not tackle such issues here.

One possible justification of the procreative model as the source of parental rights and obligations is that parents are assigned these rights and obligations because doing so is in the vital interests (perhaps even the 'best interests') of the child. This *child interest justification* contrasts with the *parent interest justification*, according to which parents are assigned these rights and obligations because doing so serves some vital interests of parents. I first attempt (in sections 1 and 2) to show that neither of these interest-based justifications adequately justify the procreative model. The child interest justification cannot be squared with the exclusivity and presumptiveness that the procreative model assigns to parental rights. Nor can it be squared with the extensive procreative liberty associated with that model. For its part, the parent interest justification cannot bridge the gap between prospective parents' interests in becoming parents and their having a right to become parents. In particular, an interest that is popularly invoked as the basis of parental rights, the interest in having the kind of uniquely intimate or loving relationship parents can have with children, is not sufficient to ground a right to bring a being into existence in order to satisfy this interest. Appeal to these interests to ground the procreative model is even less plausible if procreation is morally objectionable from the standpoint of the procreated. I argue in section 3 that in procreating, individuals create a new human person who faces her future from a set of initial conditions determined by her genetic profile, her early life material circumstances, her parental and familial relationships, cultural expectations, and so on. How that new human person can exercise her will over her lifetime to craft a life of her choosing is profoundly influenced by these initial conditions, conditions into which she is involuntarily placed by her procreative parents. We have, I contend, good moral reasons to object to our wills being encumbered by these initial conditions. Procreation always places a person into specific life circumstances that she does not choose but which substantially demarcate the horizon of possible lives she may have. Procreative encumberings are thus wrong, I argue, in something like the way in which compelling an individual into a romantic or marital relationship wrongfully encumbers her will: To subject an individual, without her authorization, to a state of affairs that substantively determines the arc of her life possibilities objectionably constrains her will.

This argument nevertheless contains a silver lining, as it paves the way to an alternative justification of the procreative model: If procreation is a wrongful encumbering, then procreators have an obligation to *compensate* their offspring for this wrong. This general obligation is in turn the source of other more specific parental obligations, as well as of parental rights. A chief advantage of this compensatory account of parental rights and obligations is that it identifies a feature of procreation that is universal but specific. Because of this constitutive wrong, *every* procreative parent has a duty to compensate *her* offspring for this wrong. The compensatory account thus succeeds in making sense of how particular acts of procreation can generate parental rights and obligations specific to the offspring one procreates. More generally, my compensatory account better vindicates the procreative model, giving individuals wide latitude to procreate, making parental rights exclusive and reasonably presumptive, and linking these rights to procreation without having to bridge the chasm between prospective parents' interest in becoming parents and their putative right to become parents. Section 6 concludes with a discussion of parental rights *vis-à-vis* children's education, and in particular, how the provision of education might serve to provide children restitution for the wrongs of procreation.

1 Child Interest Justifications of Parental Rights

Much of the popular rhetoric and legal practice surrounding parenthood and procreation assumes that children's interests are well served, perhaps even best served, when those responsible for their biological existence are assigned the distinctive rights and obligations of parenthood. In some quarters, procreation is seen as a transformative experience,[3] capable of turning otherwise somewhat self-absorbed individuals into adoring parents who love their children unconditionally and are willing to sacrifice most anything for their children's sake. Legal practices surrounding divorce, incarceration, and immigration, which often emphasize maintaining or reunifying families established via procreation, reflect a similar conviction that children are best off under the care of those who procreated them.

Such sentiments suggest a justification for the procreative model resting on children's interests. According to this justification, parental obligations are fundamental and parental rights derivative, co-originating in children's interests: The fulfillment of the moral obligations of parenthood ensures that children's interests are protected and realized; procreative parents are best suited to fulfill the moral obligations of parenthood; thus, assigning procreative parents these obligations, as well as corresponding parental rights, is justified by appeal to children's interests.[4]

As a generalization, the claim that procreative parents are best suited to fulfill the moral obligations of parenthood is probably correct. Certainly once a relationship is well established between children and their procreative parents, the disruption to this relationship that would occur if children were removed from their households and assigned to other parents would be a source of great trauma and anxiety to children. However, virility is not virtue, and there is no particular reason to suppose that having ultimate responsibility for a child's existence makes one *competent* as a parent, much the less that one is best suited (i.e., better suited than any other prospective guardian) to parent a child in that child's best interests. In advocating for a regime of parental licensing, Hugh LaFollette points to a wide range of empirical findings regarding the prevalence of abuse and neglect by parents. As it turns out, parents who incur obligations toward their children through procreation rather than adoption are in fact more likely to be incompetent parents.[5] LaFollette's licensing proposal is obviously controversial, and it is not my purpose to endorse it here. However, it does help illustrate the primary difficulty of justifying the procreative model by appeal to the best interests of children, namely, that there seems to be no special causal connection between a child's being one's procreative progeny and being disposed to act in that child's best interests. Again, this is not to say there is *no* such connection: It would be surprising if a child's procreative kin were not often the best qualified to serve as their parents (though even here we might question whether biological facts as such explain this, as opposed to, say, the relationship biological parents build with their children over time). Yet if the procreative model were grounded in the best interests of children, then parental rights would be less exclusive than the procreative model supposes inasmuch as other competent prospective parents would have conditional claims to parent children whose procreators are incompetent. Such rights would also be something less than presumptive: Less evidence would be necessary in order to override the parental rights claims of procreative parents.

The procreative model obviously has a strong grip on the customs and norms of various societies. But it is unlikely that a community primarily concerned with children's interests would bind together procreative acts and parental rights as tightly as the procreative model does. Indeed, were the procreative model grounded in children's best interests, we would likely be much more willing to decouple procreative acts from parental rights altogether. This possibility is encapsulated in what Sarah Hannan and Richard Vernon call the 'Plato worry.' Just as Plato advocated that children be redistributed in order to meet the state's interest in class specialization, the procreative model (if grounded in the interests of children) should entail a willingness to redistribute children in order to advance their interests:

> If children's interests would be better served in being raised by people other than their biological or adoptive parents—say by those who work within state-run institutions—then according to the child-centered view it would be not only permissible, but required, that they be taken from their current parents. . . . Moreover, this redistribution would not constitute a violation of the original parent's rights because under the child-centered account their rights are predicated solely on the interests of the child . . .[6]

In other words, if parental rights are rooted in children's interests, then the rights of procreative parents with respect to the children they are responsible for creating would be much more contingent than the procreative model allows.

Furthermore, the very right to procreate would likewise be more contingent than the procreative model presupposes if it is justified by appeal to children's best interests. A number of practical concerns arise in connection with proposals to limit procreative liberty. Yet there may well be some individuals for whom procreation ought to be proscribed altogether if the right to procreate rests on the interests of children. Nature sometimes bestows the capacity to procreate on those without the wisdom, patience, energy, or interest needed to parent in ways conducive to children's interests. It is hard to discern how the procreative model can rightfully bestow parental rights and obligations on such individuals under the auspices of serving children's interests.

Defenders of the procreative model may well point out the practical difficulties that would arise if, despite our culture's current attachment to the procreative model, we attempted to implement a model of parental rights and obligations that deviated from it. They may also try to salvage the procreative model by gravitating toward a less demanding criterion regarding children's interests, claiming that (say) procreative parents need only be 'good enough' in serving their children's interests in order to retain their rights as parents. Yet neither of these responses undermine the key theoretical criticism of grounding the procreative model in children's interests, namely, that the ability to procreate (or arrange for procreation) and the ability to parent are too contingently related for children's interests to provide an adequate vindication of the procreative model.

2 Parent Interest Justifications of Parent Rights

The alternative is to ground the procreative model on the interests of parents. Many possible interests of parents could be invoked here, but advocates of this model often appeal to the distinctive goods parents can enjoy thanks to their relationships with their children. For instance, Harry Brighouse and Adam Swift[7] (2006) propose that the parent–child relationship is unique among human relationships in being a relationship between unequals, in which one party is noticeably more vulnerable and needy; such that children cannot exit the relationship; characterized by spontaneous and unconditional love on the part of children; and fiduciary in that parents are entrusted with the immediate and future well-being of their children. Together these features lend the parent–child relationship a form of intimacy that makes these relationships incommensurable with other adult relationships and contributes uniquely to parents' flourishing and to the development of their capacities. In a similar vein, Christine Overall states that a fundamental "asymmetry" is built into the parent–child relationship inasmuch parents choose to create their children and hence choose to establish a relationship with their children. This asymmetry makes possible "mutually enriching, mutually enhancing love" between the parties and hence provides what Overall believes is the best reason for procreation.[8]

Can the procreative model be justified by appeal to prospective parents' interest in realizing the special goods associated with parent–child relationships? One concern is that this justification appears vulnerable to a version of the aforementioned Plato worry. At most, this appeal establishes that individuals have an interest, and hence a right, to be a parent. However, it does not establish the procreative model's claim that individuals have the right to parent *the children they procreate*. As such, the appeal to parents' interests in having a relationship with their children seems to allow, *inter alia*, for the redistribution of children away from those who procreate but have no desire for such a relationship toward those individuals who desire such relationships but are unable to procreate.[9]

That concern notwithstanding, I believe we should be skeptical that an appeal to this parental interest can generate the kinds of rights claims embedded in the procreative model. Most fundamentally, the fact that individuals may have an interest in having relationships with the distinctive sort of intimacy afforded by the parent–child relationship cannot entail that individuals have a right to bring a new being into existence in order to help realize that interest. Even if such an interest establishes a right to parent, it falls short of establishing a right to procreate.

To see why, we must first consider what sort of right the right to procreate is. According to the procreative model, procreative rights are at least negative, i.e., all other individuals (and the state) have a duty to refrain from interfering in competent adults' procreative acts and efforts.[10] Whether these rights are also positive, requiring other individuals (perhaps again, including the state) to enable or to assist in making possible procreation, is more controversial.[11] Notice that whether or not a right to procreation is, with regard to *other* already extant beings, negative or positive, this right is, with respect *to the person brought into existence*, clearly more than a negative right. In asserting a right to procreate, a prospective parent is not asserting that not yet existing beings may not interfere with her procreating. The procreator instead asserts a kind of claim *on* a not yet existing being, a claim akin to a positive right in that the prospective parent seeks a good from the child, in this case, the good of having a fulfilling relationship with that child.

Yet it hard to discern how this putative positive right might be grounded in a parental interest in having such a relationship. Whether an individual's interest is sufficient to ascribe to her a positive right that others fulfill that interest depends on both how vital the interest is, as well as on the extent or weight of the burdens that would befall others required to honor this right. Whatever interest we may have in establishing and maintaining a fulfilling relationship with our potential children does not seem to be as vital as the interests commonly thought to undergird positive rights, such as our interests in basic subsistence, healthcare, education, and legal counsel when accused of a crime. One cannot have a minimally satisfying life (at least in any minimally developed society) without these goods. But one can have a minimally satisfying life without having the distinctive sort of parent–child relationship afforded by procreation. However, there are clearly some people whose interest in this kind of relationship is deep and abiding, as is attested to by the great lengths some go to in trying to become parents, whether through atypical biological means (various forms of assisted reproduction) or through legal means (adoption). So let us allow that this interest may at least sometimes be vital enough to generate a positive right. That still leaves the question of whether the burdens that exercising this positive right imposes on those who are procreated are sufficient to outweigh the parental interests on which this right rests. Positive rights can clearly be limited in what they ask of others by way of assisting in the fulfillment of their associated interests. As Judith Thomson[12] taught us, even if the only thing that will save us from dying is the cool caress from the hand of a Hollywood icon, we do not obviously have a right to that cool caress despite how vital our interest in continued living might be. There are some burdens we may not ask others to bear even in the service of our vital interests. The question at hand is whether we may ask others to bear the burdens of procreation in the service of our interests in having the special sort of relationship often found between parents and children.

Recently, philosophers have become more skeptical that the burdens procreation imposes on the procreated can be justified.[13] Seana Shiffrin summarizes these burdens:

> By being caused to exist as persons, children are forced to assume moral agency, to face various demanding and sometimes wrenching moral questions, and to discharge taxing moral duties. They must endure the fairly substantial amount of pain, suffering, difficulty, significant disappointment, distress, and significant loss that occur within the typical life. They must face and undergo the fear and harm of death. Finally, they must bear the results of imposed risks that their lives may go terribly wrong in a variety of ways.[14]

That such burdens are not sufficient to generate a positive right to procreation—despite the vital relationship interest prospective parents may have in procreation—becomes plausible when we consider whether there are rights to other relationships that impose burdens on others. In general, our interests in having various relationships generate no positive claim to such relationships. Long-term romantic relationships are arguably sources of distinct goods as well. Adults have negative rights to pursue such relationships (within the limits established by other moral rights and considerations). Yet they certainly do not also have positive rights to such relationships. Those unable to form romantic attachments have no claim against the larger world to be provided such attachments, and no matter how much Romeo loved Juliet, he had no claim on her love. But if we lack any positive right to relationships with particular existent others it is difficult to see how we can have a positive right to *bring another person into existence*, even in order to serve our interests in having a certain form of relationship with them. For say what one will about romantic relationships, they do not impose burdens as weighty or extensive as those that Shiffrin catalogs as the burdens imposed on those we procreate. Hence, if our interest in having romantic relationships is as fundamental as our interest in having a parent–child relationship of the sort described by Brighouse and Smith and by Overall, and yet (a) the former interest is not sufficiently fundamental to ground a positive right, and (b) such relationships do not impose burdens as extensive or weighty as procreation imposes on our offspring, then it appears very unlikely that the latter interest can ground a positive right to procreation. There is, then, a reasonable basis for skepticism about the claim that procreators' interests in having relationships of "mutually enriching, mutually enhancing love" with their children entail their having the relevant right to such relationships. They may have a right that third parties not interfere with procreation, but they do not apparently have a claim against the children they procreate that they be procreated.

3 The Will and the Wrongs of Procreation

The arguments of the previous section showed that parent interests cannot justify the procreative model. This conclusion is all the more likely if exercising the negative right to procreate is a wrong to the procreated. For there cannot be a positive right to bring a person into existence if that very act is a wrong to that person.

To see what such a wrong may consist in, consider Shiffrin's account of harm:

> . . . harm involves conditions that generate a significant chasm or conflict between one's will and one's experience, one's life more broadly understood, or one's circumstances . . . all [harms] have in common that they render agents or a significant aspect of their lived experience like that of an endurer as opposed to that of an active agent, genuinely engaged with her circumstances, who selects, or endorses and identifies with, the main components of her life.[15]

Let us set aside the issue of whether Shiffrin is correct in her account of harm.[16] For my account of the wrongs of procreation will not assert that procreation wrongs by harming a person in any typical sense. Let us instead focus on Shiffrin's talk of a "chasm" between a person's will and her life or its circumstances.

The right to procreate is general, but procreative acts always result in specific individuals coming into existence. And those individuals have identities that stem not only from the genetic inheritance bequeathed them by their genetic parents, but also from the initial circumstances of one's birth. These initial circumstances are not destiny. But they are powerful determinants of the shape and quality of one's life. A person's genetic makeup; her place in the family birth order; her parent's personalities and professions; her material circumstances; the larger environment, including its political, environmental, and anthropological attributes; all of these constrain the possible ways in which a person's life can unfold. They are significant determinants of, to use Shiffrin's words, "the main components" of a person's life. Yet no person is afforded the opportunity to 'select,' 'endorse,' or 'identify with' these components, as all of these are unchosen. For the most part, an individual can only 'endure' these initial conditions and their subsequent effects.

In every act of procreation, there is therefore a 'chasm' between a person's will and her circumstances, not in the sense that those circumstances are contrary to her will but in the sense that those circumstances *encumber* her will. Procreation is on its face wrongful simply because it establishes a chasm between the will of the procreated and the life they experience due to being brought into existence. Procreation necessarily places a person into specific life circumstances—she is born into *this* family with *this* genetic inheritance in *this* society, etc.—that exert wide-ranging influence on what her life could be like. We have strong moral reasons to object to the range of possibilities among which we might choose a life for ourselves being limited in this way, much as we have strong moral reasons to object to being forced into romantic or martial relationships that similarly limit the possibilities for our lives. To compel an individual, without her consent or authorization, to occupy a state of affairs that narrows the range of options amongst which her will can choose normally wrongs her. Such a narrowing is inherent to the procreation of any given individual. Hence, procreators wrong their future children by *encumbering the future wills* of the children they create.

The encumbrance in question has two foundations. The first has already been mentioned: Simply by being brought into existence, we situate a person in circumstances not of his or her own choosing, circumstances that play a tremendous role in shaping who the individual is and what trajectories the individual's life can have. The circumstances into which a person is brought into existence—the material realities of the earliest stages of a person's life—are identity-constituting, exerting significantly more influence on her subsequent capacities, values, and attitudes than later stages. To a surprising extent, who one is and what one can reasonably expect from life is determined by social facts about one's parents. Procreation thus places us in early life circumstances that, even if highly desirable, we have no choice but to 'endure.' Let us say, then, that procreation *materially* encumbers the future will of the person so procreated, both by fashioning her identity and by establishing the initial palette of options and avenues through which she may exercise that will.

The second foundation of this encumbrance is *moral*. Recall Shiffrin's remark that "by being caused to exist as persons, children are forced to assume moral agency, to face various demanding and sometimes wrenching moral questions, and to discharge taxing moral duties." Morality makes claims on our future wills, simply by virtue of our membership in the moral community. Procreation thus places us within the moral community that will make demands upon us. Furthermore, procreation serves to place an individual into a specific web of social relations not of her choosing and hence functions to determine the specific contents of one's moral duties. That individual will have relationships with *these* siblings, *these* parents, *these* peers, etc. These relationships profoundly influence the shape of an individual's life, in addition to creating filial and other duties.[17] Thus, procreation morally encumbers a person's will both by making it true that she has moral duties and by determining what duties she has.

Again, the analogy to romantic relationships is illuminating. We observed earlier that there is not a positive right to romantic relationships. Why not? Entering into such a relationship encumbers the future wills of the parties: Such relationships shape the factual circumstances of a person's existence while also creating normative expectations regarding one's future choices and behavior (expectations of fidelity, care, etc.). Given the burdens and limitations that such expectations entail, we have strong reasons, then, to want to reserve for ourselves the latitude to determine which romantic relationships we enter into, even in cases where those relationships will be beneficial to us on the whole. Arranged marriage is thus objectionable because it encumbers our future wills in fundamental ways, even if it turns out to be an otherwise happy arrangement. Similarly, procreators assert a right to bring an individual into existence, an act which by its very nature generates wrongful burdens or claims on that individual's *future* will.

Others have argued for procreation being wrongful, but to my knowledge, none have argued that the wrong in question consists in its encumbering the wills of the procreated. No doubt the claim that procreation is inherently wrong will rub many the wrong way, so let us first address possible objections to this claim before turning the discussion in a more positive direction.

An obvious concern about my claim is that, despite having interests, the not yet procreated lack wills by which to assert those interests. Hence, it might appear that the reasons for denying (say) a positive right to romantic relationships do not apply to procreation. Prospective romantic partners can exercise their wills via consent to a relationship, but notions of consent simply do not apply to the not yet existent precisely because they lack wills with which to consent. But it is not clear that a being needs a will at a given moment in order for there to be moral reasons not to encumber her future will any more than a being needs to be susceptible to pain at a given moment in order for there to be moral reasons not to cause her future pain. However plausible the principle that it is wrong to encumber a person's future will, it does not seem to turn on a person's having a will at the time when the encumbering occurs. That the not yet existent lack wills does not entail that procreation does not wrongfully encumber their future wills, which is the very same consideration that speaks against a positive right to relationships of other kinds.[18] Perhaps the concern is with the *timing* of the wrong. I have claimed that procreation wrongs the procreated by encumbering its future will. The time at which the wrongful event occurs thus diverges from the time at which the wronging in question occurs. But I do not see that such a divergence should trouble us. Granted, prospective parents cannot disregard the will of the child they procreate until the act of procreation occurs. But this merely illustrates that when a wrongful event occurs and when a person is wronged by that event need not temporally coincide.[19]

A second objection to my argument for the claim that procreation wrongs by encumbering a future person's will is that it appears vulnerable to a version of Parfit's non-identity problem.[20]

> If in order to be harmed by being procreated in some set of circumstances C^1, a person must be made worse off by being procreated in C^1, then her existence by virtue of being brought into existence in C^1 must be worse for her than it would have been were she brought into existence in some other set of circumstances. However, had that person been brought into existence in some other circumstances C^2, that fact necessarily changes the identity of that person. Hence, being procreated in C^1 cannot be a harm to that person. We therefore cannot harm a person by bringing her into existence.

Note that the non-identity problem assumes that the wrongs of procreation consist in how procreation harms a person. However, my argument may appear to circumvent the non-identity problem because it grounds the objectionability of procreation in the fact that it encumbers a person's future will rather than in the fact that it harms her. Nevertheless, it might appear that my argument regarding the encumbering of a person's future will could be attacked with parallel reasoning:

> If in order to be wronged by being procreated in some set of circumstances C^1, a person's will must be more encumbered by being procreated in C^1, then the state of her will by virtue of being brought into existence in C^1 must be more encumbered for her than it would have been were she brought into existence in some other set of circumstances. However, had that person been brought into existence into some other circumstances C^2, that fact necessarily changes the identity of that person, and indeed, changes the initial state of her will. Hence, being procreated in C^1 cannot be a wrong to that person. We therefore cannot wrong a person by bringing her into existence.

However, whatever validity the non-identity problem has when applied to claims regarding harming a person via procreation, it is not valid when applied to my argument regarding procreative wrongs. First, the wrong I have identified is not a comparative wrong. The wrong in question is not the purported wrong of rendering a person's will *more* encumbered than it otherwise would have been. The moral reasons that make procreation objectionable do not rest on the claim that encumbering our wills in this way harms us comparatively, making us "worse off" with respect to the state of our wills than we would otherwise have been. For there is no way we would otherwise have been had we not been procreated, and no antecedent state of our wills that is encumbered by being procreated. It is rather the wrong of encumbering a person's will without their authorization. By its very nature, procreation precludes the "joining of wills"[21] necessary to permissibly encumber another's will. Second, the wrong identified in my argument is not the wrong of procreating a particular person in some specifiable set of circumstances. The wrong consists in encumbering the will of a future person *irrespective* of the precise circumstances of her procreation. The person is affected by being procreated. Thus, the wrong is not an impersonal wrong. However, that wrong does not rest on any special facts about the person's identity as a person or the procreative circumstances that establish that identity. The wrong of encumbering a future person's will is best understood as a *de dicto* rather than a *de re* wrong: a wrong done to whichever individual, or whichever rational will, is brought into existence by being procreated—a wrong to whomever the procreated individual turns out to be.

Finally, critics may contend that in proposing that procreation is inherently wrong, I thereby depict parents in a morally unflattering light. Virtually none of those who procreate intentionally mean to encumber their offspring's wills, and those who procreate unintentionally would not wish ill on their offspring. I do not deny these assertions. Procreation is not generally malicious. However, it need not be malicious in order for it to have the properties that (I contend) make it wrongful. The wrong in question is best seen as akin to a violation of a strict liability standard: Procreation is wrongful thanks to a property inherent to it, and therefore, whether procreators acted intentionally, exercised due care, etc. does not affect its wrongfulness. And even if there were some way of showing that procreators are not at fault for this wrong, procreators who take responsibility for this wrong would nevertheless exhibit the "nameless virtue" Susan Wolf describes in terms of a "willingness to give more . . . than justice requires" when one is responsible for unjust outcomes.[22]

Section 2 cast doubt on the parent-interest justification of the procreative model, illustrating how this interest does not seem sufficiently weighty, particularly when juxtaposed with the burdens of being brought into existence, to justify ascribing to would-be parents a positive right to procreation. This section provides further reason to doubt that justification of the procreative model: Given that procreation makes an arguably wrongful claim on the future wills of those we bring into existence, the interests that would justify such claims must be extraordinarily valuable. In a sense, procreation is by necessity coercive. Prospective parents exploit the very features highlighted by Brighouse and Swift and by Overall (that parents choose to procreate but children do not choose to be procreated, that children cannot exit the relationship, etc.) to force not yet existent beings into relationships the parents value. In so doing, parents treat the rational will or agency of the children they create merely as a means. Such treatment, I maintain, cannot be justified by the relationship goods that may thereby flow to parents.

4 How the Wrongs of Procreation Ground Parental Obligations

Our discussion to this point shows how an adequate vindication of the procreative model must satisfy two desiderata. First, it must rest on some feature that is universally present in acts of procreation. Parental rights and obligations must come into existence due to procreation itself. Second, in light of the Plato worry, an adequate vindication must nevertheless morally bind particular procreators to their offspring. There must be a plausible account of how a procreator has rights and obligations with respect to all and only her offspring.

The second desideratum—that parental rights and obligations must be specific to a procreator's offspring—suggests that parental obligations cannot rest on general or impersonal duties. Given that (as I have argued) procreation encumbers a person's future will undeservedly, we might think that parental obligations are duties of justice. However, an appeal to justice misses that procreators do not just happen upon the situation in which a person's future will is undeservedly encumbered. They are *responsible* for that situation. Parental obligations must instead fall under a category of obligation resting on prior acts of procreators. W. D. Ross identifies three categories of obligation resting on individuals' prior acts. The first, fidelity, does not apply to procreation. Procreators have not made any promises to their offspring that would ground subsequent obligations. Nor does the second category, gratitude. Parents were not benefitted by their children's acts. The only possibility left is duties "resting on a previous wrongful act."[23] In procreating, one wrongs one's children by encumbering their future wills. While procreative parents cannot cancel these wrongs, they can compensate their children for them.[24]

Rooting parental obligations in compensatory duties offers a superior justification of the procreative model, including its claims regarding parental rights. Parental obligations stem from the act of procreation, i.e., on parents having made the right sort of contribution to the existence of their children. It is through the wrongful act of procreation that they incur the relevant compensatory obligations. Thus, a compensatory account of parental obligations depends on a universal feature of procreation, its encumbering of the procreated individual's future will. Furthermore, because compensatory obligations are special obligations, a compensatory account also makes parental obligations specific to those one procreates: While the state of affairs that constitutes their fulfillment can be realized by someone besides the individual who incurs the obligation, they can only be *discharged* by the individual who incurs the obligation. Consider the special obligation of promise keeping: If S promises T that she will make it the case that P, S's promissory obligation to T can in a sense be fulfilled if U makes it the case that P. However, in that instance, S has not discharged her duty to T. Compensatory obligations are subject to the same underlying deontic logic: If S owes compensation to T for having wronged T, then U may 'compensate' T, thereby rendering T 'compensated' for S's wrong. But again, S has not discharged her compensatory duty to T.

A compensatory account of parental obligations is therefore invulnerable to the Plato worry. The Plato worry arises so long as we assume that the procreative model must derive its rationale from one of the parties' interests. Whether that model's rationale is that the assignment of parental rights to those responsible for procreation is in the (best) interests of children or that the assignment of parental rights (and obligations) serves a vital relationship interest of prospective parents, it is in principle possible that decoupling parental rights from procreation better serves the relevant interest. But by appealing to compensatory obligations, my defense of the procreative model dodges the Plato worry. For while it may well be true that children's procreative parents are not necessarily best situated to discharge these obligations, it does not follow, in light of the special nature of these obligations, that it would be just to distribute children and the associated right to parent children to those most able or willing to discharge those obligations. No doubt some will wish to undertake these obligations despite not having procreated. Adoption is certainly not ruled out on my account. However, to distribute children to those most willing to discharge these obligations is unjust, as it permits the procreators who incurred these obligations in the first place to circumvent them.

5 From Obligations to Rights

The source of procreative parental obligations, I have argued, is compensatory. The right to procreate, in turn, is a right to create beings to whom one is necessarily indebted simply by virtue of causing them to exist. However, the procreative model also maintains that procreation is the source of parental obligations as well. My compensatory account sees parental rights are acquiring their legitimacy from compensatory parental obligations. That is, because procreative parents have obligations to compensate their children, they must be accorded rights entitling them to exercise specific forms of care toward their children, the exercise of which provides those children the compensation to which they are entitled. The rights procreative parents have with respect to their own children—rights of guidance and control, decision-making, etc.—are ascribed to them in part so that they may fulfill these compensatory obligations. The exclusivity of these parental rights, another feature of the procreative model, flows from the exclusivity of the parental obligations. The assignment of parental rights to them largely serves to make the fulfillment of their special compensatory obligations possible. At the same time though, these rights may justifiably be curtailed or forfeited by parents who do not fulfill the corresponding obligations, in which case these rights fall on particular individuals who agree to undertake these obligations (adoptive parents) or on the community or society at large.

As I noted at the outset, in grounding the procreative model in procreative parents' compensatory obligations toward their children, I aim primarily to make sense of procreation as a source of parental rights and obligations. Although (as we shall see in the next section) education plays a distinctive role in parents discharging these compensatory obligations, parental rights and obligations are not a straightforward function of those obligations. Children have a wide range of interests and needs. Procreation, I propose, makes parents uniquely responsible for attending to these interests and needs. For by procreating, parents incur special obligations toward their children that render them morally accountable to their children in ways that strangers and others are not morally accountable to them. Thus, the currency of parental compensation takes many forms beyond direct attempts to compensate for children's wills being encumbered. I would argue that when parents provide care toward their children, such as ensuring the availability of nutritious food, they are serving to disencumber their children's wills and so provide indirect compensation. But that is not all parents are doing: They are also satisfying non-compensatory moral demands that nevertheless originate in their special compensatory relationship with their children.

Still, one might find the fact that my compensatory account of parental rights and obligations divorces these from the antecedent interests of the relevant parties puzzling. If the arguments for the previous sections are sound, this is as it should be: Neither the interests of children nor the interests of parents are sufficient to justify the procreative model of parental rights and obligations, particularly given (as I argued in section 3) that procreation wrongfully encumbers the future wills of children. Obviously, the interests of parents still bear on whether adults *ought* to procreate. But the decoupling of parental interests from their rights and obligations represents an advantage of my compensatory account. Individuals become parents for any number of reasons (and sometimes for no reason at all). By grounding parental rights and obligations in facts regarding the obligations that ensue from the act of procreation rather than the motivations for that act, my compensatory account is neutral regarding the reasons behind procreation and so can explain why those who procreate acquire parental rights and obligations irrespective of their motivating reasons (or the lack thereof). This compensatory obligations defense thus succeeds where neither the child interests nor the parental interests defenses do precisely because it attaches parental obligations to what, on the procreative model at least, generates them. the very act of procreation itself. Yet at the same time, it seems to give both sets of interests their due without ignoring either. Should parents desire to procreate, for whatever reason or for no reason at all, they may do so as long as they provide for the interests of the children thus created.

A second puzzling feature of my compensatory obligations defense of the procreative model is that it appears to codify a permission to do wrong. If, as I have argued, procreation is on its face wrong because it encumbers the future will of those brought into existence, then why should we ascribe to individuals a right to do wrong via procreation? I concur that a moral right to procreation—a pre-institutional permission to bring new human beings into existence—is implausible. This is not because one needs the state's moral permission to procreate. The wrongs of procreation are, on the view I have defended here, 'natural.' However, the absence of a moral right to procreate is compatible with there being moral considerations that militate in favor of recognizing a legal right to procreation. First, the moral right in question is not unlimited, and it is compatible with the general contours of my compensatory obligations account that the right to procreate be circumscribed by the capacity and willingness to discharge these obligations. We should, for example, be skeptical of procreative rights asserted by those with past records of child abuse or neglect, by early adolescents lacking the maturity to parent, and those with an express intent of abandoning the children they create. That said, preventing the wrongs of procreation must be juxtaposed alongside other morally important interests and considerations. Among these may be societal interests in, for example, maintaining a population level sufficient for intergenerational justice. Moreover, legal rights bring in tow burdens of enforcement that may be unreasonable or unjust in their own right. Attempting to prevent wrongful procreation may involve equally serious draconian wrongs of its own: intrusions into privacy in order to determine which parents will discharge their compensatory obligations, violations of bodily integrity in order to sterilize, compulsory abortion, and so on. That there may be no moral right to do X whilst there is a legal right to do X is not so odd after all. We may lack a moral right to break certain promises but still (and perhaps justifiably) have a legal right to break them. In any event, the state may sometimes have no right to compel people not to do what they have no moral right to do.

6 Education as Parental Restitution

I have proposed that the obligations associated with the procreative model of procreation are compensatory in nature and serve as the basis for parental rights. I conclude by considering how parental rights and obligations regarding education fit into this model as I have defended. In particular, how might parents make possible educations for their children that accord with these compensatory obligations?

The wrong of procreation, I have proposed, consists in how it encumbers the future will of a child. Many of the ways we might compensate for this wrong represent a different form of moral currency: By, for example, tending to a child's material needs, a parent is at most only indirectly 'unencumbering' a child's will. Education, however, can serve not merely as compensation, but as in-kind *restitution* for the specific wrong of procreation. A broadly liberal education, among whose purposes is to expose children to a variety of modes of life and to provide them with various generic goods and skills needed to pursue and implement those modes, can counteract the encumbrance of the will that procreation creates. Education thus offers a way of 'giving back' to the children we create the power over their future wills that procreation wrongfully encumbered.

Here Bruce Ackerman's description of liberal education in terms of a "great sphere" is illuminating:

> The entire education will, if you like, resemble a great sphere. Children land upon the sphere at different points, depending on their primary culture; the task is to help them explore the globe in a way that permits them to glimpse the deeper meanings of the dramas passing on around them. At the end of the journey, however, the now mature citizen has every right to locate himself at the very point from which he began—just as he may also strike out to discover an unoccupied portion of the sphere.[25]

In encumbering the will, procreation locates a person at a given location on this sphere. Indeed, its influence on that location is likely greater than the "primary culture" to which Ackerman refers. But one's location on this sphere determines what other locations one can perceive and travel to. That location thus establishes the horizon for one's life-shaping options and choices. There will be some locations on that sphere from which it may be difficult to travel from either because of lack of resources that make the surrounding terrain more challenging or because occupying that location has made perceiving or envisioning other locations harder. Poverty and cultural parochialism will, for example, be powerful factors in determining how mobile one is across this sphere. These differences in locations aside, however, procreation inevitably locates a person on this sphere and thereby encumbers her will to a greater or lesser degree.

One antidote to this encumbrance, admittedly imperfect, is the provision of an education to children that enables the adults they will become to travel to various locations on the sphere, and if they so choose, to resettle at a different location. Such an education seeks to assist children, in ways that do not reflect cultural prejudice, in learning about locations on that sphere other than the one they presently occupy. This does not preclude that education giving greater attention to the history, culture, etc. of children's local culture. After all, many children will opt to remain more or less at the location on that sphere where they started, and knowledge of its history and culture will be valuable in that context. Nor does this preclude parents, who presumably are co-located with their children on that sphere, from inculcating in their children affection for that location. The overall aim of parenting and formal education is not to produce human agents who occupy the view from nowhere. Its aim is instead to produce human agents who, from wherever they are on this sphere, can perceive other locations with sufficient clarity to rationally ascertain which location they wish to occupy. Still, the restitutive role of education entails that parents' rights to shape their children's education in accordance with their own values is more limited than commonly thought. A parent whose principal concern regarding her children's education is that the education instill her values in her children at any cost is compounding rather than redressing the wrongs of procreation I identified earlier. Dogmatic indoctrination, aimed not only at engendering affection or loyalty regarding the child's existing location but also at either obscuring other locations or presenting them in an instinctively hostile light, is ruled out.

Likewise, the skill set children acquire via education should not be excessively parochial. Their education should instill skills valuable in multiple locations on this sphere, including (to the extent possible) skills that will prove useful in future locations that have not yet emerged.

As noted above, the encumbrances of a child's future will that result from procreation are both material and moral. A liberal education of the kind I have been describing counteracts both kinds of encumbrance. It makes it more feasible for individuals to establish a different set of material circumstances for their lives, to modify their conceptions of themselves and the trajectories of their biographies. Liberal education counteracts the moral encumbrance of procreation in two ways. First, it invites individuals to scrutinize their own values and make independent judgments regarding the merits of alternative value systems. Second, it permits individuals to choose among different sets of possible social ties, and hence, to choose among different possible sets of specific moral obligations.

These claims ought not be exaggerated. I am not suggesting, for instance, that children ought to be raised or educated in such a way that we maximize their future options—that the more 'open' a child's future remains, the better.[26] Certain options regarding a child's future might permissibly be foreclosed to her because these options are uncontroversially awful. More generally, any process of human development is likely to put some occupations or ways of life out of the realm of the feasible. Nevertheless, that education can provide restitution for procreation's having their future wills encumbered at least suggests a desideratum for a defensible educational regime: that it expand the possible trajectories of their existence, unlike the act of procreation itself.

7 Conclusion

On its face, the compensatory account is not an especially rosy or heartening picture of the parent–child relationship. For the moral foundation of this relationship is not love, nor any good that flows to children or parents from this kind of relationship. Of course, in grounding parental obligations in compensatory obligations, I am not claiming that this is the very reason that parents do, or ought, to fulfill these obligations, nor that the fulfillment of these obligations exhausts the parental virtues. We may permissibly provide our children what we owe them from any number of motives besides the fact that we owe them.

Still, grounding procreative parental rights in parental obligations to compensate children for encumbering their future wills avoids the problems that beset grounding these rights in the interests of children or of parents. It does so by appealing to a moral bond that can only exist between procreative parents and their children. This compensatory rationale offers the best prospects for making sense of how procreative parents have both exclusive obligations toward, and rights regarding, the children they bring into existence. Granted, a central premise in my defense of the procreative model—that procreation is wrong as such—seems radical on its face. But further investigation suggests that my position is less radical than it appears. Procreators owe their children certain things, prominent among which is the real possibility that the initial conditions of their birth, conception, and upbringing do not function as fate—that, should a child so desire, she may rationally embrace a life path that diverges from those made most readily available to her by those initial conditions. My compensatory account of the procreative model merely homes in on the most philosophically plausible way to make sense of these widely shared claims.

Notes

1 As will become evident later on, I find the fact Mary Shelley chose this as the epigraph to *Frankenstein* to illustrate an important insight regarding the source of parental obligations.
2 Medical personnel may appear to be a difficult case, since they seem to satisfy (b) but do not procreate the children to whose existence they causally contribute. While I cannot fully defend this claim here, their contribution is the result of parents enlisting their assistance in procreating; they are therefore 'sub-actors' with respect to procreation and so do not satisfy (b).
3 Paul, "What You Can't Expect When You're Expecting."
4 Blustein, *Parents and Children: The Ethics of the Family*, 104–114, and Archard," The obligations and responsibilities of parenthood," 107–108.
5 LaFollette, "Licensing Parents" and "Licensing Parents Revisited."
6 "Parental Rights: A Role-based Approach," 112. See also Brighouse and Swift, "Parents' Rights and the Value of the Family," 86.
7 "Parents' Rights and the Value of the Family," 95–96.
8 *Why Have Children? The Ethical Debate*, 217.
9 Gheaus, "The Right to Parent One's Biological Baby."
10 LaFollette and others who favor *ex ante* restrictions on procreation would of course disagree.
11 Robertson, "Gay and lesbian access to assisted reproductive technology."
12 "A Defense of Abortion."
13 Shiffrin, "Wrongful Life, Procreative Responsibility, and the Significance of Harm," and Benatar, *Better Never to Have Been.*

14 Shiffrin, "Wrongful Life, Procreative Responsibility, and the Significance of Harm," 136–137.
15 Shiffrin, "Wrongful Life, Procreative Responsibility, and the Significance of Harm," 123.
16 For critiques, see Bradley, "Doing Away with Harm," and Rabenberg, "Harm."
17 Keller, "Four Theories of Filial Duty," and Jeske, *Rationality and Moral Theory: How Intimacy Generates Reasons.*
18 This argument concerns whether prospective parents have a non-comparative claim on those they procreate to bring them into existence. A different argument for comparative claims to bring persons into existence is possible, roughly, that a positive right to procreation is grounded on considerations of distributive justice. It might be unfair for some to be able to procreate but others unable to do so due to luck, etc. But notice that the validity of any comparative argument will assume that at least some prospective parents have a prior non-comparative claim to bring individuals into existence.
19 Shiffrin, "Wrongful Life," 137–138.
20 Parfit, *Reasons and Persons*, and Boonin, *The Non-Identity Problem and the Ethics of Future People.*
21 Ripstein, *Force and Freedom: Kant's Legal and Political Philosophy*, 113.
22 Wolf, "The Moral of Moral Luck," 13–14.
23 *The Right and The Good*, 21.
24 It may be inferred that the rights and obligations of those who become parents through non-procreative paths (for example, through adoption) cannot be rooted in this form of compensation. After all, a parent cannot compensate a child for the encumbrances of procreation if that parent did not procreate that child. This inference is incorrect, though. For while adoptive parents do not encumber through procreation, they nevertheless encumber through parenting, i.e., through placing the child in early life circumstances that greatly influence her subsequent identity and life trajectory. Moreover, while compensatory obligations cannot be renounced, they can be transferred. Adoptive parents, I propose, agree to acquire the compensatory obligations of a child's procreative parents (obligations stemming from encumbrances of the will due primarily to genetics). Thus, while adoptive parents' parental rights and obligations have two sources, they are nevertheless compensatory in nature and will not differ from those of procreative parents.
25 *Social Justice in the Liberal State*, 159.
26 Feinberg, "The Child's Right to an Open Future."

Bibliography

Ackerman, Bruce. *Social Justice in the Liberal State.* New Haven: Yale University Press, 1980.
Archard, David. "The Obligations and Responsibilities of Parenthood," in *Procreation and Parenthood*, edited by David Archard and David Benatar, 103–127. Oxford: Oxford University Press, 2010.
Benatar, David. *Better Never to Have Been: The Harm of Coming into Existence.* Oxford: Oxford University Press, 2006.
Blustein, Jeffrey. *Parents and Children: The Ethics of the Family.* Oxford: Oxford University Press, 1982.
Boonin, David. *The Non-Identity Problem and the Ethics of Future People.* Oxford: Oxford University Press, 2014.
Bradley, Ben. "Doing Away with Harm." *Philosophy and Phenomenological Research* 85 (2012): 390–412.

Brighouse, Harry and Adam Swift. "Parents' Rights and the Value of the Family." *Ethics* 117 (2006): 80–108.

Feinberg, Joel. "The Child's Right to an Open Future," in *Whose Child?* Edited by W. Aiken and H. LaFollette, 124–153. Totowa, NJ: Rowman & Littlefield, 1980.

Gheaus, Anca. "The Right to Parent One's Biological Baby." *Journal of Political Philosophy* 20 (2011): 432–455.

Hannan, Sarah, and Richard Vernon. "Parental Rights: A Role-Based Approach." *Theory and Research in Education* 6 (2008): 173–189.

Jeske, Diane. *Rationality and Moral Theory: How Intimacy Generates Reasons.* New York: Routledge, 2008.

Keller, Simon. "Four Theories of Filial Duty." *Philosophical Quarterly* 56 (2006): 254–274.

LaFollette, Hugh. "Licensing Parents." *Philosophy and Public Affairs* 9 (1980): 182–197.

———. "Licensing Parents Revisited." *Journal of Applied Philosophy* 27 (2010): 327–343.

Overall, Christine. *Why Have Children? The Ethical Debate.* Cambridge: MIT Press, 2012.

Parfit, Derek. *Reasons and Persons.* Oxford: Clarendon Press, 1987.

Paul, L. A. "What You Can't Expect When You're Expecting." *Res Philosophica* 92 (2015). DOI: htp://dx.doi.org/10.11612/resphil.2015.92.2.1

Rabenberg, Michael. "Harm." *Journal of Ethics and Social Philosophy* 8 (2015). DOI: http://www.jesp.org/PDF/harm.pdf

Ripstein, Arthur. *Force and Freedom: Kant's Legal and Political Philosophy.* Cambridge, MA: Harvard University Press, 2009.

Robertson, John A. "Gay and Lesbian Access to Assisted Reproductive Technology." *Case Western Reserve Law Review* 55 (2004–05): 323–372.

Ross, W. D. *The Right and the Good.* Oxford: Oxford University Press, 1930.

Shiffrin, Seana. "Wrongful Life, Procreative Responsibility, and the Significance of Harm." *Legal Theory* 5 (1999): 117–148.

Thomson, Judith Jarvis. "A Defense of Abortion." *Philosophy and Public Affairs* 1 (1971): 47–66.

Wolf, Susan. "The Moral of Moral Luck." *Philosophic Exchange* 31 (2001): 4–19.

2 Teach Your Children Well

Origins, Rights, and the Education of "My" Child

Russell DiSilvestro

> You, who are on the road must have a code that you can live by . . .
> Teach your children well, their father's hell did slowly go by . . .
> —Crosby, Stills, Nash, and Young, "Teach Your Children"[1]

> Hitherto the plans of educationalists have achieved very little of what they attempted and indeed, when we read them—how Plato would have every infant "a bastard nursed in a bureau", and Elyot would have the boy see no men before the age of seven and, after that, no women,' and how Locke wants children to have leaky shoes and no turn for poetry—we may well thank the beneficent obstinacy of real mothers, real nurses, and (above all) real children for preserving the human race in such sanity as it still possesses.
> —C. S. Lewis, *The Abolition of Man*[2]

Let's begin with an example I call *Firm Handshake:*

In the summer of 2008, California governor Arnold Schwarzenegger was greeting several schoolchildren who came to hear him welcome California athletes back from the Beijing Summer Olympics, when he suddenly encountered the grip of my nine-year-old daughter. "Wow, you have a *strong* handshake! Where'd you get that?" he asked. "My daddy!" she shot back, beaming. I smiled as she recounted the episode to me that evening, mimicking in her childish way Arnold's deep voice and Austrian accent. The thought involuntarily flashed across my mind: "even my little daughter is strong enough to impress Arnold with her handshake—it's because she's *learned* from me and because she's made of the same *stuff* as me!" This last idea particularly amused me, as I looked over her complimentary glossy photo of the governor, wearing a tight T-shirt displaying the California state seal, his arms folded across his chest to show his bulging biceps and forearms. I was a 160-pound philosophy professor whose modest physical exercise at that time consisted of occasional bike riding to my campus and occasional stair climbing to my office, so the thought that my genetic contribution to posterity might explain the governor's remark was pleasant to ponder.

However, this moment of basking in my own glory was short-lived. Later that night my daughter came into my room with Arnold's photo in her hand and a coy smirk on her face. "Daddy?" she asked. "Yes, dear?" I said. She spoke slowly and teasingly: "You . . . are . . . *small*!" She pronounced that last word with a flourish. I sighed, and replied, "Yes, dear, I know," and then grinned back at her. "Compared to Arnold, I am very small indeed."

I want my contributions to the next generation, and to my own children in particular, to be a benefit and even a blessing to them. I want this partly for their own sakes, and partly because their presence and experience in the world inevitably reflects back on me in certain ways. Yet I suspect that I might benefit from a more realistic sense of my own limitations in my abilities to benefit and bless in this regard, even when this is humbling, or humorous, or both. And I suspect I am not alone here in much of this.

The ideas of the previous paragraph come from various concrete experiences in my own life so far like *Firm Handshake*. But I hope they also reflect at least part of the wisdom contained in the two fragments I have chosen for this paper's epigraphs. Lewis is reminding his readers of how the 'obstinacy' of 'real' people might be seen as a 'beneficent' counterweight to the beneficence of intergenerational social engineers ('educationalists') who seek to mold the next generation for its own good. Interestingly, Lewis includes parents ('mothers'), non-parental caretakers ('nurses'), and children (indeed, 'above all' children!), in his list of those concrete individuals whose beneficent obstinacy we may well thank for keeping a remnant of relative sanity alive. His emphasis here is not so much on elevating any one of these groups above the others, but on calibrating our gratitude towards the stubborn livers who (at least in the past) were able to resist some of the best laid plans of men who would suggest improvements to their society's educational systems.

Likewise, Crosby, Stills, Nash, and Young are using melody to convey moral advice. Their injunction, or plea, is for parents (and in general, each generation) to listen to and understand their children (and in general, the next generation) even while they must, of necessity, do the hard work of shaping them and passing on to them what wisdom they have scraped together ('code') on their own journey ('road') thus far. Interestingly, just as Lewis emphasized both real mothers and children, these songwriters urge humility for both the older and the younger generations. The phrase "Teach your children well," which grounds the first half of the song, is paralleled by the phrase "Teach your *parents* well" anchoring the song's second half. Part of the song's perennial appeal is likely the fact that each of its listeners, if lucky, will live long enough to know what it's like *both* to be part of a younger generation *and* to be part of an older generation.

But beyond the pluriform wisdom contained in the singable melody and lyrics of this song, its titular phrase "teach your children well" contains the seeds of two philosophical questions I will seek to grapple with in this paper:

1   what makes your children *your children*—that is, (a) the individual persons they are, rather than some other individual persons (i.e. the feature[s] makes them *them*), and (b) the proper object of your attention and care, rather than the attention and care of others (i.e., the feature[s] making them *yours*)?
2   what does it mean to *teach* your children *well*—that is, to give them a *good* education, not merely in the narrow sense of academic skills, but in the broader sense of a truly beneficial upbringing?

It might appear the sensible plan for approaching these questions is to take them roughly in reverse of how I've just listed them: or, to refer to the song phrase, to take the *teach . . . well* parts first, and then move on to the *your children* parts. One might sensibly begin by investigating what it means to teach anybody well, and then, once that is established, to move on to investigating how to teach children (in general) or your children (in particular) well. However, I shall take a somewhat different approach than this apparently sensible plan; indeed, I shall take the very opposite approach. I propose to work from the inside of this phrase to its outside, from its interior points to its perimeter, from its center to its circumference, by examining the *your children* parts first and the *teach . . . well* parts last.

Questions about parental rights regarding their children's education are sometimes treated in a sort of philosophically quarantined manner. These questions are sometimes (intentionally! And understandably!) sealed off from other controversial philosophical questions in the philosophy of mind (e.g., are human persons merely bodies, or do we consist of or possess non-bodily aspects also?) and the philosophy of religion (e.g., are there divine persons, who might have claims on us for loyalty or friendship?). I believe such moral questions about parents and their children are inextricably connected with traditional philosophical questions about persons' bodies and origins and destinies. Partly because of this, I end up taking very seriously some views many philosophers quickly reject, and I end up rejecting some views many philosophers take very seriously.

Both parts of the first question above might be answered by putting some accent on the *origins* of your children. A partial answer to question 1a ("what makes them *them?*") is that their *origins* make them who they are, and so if your children had different origins, they would be different people. (Indeed, more precisely on this view, if your children had different origins, they would not exist at all, but some other people would exist instead of them.) A partial answer to question 1b ("what makes them *yours?*") is that they *originated* from you, and so you have some special rights, and/or duties, regarding them that others do not have. Of course, answers to the second question ("what does it mean to *teach . . . well . . . ?*") abound. But it is worth considering whether and how an answer to this second question might be shaped by the *origin*-focused answers given to the parts of the first question.

. . . Your Children . . . Part (a)

My first paragraph after *Firm Handshake* mentioned a desire to benefit my offspring and a need for realism in the proper managing of this desire. Consider now a second example, which comes not from my family but from an earlier article I wrote. Call it *Replacing the Complainer:*

> . . . consider the following variation on a famous example devised by philosopher Derek Parfit (1984, 359). A young couple conceives a baby girl Ana on their honeymoon. Though of modest means, they give Ana the best life they can. After feeling left out by some rich kids at school, Ana, now 15, complains to her parents that they should have waited five years to have her "so that you would have been richer and then I would have the stuff my peers at school have." One available parental reply to Ana's complaint is this: "if we had waited five years, you would not be here at all, and any child we had would not have been you." The parents' reply works, it is widely thought, because the sperm and egg that combined to produce Ana—and especially *the genetic material within these gametes*—would not have combined at all if the parents had waited five years. After five years, different sperm and egg could have combined, with different genetic material within them, but only to produce a different individual than Ana. We may call the hypothetical child produced five years later "Belle" (though it is irrelevant what we call her: even if we, or her parents, call her "Ana," the point is, she is a different individual than Ana). A simple slogan for expressing the basic idea: change the genome, *replace* the person. If Ana's parents wait five years, they *change* the genome, and thereby *replace* Ana with Belle.[3]

A third example does not come from anywhere but my own mind (so any resemblance to persons living or dead is purely coincidental), and I call it the *Slightly Obsessive Benefiters:*

Dad: I agree; Junior deserves nothing less than the very best. So when should we conceive?

Mom: Well, we want Junior's birth day to put him in the most advantageous position for achievement at school . . .

Dad: You mean "him *or her*," dear. But otherwise you're exactly right; why, I read in *Outliers* that a statistical study of professional hockey players discovered a surprising pattern; such pros were (almost) all born in a certain part of the year, making them the oldest and biggest and strongest in their grade cohorts during their school age years.

Mom: Well, let's aim for that then—we want Junior to have a competitive advantage, whether from brawn, or brains, or both. Ooh, won't he thank us later?

Dad: You mean "he *or she*," dear. But yes—I'm sure he—she—it—will thank us plenty for timing things so meticulously and beneficently. I wouldn't want to have to look anyone in the eye years from now and have to explain why we allowed them to be born in such an uncompetitive position vis-à-vis their classmates. Junior will be thanking his lucky stars he was born at the 'top' of his class!

Mom: You mean "his *or her*," dear. And "wise parents," not "lucky stars." Remember, *From Chance to Choice* and all?

Now, then. Notice that *Replacing the Complainer* and *Slightly Obsessive Benefiters* have many differences. One difference is voice: the child offspring is a speaker in one but not the other. Another difference is content: social and economic opportunities are prominent in one, educational and professional advantages are prominent in the other. Another difference is timing: the deliberation and discussion is retrospective (after the bearing and rearing of a child) in one, while the deliberation and discussion is prospective (before the bearing and rearing) in the other.

But perhaps the most interesting difference is philosophical: a key idea—"change the genome, change the person"—lies at the root of the deliberation and discussion of *Replacing the Complainer*. But the denial of that assumption seems to lie at the root of the deliberation and discussion of *Slightly Obsessive Benefiters*. Is this key idea, or some variant upon it, correct? This takes us straight into Question 1a above: what makes your children *your children*—that is, the individual persons they are, rather than some other individual persons?

The 20th-century British philosopher C. D. Broad once wrote "I have sometimes caught myself wondering what I should have been like if my father had not married my mother but had married some other woman. But I always ended by thinking that the question was meaningless."[4]

Broad assumed then what many today call "origin essentialism" or "the necessity of origin." The general idea is that, in some way, an individual's origin is essential to that individual. But this general idea is open to interpretation: in particular, it leaves open precisely which aspects of an individual's origin are essential to that individual. The typical examples given to illustrate origin essentialism are tables and humans: a given table could not have been constructed from a different hunk of wood than the hunk it was in fact constructed from, and a given human being could not have been generated by a different sperm and ovum than the sperm and ovum it was in fact generated from.[5] Origin essentialism, as these examples suggest, is supposed to be a fully general philosophical thesis that applies to all individuals whatsoever that have an origin: if origin essentialism is true, then particular versions of origin essentialism—such as origin essentialism about tables, origin essentialism about humans, and so on—should also be true. So, then, while the structure of origin essentialism may be somewhat up for grabs, the scope of origin essentialism is universal, or nearly so.

Origin essentialism is an interesting and controversial philosophical thesis in its own right. Defenders of origin essentialism have offered arguments for it as a general philosophical thesis,[6] and several recent articles have criticized these arguments.[7] However, origin essentialism *about humans* is currently taken for granted in philosophical discussions about our duties to posterity. For example, if you decide to conceive a child now instead of later, it is almost always automatically taken for granted that the child conceived now is a different child than the one that would have been conceived later, since the child conceived now is a result of a different sperm–ovum combination than the sperm–ovum combination that would produce the child conceived later.[8]

I remain deeply agnostic about origin essentialism. But I've noticed that current debates about it tend to neglect a certain sort of problem, which I shall call the Problem of Differently Constituted Precursors. This paragraph and the next briefly states this problem (an unpublished Appendix below expands on the details) in the context of origin essentialism about humans. I focus on this problem in the context of human organisms like you and I[9] partly because that is the context in which the problem can be seen most clearly, and partly because that is the context in which origin essentialism is most widely assumed to be true. But it is not hard to imagine reformulating the problem in the context of artifacts like tables.

The Problem of Differently Constituted Precursors, in brief, is this. There seem to be possible worlds in which the same gametes that produced you in the actual world possess completely different material constituents and genetic structures than the material constituents and genetic structures they possessed in the actual world, and yet you still exist after the fusion of such altered gametes. In general this is a problem for any version of origin essentialism that focuses on the "stuff" (in this case, material constituents) and/or the "plan" (in this case, genetic structure) individuals have at their points of origin.

Now, why does this matter for thinking about procreative ethics and parental rights (for example, to direct the education of their offspring)? Well, I believe there are several implications related to what it means to teach your children well—but I will discuss those in the next section. For now, let me point out two other implications that float free of what it means to teach your children well.

First, imagine for a moment that the genetic technology of the future allows us to identify the region of the human genome that is most causally relevant to a particular learning disability (I recognize this is a gross oversimplification, but bear with me here). And imagine that we learn how to modify that region of the genome prior to conception—say, by genetically "treating" one of the gametes prior to fertilization—in order to prevent the resultant individual from having a genetic defect. If origin essentialism were true, the parents (or the geneticists) could coherently say this:

> Modifying this gamete prior to conception will not benefit anyone, even if things go well, and even if the modified gamete produces a happy human person without a learning disability. The person who would have been produced by the unmodified gamete is not benefitted—she is actually prevented from existing. The person produced by the modified gamete is not benefitted either—since it's not like we've made her better off by giving her a life without the dreaded learning disability. All we've done is made it impossible for one person—who would have had the dreaded learning disability—to exist, and we've made it possible for another person, a different person—who does not have the dreaded learning disability—to exist. If anyone is benefitted by this preconception genetic alteration, it's the parents, or the community, since they now do not have to endure the various costs (financial and non-financial) of educating a person with a learning disability.

However, if origin essentialism is *not* true, then the main idea behind this speech does not get off the ground. For if origin essentialism is not true, it does not block us from saying that this preconception genetic alteration effectively allows one person—a single person, the same person—who would have had a learning disability, to enjoy her life without that disability. Here we have an illustration of how the problem of differently constituted precursors itself leads us into thinking about a procreative case slightly differently than we would have otherwise.

Second, let's assume for the moment that the problem of differently constituted precursors has done its work of calling into question the truth of origin essentialism. The inability to rely on origin essentialism has other implications in other types of case even when differing the constitution of the precursors is not in view in that type of case. Recall the slightly annoying dialogue between the two would-be parents ('Mom' and 'Dad') in *Slightly Obsessive Benefiters*. Now why did I make you, dear reader, endure such dialogue? Well, if origin essentialism is true, Mom and Dad, despite their best intentions, are *not* benefitting anyone by calibrating their conception with the public school calendar. As long as they are conceiving the old-fashioned way (and not, for example, by storing the very same gametes in a reproductive clinic somewhere), their decision to wait several months to conceive produces a numerically different individual.

But if origin essentialism is not true, then Mom and Dad's thinking here is coherent on at least this front (despite its other worrisome features): Junior might be able to sensibly thank them one day for conceiving her in one part of the year rather than another, since Junior could reason that her conception during other parts of the year was a live possibility.

. . . Your Children . . . Part (b)

Recall question 1b above: what makes your children *your children*—that is . . . (b) the proper object of your attention and care, rather than the attention and care of others (i.e., the feature(s) making them *yours*)?

Long before young Calvin (the cartoon child in *Calvin and Hobbes*) met his educational nemesis in Miss Wormwood, there was another Wormwood who received some diabolical educational advice from his uncle Screwtape:

> The humans are always putting up claims to ownership which sound equally funny in Heaven and in Hell. . . . We produce this sense of ownership . . . by confusion. We teach them not to notice the different senses of the possessive pronoun—the finely graded differences that run from "my boots" through "my dog", "my servant", "my wife", "my father", "my master" and "my country", to "my God". They can be taught to reduce all these senses to that of "my boots", the "my" of ownership.[10]

What Screwtape observes here for the first-person possessive pronoun "my" is arguably sometimes true for the second-person possessive pronoun "your." So it makes sense to ask several questions: when we speak of "my children" or "your children," in the phrase "teach your children well," where on the spectrum of "finely graded differences" do we plant our meaning? And where should we? Do we sometimes reduce the sense with children to the "my" (or "your") of ownership? If so, should we?[11]

Without claiming any special expertise here about the way folks actually talk, I submit that most people, most of the time, say (and think) "my child" with a sense somewhere between "my wife" and "my father." Or perhaps more generally, between "my spouse" and "my parent." It seems to me that this is the way most people usually talk.

But some of us sometimes use a higher sense for "my child"—one closer to "my country" or even "my God." This can quickly become less than innocent. For example, the tendency to speak of "my child" with reverence and honor is seen when a school teacher or administrator confronts a parent who thinks (what the *Slightly Obsessive Benefiters* might one day think if they are not careful) that "my child" deserves to be the best, first, top, winner, in everything, and that "my child" can do no wrong, and should not have to answer for failing to study for, or even for cheating on, the exam.

Perhaps more commonly, some of us sometimes use a lower sense for "my child"—one closer to "my dog" or even "my boots." One need not be a monster to slip into such ways of thinking or talking. Imagine how an angry mother might respond to her rebellious teenage son who blatantly refuses to respect her house rules: "as long as you are *my* kid, living under *my* roof, you'll obey *my* rules for using *my* computer—that I bought with *my* money earned at *my* job with the sweat from *my* brow!"

It's important to notice, however, that *what it means* to call some children "your" children and what actually *makes it the case* that some children are "your" children (in the specified way) are different questions. This explains the distinction between the questions "do people talk that way?" and "should people talk that way"? For example, even if you think of "your" children in the most reductive way Screwtape mentions—using the "my" of ownership, say—it is a separate question what makes it the case they are "yours" in this particular sense—that you own these people. Merely talking like you own them does not make it true that you do. And merely talking like you don't own them does not make it true that you don't.

Indeed, while I said above that "a partial answer" to the question of "what makes them *yours*?" is that "they *originated* from you, and so you have some special rights, and/or duties, regarding them that others do not have," there may be an even more challenging truth of the matter. For *origination* seems to support something potentially much stronger than "*some* special rights . . .." In particular, it is worth wondering whether origination might support something even as strong as the "my" of ownership.

How might an account of child ownership get off the ground? Here's a first stab: it is coherent, if somewhat contested, that "my" body is my own in the strongest sort of way—like ownership, or self-ownership. But then it is a fairly short step to see that "my" child should also be my own in that strong sort of way: my body is mine; my body's parts are mine; and my child is, in one sense, a combination of my body's parts. In this way self-ownership, if real, leads quickly and naturally to offspring-ownership. If you think I own the parts you should think I also own their combination. At least, this is true of other wholes with parts I own, like sandboxes and sandwiches.

But that last paragraph was seriously misleading—after all, it almost always takes two people to produce a child (I hereby set aside cloning). So let's try again. *Me and my spouse's* child is *ours* in at least one straightforward sense: *our* bodies are *ours*; *our bodies'* parts are ours; and our child is, in one sense, a combination of *our bodies'* parts. If you think *we* own the parts you should think *we* own their combination. At least, this is true of other wholes with parts that people own, like corporations that merge some of their assets.[12]

While thinkers in other time periods have advanced the idea that parents own their children like they own property or parts of their own bodies, this idea is, to put it mildly, far less popular than it used to be. Indeed, this idea probably strikes many people as it struck one anonymous reviewer—as "disturbing in many ways, of course"! But why does it strike us this way? There are surely many reasons, but I believe that one is fairly easy to state: people legitimately worry that, if parents really did own their children like property or parts of their own body, this would give parents virtually unlimited *rights* to do whatever they want to their children. It would put parents in a pernicious and despotic position over their children, with the right or entitlement or authority to determine anything and everything about their child's welfare. This would even put the child's continued life at the mercy and good pleasure of the parents, with no constraint other than the will of the parents (and whatever obligations the parents have not to harm third parties).

However, there are many ways of alleviating this worry. Rather than survey the strengths and weaknesses of several, let me cut to the chase and state one that I see as perhaps the most promising. The core worry with modeling parental rights on bodily rights or property rights can be almost entirely dissolved as soon as we realize that this property-relationship is (among other things) *enduring* and *transitive*.

The claim that this relationship is enduring means that two parents' claims to own their biological offspring do not stop once the child becomes an adult.

I realize that this move appears to make things incalculably worse, and not one bit better, for the account. "Wait a minute; you are telling me that my dictatorial father doesn't just own me when I'm a zygote, or a fetus, infant, or teenager, but . . . forever?!" Rather than quibble with the details here in ad hoc ways ("relax, it's not forever, merely as long as you both shall live"; "relax, your dad only owns you proportionate to the percentage of the mass he contributed to your origin, so it's actually your friendly libertarian mom who has the all the legitimate authority in this arrangement"), let me just state that we need to introduce the *transitive* feature at this point.

The transitive feature is this. If A is the property of B, and B is the property of C, then A is the property of C. Transitivity here suggests that you (like B) can be a property-owner of another (like A) and be property yourself (of C) at the same time. And this matters because your rights to treat your property the way you want are now quite constrained: they are constrained by your owner's rights over you. C's rights over B control, regulate, and trump B's rights over A.

For example, you may think that you have the absolute right to be as harsh as you want with your child. But this is not at all the case if it turns out that your father is using his right over you to insist that you not be harsh with your child. After all, you are your father's property too. (And so is your son, but that's a different way to reach the same point.) So it turns out you do not have any right to be harsh with your child.

But does all this really help? In other words, does transitivity really help shore up the problems with endurance? At first glance, perhaps: your genial grandfather's rights are controlling and regulating your dictatorial dad's rights. But such a slightly reassuring outcome in this case vanishes as soon as someone's grandfather is actually *worse* than his father. We could kick it up another level and appeal to great-grandfather here (if he's still alive—this depends on whether being alive is necessary for your rights to trump and regulate). But that strategy faces the same problem at the new level: what if great-grandfather is worse than grandfather? And so on.

Rather than spell out all the intricacies of this view in detail, let me follow the 'and so on.' But let's try to follow it *all the way back*. Assume the common descent of all living humans. We can trace back (mentally) the ancestral lines until we reach the very first population of organisms with whatever the relevant psychological properties are, and dub them the first individuals with rights of self-ownership, whose rights over themselves effectively entail they have rights over all of their descendants (including us). (By the way, whether that population has a size of two or larger makes no difference.)

Or, we can go back farther than this population. (Assuming this population was created directly from dust is not necessary, and is actually a methodological distraction here.) Assuming this population evolved from ever more primitive life-forms, we face the issue of whether something like the first life form (whatever it is) has the right of self-ownership that determines its rights over all future life. If this seems an arbitrary and somewhat uninspiring place to stop, we merely kick it back a level to the pre-life substances that came before this first life. And then . . .

Well? And then we are up against either eternal matter or some divine person(s). On some forms of pantheism, it looks like the divine person(s) makes the physical cosmos rather like a human person separating parts of herself from herself without destroying herself—so that divine person would have the first right of self-ownership, and through that, the right of ownership of all of the physical cosmos (and hence the right of ownership of us). But on the more familiar versions of monotheism, it looks like the divine person makes the physical cosmos *ex nihilo*—out of nothing. Without claiming any more of a theologian's mantle than is absolutely necessary for this brief sketch, it strikes me that any divine person who has the first right of self-ownership, and then makes the physical cosmos *ex nihilo*, would have just as much of a right to ownership to all of it (and hence us) as a pantheistic divine person. Perhaps the rights to creative ownership here would be analogous to the rights of an artist or author to the copyright on an intellectual product like a song or book.

The relevant point here is this: on either the pantheist or the traditional monotheist picture, the divine person's rights over me trump my rights over my child. So if the divine person does not want me to be harsh to my child, then I do not have the right to be harsh to my child. For even though I own my child, the divine person ultimately owns both me and my child.

I suspect our degree of bristle at the initial idea of parents owning their children is a function of what we take to be the most likely replacement picture: that children are owned by *the state* or (more likely) that children are owned by *themselves* or (perhaps less likely) that children are owned by *nobody at all*. Screwtape has another suggestion—one much like the suggestion I have urged in the last few paragraphs—when he scornfully considers

> . . . men's belief that they "own" their bodies—those vast and perilous estates, pulsating with the energy that made the worlds, in which they find themselves without their consent and from which they are ejected at the pleasure of Another! . . . And all the time the joke is that the word

"Mine" in its fully possessive sense cannot be uttered by a human being about anything. In the long run either Our Father or the Enemy will say "Mine" of each thing that exists, and specially of each man. They will find out in the end, never fear, to whom their time, their souls, and their bodies really belong—certainly not to *them*, whatever happens. At present the Enemy says "Mine" of everything on the pedantic, legalistic ground that He made it: Our Father hopes in the end to say "Mine" of all things on the more realistic and dynamic ground of conquest . . .[13]

Nevertheless this is still an area of much puzzlement to me, and I have changed my mind on it more than a few times in the writing of this paper. I still sympathize with one anonymous reviewer, who worried that the (alleged) fact that each parent is owned by their own parent actually "makes matters worse by making every person owned by someone else, thereby demeaning us all." Yet this worry is not fully true, since my imaginative iteration of this process did not lead to an infinite regress, but a person who functions (with apologies to Aristotle) as the ownership equivalent of an unmoved mover—perhaps an unowned owner? And if the features of this unowned owner are certain ones rather than others, the possibility opens up not of demeaning us all, but of elevating everyone with the exact opposite of the soft bigotry of low expectations. There may be a dignity in being property when that property is demanded to be great and is destined to be glorious.

In any event, I tentatively conclude that it is not necessarily a pernicious and philosophically disastrous thing to think that we literally own our children because they originated from us. But I note that this cluster of beliefs may be sensitive to our background assumptions about ownership in general, both of our bodies and of our children's bodies.

Teach . . . Well

Children, obey your parents in the Lord, for this is right. "Honor your father and mother"—which is the first commandment with a promise—"that it may go well with you and that you may enjoy long life on the earth." Fathers, do not exasperate your children; instead, bring them up in the training and instruction of the Lord.

—Paul of Tarsus, *Ephesians 6:1–4*

If you hold to my teaching, you are really my disciples. Then you will know the truth, and the truth will set you free.

—Jesus of Nazareth, *John 8:31*

The philosophy of education contained in these words is an ideal that accents the *freedom* and *flourishing* of the child or learner. Of course, not just any freedom and flourishing: with apologies to those at various points on the political spectrum, the "freedom" is not merely a negative, political, libertarian "freedom to choose" (with a wink and a nod to Milton Friedman, author of a book with that title), and the "flourishing" here is not merely whatever someone enjoys filling their time with once granted "the right to define one's own concept of existence, of meaning, of the universe, and of the mystery of human life" (with winks and nods to Anthony Kennedy, author of a line or two with that phrase).

On any view, what it means to teach your children well is partly a function of what it means to teach. So let me state a core aspect of teaching that I will take for granted in what follows. Teaching typically involves attempting to benefit a learner; the scope of benefit typically includes the learner's character, especially when she is a child, and most especially when she is "your" child; and one aspect of this character benefit involves what Colin Macleod calls "Socratic nurturing." As Macleod puts it, "Many parents believe that children should be encouraged to 'think for themselves' and that education, both at home but especially in school, should equip children with the materials and skills necessary for critical reflection on important matters. In light of its attention to the importance of the examined life, I shall label this dimension of child-rearing 'Socratic nurturing'".[14] Like Macleod, I endorse a 'strong' interpretation of Socratic nurturing—whereby "its value is located partly in the importance of expressing respect for the autonomy potential of children *per se*" (319)—and not merely a 'weak' interpretation—whereby its value is located "only if it is conducive to getting children to embrace certain putatively valuable ends favored by parents" (319).

So, then. How might teaching your children well be sensitive to the other questions discussed above? Let's take "origin essentialism" as a token example to stand in for any of the contested moral and metaphysical theses discussed above.

I do not think that answering this question is as dramatic as the following sort of formula: "If origin essentialism is true, teaching Junior well means teaching him to be a leader/philosopher/homemaker; if origin essentialism is *not* true, teaching her well means teaching her to be a follower/poet/CEO." But then what do I think?

Let's start first with what may appear obvious, even trivial. Children should be taught what is true, and should not be taught what is not true. If original essentialism is true, then children should be taught that. If origin essentialism is not true, then children should not be taught that. (By "teach" here I mean "teach as true." Of course, if Socratic nurturing is in play, parents may teach to inform their child of a view without thereby endorsing that view as true. It's not as though parents need to confiscate and burn any extant copies of *Naming and Necessity* that they discover laying around the house.)

Second, and branching out just slightly, if origin essentialism is true, don't teach (as true) any view of the world to Junior that is incompatible with origin essentialism. If origin essentialism is false, don't teach (as true) any view of the world to Junior that requires believing in origin essentialism.

Third, the truth (or falsity) of origin essentialism can also be assumed when engaged in the practice of philosophizing *about* teaching. For example, consider the following idea, which is more general and more neutral than the cluster of ideas expressed above by the *Slightly Obsessive Benefiters*: "If we wait until later to conceive Junior, then we will be in a position to give Junior a better education." This idea is necessarily false if origin essentialism is true. If origin essentialism is true, it's now or never for Junior.

Fourth, the truth (or falsity) of origin essentialism can and should be assumed when engaged in the *practice* of teaching. Assume Junior is here. The time for preconception philosophizing is over. You have got a kid on your hands. Now what? Let me suggest how the above theses might inform us with a word about character education in general and the virtue of gratitude in particular.

Sometimes pre-college schools shy away from 'character education' of their students, focusing on "the three R's" (reading, 'riting, and 'rithmetic) and studiously avoiding 'righteousness'—what Socrates calls 'justice' in *Republic* (Greek *dikaiosune*). One reason for such shying away is that "we don't need to do that since children learn their values at home." Perhaps the premise and conclusion of this highly compressed argument are sometimes true. But when it comes to character education, surely somebody needs to "do that" somewhere. Can you imagine what would happen if those at home—parents and other caretakers—adopted the school's same posture in reverse—that "we don't need to do that since children learn their values *at school*"? Unfortunately, it's not entirely a matter of imagination. Children will learn some values all right—children are like "values vacuums"—and they will learn some values at home and school *despite the shyness of those who should be teaching them well*—and one of the values they will learn, and perhaps learn so that it's hard to unlearn, is this: "character is not the sort of thing you can teach; and even if it is, it's not important enough to teach."

Teaching junior *gratitude* (which W. D. Ross identified as one of our prima facie duties) may involve teaching children to *marvel* at the wonder of their existence. How do you teach them that (to echo a famous movie) "It's a Wonderful Life"? Well, if you can't access other possible worlds directly, to show them what the world would be like without them, you can at least teach them about the radical contingency of their existence and the profound improbability that they would get to be here to experience this universe. (One must be careful here: I realized after thinking about George Bailey's treatment in the movie that it may not produce gratitude in a child but its opposite if we focus on how bad of a place the world might be without the child in it. The child may come away thinking "hey, I can see why everyone *else* should be grateful for my existence, but what about *me*? I'm doing all the work of producing value for *other* folks here!")

I shall close with one final suggestion about origin essentialism and children's education. Recall C. D. Broad's quote above. Now notice a corollary of Broad's quote: if origin essentialism is false, it actually makes sense to think the following thoughts:

(1) 'My children could have been someone else's.'
(2) '*Are* my children someone else's?'
(3) 'Are my neighbor's children, mine?'

A tip to male readers: given the dominance of origin essentialism, expressing (2) and (3) out loud could be hazardous to your health. Don't ask your wife (2) or your neighbor's wife (3).

Notes

1 "Teach Your Children," Crosby, Stills, Nash, and Young, accessed June 1, 2016, http://www.azlyrics.com/lyrics/crosbystillsnashyoung/teachyourchildren.html.
2 C.S. Lewis, *The Abolition of Man* (San Francisco: HarperSanFrancisco, 2001): 73
3 Russell DiSilvestro, "Three Christian Arguments Against Germline Engineering," *Christian Bioethics* 18 (2012): 211.
4 C.D. Broad, "The 'Nature' of a Continuant," in *Examination of McTaggart's Philosophy*, Volume 1 (Cambridge: Cambridge University Press, 1933): 275.
5 Saul Kripke, *Naming and Necessity* (Cambridge, MA: Harvard University Press, 1980): 111–14.
6 In addition to Kripke, see Graeme Forbes, *The Metaphysics of Modality* (Oxford: Clarendon Press, 1985); Nathan Salmon, *Reference and Essence*, 2nd edition (Amherst, NY: Prometheus Books, 2005); Guy Rohrbaugh and Louis deRosset, "A New Route to the Necessity of Origin," *Mind* 113 (2004): 705–25; Rohrbaugh and deRosset, "Prevention, Independence, and Origin," *Mind* 115 (2006): 375–85.
7 See Ross P. Cameron, "A Note on Kripke's Footnote 56 Argument for the Essentiality of Origin," *Ratio* 18 (2005): 262–75; Ross P. Cameron and Sonia Roca, "Rohrbaugh and deRosset on the Necessity of Origin," *Mind* 115 (2006): 361–6; John Hawthorne and Tamar Gendler, "Origin Essentialism: The Arguments Reconsidered," *Mind* 109 (2000): 285–98; Theresa Robertson, "Possibilities and the Arguments for Origin Essentialism." *Mind* 107 (1998): 729–49; Robertson, "Essentialism: Origin and Order," *Mind* 109 (2000): 299–307; Robertson and Graeme Forbes, "Does the New Route Reach its Destination?" *Mind* 115 (2006): 367–73.
8 Derek Parfit, *Reasons and Persons* (Oxford: Oxford University Press, 1984): 351–79. For other examples of authors who follow Parfit, at least in assuming origin essentialism about humans, see Allen Buchanan et al., *From Chance to Choice: Genetics and Justice* (Cambridge: Cambridge University Press, 2000); David DeGrazia, *Human Identity and Bioethics* (Cambridge: Cambridge University Press, 2005).
9 My passing remark in the text assumes, of course, that we are human organisms. For a recent defense of this view, see Eric Olson, *The Human Animal: Personal Identity Without Psychology* (Oxford: Oxford University Press, 1997). I recognize in the unpublished Appendix that one way of avoiding the Problem of Differently Constituted Precursors is to drop this assumption. But I believe that

parallel problems can be formulated that correspond to most other views about what we are.

10 Uncle Screwtape to his nephew Wormwood, C. S. Lewis, *The Screwtape Letters* (New York: MacMillan Co., 1943): XXI.

11 I hereby admit but set aside what seem to me to be several interesting but irrelevant considerations. Admittedly, the song "Teach Your Children" by itself may not be indicative of how the general population typically uses the phrase "your child." Admittedly, the way the general population talks about "your" children (second-person possessive) may have some interesting differences between the way the general population talks about "my" children (first-person possessive). Admittedly, our language sometimes uses the possessive pronoun to accent our association (or dis-association) with an individual. For example, witness the humorous way that biological parents sometimes talk about their common offspring: when mom begins by asking "guess what *our* son did today?", dad knows Junior did something good; when mom begins by asking "guess what *your* son did today?", dad knows Junior did something bad. Likewise, recall the parable of the prodigal son: when the older unforgiving brother can only speak to his father about his wayward younger sibling derisively, as "this son *of yours*," the forgiving father gently corrects the older brother: "this brother *of yours* . . . was lost and is found" (Luke 15:25–31).

12 I am not claiming that many people, or anyone, ever sat down and reasoned "things that originate from me are mine (like this fire, this tool, this shelter); this child originated from me; therefore, this child is mine." That strikes me as explaining the more clear with the less clear.

13 Lewis, *The Screwtape Letters*, XXI.

14 Colin Macleod, "Shaping Children's Convictions," in *Theory and Research in Education, Volume 1* (London: Sage, 2003): 317.

* Please contact the author directly regarding the unpublished Appendix mentioned in the text if you want a free copy.

3   Children of Choice and Educational Responsibility*

Jaime Ahlberg

Prospective parents might choose to engage in genetic selection for a variety of reasons. In many cases they aim to select against the inheritance of debilitating or dangerous genetic diseases like Huntington's and Cystic Fibrosis. In others, parents seek to enhance their children's lives by selecting for genes that would increase their competitive advantage or their access to (what the parents believe are) intrinsically valuable human experiences. Genes related to IQ, analytic or artistic ability, height, or fitness might be desirable for this purpose. Yet other parents seek to have children that enable a particular parenting experience, especially those related to the parents' own culture, values, and preferred pursuits. Parents who select for deafness in order to share Deaf culture with their child, or who would select for musical talent in order to share their love of classical music, would be examples. While scientific understanding of the genetic code, epigenetics, and the capabilities of reproductive technology determines the decisions prospective parents might make regarding the genetic makeup of their children, advancements are ongoing. There is good reason to believe that the menu of genetic interventions available to prospective parents will only become richer and more detailed over time.

In light of these technological possibilities and the demonstrated parental interest in genetic selection, philosophers have written a great deal about the ethics surrounding such practices. Much of the literature focuses on the tension between parents' and children's interests, exploring such issues as whether parents harm their future children, or otherwise act wrongly as parents, when they choose their children's genes. For now I hold these ethical questions to the side. Prospective parents in the US currently have the legal freedom to make these procreative choices, and it is becoming an established practice. Here, I want to shine a light on the social implications of individual procreative choices, and investigate how responsibility for managing the consequences of genetic selection ought to be distributed between parents and society as a whole. Importantly though, while I bracket discussion of children's rights and interests, they are still highly relevant to any investigation involving procreation and rearing rights. Children have independent moral standing, and thus have rights and interests that inform the moral responsibilities of parents and of society at large. They have rights to basic healthcare and education, the provision of a safe home environment, and opportunities for play and recreation, for example. Parents and society must collaborate to meet these needs, so any inquiry into parental and social rights and responsibilities in this domain will have to be informed by the obligations both have to children.

To focus this inquiry I concentrate on the issue of educational responsibility. I accept that there are good reasons for the public support of all children's education, and here ask about the legitimate *extent* of public support given the flexibility that parents have in forming their children's identities, and more specifically, their children's capacities for success in school. I introduce, motivate, and distill my central questions in Section I. To preview, I consider those cases in which parents intentionally design their children's genes, and in which those efforts increase the social burden of providing the resulting children with an adequate education. These cases expose a tangible way in which society has an interest in procreative decision-making. They also raise the question of what procreative liberty protects. Does it protect parents against incurring the later, social costs of their procreative choices, such as additional educational costs? In Section II I discuss the ways in which this issue is complicated by the fact that educational cost, as well as what amount to capacities correlated with success, are socially constructed. If additional educational costs are socially constructed, one might think that individual parents ought not to be morally liable for those costs. I argue that is a mistaken view. In Section III I interrogate the central reasons parents offer for engaging in genetic selection: that genetic selection is a means of constructing a closer bond with their children, and that genetic selection provides their children with competitive and intrinsic advantages. I find these reasons incapable of exempting parents from bearing the additional educational costs attendant on their procreative choices. Section IV concludes with a discussion of how my moral arguments might bear on issues of policy and practice.

I Genetic Selection and Schooling

Even without the availability of genetic selection, some parents consciously prepare their children for school as part of their efforts to ensure that their children will have the social and academic advantages required to succeed in today's society. Others are more lax about their children's development, and leave much of the training and preparation of their children's capacities to schools.[1] Greater availability of choice in procreative decision-making has the potential to greatly amplify the educational consequences of such parental decision-making. This is especially vivid in cases in which resultant children will be more costly or difficult to educate in the current schooling environment. Without falling into genetic essentialism, one might worry that selecting for genes radically narrows the range of potentialities that children bring with them when they enter school.

While genetic selection is thus a species of a broader set of parental practices that aim at preparing their children for school (or not), it is also uniquely problematic. Once decided, the genetic interventions under consideration do not allow for environmental interruption later. In this respect choosing children's genes is unlike attempting to shape their values or confer advantages in other, more conventional ways. In the latter cases, other actors may intervene, and may be successful at disrupting the parental influence. Indeed, that possibility is central to a standard argument for schooling outside of the home: the school environment is leveraged to develop in children certain capacities that are not always enabled in their familial environments. The cases that throw into relief the tension between social and parental interests in genetic selection are those in which this type of external intervention is not possible or must be pursued in a different way, because the range of children's capacities have been intentionally fixed at the genetic level.[2]

What kind of impact might genetic selection have on society's ability to achieve its educational goals? Importantly, many of the effects might be neutral, with no discernable effect on the demands for educational provision that would have existed absent the genetic manipulation. The effects might also be positive. In such cases, parental choices *reduce* the costs or other social liabilities associated with preparing their child for adulthood. Imagine a case in which a parent selects for a genetic makeup that well-suits her child for the type of schooling environment already in place: say, with a long attention span, a desire to please and be helpful, and the intellectual ability to meet educational benchmarks with ease. Lastly, however, the effects might be negative; they might make it more costly, or in some other way more difficult, to bring the child into adulthood than it otherwise would have been. These are the cases that generate the kind of question I am interested in here, because they expose the tension between parental liberty and social interest.

Cases in which this issue arises are not simply possible fictions. In 1998 for example, a study published in the *American Journal of Human Genetics* reported that 16% of deaf couples would consider pre-implantation genetic diagnosis (PGD) to test their embryos for deafness genes, and of those 29% said they would prefer to have deaf children.[3] As early as 2002 a lesbian deaf couple was profiled by *The Washington Post* for soliciting a deaf sperm donor in order to have a deaf child.[4] Similarly, parents with acondroplasia (in which the body is of typical size but the limbs are shorter), also known as dwarfism, have used PGD to select for dwarf children.[5] A 2006 study found that, of 137 IVF-PGD clinics surveyed, 3% had intentionally used PGD to select an embryo based on the presence of a disability.[6] And while it is not yet possible through PGD, there has been some suggestion that parents might want to select for 'neurodiversity.' Parents with cognitive impairments may want to select for children who share their impairments, to enable closer bonding between parent and child.[7] Or, parents might want to select for high-functioning autism spectrum neurological profiles that can bring with them the possibility for genius-level musical or mathematically related aptitude and creativity. The thought is that parents who want to rear the next Beethoven or Wittgenstein would believe that the likelihood of status benefits and social contribution would outweigh the difficulties associated with socialization and intimacy. It should also be obvious from this range of cases that *both* genetic selection that results in talent, and selection that results in disability, have the ability to generate the relevant tension. Both talent and disability are defined with reference to a normative standard and mark divergences from that standard. Both may thus problematize the delivery of an adequate education. In what follows, I use the blanket term "exceptionality" when referring to deviations from the norm that are marked by either talent or disability.

Importantly, all of these cases involve prospective parents engaging in plans they know will result in, or will at least increase the likelihood of, children with the desired genetic makeup, and participate in those plans for *that* purpose. These cases are thus importantly different from cases in which parents learn of a fetus's genetic profile *after* conception, and *then* question whether to continue a high-risk pregnancy. Not only does this latter case introduce the thorny issue of abortion, it also removes the issue of parents specifically *designing* their children to have certain genetic traits. Also different is the case of parents who, for reasons unrelated to choosing their children's genes, increase the risk of exceptionality through their behaviors (by delaying conception until the parents are much older because they wanted to focus on their careers before having children, for example).[8] Since I want to focus on the parental design project, I do not take my conclusions here to directly apply to the case in which parents did not specifically select their children's genes. Such cases introduce complications that are important to theorize if we are to fully understand the ethics of parental decision-making in a social world, but I suggest we leave these additional complications to the side for now.

Why look to the impact of procreative choice in the arena of *education*? First, social resources for education spending are not unlimited. Special education spending, for example, has increased dramatically in recent years (6.6 million children already qualify), but not nearly enough to provide for those who qualify for it, and often at the expense of spending on educational goods for students who are not legally eligible for special education resources. Purposefully increasing the number of children who will qualify for special education resources by selecting for the traits that so qualify them, especially against a background of the current status quo, thus predictably strains an already strained system.

Significantly, the procreative choices in question here are unique in that they are reasonably idiosyncratic and are each unlikely to be pursued on a large scale.[9] While the selection of children's genetic traits might become normalized as a reproductive practice, it is improbable that there will be overwhelming selection for deafness in particular, or dwarfism, or a specific neurological profile. A consequence is that the children with these traits will very likely remain minorities in schools and in society at large. The small increase in their numbers under consideration here would not be sufficient to shift the norms of the labor market or of political participation. Thus, nor would a small increase in their numbers alone be large enough to shift the norms governing schooling, or what would make for an adequate education in our world. Greater resources than would otherwise be required will have to be diverted to education in order to achieve satisfactory educational outcomes for these children.

I do not mean to ignore the contributions to the educational experience that a more diverse student body could make, or to overestimate the all things considered costs associated with more diversity. A more diverse classroom could foster in children a more accurate appreciation for the variety of human experience, and a better sense of democratic community, which could make them better citizens and cultivate within them better character traits. But even so, in order to be successful a diverse classroom has to be more accommodating in terms of the content of the curriculum as well as how the curriculum is delivered—teaching standard language skills to all *in addition* to, say, sign language, or standard math practice alongside highly advanced exercises. And the educational experience has to be accessible to all types of bodies and modes of social interaction, as well as provide the tools children need in order to participate effectively given their various starting points. The point is merely that, especially (but not only) in inclusive classrooms, the addition of students with exceptionalities would predictably raise the costs of delivering an adequate education to all.

A second reason to focus on the educational arena is that education is theoretically and practically relevant to the debates surrounding parental rights, as well as debates regarding conceptions of talent and disability. In the parental rights debates, much hinges on reconciling the authority of parents to shape their children's lives with children's educational interests, as well as with the state's interest in an educated citizenry. The educational arena is fraught territory, because it is a space in which these stakeholder interests collide. But further, it is a space in which social attitudes regarding talent and disability are adjustable. To the extent that society constructs the ways in which capacities amount to talents or disabilities, and the consequent distribution of rewards and challenges, education is integral to the shaping and reproduction of these attitudes. In the next section I explore how the social construction of these concepts and attitudes complicates the division of educational responsibility.

II The Social Construction of Disability, Talent, and Educational Costs

One might think that the prospective parents in question cannot bear much, if any responsibility for any additional educational costs, because both the cost of education and exceptionality status are social constructs. Let us start with educational costs. The values that our society chooses to adopt are a determining factor in shaping the goals and purposes of our educational system, and consequently structure our education budgets. Because individual well-being is currently so dependent upon one's performance in a competitive, capitalist labor market, the skills and dispositions that it is considered urgent for students to master include: high level literacy and numeracy, complex social interaction skills, personal ambition (to at least some degree), and proficiency in executive functioning. Schools are charged with inculcating *enough* of these traits and skills in children, such that the adults they become are competitive in the job market and at least minimally prepared for civic participation. But social commitment to a particular set of values drives the costs of educational provision, and we could decide to prioritize other values or ways of life that are less expensive to achieve. Alternative skills and dispositions that are also valuable are in tension with those mentioned above, for example: the prioritization of familial or cultural obligations over personal ambition, an emphasis on artistic capacities, or calmness and introversion. Certainly there are some justice-related constraints we would have to observe in designing and delivering educational goods. Yet, justice is consistent with society prioritizing many different ways of living, and a reordering of values would plausibly have effects on the type and amount of educational provision appropriate for children. As relates to disability specifically, one might argue that rewarding personal independence over social concern, specialization over general knowledge, and market-based contributions over other types of contributions, are social commitments that, if reconceived, might well decrease the costliness of educating children with disabilities.

Further, many scholars have observed the ways in which disability status, in particular, is socially constructed. Not surprisingly, prospective parents who select for traits like deafness and dwarfism do not see themselves as making decisions that will worsen their children's lives all things considered. Indeed, they do not see deafness or dwarfism as disabilities, but rather see them as *differences*. The insight behind identifying deafness and dwarfism, or alternative neurocognitive profiles, as differences is that there is nothing inherently disadvantaging in bodies that are deaf or dwarf, or brains that are structured differently. While it is true that deafness, dwarfism, and Down Syndrome and Autism spectrum disorders involve physiological atypical states and/or functionings, whether they are at all associated with difficulties in living is dependent upon the social environments in which they occur.[10] A powerful illustration of this is Nora Ellen Groce's historical investigation of deafness on Martha's Vineyard between the 17th and 20th centuries. She writes the following about social attitudes toward deafness in the Island:

> One of the strongest indications that the deaf were completely integrated into all aspects of society is that in all the interviews I conducted, deaf Islanders were never thought of or referred to as a group or as

"the deaf". [. . .] My notes show a good example of this when, in an interview with a woman [. . .] I asked, "Do you know anything similar about Isaiah and David?"

"Oh yes!" she replied. "They both were very good fisherman, very good indeed."

"Weren't they both deaf?" I prodded.

"Yes, come to think of it, I guess they both were," she replied. "I'd forgotten about that."[11]

Groce's work details the social and linguistic inclusion of individuals with deafness into the greater Martha's Vineyard community, in childhood, family life, and work life. The adoption of sign language among all Islanders staved the isolation of those who could not hear, demonstrating the extent to which at least deafness need not be a disabling condition. Disability rights activists generalize the point by arguing that disabilities, and conversely conceptions of normalcy, are contingent social creations.[12]

The point may be generalized even further to acknowledge the social construction of talent. In our society for example, those who have the physical capacities to play basketball at a high level and put those capacities to use can command vast notoriety and wages. But it might be otherwise. For one thing, the rules of basketball might have been different enough to privilege a different sort of athlete, or indeed different sports altogether might have come to have cultural significance. Similar points can be made about intellectual and emotional capacities, and about physical appearance. The value of these things—which particular traits are valued and how much they are valued—is always in flux, and often precarious. Consequently, so is the social position of those who possess the relevant attributes.

Since the costs associated with educating children with exceptionalities are largely (or even entirely) socially caused, and talent and disability status can vary by social environment, one might suggest mitigated parental responsibility for bearing the costs of educating children who were selected to have those exceptionalities. It is not the *parents* who are generating the additional costs by bringing these children into existence; it is *society* that shapes the costs when it commits itself to the (exclusionary) social and economic arrangement that it does, and the associated educational system. Individual parents, the thought goes, are not responsible if the trait selected incurs extra educational costs, or that their future child will face social difficulties in response to that trait. Indeed, there is nothing prospective parents could do to alter these facts while they are considering genetic intervention; it would take broad social change to do so.

Does it follow that prospective parents who want to select for the traits in question have *no* responsibility for the additional costs associated with those traits? I argue that it does not. While it is true that the educational costs, and exceptionality status, are largely socially constructed, *any* social arrangement will advantage some and disadvantage others. Further, those who are disadvantaged in one arrangement may not be disadvantaged in another. Social commitment to a particular set of values invariably ends up disadvantaging those people who would be more successful if a different set of values were emphasized, simply because they are better suited to promote those other values. Commitment to any set of values will have this effect; there is no cooperative arrangement under which no one is disadvantaged relative to some other alternative. Whether one turns out to be disadvantaged in a given society then, is almost always at least in part socially caused. The mere fact that one is disadvantaged in a social arrangement does not indicate that society ought to bear the full cost of ameliorating that disadvantage. To conclude that we would need to know more, and at the very least: is the social arrangement in question justifiable, given the alternatives?

Following the work of Allen Buchanan, Dan Brock, Norman Daniels, and Dan Wikler, a good approach to this question—especially in the context of disability—is to require that a just social arrangement balances the value of inclusion against the value of maximizing what society has to offer (including goods and activities).[13] About the value to each citizen of inclusion, Buchanan et al write:

> The choice of a dominant cooperative scheme is a matter of justice because it determines who is disabled and who is not and because whether a person is disabled has profound consequences for his or her status in society, opportunities, and overall life prospects. Because of the economic and social advantages of being able to participate effectively in the dominant cooperative scheme, individuals have a fundamental interest in not being disabled, that is, in the dominant cooperative scheme being one whose demands are matched by their abilities.[14]

And about the value of productivity, which they identify as each citizen's 'maximizing interest,' they write:

> Each individual has an important and morally legitimate interest in having access to a cooperative scheme that is the most productive and rewarding form of interaction in which he or she can participate effectively. Just as those whose abilities do not satisfy the demands of the dominant cooperative scheme are at a disadvantage, so do those who could participate in a more productive and rewarding scheme but are barred from doing so by restrictions designed to make the scheme more inclusive lose something of value.[15]

Often, given a certain population, the realization of one of these values comes at the expense of the other; including everyone in all social endeavors comes at the price of increasing the goods and rewards of participation available to all. But each citizen has an interest in both of these values being realized: in being maximally included into the social arrangement, and in living in a society that is maximally productive and rewarding from her own perspective. In order to be justifiable from the perspective of each citizen therefore, a social arrangement would have to strike a balance between these values, for all. It is a significant component of many of the leading theories of social justice that being justified from the perspective of each citizen must be at least theoretically possible. This device can be used to adjudicate issues regarding when society ought to change its ways, versus when individuals ought to bear the costs of their situations (whether those situations be a matter of choice or circumstance).

Our society is, obviously, unjust along these lines. Many of the costs persons with disabilities bear are not justifiable to them in such a way. But notice that even in an arrangement that *was* so justified to all citizens, what is aspired to is a balance for all concerned. Even in a just society, it is overwhelmingly likely that some children would be more costly to educate than others simply because their biological, emotional, and/or cognitive profiles are uncommon. Personal heterogeneities will always lead to an uneven demand on social resources, to different kinds of claims to inclusion, and to different interpretations of the 'maximizing interest.' Again, this alone is not problematic, as what is at issue is not merely whether a person experiences any disadvantage relative to alternative social arrangements. What matters is whether the social arrangement is justifiable to its citizens *on balance*. In the effort to justify itself society would presumably provide for the (at least) adequate education of all children. Further, society would ask how its social arrangement (including attitudes towards persons with disabilities) could better achieve inclusion for all, and make better efforts in that direction.[16] In the case of children with disabilities, this is what we aim for even in our imperfect and unjust society.

But what I am concerned with in this essay is not the interests of the children involved, *per se*. It is uncontroversial to say that children with exceptionalities, whether they are children of choice or not, have interests in inclusion and productivity, and all of the educational goods associated with those broader interests. The appeal to the social causes behind educational cost and exceptionality, rather, is driven by the thought that parents should not bear responsibility for the extra educational costs or need because they are not the cause of those things. According to this challenger, what we should be interested in knowing is: is it justifiable from the perspective of *parents* that the educational costs associated with their procreative choices are higher than under alternative arrangements? And then, of course, this challenger suggests that the answer to this question is 'no.'

I think this is the wrong question to ask. In a more just world, it is certainly possible that, with better attitudes toward exceptionality and more inclusive social and economic practices, the educational costs in question could be lower. But that is, of course, entirely speculative. More importantly, even if they were lower in a just world, there is an issue about what kind of information about the world prospective parents should take as fixed when they are making procreative decisions. Should they reason about their options against a background of full justice, where (say) there would not be additional costs? Or ought they to reason within the confines of their actual, nonideal context?

In procreative decision-making, there is a kind of inappropriateness in looking to distant possibilities as a way to justify one's choices. The reason is that there are real people who have to face the costs of procreative choices, and that their interests are too easily eclipsed when prospective parents look to how the world *should be*, or even how it *might be* in time, rather than looking at the way that it is. Obviously, the parents in question and the children who are created will have interests at stake.[17] But also, the broader moral community has an interest in who will come into existence, and what those people will be like. Costs are imposed on the community when children are recklessly brought into the world and abandoned, for example. In such cases there is an obligation to support those children that has gone unmet by those responsible for their existence, and upon which society then must act.[18] In similar fashion, it might be said that parents electing for exceptionalities are acting irresponsibly, when they know that their actions will impose additional social costs. As Melissa Fahmy frames the worry, procreative decision-making is a matter of civic responsibility: "One could argue that it is irresponsible to deliberately create a child who will require significantly greater public assistance in order to pursue normal development and a happy and meaningful life."[19]

Saying that society should shoulder the burden is to say that it should spend resources to support these parents' reproductive preferences, rather than on something else of value. There is a real cost to making this assessment, as pointed out earlier with regard to special education funding in the US. It has been reported, for example, that educating a child with deafness costs nearly three times what it costs to educate a hearing child.[20] Clearly, as I have already stated and as Famhy notes, in order to perform an accurate accounting of the costs imposed one would have to calculate not only the additional expense of educating these children but also the benefits they offer to society through their existence. Some have suggested that the diversity brought by the presence of persons with disabilities fosters better social attitudes, even more humanity.[21] But these benefits are speculative and difficult to quantify, and for any one child coming into existence there is unlikely to be any appreciable effect on society's level of humanity. Much more tangible and foreseeable are the costs associated with educational provision.

At this point I might be charged with being too accepting of the status quo, and too ready to express certainty regarding the future costs of educating children with exceptionalities. I readily grant that working within a transitional, nonideal space is dangerous—in doing so one must walk a line between being on the one hand too aspirational and on the other too deferential to the status quo. Yet, it is appropriate to hold much of the education system and our socioeconomic culture fixed because of the enormity of the effort that it would take to change these factors. Society would have to reconsider how persons with exceptionalities are capable of socially participating and contributing, and what they are owed in terms of their educational provision as a result. Specific educational policies and practices that would have to be revised include: quantitative measurements of educational achievements and current accountability policy; the curricula of teacher education programs; the attitudes of students without exceptionalities toward their peers with exceptionalities; the content of the curriculum in primary and secondary school and how it is delivered. All of these are worthy targets for change, but it is exceedingly unlikely that any one of them, let alone all, will change in the near future (meaning: in the roughly six years between prospective parents conceiving and their child entering kindergarten). And this is not even to speak yet of the broader cultural norms surrounding citizenship, participation and reciprocity, and understandings of exceptionality. For this reason, I do not think it is a mark of complacency to say that prospective parents should hold their current context fixed when judging the effects of their choices. It is simply to acknowledge one's place in the world, and how one's choices affect that world.

Further, especially if an optimistic view about the full social inclusion of persons with disabilities is correct, there is a sense in which the question I am asking is *necessarily* a nonideal one. On that view, a society is possible in which people with all sorts of impairments are not disabled, because the society can appreciate and support many different forms of living well. This would even be possible with regard to diminished cognitive capacity, with the recognition that the lives of people with cognitive impairments can be productive and generally integrated in society. But notice that in such a world, of course, parents would not be selecting for traits that negatively impact the costs of educational provision. They really would just be selecting for different traits, which have neutral impact. The problem I am discussing—imposing extra burdens on society because of one's procreative choices—would not arise. It is in this sense that the question I am investigating only arises in the nonideal context. But then if it is only an issue in the nonideal world, we are not necessarily required or permitted to act as we would in a world that is fully ideal. We need a transitional, or nonideal theory, to help us work through the questions about exceptionality in society. At that point, we need arguments to sort out what information to hold fixed in procreative decision-making, and I hope to have been persuasive in my argument that we should hold fixed what we know about educational costs and exceptionality status at the time the decision is being made.

III Parental Reasons for Genetic Selection

In the face of an argument connecting procreative freedom with civic responsibility then, is there a positive case the parents in question might make for social support, in rebuttal? I suggest that we first look to the reasons offered by parents who have expressed an interest in selecting for disability.

Those who have selected for deafness, and those who have selected for dwarfism, have themselves been deaf or dwarf and describe wanting children who share those aspects of their identity that place them within a community central to their lives. For example, Sharon Ridgeway, a fourth-generation woman with deafness, describes the deaf household:

> Having a shared language (sign) means we can be part of a culture with which we can all identify. We all share the same ways of life and values—like the same technology such as flashing lights in the home and text phones, as well as common beliefs, games, humor, history and poetry. Why wouldn't I want my daughter to be part of that?[22]

Indeed, the Deaf position on such cases has been described in the following way: "that it is ethical to deliberately seek a deaf baby on the grounds of a shared culture."[23] The parents in question thus actively and purposefully shape the identity of the future community in response to some set of particular values that they have. Further, they appear to do so in reaction to the status quo. The social implications of being born with these traits—that they place their possessors into a particular community, separate in important ways from the broader social world—are integral to what makes them desirable for these parents. The difference associated with the traits is thus inextricable from their value; without the difference, the unique shared experience and community would not be possible.

Importantly, in giving this kind of reason for their procreative choices and expecting state support, these prospective parents look to be giving arguments nearly identical to parents who request educational accommodations because they desire to shape their children's values, or more particularly, raise their children in a particular culture. Usually, cultural accommodation in schools takes the form of exemptions, not special resource-allocation: exemption from dress codes or the usual rules of conduct, and sometimes even exemption from school altogether. Further, public schools are not asked by society to support a particular culture's values or unique conception of the good even though they are often responsible for imparting liberal values (toleration and moral equality for instance). In general, if parents want to bring their children up to share a distinct set of values or to engage in certain types of activities—perhaps they want their child to have specific religious beliefs, or to be a soccer champion, or attend an elite private or culturally specific school—they are free to do so, but are responsible for shouldering the price-tag.[24] There are important reasons for this approach to public schooling in a liberal society, primarily having to do with the obligation to bring children into full citizenship while remaining neutral across varying conceptions of the good life.[25] Choosing one's child's genes is much like these other parenting decisions when the appeal to cultural values is made: it is designed to ensure that one's child will have a life with experiences in it that the parent deems particularly valuable. Consequently, this argument does not offer a special reason to excuse parents from shouldering the extra educational costs.[26]

Alternatively, these prospective parents might claim that a child who shares particular traits would be one with whom they could more easily bond, thus improving the parent–child relationship. Barbara Spiegel, a mother with dwarfism who wanted a child with dwarfism, had her experience captured by the *New York Times* thus:

> She underwent genetic testing [and . . .] was told that her child would grow to normal height. She would have loved the child, she said, but in an interview, she recalled thinking, "What is life going to be like for her, when her parents are different than she is?"
>
> She worried that the child would be teased excessively. Ms. Spiegel's best friend, who has average height, has a daughter with dwarfism, and the child sometimes comes to Ms. Speigel for support; maybe an average-size child would also go to others for motherly advice. For a brief time, Ms. Spiegel grieved because she felt a dwarf baby would have been "just precious." But after a week, [a lab] mix-up was detected and she got her wish.[27]

Parents indeed worry about bonding with their children, and often want to increase the chances of bonding by ensuring shared experiences. Surely, in some relationships sharing a trait may increase the chances of bonding. But it may also offer opportunities for increased friction between parent and child. Parent–child relationships are complicated and parents are often mistaken about their predications regarding what sorts of interventions will improve or worsen their relationships. This is particularly true for prospective parents, who are as yet unaware of their children's personalities or other dispositions and skills, and unaware of how they themselves will experience parenting. Put simply, this reason is extremely speculative. As such, it is not strong enough to combat the reasons against public support.[28]

A different reason parents might offer in favor of selection is that selection will be of benefit to their future child.[29] One version of this reason would emphasize the desire for the future child to have access to what the parents think are intrinsically valuable capacities, and another version would highlight the desire to enhance the child's competitive advantage.

Intrinsically valuable capacities might include those associated with artistic, athletic, or analytical ability. Importantly, many of these capacities will already be encouraged by a minimally decent schooling experience. Many agree that one of the aims of schooling in a liberal society is to secure for all children access to the tools they need to live a flourishing life. This will include the opportunities to appreciate the basic elements of human flourishing—how to keep one's mind and body healthy, how to negotiate one's economic and political world, how to exist in positive relationship with others. Children are prepared for these goals according to their needs. Some need more math practice than others. Some need to learn better how to work productively in a group. Others need to learn better how to focus or how to complete the projects they begin. Schools are tasked with ensuring that children achieve minimal benchmarks with regard to these types of skills, as they are the skills that enable students to live well *generally*. Schools are not, however, tasked with ensuring that students develop potential in any particular skill or knowledge as a part of their neutral, liberal aims. If parents desire for their child to become an excellent violinist because they believe that a good life must contain musical ability, that is their prerogative, but that particular aim is not *demanded* by a liberal agenda (though it may be part of such an agenda). Similarly, procreative choices that aim at promoting a *particular* conception of the good, while they *may* be permissible in a liberal society, cannot demand to be subsidized. Under liberal pluralism, schooling is properly aimed at securing a certain breadth of experiences, opportunities, and outcomes for children that need not be responsive to parents' particular conceptions of the good.

The desire to secure competitive advantage through genetic selection can be impugned on similar grounds. It is certainly not an aim of public education to advantage particular children over others. The proper goal is to secure for all children something like an adequate, or perhaps equal opportunity for success in the educational context. But we can say something more about why it would be particularly troubling for schools to directly subsidize parental practices that end up privileging some children over others. In these cases, parents are motivated to create offspring who are the 'brightest and the best,' most likely to secure access to wealth and esteem. Parents have operated on the basis of this reason in the educational sphere for a very long time. The purchasing of elite schooling—for its credentialing but also for its provision of social networking opportunities—is a popular way parents have attempted to secure a child's competitive advantage. But the practice of purchasing private schooling, and related practices,[30] are especially problematic when evaluated from the social perspective. For every instance that a parent is successful in advantaging her own child, she is thereby disadvantaging another's child. To agree on this as a socially supported practice would be to agree to one of two outcomes. In one outcome, parents must select for 'competitive' genes on pains of their children being disadvantaged. This may be acceptable, if the parents in question do not happen to value a life characterized by social or economic success, but most parents do not want such opportunities to be foreclosed from the beginning of their children's lives even if such opportunities are not actively promoted. Another outcome is one in which every parent selects for competitive genes, resulting in a kind of arms race for competitive advantage. Such a practice is obviously self-defeating, since competitive advantage can never truly be achieved. It is thus doubtful that the desire of parents to secure competitive advantage for their children could be justified from the perspective of each parent.[31]

Though I am skeptical that parents have legitimate rights or prerogatives to select for their children's genes on the basis of any of these reasons, none of what I have said here contradicts the view that they do have them. Instead, I have argued that such rights and/or prerogatives, if they exist, do not include the right to social support in the education sector. Arguments in the education sector regarding the proper aims of a liberal education and the legitimate scope of parental rights have helped to make the case.

IV Conclusion

Again, the argument I have presented is a moral one, and not directly about what ought to be encoded in law or policy. It is primarily directed at the view that parents are fully morally entitled not only to make procreative decisions on the basis of their particular values, but also to be insulated from the social consequences of those choices and further, socially supported in making those decisions.

I have not made any suggestions about the proper mechanism for holding parents who want to select for exceptionalities responsible for the educational costs of doing so. I am open to whatever intervention makes the most practical and moral sense, and any proposal would likely trigger numerous considerations. Two very different sorts of mechanisms might include a tax levied on uses of such reproductive assistance, or one levied upon a child's entry into public school. The former would serve as a kind of proxy for taxing parents' *intentions*, which I have suggested is the source of parental responsibility; whether or not a child results from the technological interventions the parents would be subject to payment if they take action to design their child's genes. This would also evade the problem of disgruntled parents taking any frustrations about the educational tax out on their resultant, school-aged children.

One might worry about the expressive function of a policy that taxed people for selecting for traits that are costly to accommodate in schools. Would such a policy express disrespect for persons with such traits, and especially persons with disabilities? I cannot offer a full treatment of this objection here, but I will say that I do not think such a policy need have such a consequence. First, when I have focused on disabilities I have done so because they tend to be involved in the cases that raise the issue. But as I have indicated, providing extra resources for children who are considered talented would generate the same concern, and in such a case the same argument I have provided would hold parents who choose for 'golden genes' responsible for the additional costs of educating their children. One might resist this move by claiming that the issue does not arise with respect to talent because of the expectation that talented children will offset the extra educational costs they incur by being more (straightforwardly) productive as adults. From the perspective of justice, a kind of Rawlsian argument might be marshaled: since increased investment in talented children's educations redounds to be benefit of all, including society's least advantaged, such an increase is justifiable from all perspectives. But even if this is the correct approach to selection for talent, if an increase in investment did not carry with it the expectation of net return, or did not accrue to the least advantaged, it would not be so justified. And of course, if such a policy *were* to express disrespect, that alone might be a strike against implementing it. In such a case, we should still say the parents bear responsibility for the costs they impose, but that we cannot hold them to that responsibility because of other weighty considerations. In short, commitment to a particular policy would involve arguments that go beyond the scope of this paper.

In conclusion, let me just remark that in the background of this discussion is a large and difficult debate around the morality of social inclusion: how much the majority in a population ought to accommodate for the interests of a minority. Issues like this arise in public policy all of the time, and special education funding is a paradigmatic case. Increasing educational goods to those with unusual educational need diverts resources from other socially valuable projects. This is of course not to say we should not divert resources, but rather that there is a morally relevant cost to doing so. Diverting resources channels support away from other valuable projects, even from other students. Procreative decision-making makes matters even more difficult, because it forces us to assess not only the morality of inclusion *within* our cooperative scheme but also the ethical significance of deciding on the nature of the persons who will inhabit our cooperative scheme. I have argued that prospective parents who intentionally augment the extent of educational need through their procreative choices ought to bear the burden of covering those needs, when they do so from the perspective of their own particular values. Ideally, what I have said would be nested in a more general set of arguments regarding the morality of creating the persons who will constitute our society's future generations.

Notes

* My deepest thanks go to the other contributors in this volume for their helpful feedback on an earlier draft of this essay, and in particular to Samantha Brennan, Lindsey Chambers, and Michael Cholbi. I would also like to thank Anca Gheaus, Melinda Hall, Sarah Hannan, Joshua Rust, and audience members at the Florida Philosophical Association 2014 annual meeting for comments. Last, my appreciation goes to the University of Florida Department of Philosophy faculty and students for helping to make the "From Procreative Ethics to Parental Rights" conference—at which this paper was presented alongside the others in this volume—a lively and productive event. My title is inspired by John A. Robertson's book, Children of Choice: Freedom and the New Reproductive Technologies (Princeton, NJ: Princeton University Press, 1994).

 1 See Annette Lareau's important book on the different parenting styles of American middle-class and working-class parents, and the implications for children's lives as children and the opportunity sets they face as adults. *Unequal Childhoods: Class, Race and Family Life*, 2nd edition (Berkeley: University of California Press, 2011).

2 Of course, it may certainly still be possible to intervene on some capacities, or very general ones. It is probably virtually always possible to promote children's autonomy for example, even when their genes have been deliberately selected. My only claim is that there are cases of selection that put real limits on what is possible in the educational context, or the ways in which it is possible to achieve educational aims.

3 Anna Middleton, J. Hewison, R.F. Mueller "Attitudes of Deaf Adults Toward Genetic Testing for Hereditary Deafness," *American Journal of Human Genetics* 63 (1998): 1175–80.

4 They were successful. See Liza Mundy, "A World of Their Own," *The Washington Post Magazine*, April 1, 2002, Accessed on September 24, 2016, https://www.washingtonpost.com/archive/lifestyle/magazine/2002/03/31/a-world-of-their-own/abba2bbf-af01-4b55-912c-85aa46e98c6b/. Also see M. Darshak and M. D. Sanghavi, "Wanting Babies Like Themselves, Some Parents Choose Genetic Defects," *The New York Times*, December 5, 2006, Accessed on September 24, 2016, http://www.nytimes.com/2006/12/05/health/05essa.html?_r=0.

5 This case is slightly more complicated than selecting for deafness or selecting for neurodiversity, because the genes associated with acondroplasia are also implicated in a fatal condition. When both parents have the gene, their offspring have a 25% chance of being average size, 50% chance of being little, and 25% chance of having a condition called "double dominant mutation" which is usually fatal soon after birth. Dwarf parents using IVF thus often use PGD to screen for the fatal condition, and then are faced with the decision of whether to implant the embryos that will be little or the embryos that will not be little, since the genetic makeup of each embryo is known. When two dwarf parents conceive naturally, expectant mothers will often use amniocentesis to screen for double dominant mutation and abort when it is present. See Darshak M. Sanghavi, op. cit.

6 Susannah Baruch, David Kaufman, and Kathy L. Hudson, "Genetic Testing of Embryos: Practices and Perspectives of U.S. IVF Clinics," *Fertility and Sterility* 89 (2006): 1053–58. Cited in Sanghavi, op. cit.

7 Julian Savulsecu mentions this possibility in "Deaf Lesbians, 'Designer Disability,' and the Future of Medicine," *British Medical Journal* 325 (October 2002): 7367. Parents with Down Syndrome may be interested in selecting children with Down Syndrome, for the same reasons parents with deafness express an interest in rearing children with deafness: the belief that shared experiences lead to better bonding and make possible the sharing of a culture.

8 Thank you to Joshua Rust for challenging this essay's central arguments with this more complicated, and much more common, case.

9 Though films like *Gattaca* suggest an alternative possibility. In that film, practices of parents selecting for mental and physical enhancements are so widespread that the norms of human functioning shift. About these cases, the central argument that I offer in this paper will imply that parents who *do not* engage in selection are responsible for bearing the costs associated with their decision. I should say that I think this case introduces additional considerations that might affect the division of parental and social responsibility: namely, personal responsibility in the context of collective action problems. A full account of the ethics of procreative decision-making would have to address this.

10 The World Health Organization's International Classification of Functioning, Disability, and Health (ICF) makes the following useful distinctions. An impairment occurs where there is atypical bodily functioning or structure. A disability arises when one has difficulty negotiating a given environment with a certain impairment. Handicap is further distinguished as the competitive disadvantage one experiences as a result of disability.

11 Nora Ellen Groce, *Everyone Here Spoke Sign Language: Hereditary Deafness on Martha's Vineyard* (Cambridge, Massachusetts: Harvard University Press, 1985): 4–5.

12 I do not intend to endorse the conclusion of the disability social model theorist Michael Oliver, who claims that disability is *entirely* socially caused. He writes: "it is not individual limitations, of whatever kind, which are the cause of the problem but society's failure to provide appropriate services and adequately ensure the needs of disabled people are fully taken into account in its social organization." Michael Oliver, *Understanding Disability from Theory to Practice* (New York: St. Martin's Press, 1996): 32. Rather, some of the physiological aspects of disability may be implicated in the difficulties in living with disability, whatever the social environment occupied. Chronic pain would be a good example of this. I mean only to point out that there are many ways in which disability status is a matter of social environment, as can be seen through the Martha's Vineyard case. See also the work of Lorella Terzi, *Justice and Equality in Education: A Capability Perspective on Disability and Special Educational Needs* (London: Continuum International Publishing Group, 2008): 52–58.

13 Allen Buchanan et al., *From Chance to Choice: Genetics and Justice* (New York: Cambridge University Press, 2001).

14 Ibid., 291.

15 Ibid., 292.

16 See Buchanan et al. on this point, Ibid., 303.

17 And ethical assessment of any particular procreative decision will have to issue from a myriad of factors, including the non-identity problem, the nature of possible benefits and harms, and the extent of risk that it is acceptable to incur on behalf of a nonconsenting other. These are difficult issues that, thankfully, I do not have to engage in this paper.

18 This is not to deny that children are public goods or that society must, in various ways, offer assistance to parents in the rearing of children. It is only to say that procreative choices can have vast consequences for our social community as a whole, and arguments thus need to be given regarding the nature and extent of social support.

19 Melissa Seymour Fahmy, "On the Supposed Moral Harm of Selecting for Deafness," *Bioethics* 25 (2011): 133. To be clear, Fahmy does not endorse this view.

20 B.P. Tucker, "Deaf Culture, Cochlear Implants, and Elective Disability," *Hastings Center Report* 28 (1998): 10. Cited in Fahmy, op. cit. 133.

21 Fahmy cites Sharon Duchesneau, a deaf mother, as claiming that deaf children make the world more diverse, and that that diversity translates into a more humane world. Op. cit.

22 Quoted in H-Dirksen L. Bauman, "Designing Deaf Babies and the Question of Disability," *Journal of Deaf Studies and Deaf Education* 10 (2005): 313. Bauman correctly observes that Ridgeway's claim about shared culture could not ground a right to use PDG to select a baby with deafness, since if Deafness is cultural and not physiological then it would surely be available to babies who can hear, as well.

23 Ibid., 312.

24 Interest theories of rights do not necessarily protect this kind of parental choice. See, for example, Harry Brighouse and Adam Swift, "Parents' Rights and the Value of the Family" *Ethics* 117 (2006): 80–108 and Sarah Hannan and Richard Vernon, "Parental Rights: a role-based approach," *Theory and Research in Education* 6 (2008): 173–89. Choice theories might protect the right to make this choice, but do not necessarily imply that society should shoulder the costs of the choices made.

25 See Mianna Lotz, "Liberalism and the Status of Family Making," in *Procreation, Parenthood, and Educational Rights*, Edited by Jaime Ahlberg and Michael Cholbi; and Marc Ramsay, "Liberalism, Parental Rights and Moral Education,"

in *Procreation, Parenthood, and Educational Rights*, Edited by Jaime Ahlberg and Michael Cholbi, both in this volume.

26 This is not at odds with the view that parents and children have an interest in sharing a particular kind of relationship, and that the practices mentioned (and particularly the sharing of enthusiasm regarding cultural or religious heritage) ought in some cases to be protected. It is merely to claim that society does not have the obligation to foster or support this kind of connection in the schooling environment. For an argument establishing parent–child associational rights, and their limits in the education sector, see Harry Brighouse and Adam Swift "Family Values and School Policy: Shaping Values and Conferring Advantage," *Education, Justice, and Democracy*, Edited by Danielle Allen and Rob Reich (Chicago: University of Chicago Press, 2013): 199–220.

27 Sanghavi, op. cit.

28 Beyond this observation, Harry Brighouse and I have argued elsewhere that, even if parents have the right to forge a certain kind of relationship with a child they are rearing, they do not have the right that that relationship be made as easy or as desirable as possible. See Jaime Ahlberg and Harry Brighouse, "An Argument Against Cloning," *Canadian Journal of Philosophy* 40 (2010): 539–66.

29 I hold to the side any complications introduced by the non-identity problem. For further discussion on that issue, see especially Robert Noggle's contribution to this volume, "A Chip Off the Old Block: The Ethics of Shaping Children to Be Like Their Parents."

30 Consider the practices of moving to the school district with the best schools, and of purchasing educational experiences for one's child after school and over the summer.

31 The literature on the morality of enrolling one's child in private school explores these arguments in more detail. See: Harry Brighouse and Adam Swift, "Legitimate Parental Partiality," *Philosophy & Public Affairs* 37 (2009): 43–80; Adam Swift, *How Not To Be a Hypocrite: School Choice for the Morally Perplexed Parent* (New York: Routledge, 2003); Matthew Clayton and Andrew Stevens, "School Choice and the Burdens of Justice," *Theory and Research in Education* 2 (2004): 111–26.

Bibliography

Ahlberg, Jaime and Harry Brighouse. "An Argument against Cloning." *Canadian Journal of Philosophy* 40 (2010): 539–566.

Baruch, Susannah, David Kaufman and Kathy L. Hudson. "Genetic Testing of Embryos: Practices and Perspectives of U.S. IVF Clinics." *Fertility and Sterility* 89 (2006): 1053–1058.

Bauman, H-Dirksen L. "Designing Deaf Babies and the Question of Disability." *Journal of Deaf Studies and Deaf Education* 10 (2005): 311–315.

Brighouse, Harry and Adam Swift. "Family Values and School Policy: Shaping Values and Conferring Advantage," in *Education, Justice, and Democracy*, edited by Danielle Allen and Rob Reich, 199–220. Chicago: University of Chicago Press, 2013.

Brighouse, Harry and Adam Swift. "Legitimate Parental Partiality." *Philosophy & Public Affairs* 37 (2009): 43–80.

Brighouse, Harry and Adam Swift. "Parents' Rights and the Value of the Family." *Ethics* 117 (2006): 80–108.

Buchanan, Allen, Dan Brock, Norman Daniels and Dan Wickler. *From Chance to Choice: Genetics and Justice*. New York: Cambridge University Press, 2001.

Clayton, Matthew and Andrew Stevens. "School Choice and the Burdens of Justice." *Theory and Research in Education* 2 (2004): 111–126.

Fahmy, Melissa Seymour. "On the Supposed Moral Harm of Selecting for Deafness." *Bioethics* 25 (2011): 128–136.

Groce, Nora Ellen. *Everyone Here Spoke Sign Language: Hereditary Deafness on Martha's Vineyard*. Cambridge, MA: Harvard University Press, 1985.

Hannan, Sarah and Richard Vernon. "Parental Rights: A Role-Based Approach." *Theory and Research in Education* 6 (2008): 173–189.

Lareau, Annette. *Unequal Childhoods: Class, Race and Family Life*, 2nd Edition. Berkeley: University of California Press, 2011.

Middleton, Anna, J. Hewison and R.F. Mueller. "Attitudes of Deaf Adults toward Genetic Testing for Hereditary Deafness." *American Journal of Human Genetics* 63 (1998): 1175–1180.

Mundy, Liza. "A World of Their Own," *The Washington Post Magazine*, April 1, 2002.

Oliver, Michael. *Understanding Disability from Theory to Practice*. New York: St. Martin's Press, 1996.

Sanghavi, Darshak M. M. D. "Wanting Babies Like Themselves, Some Parents Choose Genetic Defects," *The New York Times*, December 5, 2006.

Savulsecu, Julian. "Deaf Lesbians, 'Designer Disability', and the Future of Medicine'." *British Medical Journal* 325 (October 2002): 7367.

Swift, Adam. *How Not To Be a Hypocrite: School Choice for the Morally Perplexed Parent*. New York: Routledge, 2003.

Terzi, Lorella. *Justice and Equality in Education: A Capability Perspective on Disability and Special Educational Needs*. London: Continuum International Publishing Group, 2008.

Tucker, B. P. "Deaf Culture, Cochler Implants, and Elective Disability." *Hastings Center Report* 28 (1998): 6–14.

4   The Problem of Choosing (For) Our Children

K. Lindsey Chambers

Parents have an interest in sharing their values, beliefs, and projects with their children.[1] At the same time, children have an interest in being both capable of and free to develop their own values, beliefs, and projects. The interests of parents and children can conflict, and a great deal of attention has been given to how we ought to adjudicate this conflict with respect to child-rearing and education.

This tension has been pushed further back in the parenting timeline by the advancement of reproductive technology. From donor selection to embryo testing and selective implantation during in vitro fertilization, parents have greater opportunity to impose their own values on their children by selecting for the traits their future children will come to have, potentially at the expense of the child's interest in being both capable of and free to determine for herself who she will be and how she will live her life.

Preconception reproductive decisions differ from child-rearing decisions in that they can also determine *which* child is created.[2] In cases where a procreator's decision determines which child will come into existence, much has been made about the metaphysical possibility of the created person's being harmed by that decision. Some believe that it is impossible to harm a person by creating her because being created cannot make a person worse off.[3] Procreators, then, do not wrong the persons they create, though they may count as acting wrongly in some impersonal sense.[4]

Even if it is not possible to make a person worse off by creating her, it does not follow that the person created has not been wronged in some other way. Though the person created does not exist at the time of the procreator's action, her interests are not thereby moot. The procreator is still *creating another person*, so it stands to reason that her decision should in some way be constrained by the value of the person she creates.

One framework for thinking about how a procreator's decisions should be constrained by the interests of future persons is to consider the role obligations that procreators incur in the decision to create children to parent.[5] For many procreators making use of reproductive selection, their end is not just to create a child but to create a child in order *to parent* that child. A procreator who procreates in order to parent may be constrained by the obligations she has as parent to that (future) child.

In this paper, I will argue that the parental role constrains the ends that are appropriate for a parent to pursue when she creates a child in order to parent that child. The parental role is both justified and constrained by the moral status and predicament of children.[6] Parental obligations, both before and after conception, are largely directed at relieving the child from that predicament by facilitating the child's coming to be her own person, capable of forming and revising her own system of beliefs, values, and projects. Parents wrong their children when they fail to take that end as a limiting condition of their actions.[7]

In section §1, I will elucidate the connection between the moral situation of children and the moral end of parenting. In section §2, I will consider the consequences of the moral end of parenting on the appropriateness of a parent's transmitting her religious beliefs to her child. I will argue that it is permissible for a parent to transmit her beliefs when doing so does not hinder the moral end of parenting and the parent has made that the condition of her action. In section §3, I will show that prospective parents must also condition their actions on the moral end of parenting in their reproductive selection decisions. Specifically, I will argue that the requirement generated by the moral end of parenting undermines arguments in favor of reproductive selection that appeal to the parents' interest in having a child who shares her beliefs and values.

§ 1 The Moral Status and Predicament of Children

Persons are beings who have the moral right to determine for themselves what they believe, what they care about, and what they do. Persons are distinguished from other beings in part because they *can* reflect on and evaluate their own beliefs and values. Persons need not act on every whim and desire they encounter; they can decide *whether* a given desire is to be acted on, whether a given belief is to be believed, a proposed action to be done. I may want to eat a cupcake for lunch, but part of being a person is having the capacity to think about that desire and decide whether I should and whether I will act on it (I did).

Controlling another person's life may sometimes make her happier, but a person whose life becomes the product of another person's decisions and not her own is missing something important. I might, for example, be much healthier if someone follows me around and throws away the junk food I buy, constantly replacing it with fruits and vegetables. After the frustration turns to reluctant acceptance, I may come to quite enjoy the carrot sticks I am left to eat for lunch. However, an important component of my life would be missing: my action would be the product of another person's choice, not my own. I may flourish physically, but I do not flourish *as a person*, because I am not fully acting as a person.[8]

The value of a person determining her own life is not merely an instrumental one. People may do a terrible job of figuring out what to believe and do, and even when they do a fine job, life circumstances don't always work out how they would like them to. Exercising one's agential independence, as I'll call it, is no guarantee for a happy life. However, no matter how happy a person may be, she cannot fully flourish *as a person* if she is prevented from acting as a person. I will not argue here for this account of human flourishing. I assume that, for those who are able to act as persons, their flourishing depends at least in part on their doing so. We respect other persons as persons, then, by giving each other the freedom to decide and act for themselves, even if some persons do not act as well for themselves as others would do for them.

Importantly, persons start out their lives as children. Children lack the capacities that enable persons to make their own decisions about what to believe, care about, and do. Children begin life with little control over their bodies, their thoughts, or their desires. Children also lack the skills and knowledge they need in order to successfully navigate the world on terms that could count as their own. As Tamar Shapiro writes, ". . . [T]he condition of childhood is one in which the agent is not yet in a position to speak in her own voice because there is no voice which counts as hers."[9]

Despite lacking the capacities to act as persons, children still have the moral status of persons.[10] Though they are in the care of adults, they are not the property of those adults as if they were *things*.[11] Ultimately, children, like adult persons, aren't *for* anything. They are valuable as persons independent of what they can do for others.[12] We respect children as persons, not by leaving it to them to determine their own lives (they can't), but by helping them become beings who can act as independent persons.

To become persons who have the physical, cognitive, and emotional capacities necessary to act as independent persons, children require and have a moral claim on the rest of us for the care, support, education, and resources necessary to do so.[13] A child's interest in receiving that care generates an obligation on everyone to ensure that the child receives it. Some adults choose to assume primary responsibility for providing that care to particular children by becoming the parents of those children.[14] The social role of parent is a response to both the moral status of children and the moral predicament of children. Children are valuable as independent persons, but they lack the capacities and resources they need to act as persons. Parents assume responsibility for helping children develop the capacities and acquire the resources they need to do so. The parental role, then, has an important moral purpose: we have a collective obligation to care for children and to help relieve their predicament, and we've organized our social institutions such that parents can and do assume responsibility for discharging that obligation.[15]

A person can enter the parental relationship with a child either by creating a child or by choosing to parent an already existing child.[16] When a parent assumes responsibility for a child, she assumes responsibility for a person whose value is fixed and independent of her utility with respect to the parent's other ends. The parental role is grounded in the interest the child has in becoming an independent agent, and so the actions of parents ought to take that end as their condition.

Part of facilitating a child's agential independence may involve other aims, such as raising a happy and emotionally well-adjusted child or developing an intimate parent–child relationship.[17] However, these aims are not sufficient on their own. Parents must pursue these aims in conjunction with and on behalf of their child's eventual independence. Imagine a child whose parents act in ways that keep her reliant on them—perhaps they spoil and shelter their child from the outside world. The child may want for nothing, and she may be content with her life. However, her parents' keeping her dependent on them violates their duty to her as their child. Neither happiness nor a loving parent–child relationship is a substitute for the child's eventual self-determination. Children must have the opportunity to live their own lives, even if doing so makes them less happy than they would otherwise be. Aiming at raising a happy child or at developing an intimate parent–child relationship ought to be conditioned on the aim of facilitating that child's independence. Where the child's happiness or attachment to her parents *furthers* her agential development, it's an appropriate aim. Where some other aim comes at the cost of the child's independence, it's not an appropriate aim.

Though parental obligation is primarily directed at facilitating the child's coming to be her own person, parents must make innumerable decisions on behalf of their children in order to do so.[18] Just in discharging their obligations, parents stand to greatly influence what their children will one day come to believe and care about. Sometimes this influence is deliberate, like enrolling a child in clarinet lessons, while other times the influence is incidental, like what friends the child meets at camp or the fondness for cheese curds the child develops after attending the county fair. All of these influences, whether deliberate or not, shape the child's development, and, in particular, they have the potential to shape what sort of person the child eventually becomes.[19]

Parents also have their own interest in explicitly sharing their own beliefs, values, and commitments with their children.[20] Parenting is a full-time job, and a parent doesn't cease to be her own person when she is in the role of parent. In fact, the opposite is true: parents parent by living alongside their children as persons in their own right, with their own beliefs and values. When parents go about living their lives in front of their children, they can't help but model social and behavioral norms, express emotions, resolve (or fail to resolve) conflicts, possess (or lack) cultural capital, and, ultimately, operate with some orientation toward the world and their place in it. A parent's own capacities and understanding of who she is and what matters to her will have a profound impact on her children—whatever else she does as a parent.[21]

The parent–child relationship is just that, a relationship between two morally equal persons. Children aren't the property of their parents, nor are parents slaves to the needs of their children.[22] It's within the context of the parent–child relationship that parents have an interest in being able to exercise their own beliefs and values. If a parent is committed to eating organic food, for example, then she has an interest in preparing organic meals both for herself and for her child. If a parent is religious, she has an interest in participating in her religious practices with or around her child.[23]

The parental role, then, though grounded in the child's interest in exiting the predicament of childhood, is also sensitive to the parent's interest in being herself within the context of the relationship she has with her child. Part of being in an intimate relationship, like that of a parent and child, involves sharing oneself with the other person, both by talking about one's values and by sharing experiences and doing things together. A parent must have some leeway to share her values with her child as part of being true to herself within the context of their relationship.[24]

However, though both the parent and child are equally morally valuable, the parent nevertheless incurs an obligation to take the child's interest in becoming an independent agent as a limiting condition of her actions, even where that might limit her own freedom to transmit her beliefs and values to her child. Whatever a parent does, she must constrain her actions so as to facilitate the child's coming to have the capacities necessary to live her own life, because it's her duty to respect her child as an independent person. In what follows, I will explore how the tension between parents' and children's interests might be recast in terms of the parent's obligation to make the moral end of parenting the condition of her actions.

§2 Religious Education

Consider the (somewhat) controversial practice of educating one's child in a particular religious tradition. Where does one draw the line between an appropriate exercise of the parent's own religious beliefs and the child's interest in being free to decide for herself what to believe? What, for example, could explain why it could be impermissible for a parent to indoctrinate her child into a religion but not impermissible to include her child in her religious practices?

One familiar place to draw the line is to look at whether the child's participation in the parent's religious practices *harms* the child. Arguments against indoctrination, for example, tend to take this form: indoctrination is wrong when and because it *harms* or threatens to harm the person being indoctrinated.[25] Indoctrination is the practice of instilling beliefs in a person in a way that bypasses the person's reason,[26] making those beliefs resistant to later rational revision. The harm is understood in terms of the damage that indoctrination does to a person's rational capacity: the person is stuck with some set of beliefs, not because she has rationally reflected on and accepted them, or has, on reflection, chosen not to reflect on them, but because they were psychologically reinforced in a way that prevents her rationally reconsidering them.[27]

If harm is the relevant standard, then indoctrination might not be the only practice ruled out as inappropriate parenting. Any serious initiation, teaching, or privileging of the parent's belief and value system has the potential to be harmful to the child's future emotional state. If a child is raised with a serious commitment to a particular worldview, then her later abandoning that worldview for another might only be possible at a high emotional cost. If, for example, the religious child comes to abandon her religious beliefs, it may cost her the community she's grown up in, it may change the nature of her relationship with her parents, and it may make her feel disoriented about the world and her place in it.

If the thing to avoid is *harm*, then parents might need to refrain all together from imparting their particular belief system, religious or otherwise. Not only would religious parents potentially harm their children by sending them to religious schools or taking them to religious services, but parents with deep political convictions, views about the ethical consumption of food, etc., would all risk harming their children if their children later reject their parents' beliefs. The child raised as a vegan who becomes a meat-eater may experience the same emotional distress and familial tension as the conservative who becomes a socialist, or the atheist who becomes a Christian.

Parents should not try to avoid causing their children pain at any cost (if that were possible). Parents should aim to create the conditions necessary for their children to be capable of determining, for themselves, what they care about and what they will do with their life. That end is directed at developing the child's capacity for forming and revising her beliefs about what matters. If developing that capacity is the ground of the child's interest and the parent's obligation, then the morally relevant harm is the harm a parent's action might do to the child's development of that capacity. Indoctrination is a serious wrong on this account, not because the child is stuck with some set of beliefs that she didn't arrive at by her own rational consideration, but because the child's very capacity to rationally consider her beliefs has been damaged.

Moreover, it may be that a condition of a child's coming to have the capacity to form any serious commitment to a belief or value system is that she first learn some particular belief system "from the inside."[28] Even if a parent tries to give her child a neutral upbringing, she is still raising her child with a particular worldview. Suppose a religious parent raises her child with a serious commitment to liberal pluralism in an effort to avoid unduly influencing her child's eventual religious beliefs. The commitment to liberal pluralsim, however, is itself a substantive commitment about what people are like and how they should treat one another within a scheme of social cooperation. Whatever the parent teaches her child, she can't escape teaching her child some particular worldview—even if the worldview is more inclusive than others. The child, then, will learn how to think about what the world is like, who she is, and what her place in that world is from within some particular system of beliefs and values. If developing the child's agency requires robust education from within some belief and value system, then parents would not only be permitted to teach their children a particular worldview, they would be morally required to do so, and to do so on the condition that the child's growing up inside that worldview will not damage her capacity to become an independent agent later.[29]

The emotional pain the child experiences when she rejects the belief system she's been raised with is not unimportant. The child's potential emotional distress gives parents a strong reason to make it clear to the child that their love and support as that child's parents are not conditioned on the child's continuing to share their beliefs. Parents can take their children to church, so to speak, but if the child later rejects the parents' religion, the parent is not thereby entitled to reject the child. Parents, though permitted to share their beliefs with their children, are not permitted to stop parenting their children if their children fail to share those beliefs.

Harm isn't thereby irrelevant to the moral evaluation of parenting, but harm understood as making the child 'worse off' in some general sense doesn't track what's at stake. It is a grave harm to children when their parents continually act against or without regard to their development as independent agents, but that leaves it open that acting *for* the child's development as an independent agent might come at some other cost to the child. Indoctrination hinders the moral end of parenting not because it makes the child worse off generally, but because it directly violates the parent's obligation to facilitate the child's development into an independent person. That it might one day be emotionally difficult for a child to change or revise her beliefs, however, isn't on its own an obstacle to the child's developing the capacities to be her own person. In fact, it may be a price of that development.

The question isn't whether parents greatly influence what their children come to believe and care about, the question is whether their actions are consistent with the moral end of parenting and whether they *condition* their actions on the moral end of parenting. Some kinds of actions, like indoctrination, are themselves unsupportable by the moral end of parenting, whatever the parent's ultimate reason for action. Other kinds of actions might be justifiable within the parental role; however, an action's being justifiable with respect to the moral end of parenting doesn't guarantee that a parent acts *for that reason* or *on that condition*. A parent might fail, not by actually hindering the realization of that end, but by failing to make that end the condition of her action. This mistake is a subtle but important one. As a parent, a person takes on a role, the standard for which is determined by the moral status and predicament of the child.[30] To assume the role of parent and yet fail to be guided by the moral end of parenting in one's parental decisions, or to make the realization of that end conditional on its being instrumentally valuable to one's other ends or projects, is to make a mistake as a parent.

Failure, then, is not relegated to cases where a child is *in fact* made incapable of later making up her own mind about some set of beliefs or values. A parent can make this mistake even when the child happens to successfully develop into an independent agent in the world. A parent who aims to bring it about that her child becomes a person with particular beliefs and values might do all the same things as a parent who is merely sharing her own beliefs on the condition that doing so doesn't hinder the moral end of parenting. The difference lies in the condition: the former's condition is successful belief transmission while the latter's condition is capacity facilitation. In either case, the child may come to share her parent's belief system, yet only the former case counts as an inappropriate end with respect to the moral end of parenting.

What, then, is an acceptable end or aim for a parent to pursue in exercising her own beliefs and values within her role as a parent? The answer, I think, is found in the nature of the relationship between the parent and her child. A parent, as noted above, has an interest in being able to exercise her own beliefs and values within the context of her role as a parent. She has an interest not only in being able to express her beliefs and commitments to the child, but also in living out those commitments *with* her child. However, if the child rejects the parent's commitments, the parent is not thereby released from the role of parent. The parent must still facilitate the child's coming to be her own person. She is not permitted to make her relationship with her child, both her care and affection, dependent on whether her child eventually comes to share her values and commitments.[31]

A parent can introduce her child to her beliefs and values if she takes the exercise of her own beliefs and values to be appropriate only on the condition that she is at the same time equipping her child with the skills and knowledge of the world that will enable her child to eventually make up her own mind about what matters.[32] A parent may, for example, bring her child with her to a religious service, or even send her child to a religious school, and yet be doing so on the condition that doing so will enable the child to eventually make up her own mind about whether to believe and practice that religion or any religion at all.

The difference between a parent who acts on the right condition and a parent who doesn't may be most evident in cases where a child later rejects the parent's belief system.[33] A parent who is committed to the moral end of parenting will respond differently to the child's doubts, questions, and outright rejection than a parent who is committed to replicating her own religious beliefs and commitments in her child. A parent committed to the moral end of parenting would encourage the child's critical assessment of the belief system she was raised in, make it clear to the child that the parent's love is not conditional on the child's sharing the same beliefs system, etc., without having to disavow her own beliefs or even support the values the child adopts.[34]

For a parent to make the moral end of parenting the condition of her actions doesn't require that the parent expose her child to some à la carte array of prospective belief systems, pretending to be impartial to the merits of each, in order to count as being committed to the moral end of parenting.[35] Doing so would not only be disingenuous to the parent's own commitments, but it would also fail to model to the child what it is to care deeply about something, to think seriously about whether those commitments are worthwhile, and to engage with others who don't share those commitments. A child who learns some particular belief or value system from within and in the context of a loving and secure relationship with her parents, however, is well positioned (as ever she could be) to navigate the world as her own person. She knows what it is to care about something, and she has a support system within which she can sort out what *she* ultimately finds worthwhile.

Importantly, the parent–child relationship, unlike other relationships, is characterized by only one party—the parent—being able to choose to enter the relationship. And even when the parent does choose to enter the relationship, she does so without knowing much, if anything, about who the child is or who the child will be. It's a relationship where the parent commits to caring for the child, by loving her and respecting her as an independently valuable person, before knowing who that child will be. Something goes wrong when that commitment is itself conditioned on the child's coming to be *someone in particular*.[36] A parent who suspects that she could not continue to love her child if her child does not come to share some belief or value system shouldn't enter the parent–child relationship to begin with. Once in the role of parent, she will be obligated to provide that care irrespective of what her child comes to believe or care about, because once a parent is parenting a child, that child is dependent on the parent(s) she has for *their* love and support—another adult won't do. Once the relationship is underway, the parent is in it for the long haul. To enter that relationship and *not* be committed to the moral end of parenting is as much a mistake as failing to condition one's child-rearing on the moral end of parenting.[37]

The moral end of parenting, then, not only constrains the actions of parents who are parenting existing children, it also bears on how a parent enters the parental role to begin with. A parent should not create a child to parent and at the same time fail to take that child's coming to be her own person as the ultimate end of creating her. A parent who creates a person to parent in order to satisfy her own ends, without regard for her responsibility to her child as an independent person, fails in her obligations as a parent. The prospective parent's failure is a mistake not because the child will be harmed or otherwise made unable (or less able) to determine her own beliefs or values, but because the parent fails to condition her actions on the moral value of the child and the obligation she incurs by choosing to enter the parental role. In what follows, I will consider the implications of the moral end of parenting on the practice of reproductive selection.

§3 Reproductive Selection

Prospective parents might use reproductive selection for a number of reasons. Some may want to use selection to avoid passing on certain hereditary diseases, like cystic fibrosis or Tays Sachs. Others might use selection to create children who resemble them, by, for instance, selecting sperm or egg donors who resemble the prospective parents. Some may want to give their children a competitive edge, such as greater height or higher intelligence, while others might want to select traits that they anticipate will make it easier for them to parent their child, such as the child's sex or, if it becomes possible, temperament.

Of the variety of reasons that prospective parents might employ selection, one kind of reason stands out as potentially problematic with respect to the child's agential independence: the prospective parents' desire to pass on their beliefs and values to their children by selecting for physical traits that embody those values and/or enable the prospective parents to transmit those values to their children. The decision of some deaf parents to select for deaf children, for example, is sometimes defended by appealing to the deaf parents' interest in sharing Deaf culture and the unique benefits available to members of the Deaf community with their children.[38] One could employ that strategy to defend the selection of a wide range of traits—from the child's sex to her musical aptitude.

I won't address the particular practice of selecting for deafness here. There are hard questions about whether deafness is a difference or a defect and whether what makes deafness a hardship for those who have it is primarily of a social or physical nature. What I am interested in is the appeal to the parents' own conception of what kind of life is valuable to live as a way to justify their creating a person with a particular physical trait.

In order to isolate the parent's aim from considerations about the child's being harmed, I will consider the case of selecting for musical aptitude. Musical aptitude is a trait many would say is either a benefit to those who have it or at least not a burden, though people differ as to whether (and to what extent) they value that particular aptitude.[39] Selecting for musical aptitude in one's child also doesn't seem like an outright hindrance to the moral end of parenting. If it's not appropriate for a prospective parent to select for musical aptitude, it is when and because the selection itself isn't *for the child*.

When prospective parents act in order to become parents, they assume the role and subsequent obligations of being a parent. For example, a parent can be under parental obligations in her pursuit of adopting a child, even before she successfully adopts and enters a relationship with a particular child. Suppose that a prospective parent decided to become a parent by purchasing a child. She would not only act wrongly insofar as she participates in the commodification of another person, but she would also act wrongly as a prospective parent. Her purchase of a child is wrong in a way that's distinct from the wrong committed by the person who brokers the child's sale. Though both act wrongly by treating the child as a thing that can be bought with a price, the parent also acts wrongly *as a parent* in her failure to appreciate and act in accordance with the moral worth of the being for whom she plans to assume primary responsibility.

Prospective parents can also act well as parents before they begin parenting a particular child. As with other roles that serve a moral purpose, parents can and do prepare to take on the role of parent. Prospective parents, adoptive or biological, take parenting classes, read parenting books, plan financially, gather the necessary resources for caring for a child, enlist help and advice from friends and family, etc. These actions suggest that a person can begin to assume parental responsibility, and act well as a parent, before she is a parent to a particular child.

A prospective parent assumes the responsibilities of a parent when she *intentionally* sets out to create a child in order to parent that child. The prospective parent's creating the person to parent is part of her parenting, and it, like her subsequent parenting actions, falls under the obligations for what counts as parenting well. Prospective parents' procreative decisions, including selection decisions, can be evaluated in terms of their appropriateness with respect to the moral end of parenting and whether the prospective parent makes the moral end of parenting the condition of her selection.

Parents, including prospective parents, don't have an independent right to shape their children however they want. Selection decisions, if made at all, should be made on the condition that they facilitate the child's coming to have the capacities she needs to be an independent agent in the world, because that's the only justification for selection that could count as respecting the child as a person who is valuable in her own right and who, if created, would be in a moral predicament that the parent is responsible for relieving. Selection decisions not made on that condition are not bad because the child will have some trait that's not worth having, just like someone else deciding what I will eat for lunch needn't result in my having a bad lunch—their lunch choice could be both healthy and delicious. The problem is in the choosing, not the lunch itself.

Parents are only permitted to act on behalf of their actual children because their doing so is a necessary condition of their children's coming to have the capacities they need to navigate the world on their own terms. For selection decisions, it's not enough for the trait to be neutral with respect to the child's coming to be an independent person. Someone choosing my lunch for me may be neutral with respect to my agential capacities, but it's still an imposition on my agential independence. Selecting for traits that are not necessary for facilitating a child's future independence is akin to choosing a stranger's lunch: the choice could be a good one in lots of other ways, but the choosing itself is problematic. Prospective parents who select for a trait to further their own ends treat their children as if their very existence is worth bringing about merely as a means for the parents to exercise their own conception of what makes life worthwhile. But a child is not *for* anything. A child is valuable as a person in her own right. If she's created at all, she should be created in a way that treats her as a person who will someday come to have her own beliefs about what's valuable, not as a vehicle for her parent's values.

To see how a parent might act wrongly as a parent by selecting for a person with a particular trait, consider the following three scenarios:

1   *P values music/musicianship and selects for musical aptitude as a way of bringing it about that her future child also values music/musicianship.*
2   *P values music/musicianship and selects for musical aptitude in order to share her love of music with her future child.*
3   *P values music/musicianship and selects for a child with musical aptitude as an expression of (or an instantiation of) the value of music/musicianship.*

Scenario (1)

If, as I've suggested above, parents must enter the parental role on the condition that their doing so will facilitate the child's coming to be her own person, then scenario (1) seems to be a straightforward violation of that end. Even if in scenario (1) the child doesn't in fact become the next Yo-Yo Ma, the aim of creating a person with a particular life-shaping value is inconsistent with the aim of facilitating that person's coming to determine for herself what's valuable to do with her life. The problem isn't that musical aptitude is itself bad, or even that selecting for musical aptitude could ever ensure a child's later life plans; rather, the problem is the parent's aim of creating a person in order to bring it about that the person created adopts a particular way of life. That aim subordinates the value of the child to the end of bringing it about that a person has some trait that the parent values.

Suppose that instead of musical aptitude P selects for a child with a particular sexual orientation or a disposition toward religious belief.[40] On the view I'm proposing, these cases should make us uneasy. It's not that any one sexual orientation or religious affiliation is good or bad. The problem is that it would be inconsistent with being in the role of a parent to select for such traits on behalf of one's child just because one values that particular way of life. To do so is to subordinate the value of the child to the value of the child's having some trait.

Scenario (2)

In scenario (2), the parent's aim is not obviously at odds with the moral end of parenting. In this scenario, P selects for musical aptitude in order to share her own love of music with her child. You might think that a prospective parent can justifiably use reproductive selection in order to create a child that is better positioned to share her parent's values. In *Ethics and Human Reproduction*, for example, Christine Overall presents a potential feminist justification for preconception sex-selection that takes on a similar structure to scenario (2).[41] Overall appeals to a woman's desire to share the unique experiences of being a woman with her child as a reason for selecting for a female-sex child. On her view, being a woman isn't just a matter of biology. Women, whether by sex at birth or gender identification, experience life in a unique way that includes certain hardships and burdens that a person cannot fully understand without experiencing them herself. Overall imagines that a woman might legitimately prefer to select for a female child in order to share those experiences that are unique to women as part of the intimate relationship she will have with her child.

On the view I've proposed, though a female parent may better be able to share her particular experiences as a woman with a female child, that alone does not justify intentionally bringing into existence a person on the condition that the person will be capable of sharing those experiences. What's troubling about Overall's example is that a condition of the parent's being able to share herself with her child is that the child experience a similar *hardship* to the parent.[42] The parent, then, doesn't merely value the trait in question (being a biological female), the parent also intentionally selects a trait that will bring about additional burdens for the child *for the sake of* being better able to share her own conception of value with that child.

Suppose, on the other hand, that the woman recognized that there are burdens faced by both sexes, though the kinds of burdens that are faced by each sex differ from each other.[43] The woman might opt to select for a female child, not to share her burdens with her child, but to be better positioned to help her child navigate the burdens that are unique to being female. Or, suppose she wants to select for a female child because she suspects that, for similar reasons, she *couldn't* adequately rear a male child. You might think parents can—and perhaps should—take measures to parent children they are better suited to parent (though I suspect prospective parents are not well positioned to make such judgments before they've parented a child).[44] In the woman's case, she wouldn't be selecting in order to impart her own values to her child, she'd be selecting in order to better parent her child. Her selection is not obviously permissible, but her reasons come closer to the kind of justification for selection that could count as respecting the person she intends to create.

In scenario (2), P proposes to choose for her future child just so she can more easily share her beliefs and values with the child. This line of justification for selection treats the child's existence as a mere means for the parent to satisfy her own desire to share her values and commitments with someone like her. Unless the parent has some additional reason to think that it's all things considered better for the child to have the trait than not, where better for the child is understood in terms of the child's future capacity to be her own person, it's hard to see how selecting for that trait could be consistent with being a parent that respects the independence of her child by acting for the child's well-being and future, not for what the child can be and do for the parent.

It's perhaps an unsettling consequence of the view I'm considering that a parent's desire to have a child *like herself* is not, in itself, sufficient justification for employing reproductive selection. I think the intuition behind it, however, maps onto something many parents already know to be true. Though opting into parenthood may be part of a person's overall life plan (and so may be the motivating reason for a person's decision to take on that role), once in the role of parent, her own projects and plans are no longer the parent's primary concern.[45] The child's development into a healthy, independent person takes precedence as the parent's primary (though not only) aim.

The priority of the child's needs over the parent's interests is part of what marks the different nature of a parent's relationship to her child and a person's relationship to a romantic partner, friend, or even another family member, like a sibling or cousin. Though a parent may have an interest in having the kind of relationship that she can only have with a child in her care, that relationship is still a fiduciary relationship: one where the parent assumes primary responsibility for the well-being and development of a dependent and vulnerable person.[46] It's on the parent, then, to sometimes subordinate the ideal exercise of her own values and projects where failing to do so would be inconsistent with facilitating the child's coming to be *her own person*—a feature that doesn't show up (at least not to same degree), in other relationships.[47]

Scenario (3)

In scenario (3), the parent's aim is to express her love of music by selecting for musical aptitude. Selecting for musical aptitude is the parent's way of endorsing the value of music in a flourishing or meaningful life. The parent's valuing music is expressed by her creating a person who will (hopefully) be well positioned to appreciate and partake in the distinct joys and benefits that music and musicianship have to offer.

What's interesting about scenario (3) is that it's partly aimed at benefitting the child. The parent values some trait or aptitude x, and the parent aims at benefitting her child by positioning the child to better appreciate and partake in x. However, though there is a sense in which the parent aims at benefitting the child and not at determining the child's life course, the ultimate justification still rests on the parent's valuing that particular trait within or as part of her own conception of what makes life valuable. In this case, the parent values the role of music in contributing to a person's living a good life. Her choice to select for musical aptitude in her child is both an expression of that value and a way of positioning the child to enjoy that value herself. A prospective parent's creation of a person to parent, however, is not the appropriate avenue for her expressing or endorsing her particular beliefs and values. The value of the person she creates is not conditional on that person's being an expression of some other value, and so the child shouldn't be brought into existence on the condition that her life will express the parent's commitment to it.[48]

It's worth noting that on my account of parental obligation, a parent can enroll her child in music lessons but a prospective parent can't select for musical aptitude, though both actions may be motivated by the parent's valuing the role of music in living a good life. The relevant distinction depends on the context of the parent–child relationship. Parents who are in the midst of an intimate, pervasive relationship with their children must have some freedom to express their own beliefs and values within the context of that relationship, so long as they do so on the condition that they are also facilitating their children's independence. However, before the child is conceived, prospective parents are not yet in a *relationship* with their future children.[49] Their decisions, then, cannot be justified as an exercise of their interest in sharing who they are with the persons to whom they are intimately connected and for whom they must equip with some practical starting point. Imagine that a stranger, not a parent, chose where the child would go to school, what sports she would play, etc. Those choices needn't be malicious for the choosing itself to be inappropriate. The stranger shouldn't choose for the child any more than she should choose such activities for another adult, even if she would make excellent choices. Absent a relationship with the child and a commitment to taking responsibility for the child, the stranger has no moral standing to impose her own beliefs and values on the child, even if doing so wouldn't otherwise harm the child.

Nevertheless, it's still an open question whether a parent could opt to select for (or against) some trait as the result of an appropriate parental aim. If some trait or bundle of traits are necessary for a person's developing the capacities they need to act as an independent person, then, arguably, prospective parents ought to be allowed to select for such traits *for that reason*. There may even be adequate child-centered reasons to select for traits that aren't essential to agential independence, but that stand to expand an agent's opportunities in ways that would make the child *more* able to determine her own life. Suppose, for example, that the future child in scenario (3) *couldn't* enjoy music unless P selected for it. P may very well be justified in selecting for musical aptitude as a way of expanding the opportunities available to her future child.[50]

Prospective parents must at least refrain from using selection to further their own ends. Even if the child who results has an all things considered good life, her very existence is the result of an action that disrespects her independence as a person. Her parents wrong her not because she suffers or is otherwise burdened by their selection, her parents wrong her because they've treated her as if her value depends on her usefulness to their own ends. The question that prospective parents should consider, then, is whether they are selecting some trait for their own sake or for the sake of their future child's most fundamental interest in living her own life.

§4 Conclusion

Parents choosing for children, even outright choosing their children, must not violate their obligation as parents to facilitate their children's coming to have the capacities necessary to operate in the world as independent persons, capable of determining for themselves what to believe about the world and their place in it. Parents don't violate this end just by influencing what their children come to believe and care about. On the contrary, parents may have an obligation to equip their children with some practical starting point, some way of understanding the world and what matters. However, their doing so is not justified by their own interest in or right to settle these questions on behalf of their children. Rather, the justification comes from the child's interest in developing the capacities to eventually settle such questions herself.

Parents, then, may share their own beliefs and values *on the condition* that doing so is part of their facilitating the child's coming to develop the capacities to determine her own beliefs and values. Parents may, on that condition, teach their children a particular system of beliefs and values, and if the child later comes to share those values, the parent has not thereby parented poorly. However, a parent whose aim is to determine for her child what her child will believe and care about, regardless of her success, fails to act on the condition that her parenting facilitate her child's coming to be her own person.

Prospective parents who choose to enter the parental role by intentionally creating children to parent are under the same obligation to condition their actions on the independent value of the person they intend to create. Unlike the case of a parent sharing her beliefs with her child within the context of an existing relationship with that child, the practice of using reproductive selection to transmit or express her values is not consistent with treating the child as a person in her own right. Unless the selection is for the sake of the child's coming to have the capacities she needs to be her own person in the future, the prospective parents wrong their child. Selecting for a trait, then, can be inappropriate not because the trait is itself bad for the child, but because selecting it subordinates the child's value as a person to the parent's own ends. Parents, then, are only permitted to choose for their children when they are truly choosing for the sake of their children.[51]

Notes

1 I have in mind the overall collection of beliefs and values that shape how a person lives her life. People act under some conception of what's good to do, what the world is like, and what their place is in that world. Those beliefs and values can be present and effective without necessarily forming a systematic, consistent, and well-thought out life plan or overarching conception of what gives life meaning.
2 Derek Parfit, *Reasons and Persons* (Oxford: Clarendon, 1984).
3 David J. Velleman, "The Identity Problem," *Philosophy & Public Affairs* 36, no. 3 (1998): 221–44; Matthew Hanser, "Harming Future People," *Philosophy and Public Affairs* 19, no. 1 (1990): 47–70.
4 Parfit argues that we should give up the idea that there is a personal, or person-affecting, wrong. However, he still thinks a procreator can act wrongly by violating a general consequentialist principle by failing to bring about the better state of affairs in the world. See Parfit's *Reasons and Persons*, 378.

5 There may be a general constraint on anyone who creates a person, regardless of whether he or she occupies a role like that of parent to the child. For instance, a Kantian might object to anyone's creating another person merely to serve her own ends. Though I think there is an argument to be made about a wrong that is not role-based, I think starting with the role requirement on parents can help get traction on the kinds of considerations that should bear on the creation of a person.

6 Tamar Schapiro, "What Is a Child?" *Ethics* 109, no. 4 (1999): 715–38. I am using Schapiro's language of 'predicament' to describe the state of children because I think it captures something important: children are in a state of dependency now, but they are, with our help, on their way to becoming independent agents. Their success in becoming independent agents depends on many factors—some of which are up to us.

7 My discussion, though it may bear on questions about the extent of parents' legal rights, is not directly addressing what a parent should be free to do to or with her child. My target is the moral end of parenting, not the legal rights she should have (or not have) in procreating and child-rearing.

8 If I hired someone to do that, knowing that I should eat more healthy lunches but also knowing that I'm terrible at following through with that aim, the lunch-snatching would at least be connected to *my own decision*, albeit indirectly.

9 Schapiro, "What Is a Child?" 729.

10 K. Lindsey Chambers, "Choosing Our Children: Role Obligations and the Morality of Reproductive Selection" (Ph.D. diss., University of California Los Angeles, 2016). I am assuming a Kantian view of the moral status of persons, where a human being counts as a moral person in virtue of the general rational (and by extension, moral) capacities of human beings. Importantly, an individual human being's moral status does not depend on her particular rational capacities. Though that claim is not uncontroversial, I think there are good reasons for not making an individual's moral status dependent on her *current* skill level in exercising her agency. In my dissertation, I discuss our obligations to persons who are not yet able to exercise their agency, including future persons.

11 Immanuel Kant, *The Metaphysics of Morals*, trans. Mary Gregor (Cambridge: Cambridge University Press, 1996): 64–5; Kevin N. Maillard, "Rethinking Children as Property: The Transitive Family," *Cardozo Law Review* 32, no. 1 (2010): 225–63. Kant writes that a child is not like a table, something that can be discarded at the will of the parent. Kant's discussion may seem misleading insofar as he is, in that very passage, describing a person's right to the child 'as if a thing.' What he means, however, is not that the child has the moral status of a thing, but that the state of the child, and the corresponding responsibility of the parent with respect to the child, requires that the parent be allowed the freedom to exercise some control over the child (as if a thing). The parent's right to the child, as if a thing, is still grounded in the child's value (and needs) as a person, and not in the claim a parent has to her as property. Contrast this view with how children are sometimes treated in in custody disputes. Maillard discusses how the law sometimes treats children as the property of their parents.

12 A child's value, then, doesn't depend on whether she makes her parent happy or contributes to society as a public good. Any benefit she provides to others is secondary to her value as a person.

13 Not all children will be capable of reaching this state. The moral implications of caring for a child who cannot become an independently operating agent, though important, are beyond the scope of this paper.

14 Anne Alstott, *No Exit: What Parents Owe Their Children and What Society Owes Parents* (Oxford: Oxford University Press, 2004). As Alstott notes, we could have set things up differently, but we haven't. We have structured society

so that particular persons tend to assume primary responsibility for the care of a child.

15 Erin Taylor, "All Together Now: Conventionalism and Everyday Moral Life," <http://philpapers.org/rec/TAYATN>. Taylor argues that social conventions can generate distinct moral obligations where the conventions play a role in dividing our moral labor. The family is itself a social institution, governed by social and legal practices, expectations, and norms.

16 David Archard, "The Obligations and Responsibilities of Parenthood," *Procreation and Parenthood*, eds. David Archard and David Benatar (Oxford: Oxford University Press, 2010): 103–27. There is debate about whether a parent can incur parental obligations just by creating a child, even if she does not herself wish to discharge the duties of being a parent. Archard, for instance, argues that procreators incur an obligation to ensure that their progeny are parented by someone. I am interested in procreators who procreate in order to become parents.

17 Harry Brighouse and Adam Swift, *Family Values: The Ethics of Parent-Child Relationships* (Princeton, NJ: Princeton University Press, 2014). Brighouse and Swift defend the value of the parent–child relationship, both to the parent and to the child.

18 Samantha Brennan and Robert Noggle, "The Moral Status of Children," *Social Theory and Practice* 23, no. 1 (1997): 1–26; Sarah Hannan and Richard Vernon, "Parental Rights: A Role-Based Approach," *Theory and Research in Education* 6, no. 2 (2008): 173–89. Parental rights can be justified as a way of meeting the child's interests if the parent is best situated to meet the child's needs. Parental rights, then, can piggyback off of the child's interests if parents need some rights or freedoms to discharge their duties to their children.

19 Annette Lareau, *Unequal Childhoods: Class, Race, and Family Life* (Berkeley: University of California Press, 2003). Examples range from the behavioral norms passed on to children to the child's acquisition of vocabulary.

20 See again Brighouse and Swift, *Family Values*.

21 Susan A. Dumais, "Early Childhood Cultural Capital, Parental Habitus, and Teachers' Perceptions," *Poetics* 34, no. 2 (2005): 83–107.

22 That is, parents are not obligated to always do what is in the *best* interest of the child. Meeting the moral end of parenting is the bar, after which a parent might appropriately meet her own needs at the expense of her child.

23 Of course, the child has an interest in being well-nourished, and if a parent's dietary restrictions fail to adequately nourish the child, the parent's interest may be overruled by the child's interest. However, even if the interest is overruled by a stronger consideration, the parent still has an interest in preparing meals that align with her beliefs about moral food consumption.

24 This idea resists a purely child-interest view of parental rights. Though again, I am not giving an account of parental rights, only describing the kind of interests parents have in the parent–child relationship.

25 Ivan Snook, *Indoctrination and Education* (London: Routledge and K. Paul, 1972).

26 Tim McDonough, "Initiation, Not Indoctrination: Confronting the Grotesque in Cultural Education," *Educational Philosophy and Theory* 43, no. 7 (2011): 706–23.

27 Michael Hand, "Religious Upbringing Reconsidered," *Journal of the Philosophy of Education* 36, no. 4 (2002): 545–57. Hand is concerned not just with resistant beliefs, but beliefs that, though revisable, are imparted by way of an adult's intellectual authority. For Hand, the adult wrongs the child if the belief she imparts is harmful or, if not harmful, is not in some way beneficial. Either way, the focus is still on whether the belief-imparting is a harm to the child or not.

28 Thanks to Barbara Herman for both the point and the turn of phrase.
29 Some belief and value systems may be ruled out, including some religious world-views, if children raised from within them are likely to be incapable of rational reflection later on.
30 People might assume this role for a variety of reasons, many of which may make no reference to the moral status and needs of the child. However, the role is what it is based on the moral obligation it is there to meet—regardless of the other interests potential parents take in the role. Once a person assumes the role of parent, she incurs the obligation to discharge the duties that attend it.
31 Or, as Hannan and Vernon put it, "parental care and affection cannot be conditional upon their children sharing the same interests." Hannan and Vernon, "Parental Rights," 176.
32 Matthew Clayton, *Justice and Legitimacy in Upbringing* (Oxford: Oxford University Press, 2006). Clayton offers a similar constraint on parents. Parents ought not *intend* to indoctrinate their children into a particular conception of the good, though they may "reveal their enthusiasm" for a particular conception of the good, which may well lead to the child's also adopting that system of beliefs and values.
33 I owe this point to Daniela Dover.
34 If part of her belief system is that she cannot continue to parent her child without disavowing her beliefs, then she ought to disavow her beliefs.
35 I am grateful to Barbara Herman for pressing this point.
36 Michael Sandel, *The Case Against Perfection: Ethics in the Age of Genetic Engineering* (Cambridge: Belknap of Harvard University Press, 2007). Sandal makes a helpful distinction between accepting and transformative love. Parents must have the right balance of both: a willingness to accept their children for who they are and a preparedness to bring about their child's well-being by changing who their children are (through education, discipline, etc.). Parents act in transformative love when they facilitate their child's coming to have the capacities they need to be independent persons, and they act in accepting love when they allow that process to lead where it may.
37 If the child becomes a violent toward her parents or poses a risk to herself, those parents may need to discharge their parental duty by handing her care over to professionals.
38 Edward Dolnick, "Deafness as Culture," *The Atlantic Monthly* 272, no. 3 (1993): 37–53. Melissa S. Fahmy, "On the Supposed Moral Harm of Selecting for Deafness," *Bioethics* 25, no. 3 (2011): 128–36. There may also be child-centered reasons for deaf parents to select for deaf children. In particular, deaf parents may think that they can better parent deaf children if they can more easily share a language and culture with their child. That line of justification is not the target of this paper.
39 A parent might, for instance, select a sperm donor with musical aptitude. She wouldn't be able to guarantee that the child she creates will have any musical aptitude, but my concern with her end applies whether or not she's ultimately successful in bringing the aptitude about.
40 In either case, though it's unlikely that genetics have a decisive influence in a person's psychology, there is reason to think there may be some genetic influence, in which case it's at least theoretically the sort of thing that a prospective parent could select for in her offspring.
41 Christine Overall, *Ethics and Human Reproduction: A Feminist Analysis* (Boston: Allen & Unwin, 1987).
42 A similar problem arises when this kind of justification is given for selecting for deafness and dwarfism.
43 Thanks to Barbara Herman for pointing out the possible alternate motive.
44 David J. Velleman, "The Gift of Life," *Philosophy & Public Affairs* 36, no. 3

(2008): 245–66; L. A. Paul, "What You Can't Expect When You're Expecting," *Res Philosophica* 92, no. 2 (2015): 1–23. You might think that a child who is better able to share in her parent's beliefs and values, even in understanding similar hardships, will be better parented, better cared for, or better loved. Even if that's true, that's a different, child-centered, claim. Velleman makes the point that children have an interest in having parents like them, but that's a different kind of justification from a parent's interest in having children like them. Paul argues that parents can't know what parenting will be like before they become parents. If Paul is right, then it's unlikely that parents can accurately predict what sort of children they can best parent.

45 Importantly, that is not to say they are of no concern, only that the parent assumes a role that involves putting the child's needs before her own.

46 Harry Brighouse and Adam Swift, "Parents' Rights and the Value of the Family," *Ethics* 117, no. 1 (2006): 80–108.

47 Of course, we have lots of influence over the beliefs and values of persons we're in others kinds of relationships with who are not our children. The difference, however, is that those relationships are voluntary, on both sides, whereas the child has no choice (at least initially) in who parents her. I owe Seana Shiffrin for noting the difference.

48 Seana V. Shiffrin, "Wrongful Life, Procreative Responsibility, and the Significance of Harm," *Legal Theory* 5, no. 2 (1999): 117–48. You could worry that *any* act of creation is, to some extent, an expression of the prospective parent's conception of life as good and worth creating, a view that not everyone shares. Shiffrin raises a similar concern: procreating parents may count as making a morally problematic choice on behalf of the child that life, with its mixed benefits and burdens, is worth bestowing on the created person.

49 Relationships require some interaction with the other person. I think a relationship with a child can start as early as the child's first perceivable interaction with the world: the quickening. It's a milestone that's become less significant in contemporary society, but it might still be morally significant insofar as it marks the first interaction between the child and the parents (not just the birth mother, but also the other adults who are involved in the pregnancy and are committed to parenting the child).

50 Such cases require further investigation. They are not obviously permissible, but if they aren't permissible, it's not because the prospective parents were pursuing their ends at the expense of their future children.

51 Thanks to the participants of the *From Procreative Ethics to Parental Rights* conference and the members of UCLA Philosophy Department's *Ethics Writing Seminar* for their helpful feedback on earlier versions of this paper.

Bibliography

Archard, David. "The Obligations and Responsibilities of Parenthood." In *Procreation and Parenthood*, edited by David Archard and David Benatar, 103–127. Oxford: Oxford University Press, 2010.

Brennan, Samantha and Robert Noggle. "The Moral Status of Children." *Social Theory and Practice* 23, no. 1(1997): 1–26.

Brighouse, Harry and Adam Swift. *Family Values: The Ethics of Parent-Child Relationships*. Princeton: Princeton University Press, 2014.

Brighouse, Harry and Adam Swift. "Parents' Rights and the Value of the Family." *Ethics* 117, no. 1 (2006): 80–108.

Chambers, K. Lindsey. "Choosing Our Children: Role Obligations and the Morality of Reproductive Selection." Ph.D. dissertation, University of California Los Angeles, 2016.

Clayton, Matthew. *Justice and Legitimacy in Upbringing*. Oxford: Oxford University Press, 2006.

Dolnick, Edward. "Deafness as Culture." *The Atlantic Monthly* 272, no. 3 (1993): 37–53.

Dumais, Susan. "Early Childhood Cultural Capital, Parental Habitus, and Teachers' Perceptions." *Poetics* 34, no. 2 (2005): 83–107.

Fahmy, Melissa S. "On the Supposed Moral Harm of Selecting for Deafness." *Bioethics* 25, no. 3 (2011): 128–136.

Hand, Michael. "Religious Upbringing Reconsidered." *Journal of Philosophy of Education* 36, no. 4 (2002): 545–557.

Hannan, Sarah and Richard Vernon. "Parental Rights: A Role-Based Approach." *Theory and Research in Education* 6, no. 2 (2008): 173–189.

Hanser, Matthew. "Harming Future People." *Philosophy and Public Affairs* 19, no. 1 (1990): 47–70.

Kant, Immanuel. *Groundwork of the Metaphysics of Morals*. Translated by Mary Gregor. Cambridge: Cambridge University Press, 1998.

Kant, Immanuel. *The Metaphysics of Morals*. Translated by Mary Gregor. Cambridge: Cambridge University Press, 1996.

Lareau, Annette. *Unequal Childhoods: Class, Race, and Family Life*. Berkeley: University of California Press, 2003.

Maillard, Kevin N. "Rethinking Children as Property: The Transitive Family." *Cardozo Law Review* 32, no. 1 (2010): 225–263.

McDonough, Tim. "Initiation, Not Indoctrination: Confronting the Grotesque in Cultural Education." *Educational Philosophy and Theory* 43, no. 7 (2011): 706–723.

Overall, Christine. *Ethics and Human Reproduction: A Feminist Analysis*. Boston: Allen & Unwin, 1987.

Parfit, Derek. *Reasons and Persons*. Oxford: Oxford University Press, 1984.

Paul, L. A. "What You Can't Expect When You're Expecting." *Res Philosophica* 92, no. 2 (2015): 1–23.

Sandel, Michael. *The Case Against Perfection: Ethics in the Age of Genetic Engineering*. Cambridge: Belknap of Harvard University Press, 2007.

Schapiro, Tamar. "What is a Child?" *Ethics* 109, no. 4 (1999): 715–738.

Shiffrin, Seana V. "Wrongful Life, Procreative Responsibility, and the Significance of Harm." *Legal Theory* 5, no. 2 (1999): 117–148.

Snook, Ivan. *Indoctrination and Education*. London: Routledge and K. Paul, 1972.

Taylor, Erin. "All Together Now: Conventionalism and Everyday Moral Life." <http://philpapers.org/rec/TAYATN>.

Velleman, David J. "The Gift of Life." *Philosophy & Public Affairs* 36, no. 3(2008): 245–266.

Velleman, David J. "The Identity Problem." *Philosophy & Public Affairs* 36, no. 3 (1998): 221–244.

5 A Chip off the Old Block

The Ethics of Shaping Children to Be Like Their Parents

Robert Noggle

Introduction

I am proud of all of my children's accomplishments, but two recent accomplishments by my oldest child made me especially proud: The first 5K run she and I did together (as part of a wonderful program called "Girls on the Run"), and when she passed her first belt test in the karate school where I train. In both cases, my daughter was following in my own footsteps, pursuing activities that I pursue and value. I was also proud of her when she did a solo in the church choir, but since I'm neither religious nor musical, this achievement didn't have the same "icing on the cake" for me. There is something especially stirring about seeing one's child following in one's footsteps, knowing that she is "a chip off the old block."

But for some parents, the child's traveling down the parent's path isn't just *icing* on the cake: it *is* the cake. Some parents don't just *hope* that their children will be chips off the old block; they rather *insist* on it, and they feel that they have a right to do so. Perhaps most often, this insistence is manifested in parental attempts to ensure that children adopt the parents' religion, value system, or worldview—what Rawls would call their "comprehensive doctrines." But parents often try to shape other things about their children to make them more like their parents. Parents with a love of and ability to create music might seek to instill that same love and ability in their children. Families with traditions of attachment to certain careers might push their children to become doctors or lawyers or soldiers just like their parents and grandparents before them. Small business owners and farmers often expect to turn those enterprises over to their children who will tend to them in their turn. The legitimacy of such practices is commonly taken for granted as part of what many parents assume is their right to raise their children however they see fit, subject only to minimal requirements that they avoid abusing or neglecting them.

In some cases, parental efforts to shape their children are motivated not only by the desire that their children be like them, but also by the desire to perpetuate the parent's values, culture, religion, and way of life. Indeed, sometimes the very survival of these things depends on children following in their parents' footsteps. This fact may seem to the parents to provide additional justification for shaping their children. The much-discussed case of the Old Order Amish comes to mind here. Typically, the Amish limit their children's formal schooling to the 8th grade, and whenever possible, they conduct that schooling in local schools run by the Amish themselves. After the 8th grade, Amish children typically learn a traditional Amish trade through an apprenticeship system. This system effectively prepares children for an Amish career and way of life. But it also creates significant hurdles for pursuing careers other than farm work or a limited number of skilled trades, and thus for leading prosperous lives in contemporary non-Amish society.

The Amish seek to lock their children into their lifestyle by manipulating the social and educational environment in which the child develops—what we might call the "environmental shaping" of children. Recently, it has become possible to shape children more directly, by manipulating their genetic makeup. Consider Sharon Duchesneau and Candy McCullough, a Deaf couple who wanted children, and preferred that they be deaf, just like their parents. They decided to employ in vitro fertilization and selected a man with five generations of deafness in his family to serve as a gamete donor. Their motivation appears to have included both the desire that their child be like them, and the desire to help perpetuate their own Deaf culture into the next generation. Their decision raises worries similar to those raised in the case of the Amish children: While it facilitated their children's entry into Deaf culture, it also raised significant hurdles for life outside that culture. In this way, the Duchesneau-McCullough children's intentionally selected deafness is rather like the lack of education beyond the 8th grade, in that it creates an obstacle for the children if they decide that they do not want to be chips off the old block.[1]

Duchesneau and McCullough used a fairly low-tech form of genetic shaping. More complicated methods—some available already, and others on their way—will allow parents to engage in ever more fine-grained genetic shaping. It is already possible to use pre-implantation genetic diagnosis to select for implantation only those embryos that possess certain genes. Dena Davis reports that this technique has been used by parents with achondroplasia (a form of dwarfism) to ensure that their children will share this condition.[2] In the near future, it will probably be possible to engage in more direct genetic engineering of children, by replacing small numbers of genes in an early-stage embryo, for example. In the farther future, it may become possible to create a baby with a genome made more or less to order, or perhaps even to create the ultimate chip off the old block: a human clone.

Genetic shaping has often been analyzed in the context of debates about the permissibility of creating "enhanced" children. But as we have just seen, parents might employ genetic shaping methods not to create super-children, but to create children that are simply more like their parents, and more likely to follow in their parents' footsteps. The most obvious way to do this, of course, would be to use genetic shaping to increase the number of genetically influenced traits the child has in common with the parent. But parents might employ genetic methods indirectly to do the kind of shaping now done primarily through education and other environmental methods. Although genetic methods may not be able to directly influence a child's choices and values, they might be used to grease the wheels by ensuring that their children are good matches for paths that the parents value, and to erect barriers to competing paths. Parents with sexist worldviews might use genetic shaping to decrease their daughters' intelligence and ambition; intellectual parents might seek to increase their children's intelligence while decreasing traits that might make them good at athletic endeavors that could distract them from the life of the mind.

Yoder, Feinberg, and the Open Future

Philosophical thinking about the parent's rights to engage in environmental shaping has been heavily influenced by the case of *Wisconsin v Yoder*,[3] and Joel Feinberg's discussion of it in his article, "The Child's Right to an Open Future."[4] Feinberg's central claim is that a child has a right to an open future, that is, a right not to have important decisions made for her simply because she cannot make them yet on her own. Although this idea seems simple enough, it admits of two rather different interpretations, and Feinberg seems at various times to endorse each.[5] In some passages, Feinberg seems to endorse the right of children to "be permitted to reach maturity with *as many* open options, opportunities, and advantages *as possible*."[6] This suggests a right to a *maximally open* future, with parents making no more decisions for children than absolutely necessary. In other passages, Feinberg seems to suggest a more moderate view, writing that the Amish parents "are permitted and indeed expected to make every reasonable effort to transmit by example and precept their own values to their children,"[7] which certainly suggests that parents are allowed to try to shape their children's values. Indeed, he writes that, so long as the parent does not try to insulate the child from outside influences that may be contrary to the parent's values, the parent "is free to provide any kind of religious upbringing he chooses, or none at all, . . . to attempt to transmit his own ideals, moral and political, whatever they may be, to his child; in short, to create whatever environment of influences he can for his child, subject to the state's important but minimal standards of humanity, health, and education."[8]

Perhaps the closest thing to a recent philosophical defense of the maximal openness interpretation of the right to an open future appears in work by Matthew Clayton. Clayton argues, provocatively, that it is wrong for parents to have their infant children baptized, since this "enrolls" them into their parents' comprehensive doctrine.[9] Such "enrollment," he claims, violates their right to choose their own comprehensive doctrines when they are old enough. Moreover, he suggests that even taking a child to church may wrong the child, if it causes her to adopt a comprehensive doctrine that it may later be distressing for her to shed.[10] Clayton's argument is based on an analogy between the state and the parents: In both cases, he argues, a coercive authority operates, and to avoid infringing on the rights of its subjects, it must remain neutral on the question of what comprehensive doctrine its subjects should adopt.

In the abstract, at least, the arguments for the maximal openness interpretation of the child's right to an open future seem compelling. I have no right to shape *your* values, or decide what church you shall attend. Nor do I have the right to make a decision about your future simply because you are unable to make it right now. For instance, if it's 3:00 a.m. and you are asleep, I can't just "volunteer" you for a burdensome committee assignment simply because your unconsciousness temporarily precludes you from deciding for yourself. Since my children are persons, and since they will (if all goes well) develop autonomy, what right do I have to decide what values they shall hold or what church they shall attend, or to make any other decisions that will constrain their future choices? Of course, it may be necessary for their well-being or the future development of their autonomy for me to make *some* decisions for my children. So perhaps it's fine for me to decide on their behalf that they will brush their teeth, eat vegetables, and learn their multiplication tables. (By analogy, it is often permissible to make decisions on behalf of an incapacitated adult where those decisions are necessary to preserving that person's life or well-being.) But why shouldn't I be required to avoid making any more decisions for them than absolutely necessary? Why shouldn't I be required to bring them into adulthood with as many options—as maximally open a future—as I can give them?

Despite the logical appeal of this argument, it is not widely accepted, even among liberal theorists who take children's rights seriously.[11] It is not difficult to understand why. After all, the maximal openness interpretation of the child's right to an open future would impose serious obstacles to many parents' ability to live according to their own comprehensive doctrines. Taken at face value, the maximal openness interpretation would appear to forbid parents from taking their young children to Sunday School, for fear that they may unjustly instill values and religious views that they may find it difficult or traumatic to give up later. We can easily imagine religious parents—even if they are good liberals—retorting that "It's not brainwashing, it's just Sunday School!" Having to choose between skipping church or hiring a babysitter so that one can insulate one's children from one's own religious observances would seem to be a rather large imposition on the parent's religious rights. A separation of church and state is fine, but the idea that parents must erect a wall separating their religious life from their children seems far-fetched. Of course, such a view would not only apply to religious views and values, but to any value or decision that an autonomous person has the right to make for herself. Perhaps I should worry that encouraging my children to prepare for college illegitimately biases them against the skilled trades. Or perhaps I should worry that my family's "girls can do anything boys can do" mantra unfairly biases my children against adopting more traditional gender roles later in life. Perhaps I should worry that, rather than celebrating my daughter's decision to do Girls on the Run again, I should encourage her to take ballet lessons instead, so as to keep her options more open. Most parents—myself included—would find such suggestions to be implausibly radical.

Not surprisingly, most liberal theorists who take children's rights seriously have sought a middle ground between countenancing extreme efforts to shape children on the one hand, and the maximal openness interpretation of the child's right to an open future on the other. This moderate interpretation of the child's right to an open future asserts that it is legitimate for parents to bring up their child in the parent's own comprehensive doctrines, so long as (1) they do not try to "lock in" that comprehensive doctrine so that the child is unable to question or reject it later, (2) they foster (or allow schools to foster) critical thinking capacities sufficient for the child eventually to reflect on their parents' comprehensive doctrine, and (3) they do not work to deprive the child of other options or the knowledge of them.

Of course, the fact that the moderate interpretation of the child's right to an open future is a better fit with our intuitions and practices is not, in itself, a decisive argument for it. Moreover, the argument for the maximal openness interpretation remains quite compelling, at least in the abstract. Given the presumption that infringements to autonomy must be both justified and as minimal as possible even when they are justified, what reason could there be for *not* giving children the most open futures possible?

One reason might involve the rights of the parents, and in particular the parents' right to autonomy. Indeed, the reason why most parents would chafe under the requirement to provide maximally open futures for their children is that such a requirement would appear to constrain their own autonomy. Certainly parents have the right to live according to their own values, beliefs, and life plans, and, one might think, they have a right to some say in how they raise their children. So we might think that parents have the right to decide, for example, that they will raise Christian or Muslim or Agnostic families because doing so is part and parcel of their own commitments to those worldviews. This is certainly the reasoning behind the Supreme Court's decision in *Yoder*: The majority determined that the parent's own rights to freely exercise their Amish religion included the right to raise their children in that religion.

Of course, the parents' rights to direct their children's upbringing are not absolute. As Justice Rutledge wrote in the 1944 case, *Prince v. Massachusetts*, "Parents may be free to become martyrs themselves. But it does not follow [that] they are free, in identical circumstances, to make martyrs of their children before they have reached the age of full and legal discretion when they can make that choice for themselves."[12] Whatever autonomy-based rights parents may have to shape their children are limited by the child's own rights, including the rights to make decisions for themselves when they are able.

Hence, it is very tempting to see parents as having autonomy-based rights to direct their children's upbringing—to shape them, in other words—but to see those rights as being constrained by the child's own rights, including and especially the right to an open future. But on the flipside, it is tempting to see the parental autonomy rights as the reason why the child's right to an open future does not require parents to provide a *maximally* open future. This suggests a very appealing picture in which the right answer about how much a parent is allowed to shape a child is determined by a balancing or equilibrium of two opposing rights. On the one hand, parents clearly have the right to live according to their own comprehensive doctrines, and this right may be thought to include or imply a right to raise their children within those comprehensive doctrines. But these rights do not seem to be absolute. And one explanation for why they are not absolute is that they are limited by the child's right to an open future. We might think, then, of the moderate interpretation of the right to an open future as the outcome of an equilibrium or balance between competing rights. In other words, we might think of the child's right to an open future, *taken in isolation*, as being maximally expansive. But in practice, it is limited by the countervailing weight of the parent's rights to live their own lives. By the same token, we might think of the parent's right to live her own life, taken in isolation, as being maximally expansive. But in practice, this right is limited by the countervailing weight of the child's rights, including the right to an open future.

It is important to emphasize that on the balancing model, each right would be expansive but for the countervailing moral force from the other: The child's right to an open future *would* require parents to provide a *maximally* open future, *but for* the countervailing moral force of the parent's autonomy rights. The parent's autonomy rights *would* permit extreme parental shaping (e.g., of the kind practiced by the Amish), *but for* the countervailing moral force of the child's right to an open future. Notice that this is how we often think of liberty rights: The old saw that my right to swing my arm ends where your nose begins implies that, taken in isolation (your nose being absent from the picture), my right to swing my arm is maximally expansive. But once your nose enters the picture, the countervailing moral force of your right not to have it hit limits my right to swing.

So the balancing model taps into a very natural way to think about how rights interact, and in so doing it provides a blueprint for generating the moderate view about parental shaping: The child's right to an open future makes it immoral for the parent to try to lock in her comprehensive doctrine, while the parent's autonomy rights prevent the child's right to an open future from requiring parents to provide the child with a maximally open future.

I believe that this balancing model is implicit in much of our thinking about parental rights. The majority of the Justices in *Yoder* are clearly balancing the parents' free exercise and other autonomy rights against the rights of the children (primarily their right to a decent education). Much of the commentary on *Yoder* seems to take this balancing model for granted, and simply quibbles about whether the court got the balance right or balanced the right things (some commentators fault the court for not including the children's free exercise rights in the balance).

But the balancing rights model is not confined to discussions of legal cases like *Yoder*. For example, William Galston, writing about ". . . the desire of parents to pass on their way of life to their children," notes that "few parents . . . are . . . immune from the force of this desire. What could be more natural? . . . Still, your child is at once a future adult and a future citizen. Your authority as a parent is limited by both these facts."[13] Similarly, Colin Macleod discusses a parental "prerogative of provisionally privileging the conception of the good that they favor."[14] This "prerogative" appears to result from the interplay of two moral considerations: "the parental interest in having children share a familiar commitment to a common conception of the good,"[15] and the child's interest in acquiring autonomy. Hence, Macleod writes, "the exercise of parental autonomy is constrained by the requirement that children be afforded free and full access to the deliberative resources available in the pluralistic public culture."[16] It is natural to read his derivation of "constrained parental autonomy" as arising from a balance between parents' morally protected interest in having their children share their comprehensive doctrine and the child's morally protected interest in developing the capacity for self-determination.

Despite its appeal as a way to justify intuitively plausible limits to both the child's right to an open future and the parent's right to direct the child's upbringing, I think that we should reject the balancing model. Here's why: For all its intuitive appeal in cases of environmental shaping, the balancing rights model has unsettling consequences when applied to certain kinds of genetic shaping.

Open Futures and the Non-Identity Problem

As we noted earlier, it is tempting to criticize Duchesneau and McCullough for trying to lock their children into the Deaf community, much as many of us would criticize the Amish for trying to lock their children into the Amish community. Yet there is a serious obstacle to making that charge stick—an obstacle that arises from what has come to be called the non-identity problem.

The non-identity problem arises because certain methods of genetic shaping have the following curious property: Had the child not been shaped a certain way, that child would not exist. The methods used by Duchesneau and McCullough to ensure that their child would be deaf have this property: had they not selected the sperm donor they did, then that particular child would not exist. Some other child might have existed, but that child would not have been the same child as the one who did come into existence, since this other child would have been created from at least one different gamete. This being the case, it is difficult to make what would otherwise seem like a natural claim, viz., that his mothers' procreative decision harmed him (either by making him deaf or by closing off his options). So long as his life is worth living—as it surely is—it seems as though he has not been harmed, since the only alternative to his being born deaf was his not being born at all. The non-identity problem arises in any situation—call it a "non-identity situation"—where the conditions necessary to a person's creation unavoidably cause that person to have a condition that we would normally count as an impairment. For our purposes, we can think of a constrained future as a form of impairment, relative to a more open future. The non-identity problem seems to block the claim that Duchesneau and McCullough did anything wrong in shaping their children to be deaf, for had they not done so, these particular children would not even exist.

Like most philosophical problems, the non-identity problem does not so much suffer from the lack of a solution as from multiple solutions, each of which requires us to give up some claim that seems intuitively plausible. These solutions fall into three main categories: (1) biting the bullet by claiming that it cannot be wrong to deliberately create an impaired child in a non-identity situation, so long as the child's life is worth living; (2) claiming that, contrary to appearances, the child is harmed or has her rights violated; and (3) claiming that a procreative act undertaken in a non-identity situation can be wrong even though it neither harms nor violates the rights of the resulting child.

According to the bullet-biting approach, a child born in a non-identity situation can only be harmed if her impairments make her life not worth living. Otherwise, she cannot be said to be harmed, since the only available alternative to being born in the impaired condition was not being born at all. But if the child has not been harmed by the process on which her very existence depends, then how can she have any legitimate moral complaint against her parents for undergoing that process? And if the child has no legitimate moral complaint against her parents, then how can the parents be said to have acted wrongly? According to the bullet-biting view, so long as the child's life is worth living, she has no basis to complain about interventions on which her very existence depends, and consequently, the parents do not act wrongly in employing those interventions. On this view, shaping a child, even in ways that drastically narrow her future options, cannot be wrong if that child's existence depends on having been shaped that way, and if her life with its narrowed options is still better than no life at all.

This approach to the non-identity problem appeals to those who favor "genetic libertarianism," according to which parents have vast moral freedom to shape their children however they wish. However, it suffers from serious counter-examples. Consider the Gammas in Aldous Huxley's *Brave New World*. The Gammas are humans who are only capable of doing menial tasks, but who are happy to do them. Imagine that Gamma-like children are created by pre-implantation genetic selection (perhaps by Gamma-like parents who want their own children to be chips off the old block): Embryos are tested for the genes for various Gamma-like traits, and only those embryos with genetic profiles that will result in Gamma-like children are selected for implantation. Thus, for the resulting Gamma-like child, the following will be true: The only way the parents could have avoided creating a Gamma-like child would have been to avoid creating that *particular* child at all, since they would have had to choose a different embryo to implant. This being the case, on the bullet-biting view, so long as her life is still worth living, she has not been harmed, and so she has no basis to complain about her parents' decision, and so the parents did nothing wrong. So, on the bullet-biting view, we must deny the common sense intuition that it would be wrong to employ a technique like pre-implantation genetic selection to create a Gamma-like child. That's a hard bullet to bite.

Those of us who are unwilling to bite the bullet have two remaining options: Claiming that genetic shaping in non-identity situations, can, contrary to appearances, harm or violate the rights of the child, or claiming that genetic shaping in non-identity situations can be wrong even if it does not harm or violate the rights of the child.

There have been attempts to show that, despite appearances, the child in non-identity cases really is harmed. Such attempts typically begin with the observation that the non-identity problem gets much of its initial bite from the assumption that harm must always be comparative: An action harms me only if I would have been better off had that action not been done. Once we adopt this conception of harm, we seem forced into the non-identity problem, since it is difficult to see how I can be harmed by something without which my worth-living life would not have been possible. However, some philosophers have argued that this is not the only coherent conception of harm.[17] For example, one might claim that certain conditions are harms just in case they are the sorts of things that impair normal functioning, create suffering, significantly narrow one's life choices, etc.

But even if we can coherently speak of the child in a non-identity situation being harmed, the fact that the harm was necessary to the child's very existence makes it plausible to regard the child's assessment that her life is still worth living as a sort of retroactive consent to the harm. In other words, it is plausible to assume that a child will give her consent to whatever harms are necessary for her to exist, assuming that she regards her existence even in the harmed condition as being preferable to non-existence.

This same problem befalls proposals to claim that bringing an impaired child into existence in a non-identity situation violates that child's rights. Even if genetically shaping a child in a non-identity situation violates her right to an open future, given that the only available alternative to her condition is non-existence, she can be reasonably expected to waive the right to the open future that she never could have had anyway. Since it is generally thought to be permissible to do a thing that would otherwise violate a right if the right-holder waives the right, it would appear that genetic shaping in non-identity situations would be permissible even if it results in a child with a less than satisfactorily open future.

Although some philosophers continue to seek solutions to the non-identity problem that salvage the idea that creating an impaired child in a non-identity situation somehow wrongs the child, the prospects for such a solution look pretty grim. If we are unwilling to bite the bullet, that leaves the third approach, namely conceding that the child is neither harmed nor the victim of a rights violation, but nevertheless maintaining that his parents have acted wrongly.

How would that position work? One influential account is given by Joel Feinberg.[18] Feinberg imagines a child born with a withered arm, whose mother "had only two options with respect to his birth. One was to do what she did, which led to his being born with the withered arm. The other . . . would have led to his never having existed at all, which even the child acknowledges was the worse fate."[19] Feinberg concedes that "I do not think the child can establish a grievance against her so long as he concedes that his handicapped existence is far preferable to no existence at all. For if he were to claim that she wronged him by doing what she did, that would commit him to the judgment that her duty to him had been to refrain from doing what she did; but if she had refrained, that would have led to his never having been born, an even worse result from his point of view."[20] Feinberg concludes that "There is no doubt that the mother did act wrongly, but it does not follow that her wrongdoing wronged any particular person, or had any particular victim. She must be blamed for wantonly introducing a certain evil into the world, not for harming, or for violating the rights of, a person."[21]

So long as we are clear that the "certain evil" is the impairment rather than the person who has it, Feinberg's point seems appealing. Applied to the kinds of cases at issue here, Feinberg's reasoning suggests that creating a child with a less than satisfactorily open future in a non-identity situation is wrong, but not because it violates the child's rights. Instead, it is what Feinberg calls a non-grievance wrong, something that is wrong even though it does not do anything wrong *to* any person. Since no one has a legitimate grievance against the wrongdoer, the wrong is, in effect, victimless. This idea of a non-grievance or victimless wrong is certainly an odd idea, given how natural it is to think that every wrong thing must be a wrong thing that is done to someone who is its victim. However, given the problems with the claim that a child can be victimized by an action that was a causally necessary condition of her very existence, and the unpalatability of biting the bullet, this victimless wrongdoing approach seems like the least bad solution to the non-identity problem.

Balancing Rights and the Non-Identity Problem

So far, so good. Except for this: If genetic shaping in non-identity situations does not violate anyone's rights because it is a victimless or non-grievance wrongdoing, then we will have difficulty maintaining that extreme *genetic* shaping is immoral if we adopt the competing rights model of the moral status of *non-genetic* shaping discussed earlier.

The problem is that a victimless or non-grievance wrong seems too insubstantial to counterbalance the moral clout of a parents' autonomy-based *rights*. This kind of worry has been given explicit voice in a slightly different context by John Robertson: "If ART [assisted reproductive technologies—rn] harmed offspring, a strong case for limiting them might exist. But if due to the non-identity problem harm to offspring is questionable or non-existent, then harm to offspring in those cases cannot justify limiting use of ARTs. This is particularly true in those cases in which use of the ART implicates the procreative liberty of infertile couples and others who use them."[22]

A similar worry applies to cases of genetic shaping. If we rely on the child's right to an open future to provide a counterweight that prevents parental autonomy rights from expanding to permit extreme shaping, then we encounter a serious problem in situations where parents employ genetic shaping methods in non-identity situations. Because we can expect the child to waive her right to an open future when having her future narrowed is an unavoidable part of her coming into existence, that right becomes unavailable to provide any counterweight to the parents' autonomy rights. Without the countervailing moral force of the right to an open future, the parents' autonomy rights expand to permit far more extensive genetic shaping than most of us think is permissible. In fact, with the right to an open future out of the way, parents would become *more* free to employ *genetic* shaping methods than they are to employ *environmental* shaping methods. For those of us who have the same qualms about unconstrained shaping of either sort, this is an unwelcome conclusion. It is even more unwelcome for those who think that genetic shaping is more problematic than environmental shaping.

One might wonder why the parental rights would remain unconstrained in a non-identity situation; after all, we have argued that creating a child in an impaired condition can still be wrong, even if the wrong is a victimless wrong. The reason, as Robertson notes, is that a mere victimless wrong seems insufficiently robust to outweigh the parents' autonomy rights.[23] A right, after all, is not easily outweighed (otherwise it would not be a right). Hence, it is hard to see how a mere free-floating, impersonal, victimless wrongdoing could outweigh the parents' autonomy right. Nor does it help to ground the victimless wrongdoing in consequentialist considerations, for example, by claiming that the reason that it is wrong to create a child in an impaired condition in a non-identity situation is that doing so makes the world a less good place than it otherwise could have been. For the point of a right is precisely to insulate agents (at least partially) from considerations of utility. If my right to do X can be blocked simply because my X-ing makes the world go less well than not X-ing, then I don't really have a *right* to X. Indeed, if we take Mill's Harm Principle seriously, we should be disinclined to say that parental autonomy can be infringed for anything less than harming or violating the rights of another person.[24]

Of course, one might suggest that even though creating a child with a less than satisfactorily open future in a non-identity situation is a victimless wrong, it is still sufficiently weighty to provide a counterweight to the parents' autonomy rights. But unless we can find a reason to justify treating this victimless wrongdoing as being as morally weighty as a harm or a rights violation to another person, such a claim seems ad hoc. Even if the reasons generated by a victimless wrongdoing have some weight, it is difficult to see why they would have enough weight to provide anything comparable to the counterweight otherwise provided by the child's right to an open future. To see why, we must go back to the balancing model. Recall that the balancing model involves positing a parental right that creates countervailing moral force sufficient to keep the child's right to an open future from becoming maximally expansive. In order to do that, the parent's autonomy rights must be very weighty indeed—weighty enough to significantly constrain rights held by the child that protect her future autonomy. But unless the wrongness of this victimless wrongdoing is grounded in something as weighty as the child's right to an open future, then when the child's right ceases to operate (as it does in the non-identity situation), it will not be able to produce as much moral counterweight as the child's right would have provided. Normally, if I have a right to do X, then the only thing that can override my right in a particular situation (and thus make it immoral for me to X in that situation) is the fact that my X-ing will harm someone or violate someone's rights. But if we accept the "victimless wrongdoing" approach to the non-identity problem, then any right that the parent has to shape her child cannot be overridden, since the shaping neither harms nor violates the rights of the child so created.

To summarize: If we adopt the opposing rights view for environmental shaping, we will face a serious problem when we move to cases that involve genetic shaping in non-identity situations—at least if we take what seems like the most promising approach to the non-identity problem that treats the wrong done as a victimless wrong that does not violate the rights of the child. For in non-identity cases, the child's right to an open future is likely to be waived, so that it can no longer operate as a counterweight to limit the application of the parents' autonomy rights. Lacking this moral counterweight, the parents' autonomy rights would become maximally expansive, in much the same way that my right to swing my arm becomes maximally expansive once your nose is out of the way. These now expansive parental autonomy rights would then seem to permit very extreme forms of genetic shaping. Consequently, if we are to avoid having the non-identity problem block our moral criticism of extreme genetic shaping, then we must either find an alternative to the non-complaint solution to the non-identity problem, or we must avoid the model of parental authority that sees it as a balance between an otherwise expansive parental authority and an otherwise expansive child's right to an open future. I am skeptical of finding an alternative to the non-complaint approach to the non-identity problem. I am more hopeful about the prospects for basing a moderate view of the limits of permissible parental shaping on something other than the balancing model.

Denying a Parental Right to Shape

To avoid having the moderate position on the right to an open future unravel when we encounter non-identity situations, we must abandon the balancing model and find another way to avoid *both* the maximal openness interpretation of the right to an open future *and* the claim that parents have almost unlimited authority to shape their children however they wish. Fortunately, recent philosophical work on children's rights provides resources that may allow us to do this. Several philosophers have recently argued that parents may legitimately engage in many behaviors that shape their children in ways incompatible with the maximal openness interpretation of the right to an open future, but without basing these arguments on a parent's free-standing moral right to shape their children.

Before examining these arguments, it is important to distinguish two very different ways to justify a limited parental prerogative to shape their children. One is to derive that prerogative from a right that protects (and thus gives moral weight to) the *parent's* interest in shaping their children. For example, such a right would justify enrolling a child in Sunday School, or Girls on the Run, or Boy Scouts, in terms of the *parent's* interest in helping to direct the child's developing interests and values. By contrast, we could think that such things are permissible (if they are) because they are *in the interests of the child*. In this way, we might attempt to derive limited parental prerogatives to shape their children not from the parents' interests, but from the child's interests.

The idea that a *parental* right might actually derive from the *child's* interest is hardly new. The idea that parental rights are like fiduciary or stewardship rights, which has been extremely influential in recent work on children, has precisely this feature. The idea is to model parental rights on the rights of a steward or fiduciary agent, so that in both cases, the right exists only to enable one person to protect the interests of some other person. This distinction will be difficult to track if we use the same term to refer both to rights that protect the right-holder's interests and to rights that protect some other person's interests. Consequently, I will use the term "prerogative" to refer to a parent's moral permission that derives from the child's interests, and I will use the term "right" to refer to parental rights that protect the parents' own interests.

Now, if we can derive a limited parental prerogative to shape one's children from the child's interests rather than from the parents' autonomy rights, then we might avoid the balancing model that unravels when we encounter the non-identity problem. For if we don't need to appeal to a free-standing parental right to shape to prevent the right to an open future from becoming maximally expansive, then we need not worry about the parental right to shape becoming maximally expansive in non-identity situations where the right to an open future is inoperative.

This assumes, however, that we can find a way to ground a limited parental prerogative to shape their children in the interests of the child. (Otherwise, we risk the opposite problem—namely that the child's right to an open future will, lacking anything to counterbalance it, expand so as to require parents to provide a maximally open future.) Fortunately, recent work in the ethics of parents and children provides some hope of finding considerations that would justify limited parental shaping, not because it serves the parents' interest in shaping, but because it serves the *child's own* interests.

To see how this suggestion might work, let's begin with an insightful paper by Claudia Mills, who argues that "it is both impossible and undesirable to try to provide children with an 'open' future in any meaningful sense."[25] It is impossible, she argues, because it is impossible for parents to be strictly neutral among potential options. There is simply no neutral "default" setting that parents can keep switched on, so as to avoid any slight steering of the child one way or another. Mills recounts a friend's practice of having his son sample a different religion or denomination each week. Although this might seem like a good way to keep the child's religious options maximally open, Mills predicts that "This little boy is not going to grow up to have any religion at all" because a "weekly survey of various creeds and rituals" does not impart "the experience of *belonging* to a religion."[26] Such a "smorgasbord" (as Mills aptly puts it) is very superficial: not only does it provide insufficient time to engage with the complexity of each religion, but it provides insufficient time to learn what it is like to be part of a faith community structured by that religion. But perhaps more importantly, such an approach steers the child to a view of religion as a thing for which to "shop around" rather than something that grounds one's view of the world, anchors one's value system, and shapes one's identity. In attempting to expose the child to many religions, the smorgasbord approach fails to show the child what it is like to have a longstanding commitment to a single religion. Arguably, that is what it really means to have a religion.

Mills argues that similar considerations make it undesirable for parents to try to maximize openness in terms of pursuits, talents, and potential career choices. She argues that having a child hop from sport to sport, musical instrument to musical instrument, and after-school activity to after-school activity, doesn't provide enough time for the child to meaningfully discover which she most prefers and which she has most talent for: "Precisely what will be missing from the list is experiences that require *time* to assimilate and absorb, experiences that are slow and deep, rather than easily scheduled in a escalating spiral of extracurricular activities." And, one might add, a superficial hopping around approach seems unlikely to help teach one of the most important lessons that such pursuits can teach: the value of persevering through setbacks, practicing on days when you don't feel like it, and so on. In short, the more we try to maximize openness in our child's options, the more we fail to give them the experience of being committed to one community or pursuit or value. Instead, we risk imparting a view of life in which commitments are disposable, worldviews are things for which to shop rather than frameworks that ground one's sense of the world and one's place within it, and perseverance is unnecessary because if at first you don't succeed, try a new sport—or get a new religion.

A second and complementary line of thought has been developed by Harry Brighouse and Adam Swift.[27] Although they argue that parents' interests play a role in justifying the family as an institution, they derive the content of parental rights from the interests of children, claiming that a "parent should have just those rights that it is children's interests for them to have."[28] Hence, on their view, parental rights are a form of fiduciary or stewardship rights that protect the *child's* interests rather than the parents' interests. (And thus, for reasons of clarity mentioned above, I'll refer to them as prerogatives rather than rights.)

What is most distinctive about Brighouse and Swift's account of the moral prerogatives of parents is their observation that part of what they protect is the child's vital interest in "relationship goods" provided by the family. Hence, parental prerogatives, in part, make it possible for parents "properly to discharge the parental role, on the understanding of that role which ties it to our conception of familial relationship goods."[29] These relationship goods include the goods intrinsic to childhood as well as the ability to develop capacities needed for fully functioning adulthood, all within a relationship that provides a stable, loving, and nurturing foundation for well-being and healthy psychological development. According to Brighouse and Swift, family relationships that provide these goods "require parents to be free to engage with their children in ways that produce mutual identification and reflect the parents' judgments about what is valuable in life."[30] Such relationships involve the sharing of the parent's self with the child, and since the parent's self includes his or her values, they involve the parent's sharing of her values with her child. This, however, will inevitably help to shape the child's own values: "there can be no value sharing without at least some degree of value shaping."[31] This is because "a close, loving relationship will surely involve parents' honestly revealing their enthusiasms and aversions, their sense of what matters in life and what is trivial. . . . Because people's values are central to who they are, because successful parenting requires parents to share themselves with their children, and because value sharing implies at least some degree of value shaping, value shaping is an inherent part of that kind of relationship."[32]

Hence, according to Brighouse and Swift, some parental shaping of the child's values is an inevitable by-product of the parent's sharing of herself with the child—a sharing that is itself in the best interest of the child because it provides vital relationship goods to the child. In light of this, a requirement of maximal openness and parental neutrality turns out not to be in the child's best interest: "The idea that parents should constantly monitor

themselves in their relations with their children in order to screen out anything that might have any influence on their children's emerging values is
ludicrous. It would risk distancing them, creating artifice in the relationship,
and depriving their children of the possibility of the warm, spontaneous
genuine relationship that they need."[33]

Although Brighouse and Swift emphasize the legitimacy of shaping that is
a by-product of sharing, they also see a role for some legitimate direct and
deliberate instilling of their values. Here again, though, they see this as being
in the interests of promoting the relationship goods that children need, and
they are careful to emphasize that it must not compromise the child's ability to subject those values to critical reflection when she is older: "When a
Christian and cricket-loving parent takes his daughter to a cricket match, or
to church, that is not usually an unthinking and automatic sharing of self
between parent and child. It is more likely a deliberate decision to introduce
the child to an activity, or a worldview, that the parent judges valuable. As
long as that kind of deliberate shaping of values is needed for a close relationship between parent and child, and as long as it is done in a way that is
consistent with the duty to develop the child's capacity for autonomy, then,
on our account parents have a right to engage in it. . . . The shaping of values is itself, under this aspect, a means to a familial relation of the kind that
lies at the heart of our theory."[34]

A third resource for deriving the legitimacy of some limited parental shaping from the interests of the child rather than the parents comes from the
observation that children must be supplied with an initial cognitive-evaluative
worldview before they can develop the intellectual skills to reflect on and
revise any values or other elements of a comprehensive doctrine. As a number of theorists have noted, without a background or default sense of how
the world works and what is good and bad, one cannot organize one's experience at all, much less develop the critical-thinking skills needed to reflect
on the adequacy of that initial default sense. Choices—even choices about
whether to retain, revise, or reject a set of values or a worldview—must start
from somewhere. One cannot make any choice, autonomous or otherwise,
without some values to serve as an evaluative point of reference. Since it
is impossible for anyone to choose the values on the basis of which she
chooses the values on the basis of which she chooses the values . . . ad infini-
tum, it appears that genuine choice requires some initial evaluative starting
point, even if that starting point is to be subject to critical evaluation. Since
children are best served by having an initial evaluative framework, it seems
reasonable to allow parents to offer their frameworks to the child, at least
insofar as the parents' values are morally decent, and at least insofar as the
parents refrain from trying to lock in those values.

Similarly, normal cognitive development requires that children have some
sort of initial sense of how the world works—a sense that may well include
elements of a particular comprehensive doctrine. Moreover, in order for
the child to make an eventual decision about religious components of a

comprehensive doctrine, she will have to be introduced at some point to the concept of religion itself. How this is done will inevitably nudge the child into one direction or another. As Mills observes, there is no neutral way to do this: Parental affirmations of atheism or even agnosticism privilege certain views about religion no less than parental affirmations of a particular creed. And, far from being the epitome of neutrality, the smorgasbord approach of sampling many different religions carries with it certain attitudes about religion no less than does the announcement to the child that, say, "Mommy and Daddy are Methodists." Even if we try—as we should—to avoid locking in our religious attitudes in our children, we cannot simply avoid letting them know our views, nor can we avoid the fact that they will probably imitate us, at least for a while.

Finally, it is worth noting that the parents' free exercise of their own religions and pursuits will, as a matter of course, make certain options more salient, more available, and more appealing to their children than alternatives. A child of Catholic parents will almost inevitably learn more about Eucharist than the Hadj. The fact that I practice karate increases the chance that my children will practice karate, and decreases the chance that they will take up ballet. Partly this is a matter of logistics: It's easier to pack a kid along to go somewhere you were going anyway. But it's also part of the fairly natural tendency of children to see what their parents do as worth doing. Children, as it turns out, often want to be chips off the old block. This means that things that parents value are likely to be valued by their children as well, whether that is something as deep as a religion or as inconsequential as a favorite sports team.

Although these considerations vary in the extent to which they apply to every form of shaping, taken together, they suggest that we can develop a plausible liberal, child-respecting account of a limited parental prerogative to shape, and that we can do this without according to parents an independent, free-standing right to shape their children in their own image or according to their own values. On this account, a limited parental prerogative to engage in some activities that will have the effect of shaping the child in their own image or according to their own values derives from the interests of the child rather than the parent. Hence, we do not need to see the limited prerogative to shape our children as the outcome of a balance between a child's right to an open future which, left unconstrained, would require a maximally open future, and a free-standing parental right to shape their children. And thus we avoid the problems created by the unraveling of this model when it is confronted with the non-identity problem.

Conclusion: Blocking Unrestricted Genetic Shaping

The considerations explored in the previous section suggest that we may be able to defend a moderate interpretation of the child's right to an open future without positing a free-standing parental right to shape their children, and deploying it to constrain a right to an open future that would otherwise become maximally expansive. Instead, we might derive limited parental prerogatives to shape from the interests of children. This is vital, because in non-identity situations, the child's right seems not to come into play, so it is unavailable to provide a counterweight to the free-standing parental autonomy right, which would then threaten to become maximally expansive. In this way, the non-identity problem gives those who believe in sharply limited parental rights to shape their children by either environmental or genetic methods a strong reason to derive the limits to the right to an open future from the interests of the child rather than the parent. Hence, it appears that considerations about genetic shaping can provide important reasons to revise how we think about non-genetic shaping. If we believe that there are limits to the kinds of shaping that parents are permitted to do by genetic means, and that those limits do not disappear in non-identity situations, then we would do well to avoid thinking about the limits to non-genetic shaping in terms of a battle or a balance between competing rights.

Of course, these conclusions will be less interesting to those who do not hold the moderate view of the child's right to an open future, or those who believe that parents have far greater moral latitude to shape their children in non-identity situations than in other situations. Finally, those stalwarts who think that there is hope for solving the non-identity problem in ways that retain the claim that creating a child who is inevitably impaired by the events necessary to his or her very existence is nevertheless wronged will not feel the force of the problem posed here.

While I acknowledge that the problem I have explored, and the solution I have suggested, will not appeal to everyone, I hope that this exploration has served to illuminate a broader point that stands regardless of one's acceptance—or not—of the position I have outlined. That broader point is that work on procreative ethics may intersect in interesting and unexpected ways with work on parental rights, especially when we begin to ask deep moral question about how far parents may go when they act on the fairly common desire to have a child who is a chip off the old block.

Notes

1 In this paper, I put aside the vexed question of whether and to what extent deafness is a disability, and to what extent the obstacles faced by deaf persons are created by discriminatory social arrangements rather than their deafness. Instead, I simply focus on the permissibility—or not—of using genetic methods to attempt to "lock in" the culture that the parents seek to instill in their children.

2 Dena S. Davis, *Genetic Dilemmas: Reproductive Technology, Parental Choices, and Children's Futures* (London: Routledge, 2000): 61–3.

3 406 US 205 (1972).

4 Joel Feinberg, "The Child's Right to an Open Future," in W. Aiken and H. LaFollette, eds., *Whose Child? Parental Rights, Parental Authority, and State Power* (Totowa, NJ: Littlefield, Adams, and Co., 1980): 124–53.

5 The ambiguities in Feinberg's formulation of the right to an open future are brought out in Bertram Bandman, "A Friendly Critique of a Child's Right to an Open Future," *Philosophy of Education Yearbook* (2001): 438–44; and in

Mianna Lotz, "Feinberg, Mills, and the Child's Right to an Open Future," *Journal of Social Philosophy* 37 (2006): 537–51.

6 Feinberg, "The Child's Right to an Open Future," 130, emphasis added.

7 Ibid., 133.

8 Ibid., 139f.

9 Matthew Clayton, *Justice and Legitimacy in Upbringing* (Oxford: Oxford University Press, 2006), and "The Case against the Comprehensive Enrollment of Children," *Journal of Social Philosophy* 20, no. 3 (2011): 353–64.

10 Ibid., 363. Interestingly, though, he also suggests that it is permissible to take one's child to a church service merely to allow her to "witness the nature of Christian worship if one's aim is to develop her capacity to deliberate and act autonomously rather than to participate as a Christian" (ibid.).

11 Indeed the ambiguities in Feinberg's article suggest that *Feinberg* may not accept it, and I gather from conversations with people who know him that Clayton may not hold quite as extreme a view as some of his written remarks suggest.

12 321 US 158 (1944).

13 William Galston, *Liberal Purposes* (Cambridge: Cambridge University Press, 1991): 252.

14 Colin Macleod, "Conceptions of Parental Autonomy," *Politics and Society* 25, no. 1 (1997): 117–140, 129.

15 Ibid., 130.

16 Ibid.

17 For example, see Elizabeth Harman, "Can We Harm and Benefit in Creating?" *Philosophical Perspectives* 18 (2004): 89–113.

18 Joel Feinberg, *Harm to Others* (Oxford University Press, 1984); see also "Wrongful Life and the Counterfactual Element in Harming," *Social Philosophy and Policy* 4, no. 1 (1986): 145–78.

19 Feinberg, "Wrongful Life and the Counterfactual Element in Harming,", 169.

20 Ibid.

21 Ibid.

22 John A. Robertson, *Children of Choice: Freedom and the New Reproductive Technologies* (Princeton, NJ: Princeton University Press, 2004): 19.

23 Of course, Robertson is concerned with parental autonomy with regard to reproduction, but the point applies equally to other exercises of the parents' autonomy, such as the free exercise of their religious views, "expressive liberty," etc.

24 This inability to square the Mill's Harm Principle (that only those actions that harm or violate the rights of another person ought to be prohibited by the State) with the conviction that some choices parents might make in non-identity situations are nevertheless so wrong that they ought to be made illegal is the source of considerable worry for Fienberg. See Feinberg 1984, 100–104.

25 Claudia Mills, "The Child's Right to an Open Future?" *Journal of Social Philosophy* 34, no. 4: 499–509.

26 Ibid., 502.

27 See Harry Brighouse and Adam Swift, *Family Values: The Ethics of Parent-Child Relationships* (Princeton, NJ: Princeton University Press, 2014). A brief suggestion along these same lines can be found in David Archard, *Children: Rights and Childhood* (London: Routledge, 1993): 131.

28 Ibid., 54.

29 Ibid., 150.

30 Ibid., 151.

31 Ibid.

32 Ibid., 152.

33 Ibid., 154.

34 Ibid., 155.

6 Liberalism and the Status of Family Making

Mianna Lotz

I Introduction

The apparently 'exceptional' status of the family has long posed vexed questions and challenges for liberal theory and society, not least of all in relation to one of its constitutive activities—the bearing and rearing of children. Additional to what we might term the 'external' justification challenges confronting political liberalism in determining the precise details of a just distribution of social resources, liberalism also confronts an 'internal' justification problem that I will refer to as the *family justification problem*. Specifically, this is the challenge of explaining how its orientation towards the family is consistent with certain of its core political commitments.[1] Without such justification there might appear to be a tension between those commitments and the way in which the resources and cost burdens are distributed amongst citizens, families, and non-families alike.[2] The precise nature of this supposed tension requires unpacking, and that is the task of the first part of this chapter. The second and third parts consider two possible proposals for resolving the apparent tension and bringing liberalism's stance with respect to the family and children more clearly into alignment with those *prima facie* conflicting commitments. I ultimately set aside both of those proposals, on the grounds that while they may resolve the suggested tension, they would do so at the cost of mischaracterizing either the nature of family making or the good of children. The final part of the chapter proposes an alternative justification that brings the state's own distinct interests more fully into view than has been common practice in recent discussions of philosophical questions of the family and children. The focus of the discussion here is necessarily conceptual and foundational. Rather than addressing specific questions of the nature and limits of parents' and children's interests, rights, and duties its focus is instead on the philosophical and political parameters within which those interests, rights, and duties can be examined and their scope and limits determined.

II Liberalism's Family Justification Problem

How does this alleged internal tension amongst liberalism's core commitments arise?[3] It does so in at least the following related ways. First, the tension may seem to arise due to the *direct provisions* that liberal states accord parents, children, and families. These provisions amount to a special allocation of social resources, facilitated via such measures as family tax exemptions and benefits; publicly funded ante-natal and childbirth medical services; government-sponsored 'baby bonuses' for new parents; subsidized pre-school childcare facilities; publicly funded education systems; public recreational facilities for children; publicly funded health and dental care; paid employment leave in the form of maternity, paternity, and parental leave; and the like.[4]

Second, in implementing these provisions liberal states impose a significant *cross-subsidization* of families and children by non-families and non-parents. This occurs primarily via the tax imposts that are borne by all citizens rather than exclusively or disproportionately by those who have families. Yet such cost sharing seems *prima facie* in conflict with core tenets of egalitarian liberalism in particular, specifically in its widely accepted responsibility-sensitive forms. According to responsibility-sensitive egalitarianism, in certain conditions individuals may appropriately be held responsible for the choices they make, and this may extend to bearing the costs of those choices. In the case of having children, the costs—in particular the *care costs*, as Serena Olsaretti refers to them—are of course substantial.[5] But they are distributed far more broadly than we might expect a responsibility-sensitive model to allow.[6] Thus a *prima facie* liberal egalitarian fairness claim may hold that those who choose not to have children ought not to be burdened with costs generated by those who do.[7] Assuming for the moment that having children is indeed a choice (a point to which I will return shortly), such responsibility-*in*sensitive cost sharing seems to stand in need of justification.

As an implication of this apparent discrepancy with its egalitarian norms, liberalism's commitment to *neutrality* likewise appears strained by its special provisions for families and children. Standard forms of liberalism are supposed to be committed to neutrality towards so-called 'comprehensive' conceptions of the good, at least those that are justice-respecting. Rawls' original model was one of a political framework neutral between 'competing comprehensive doctrines' so as to allow individuals the maximum liberty, compatible with the like liberty of others, to pursue and live according to their own conceptions of the good life, and to carry out what John Stuart Mill referred to as their own 'experiments in living.'[8] Individual 'life plans' are to be pursued within the framework of liberal equality and therefore within an individual's just share of social resources, receiving no disproportionate support or resource allocation as compared to the life plans of others.

Here too the state's orientation to the family appears to breach its own commitments, specifically to liberal neutrality. As we have seen, family making receives a significant and disproportional allocation of social resources, as compared to other—perhaps all other—chosen life plans. What is the basis for such differential treatment? Does liberalism regard the family as having a special status—albeit not usually articulated—which justifies its apparently exceptional treatment? What might be the basis for the ascription of special status?

In the following section I consider two possible answers to that question. The first explores the idea of family making as a special kind of 'project,' where the specialness might be thought to derive from the value that parenting has for those individuals who engage in it. The second proposes a specific conception of children themselves—as 'goods,' of either a 'public or a 'socialized' kind. Ultimately I reject both of these approaches, for reasons to be explained.

III Family Making as a Special Project?

One approach to justifying the liberal state's apparent non-neutrality towards the family might be to base it on an argument that family making is a special kind of project, warranting the suspension of liberalism's usual neutrality constraints. The idea that parenting might be thought of as a project is accepted by Robert Taylor, as evident in his setting out of the neutrality problem that he too sees confronting liberalism:

> If special state support is provided for parenting projects but not for other kinds of projects . . . that can be just as demanding and all-consuming, then a case can surely be made that such support is non-neutral with respect to (justice–respecting) conceptions of the good life and therefore prima facie inconsistent with liberal principles of distributive justice.[9]

As I will explain, it is my view that family making ought not be conceived of as a 'project,' even one of a special kind. However, before we get to the reasons for that view, consider two further points made by Taylor. Although he does not make such a goal explicit, both points could serve to support a conception of family making as a project. Taylor's main purpose in raising them, however, is to show that each fails to provide the basis for removing family making from the scope of activities to which the neutrality requirement applies, and therefore leaves intact the problem of liberalism's exceptional treatment of the family that is our concern here.

Taylor notes that if we conceive of family making as a project, two questions immediately arise, some possible answers to which might remove the problem of the breach of liberal neutrality by removing the requirement of neutrality itself. These questions are: Is family making freely and voluntarily chosen? And, (if it is), is it reasonably thought of as obligatory? First, if it can be shown not to be freely chosen, then that would undermine the case for requiring state neutrality, given that such a requirement is premised upon the rational capacity of individuals to assume responsibility for their goals and plans and to accommodate their life plans within a just share of social resources. Expressed in more Millian terms, the value of leaving individuals free to experiment with their own conceptions of the good can only be realized by *chosen* projects. Accordingly, if family making is in all relevant respects *non-voluntary*, then the liberal state is not obliged to be neutral, and is entitled to treat it differently from the way it treats voluntary projects. The same applies if, second, it could be shown that parenting projects are in fact voluntary but in some sense *obligatory*. As Taylor points out, there are a number of potentially problematic implications of such a view, in particular in relation to the enforcement of the duty. But the key point is that an activity that is obligatory within a liberal society is not an activity towards which the liberal state is required to maintain neutrality.

Taylor makes a convincing case for the repudiation of both potential claims, however. He does so on the grounds that, first, within *liberal* societies at least, reproductive planning and restraint is both possible and highly prevalent, and adoption possible, thereby undermining an involuntariness claim;[10] and second, the coercion required by an acceptance of a duty to procreate would not be compatible with liberal principles.[11] It seems clear that we ought to consider family making to be both voluntary and non-obligatory, putting it back on a par with other projects towards which the state does owe neutrality. And yet the state is evidently non-neutral towards the family project. The discrepancy persists and the challenge for political liberalism has not been dissolved.

Perhaps it is possible to argue that even though family making is both voluntary and non-obligatory, it is nevertheless a project that is distinct in important respects from other projects towards which the state must be neutral—in other words, perhaps it could be claimed that family making is a 'special' kind of project—perhaps a kind of 'ground project'[12]—deserving of special protection and provisions? I think the most plausible argument in support of such a view is that the activity of bearing and rearing children is an activity with unique and significant value for those who engage in it. Perhaps it could be argued that projects that are of such considerable and exceptional value for liberal citizens deserve special recognition and status within liberal society, as well as a special allocation of social resources. Indeed, it could perhaps be argued that the liberal state has a legitimate special interest in anything that its citizens have a significant interest in. Let us consider the case for family making being of special value, before we consider whether its value is sufficient to ground a defense of liberal non-neutrality.

The kind of account I have in mind is sometimes developed into a fully-fledged *'parent-centered'* account of the value of raising a family, one that gives priority to the interests of parents above those of present or future children.[13] However, in elaborating the value claims that follow I do not mean to suggest that all versions of those views must necessarily prioritize parents' interests; they may do so, but my purpose is solely to convey a sense of the kind of value that parenthood has been claimed to have for parents themselves (irrespective of how that value and those interests are to be weighed against other goods and interests in family making).[14] A variety of (overlapping) accounts have been proposed, which I will categorize and briefly summarize. An *intimacy argument* claims that the family enables the development of a special form of intimacy between its members (given certain conditions standardly accepted within liberalism, such as a substantial degree of familial privacy), where intimacy is regarded as itself inherently valuable.[15] A *relationship goods argument* claims that the family provides unique opportunities for realizing the goods inherent in being part of loving relationships.[16] A *satisfaction argument* bases itself on claims of the special kinds of satisfaction that a parent derives, including delight in the child's observations of the world and in her successes, and the satisfaction gained from providing for and observing the child's 'cognitive, emotional, physical and moral development.'[17] A more general *argument from flourishing* points to the allegedly distinctive and important contribution that parenting makes to adult flourishing. This arises from the opportunities families provide for adults to "raise their children in a manner consistent with their deepest commitments" as an aspect of their own identity development and self-actualization;[18] to "form [their] child's values and life plans";[19] and, more broadly, to reflect on and test the merits of different conceptions of the good.[20]

I want to suggest that a number of problems confront the claim that the distinctive value of the parenting experience entails that parenting is a project of special status occupying an exceptional position within the parameters of liberal political principles. One such problem is that at least in the absence of further explanation, it still seems rather arbitrary for the satisfactions and value of parenting to be uniquely chosen as grounds for special status, given that for some individuals there may be other projects—including other relationships—that are just as, or perhaps even more, satisfying than a parenting role is or would be. A second problem concerns the reach of the claim: if the claim is true (its merit deriving from the plausibility of one or other of the value accounts supporting it) then it is difficult to avoid the implication that parenting must be in the interest of and good for *all* adults (and perhaps even the further implication that as such, all reproductively capable adults morally *ought* to pursue parenthood, and can decline to do so only on pain of irrationality). But I do not believe this to be an acceptable implication; nor is it one that the proponents of the various value accounts would embrace. It clearly is not the case that all adults possess the attributes that make a person well suited for the parenting role; and even if an adult is in possession of such attributes, it clearly is not the case that the proposed parenting goods are *necessarily* realized in parenting, given the range and significance of the external factors that impact upon the family and can block the realization of those goods. For these and other reasons, the suggestion of any kind of moral obligation to parent is, I believe, to be avoided.[21] We are certainly correct to acknowledge the importance and value of bearing and rearing children for many individuals; but we should stop short of advocating it as any kind of ideal 'project' for all.

A more fundamental concern, however, seems to be that the significant potential moral value of parenting for (some) parents, does not readily provide an account of the *political* value of parenting, of the kind that is presumably needed to explain why the liberal state is appropriately non-neutral in its orientation to the family. To remain liberal (at least in a Rawlsian sense) as opposed to liberal perfectionist (in a more Millian sense) the liberal state "must be restricted by a core set of *political* principles that are, or can be, the subject of consensus among all reasonable citizens."[22] Unless we can construe it in *political* terms, as well as attain consensus in relation to it among all rational individuals, moral claims of the parent-centered value of parenting do not seem to be of the right kind to be capable of explaining and justifying the exceptional status of the family within liberalism. To seek to justify the value of parenting by providing a comprehensive account of the good of it is, therefore, to respond to a question that arises at one level (in this case *political*) with an answer that is only available at a different level (in this case, *moral*).

A final substantive concern might be noted in relation to this proposal. That is that, contrary to Taylor's assumption, the notion of a 'project' is not one that is unproblematically extended to the bearing and rearing of children. I would argue that parenting is so incommensurate with any other activities to which we might apply the concept, as to not appropriately be classifiable as a 'project' of any kind. There is therefore a sense in which to conceive of procreation and parenting as a 'project' is to make a kind of category mistake.[23] 'Project' is broadly definable as *an individual or collective enterprise carefully planned to achieve a particular aim*. But raising a child is not a clearly defined and ends-directed activity comparable to 'climbing Mount Everest,'[24] developing a permaculture garden, making a movie, renovating a house, writing a novel, or any of the other activities commonly referred to as 'projects.' Moreover, parenting is enduring, demanding, emotionally consuming, and irrevocably personally transformative to an extent that I believe sets it fundamentally apart from any of those other kinds of endeavor or enterprise.[25] It is also an enterprise that, once undertaken, cannot be abandoned readily or without very serious implications. Finally, there seems to be a distinctly proprietorial sense attached to the notion of a project that is, I believe, inappropriate for thinking about procreation and parenting. Some accounts of parenthood do construe it in proprietarian terms; and some parents appear to parent in a way that suggests that that is the way they regard it also. But I would suggest that these are not accounts we ought to embrace.[26] At best I think family making may be thought of as something more akin to a 'life plan' than a 'project.' However, that conceptual correction does nothing to remove the difficulty that concerns us here, since according to political liberalism, justice-respecting individual life plans call for state neutrality just as surely as justice-respecting individual projects do. The family justification problem thus remains even if we supplant talk of 'projects' with talk of 'life plans.'

IV Children as Goods?

Let us turn, then, to a second possible strategy for justifying liberalism's non-neutral orientation to the family. Here I focus in particular on the non-neutrality of state-imposed cost subsidization of families and children by all members of the liberal society, irrespective of whether they have children. This distribution of costs among parents and non-parents raises what Serena Olsaretti has referred to as 'the question of parental justice.'[27] The question posed is: Do non-parents in a just society have an obligation to share with parents some of the costs of having children? One approach to addressing the parental justice question is to propose that it is because children are in some sense 'goods' that the sharing of costs related to raising them is, in fact just. If it is just for all to share the costs of children, then it is presumably also just for the liberal state to implement and enforce such cost-sharing, explaining away what otherwise might look like a problematic breach of the requirement of state neutrality. Let us consider, then, two versions of the 'goods' argument.

(a) Children as 'Public Goods'

The most prevalent pro-cost-sharing argument is the 'public goods' argument. That children are in some sense public goods is a view endorsed by David Archard:

> In the absence of such extensive family support [as is provided by the liberal state] very many of those who wish to be parents would have enormous difficulties in doing so. This means either that significant numbers of people would not be able to have children or that many children would be inadequately cared for. Either way society as a whole would suffer. It would fail to generate in sufficient numbers or to the sufficient level required a future generation of well-functioning adults.

> Children are a public good from which all members of society ben-
> efit. . . . The public good of children is enjoyed non-exclusively and
> equally by all within society.[28]

The 'public goods' argument accordingly holds that the obligation of
non-parents to share in the costs of children derives from the fact that
non-parents *benefit* from children and from the work that parents do in
raising them; and they do so, specifically, from the production of a sufficient number of well-functioning future adults to contribute in the necessary
ways to the ongoing welfare and reproduction of liberal society.

Going beyond Archard's more general account of the good of children,
proponents of the 'public goods' view take it to be specifically the production of future taxpayers of the welfare state that is the most important way
in which "children are supposed to be or create public goods."[29] As Rolf
George states, "children grow up and become, among other things, providers of pensions, maintainers of society.'[30] Developing the view, Serena
Olsaretti breaks down the component steps of the public goods argument
in the following way:

(i) Parents bearing and rearing children creates benefits for others;
(ia) These benefits are positive externalities and, more specifically, are public goods;
(ii) There is a plausible version of the fair play principle, such that under
certain conditions producers of benefits have enforceable claims against
those who receive the benefits;
(iii) The conditions specified by a plausible version of the fair play principle
obtain in the case of parents' producing the benefits and non-parents'
receiving them.[31]

Thus, Olsaretti explains, it is argued that "nonparents would be unfairly free
riding on parents if they accepted the benefits but did not share the costs."[32]

Importantly, Olsaretti ultimately rejects the 'public goods' argument as a
defense of cost sharing; but before we consider her critique and proposed
alternative to it, it will be helpful to briefly recall Rawls' account of the
key features of public goods. According to Rawls, public goods have two
characteristic features—*indivisibility* and *publicness*—which he explains as
follows:

> [T]here are many individuals . . . who want more or less of this good, but
> if they are to enjoy it at all [they] must each enjoy the same amount. The
> quantity produced cannot be divided up as private goods can and pur-
> chased by individuals according to their preferences for more and less.[33]

Rawls identifies national defense as a classic case of a public good, and
it provides a relatively rare clear example. Individual citizens cannot

be in receipt of differential benefits of national defense, nor can they opt out of receipt of such benefits; and the enjoyment of the benefit by any citizen does not deplete or in any way impact upon the enjoyment of it by others. Olsaretti uses the terms *non-excludability* (it is either impossible or too costly to exclude anyone from receipt of the benefit); *non-avoidability* (it is not possible for someone to opt out of or refrain from receiving the benefit); and *non-rivalry* (the amount of the benefit that is received by some does not diminish the amount able to be received by others).[34]

As indicated, however, Olsaretti does not accept that the 'public goods' argument accurately depicts the benefits of children, and she therefore ultimately denies that the argument succeeds in justifying cost sharing. One of her points of disagreement is with the idea that the benefits of children can be thought of as positive externalities. She rejects this because whereas *unintentional* third-party benefit is required for externalities, by contrast, she believes, "the benefit that parents produce is an outcome that is *intended*, it is something they *aim* at," and " . . . they aim at it partly *because* it is beneficial for third parties."[35] She says:

> It is clearly not true that parents create a benefit unintentionally, in the sense that they do not intentionally bring about the outcome that is beneficial to third parties. They clearly do intentionally take steps to ensure, or maximize the probability, that they bring up children who will become economically active and productive members of the society, and this is the outcome that is beneficial to third parties.[36]

I find Olsaretti unpersuasive on this particular point, however, as I think her objection either conflates *intentional* benefitting with *foreseen* benefitting; or conflates an intention to achieve an end that will, ultimately, produce third-party benefit, with an intention to bring about that third-party benefit.[37] Similar skepticism regarding procreation as intentional third-party benefitting is expressed by Paula Casal:

> . . . parents standardly do not decide to have children in order to produce a public good. Instead, the beneficial effects are unintended consequences of their decision.[38]

Indeed it seems a misrepresentation and over-estimation of parental intention to suggest that parents intentionally benefit society when they raise children. Procreation and parenting are first and foremost—and for many, exclusively—activities that individuals engage in based on some conception of *their own* good and desires, in combination with a conception of the *good of the child*. Rolf George suggests that in Western societies at least, most people have:

. . . only one motivation for having children . . . namely, the expected gratifications of parenthood. These may range from the enjoyment of infant cuteness to pride in the children's achievement to such things as the perpetuation of a name or keeping wealth or a business in the family . . .[39]

Parental gratifications aside, while the raising of successful and productive children is a goal that parents ideally and commonly do have, I would suggest that that specific goal has as its central object the benefitting of the children themselves, in their expected future lives in liberal society, rather than the production of benefits to third parties—even if such benefits are undeniable and foreseeable, including to parents themselves. I do not, therefore, regard Olsaretti's specific objection to the public goods argument to be persuasive.

Setting that disagreement aside, however, Olsaretti also rejects the 'public goods' argument on the grounds that she doesn't believe that the benefits of children meet the criteria of being non-excludable, non-avoidable, and non-rivalrous. She thinks that it is at least in principle possible for non-parents *not* to receive the benefits produced by the taxes of the next generation; and further, that non-parents' consumption of tax-funded benefits does lessen the amount of benefit available over all.[40] These are persuasive claims as far as I can see, and clearly present problems for the argument that children are public goods, whatever our conclusions regarding the intentionality question. But let us leave those problems to one side and consider now Olsaretti's proposed alternative cost-sharing justification: namely that costs are appropriately shared by non-parents because children are 'socialized goods.'

(b) Children as 'Socialized Goods'?

Olsaretti's position is that the (central) benefits produced by parents in bearing and bearing children are not public goods, but rather, *deliberately socialized goods*. Elaborating on the nature of the benefits, she explains that " . . . all recipients of welfare benefits and publicly funded goods, including nonparents, are benefitting from the contributions of someone's children, and hence, indirectly, from parents' having and rearing children."[41] Going further than a mere benefits claim, however, Olsaretti's commitment to the idea that those benefits are *intentionally* produced, remains in evidence, as the following passages indicate:

[O]ur society intentionally and forcibly redirects some of the benefits of children to nonparents, and thereby sets up a cooperative scheme that, in the absence of nonparents' cooperation, is unfair to parents.[42]
[O]ur social and economic institutions *are intentionally so structured as to ensure that* the product of parents' labors is socially beneficial for everyone, including nonparents.[43]

And elaborating further, she says:

> [T]he benefits-producing activity parents intentionally engage in, and by dint of which they have claims of fairness against nonparents, is that of having and rearing children *in the context of a scheme that redistributes the benefits of children to nonparents and parents alike.*[44]

So far so good; I have no disagreement with Olsaretti in relation to these claims, which are ultimately about benefits intentionally produced *via our social and economic arrangements*. However, in a footnote she adds a qualification, worth representing here because it serves to reinstate my original concern regarding her claims in relation to *parental* intentionality:

> While most parents do not explicitly formulate to themselves the specific intention of raising children who will provide tax contributions, they do implicitly intend that outcome as part of a more complex goal they aim at in raising their children.[45]

Combined with her view that the benefits received by non-parents are excludable, avoidable, and rivalrous, the fact that the benefits are produced through a coordinated and cooperative collective arrangement entails for Olsaretti that the proper characterization of the benefits of children is as *socialized* rather than public goods. For Olsaretti, then, the socialized nature of the benefit establishes on grounds of fairness the obligation of non-parents and parents alike to share the costs involved in raising children. Her purpose in insisting on the *intentional* nature of the benefit-production is that it establishes the kind of "mutually advantageous cooperative venture" that can explain why 'free-riding' or taking advantage of other peoples' cooperative efforts, is unjustified, and obligations of cost-sharing are justified:

> The socialized goods argument can appeal to a principle which holds that a person's intentional contribution to a cooperative, benefits-sharing scheme, as a result of which she incurs some costs, grounds enforceable obligations on the part of those who receive the benefits.[46]

As already indicated, I have problems accepting Olsaretti's claims about parental intention. More generally, however, it is also just not clear why we ought to regard intentionality—parental or otherwise—as necessary in order for a 'fair play' justification to ground a cost-sharing obligation. As a first pass, it seems to me that the *mere fact of receipt of a known benefit*, produced by those who have and raise children, whether intended or not by the benefit-producers themselves, ought to be sufficient to ground obligation, given that (if Olsaretti is correct,) the benefit in question (tax contributions) is avoidable and excludable. That is, if it is the case that non-parents could avoid receipt of the benefits, yet they knowingly and voluntarily accept those benefits, then that voluntary acceptance seems to me to provide sufficient ground for a fairness-based obligation to contribute to the costs involved in generating those benefits. If we accept my analysis of an alternative basis for an obligation to share costs, then the role and significance that Olsaretti attributes to intentionality—and especially parental intentionality—in establishing cost-sharing obligations, becomes redundant.

As indicated, Paula Casal agrees that the public benefits of children are not (typically) intended by parents; however, her position ultimately differs from my own in that she does not believe that known receipt of benefit is sufficient to establish a fairness-based claim for cost sharing. She refers to the intuition underpinning the fairness principle in Rawls' original account of public goods, which states that where "a number of persons engage in a mutually advantageous cooperative venture according to rules, and thus restrict their liberty in ways necessary to yield advantages for all," then fairness requires that those who have "voluntarily accepted the benefits of the arrangement or taken advantage of the opportunities it offers to further [their] interest" are not morally permitted to free ride but must, rather, contribute a "fair share."[47] But, Casal argues, "[w]e do not usually think that we are under any obligation, let alone an enforceable one, to reward people for a benefit they produced unintentionally, when doing something they love doing."[48] Accordingly, she states:

> My conclusion then is that both sacrificing, and doing so in order to provide a public good, are two necessary conditions for the plausible application of the principle of fairness.[49]

Casal illustrates her position with the case of the beach-cleaning environmentalists.[50] She asks us to consider a group of environmentalists who decide to clean a commonly owned beach, so that a public good is produced: a clean beach for everyone to enjoy.[51] In view of the personal sacrifice that they make for the purpose of achieving the public good (enjoyment of a clean beach), Casal thinks that the environmentalists do have a fairness-based claim against the beachgoers free-riding on their efforts, and that those beachgoers ought therefore contribute a fair share towards the ongoing costs of the beach-cleaning.

We can spell out the implications of Casal's emphasis on sacrifice and intent for our argument as follows. Procreation amounts to the unintended benefitting of others as a by-product of the pursuit of an activity that parents engage in primarily for reasons of their *own* enjoyment and preference. While there are personal sacrifices and costs involved, those are *not* costs and sacrifices accepted by parents *in pursuit of the provision of public good*, but rather, costs and sacrifices accepted by parents *in pursuit of realization of their own goals, preferences, and enjoyments.* The (unintended) beneficiaries of procreation do not, therefore, incur a fairness-based obligation to share in the costs or make sacrifices of their own in response to receipt of those benefits. In other words, if the third-party benefits are merely by-products of people pursuing their own personal goals (unlike in the beach-cleaning environmentalists case) then the enjoyment of those benefits does not establish a fairness-based obligation to share in the costs. However if, by contrast, the beach-cleaning was being carried out purely out of the enjoyment of beach cleaners who clean beaches simply because they love doing so, then—whatever benefits might in fact collaterally be enjoyed—the third-party beach enjoyers do not have a fairness-based obligation to contribute to the costs of the beach cleaners. For Casal, parents are like the self-motivated rather than public-motivated beach cleaners: they fundamentally pursue their (collaterally benefits-producing) activities for their *own* enjoyment, and not for the public good. Hence, no fairness-based claim for cost compensation or contribution is available to parents.

Or so concludes Casal. However, it remains my view that if the procreative benefits *could* be refused, yet the third-party beneficiaries *do not* refuse them, then the mere fact of their (avoidable) acceptance of those benefits *does and should* count sufficiently for an obligation to share in the costs of producing those benefits. Importantly, the beneficiaries of procreation are not, after all, analogous to the beachgoers, who merely occasionally visit the beach and do so only for (comparatively) brief periods of time. The third-party beneficiaries of procreation willingly and avoidably accept the benefits in *a continuous and ongoing way*; indeed it would not be a gross exaggeration to say that by contrast with the free-riding beachgoers, the beneficiaries of procreation languish their entire lives on (metaphorical) Benefits Beach.

And a further point can be made. Given their continual and ongoing receipt of the benefits in question, if it somehow happened that these beachgoers were offered the opportunity to contribute to the ongoing costs incurred by the lovers of beach cleaning—a 'Beach Tax,' let us imagine—yet they refused to contribute *in spite of knowing and intending that they would continue their enjoyment of the beach*, this, I suggest, contra Casal, both *could and should* be regarded as an unfairness—notwithstanding and quite irrespective of the beach cleaners' love and free pursuit of beach-cleaning. Hence, while I think Casal's injunction that fairness should be determined not by reference solely to aspects of the *consumption* of benefits but also by reference to aspects of their *production*, nevertheless the fact that the benefits producers are producing benefits in the course of pursuing a venture that they love and freely choose (and are hence not making a personal sacrifice in the required way) should not persuade us to accept that the benefits consumers have no obligations whatsoever to share (at least some of) the costs of producing those benefits. Accordingly Casal's proposed disanalogy between the beach cleaners and the procreators does not succeed in removing the grounds for a fairness-based claim to cost sharing. On this view, the crucial work in grounding a fairness claim for cost-sharing is done by the fact of (ongoing) avoidable public benefit; and that claim would not be automatically and decisively undermined by a discovery that the benefits producers did not intend the public benefit, nor by the fact that they enjoy and freely pursue their benefits-producing activity, as Casal would have us accept.

To sum up: A proposed move away from the classification of children as public goods might well serve Olsaretti's objective of avoiding an account that insists that the benefits produced by parents are unintentional (and therefore avoiding the characterization of children as 'positive externalities'). Children cannot be positive externalities and therefore public goods, Olsaretti says, since parents *do* intend the third-party benefits that they bring. A distinct account of their good—as socialized—allows for reinstatement of a cost-sharing obligation, as Olsaretti wants. I have indicated that I am not persuaded by Olsaretti's insistence on parental intention as the means by which to establish a fairness-based claim for cost-sharing, and in the process have also clarified why I do not think that Casal's objection to fairness-based claims for cost-sharing ultimately succeeds either. Setting aside those arguments, however, the question of whether or not a 'socialized goods' account will ultimately yield a superior account to the 'public goods' account, is a distinct matter. In fact, I think we have good reason to reject both the 'public goods' and 'socialized goods' arguments for cost sharing, quite aside from the very specific problems raised above. Let me turn to those reasons now.[52]

(c) Against any 'Goods' Account of Children

The first two concerns relate to clarity and precision in terms of what exactly it is that we characterize as the public (or socialized) 'good' itself. First, it seems to me that the accounts provided by both the public and socialized goods arguments are over-inclusive: they cannot isolate parents or children as benefit-producers distinct from other benefit-producers. For example, if children are to be thought of as public (or socialized) goods in virtue of their role in providing the tax base for the welfare state, then every tax-paying citizen is likewise a public (or socialized) good. If the central good provided by children is provided by all tax-paying citizens, then that would seem to provide justification for the costs of all citizens to be equitably shared amongst all beneficiaries (i.e. all citizens equally). This does not seem to be an intended implication of the public (or socialized) goods accounts, and in the absence of further explanation of what it is that is special about the case of children, it seems to undermine the grounds for sharing *child-related* costs in particular.[53]

Second, Olsaretti's argument depicts children themselves as the goods, as do the original public goods arguments. But it is unclear why we should construe children themselves as the goods, rather than the *parental activities that produce the benefit*—that is, reproduction, parenting, and education—as *a good*, in society.[54] In other words, if it is inter alia the provision of future taxpayers to support the welfare system that is the benefit, then it is not clear why it is not the *taxpayer-generating activities* that we ought to regard as the relevant good. Indeed, it is not clear why we are not simply talking in terms of reproduction, parenting, and education as *forms of labor that are of public value and good*. In the absence of a compelling argument against regarding the good in that way, this seems a more accurate conception than the one on offer. Ultimately, however, I suspect that the force of this objection depends to a considerable extent upon the force of a deeper concern I have, namely about the designation of children as 'goods' of any kind, public or socialized.

My deeper objection is a more ideological one. The concepts 'public goods' and 'socialized goods' are fundamentally economic concepts. Their use frames the argument for valuing the contribution of parents (or children) within the terms of economic value and contribution (as indeed is the intention of proponents). In construing obligations to share costs as determined by what has been or will be received in turn, however, such accounts provide an overly transactional, compensatory, and ultimately, I think, self-interest-referring basis for accepting distribution of the costs of raising children amongst parents and non-parents alike. To base a pro-cost-sharing argument on an economic rationale seems unfortunate for those reasons.[55] It is also surely inadequate as a justification for the liberal state's non-neutral orientation to families and children. Of course, any moralized justification for sharing procreative costs will confront the problem that it will not secure overlapping consensus amongst all reasonable liberal citizens; and structurally it appears to constitute an appeal to comprehensive doctrine, ruled out by the original principles of political liberalism. But an alternative may be available. Recall the earlier-mentioned requirement that reasons justifying the principles upon which liberal society is arranged, ought to be *political* in kind—not substantive or moral, nor, we can add, economic. Economic grounds are not sufficiently foundational to justify liberal non-neutrality. Thus, whatever the merits of the public or socialized goods arguments in establishing fairness grounds for cost-sharing, it turns out that they cannot be of service for our intended purpose here, of establishing a foundational *political* justification for the state's exceptional non-neutrality towards the family and the bearing, rearing, and educating of children. We would be wise, therefore, to eschew any strategy that involves categorization of children as 'goods' of either a public or socialized kind.

V Alternative Solution and Implications

A more promising source of justification of the liberal state's non-neutrality towards the family is to be found, I suggest, in an account of the *political* value of procreation and parenting to liberalism and the liberal state itself.[56]

Such an account will set the parameters within which questions about parental rights and authority can be addressed, as well as, potentially, help to clarify the state's obligations with respect to the education of children. While it is not my purpose here to settle substantive questions about the scope of parental and state rights and obligations, the more foundational proposals offered here should serve effectively to indicate the upper limits of those rights and obligations.

David Archard and Colin Macleod are amongst the seemingly few contemporary philosophers who explicitly acknowledge the distinct interest of the liberal state in procreation and parenting. They say:

> There is one very important reason for thinking that [the state has an independent set of interests of its own in respect of children]. This is that the state should secure the conditions for the reproduction of its institutions and their essential social, political, economic and cultural preconditions.[57]

Developing such a view further, it could be argued that the liberal state's foundational interest in preserving the conditions required for its own existence entails that both procreation and parenting can be included as amongst those conditions in which the state is not required to be disinterested (as indeed can public education and health systems). In fact children themselves, as proto- or emergent persons, are probably more accurately depicted as amongst the *preconditions* for liberalism; and if the liberal state has a legitimate interest in the conditions for its own existence, then it surely also has a legitimate interest in its preconditions. I believe that this interest is sufficiently foundational so as to not be in breach of liberalism's core political principles.[58]

Rawls does not himself directly provide us with this solution, though he certainly acknowledges the role and importance of the family in reproducing political society over time.[59] As David Archard has noted, Rawls' position with respect to the relationship between the family and principles of social justice appears to have been ambivalent, though he did not believe that the family ought to be abolished in favor of some other arrangement for producing justice-respecting citizens of liberal society. Rawls' ambivalence was over whether or not the family lies "beyond justice"—that is, outside of the reach of the accepted principles of justice, both in terms of its internal constitution and in terms of its contribution to liberal society and, most problematically, the effect of its existence on the distribution of social goods within liberal society.[60] The account I am proposing here does not argue or entail that the family lies beyond justice; its claims entail only that *some forms and manifestations of* state non-neutrality towards the bearing, rearing, and educating of children, can be just; state non-neutrality towards the family and children is not, in principle at least, necessarily in conflict with core liberal commitments. While it does not propose a solution to Rawls' ambivalence, it does, I think, offer an account of the state's special interest in the bearing, rearing, and educating of children with which Rawls could agree.

Robert Taylor also acknowledges the possibility that the state has an interest in procreation in virtue of its interest in its own preservation;[61] but he fails to draw the right conclusions from it—or rather, he overlooks one important potential implication. Taylor rightly argues that the existence of a state interest in procreation cannot underwrite either a strong or weak enforceable obligation to parent, for the reason that, inter alia, we cannot presume that citizens will care for "the preservation of political society after their deaths"; and moreover, the external enforcement of such an obligation will, unavoidably, be highly coercive. As indicated, I agree that the state's interest in procreation cannot justify enforceable obligations to parent. Yet it presumably *can* provide a justification for the state's non-neutrality with respect to family making. If the state can be viewed as having a legitimate interest in some activity then its non-neutrality towards that activity is presumably defensible. This can certainly be claimed in respect of liberal political institutions and processes: the liberal state is perfectly entitled to use a share of its resources to preserve those institutions and practices that are necessary for its own political preservation and reproduction.

An interesting and more substantial justification of the family is provided by Veronique Munoz-Darde.[62] She suggests that we view the state as having an interest in whatever conditions are necessary to maintain a background of diversity against which people can make a wide range of choices about how to live; and furthermore that the family contributes to this by contributing opportunities for deliberating about and developing one's own conception of the good life and discovering its merits.[63] As Munoz-Darde points out, "the diversity of families makes it possible for the worth of different ways of life to be available as options, and hence creates the conditions necessary for pluralism."[64] While I think Munoz-Darde's argument is promising, I am not here undertaking to endorse a view as substantive as this. Again, the position I am defending is the more foundational one that the liberal state has a legitimate self-constitutive interest in activities and life plans that produce future citizens who can participate productively in the liberal economy and public affairs, and thereby secure the benefits of a stable welfare state. Those activities that contribute to the generation of productive liberal citizens are activities towards which the liberal state is not required to be neutral, and towards which it is therefore permitted to allocate a (just) disproportionate share of social resources, either directly or through indirect distributive means such as taxation. The problem of the state's non-neutrality towards the family is therefore resolved without the need for problematic reference to the special interests of some individuals, or the economic value of children—both of which, I have argued, are undesirable solutions. Finally, establishing the basis for acceptable state non-neutrality with respect to the family and children does not entail that the family or its impact on the distribution of resources lies "beyond justice."

VI Conclusion

In recent philosophical work the defense of parent-centered interests in childraising has been offered by way of correcting for a perceived overemphasis on children's rights and welfare. Harry Brighouse and Adam Swift, amongst others, have justifiably sought to restore parental interests to the picture, highlighting the special significance and value that parenting can have for those who undertake to raise children, but without embedding such interests in the kind of proprietarian conception of parenthood that they have historically been grounded in.[65] Perhaps less popular but, I argue, nevertheless important, is the restoration of an account of the state's own interests, not least of all because of the role of those interests in accounting for what might otherwise appear to be a problematic exceptionalism in regards to the bearing, rearing, and educating of children. Clarifying the state's distinct and legitimate interest in procreation, parenting, and education suggests that parents' and children's interests do not exhaust the moral terrain of consideration in the way that many contemporary discussions of parents' and children's rights assume or endorse. That recognition in turn highlights that in having children, raising them, and making significant decisions about their lives—including about their educational opportunities—we engage in activities that are in an important sense not individual and private. As I have argued elsewhere, distinctly *collective* procreative interests are ineliminably bound up with individual procreative conduct, and this applies to parenting conduct as well.[66]

What might be the general implications of accepting such an account, in particular in terms of procreation, parenting, and children's education? I think these include that the liberal state is permitted to actively encourage and support procreation, family making, and children's education to an extent that is compatible with preservation and even enhancement of the conditions for its *own* continuation, including by distributing additional resources to families and by implementing just systems of cost-sharing amongst all citizens, even those who opt out of parenthood. Furthermore, because it is not simply citizens but *justice-respecting* citizens that liberalism requires, the state may allocate a substantial and disproportionate (yet just) share of social resources to the provision and support of a public education system that is well suited to developing in children a robust understanding of the liberal conception of justice on which society is built.[67] For it to do so on the self-constitutive grounds I have defended here, is not tantamount to adoption of a substantially pro-natalist view nor to endorsement of a substantive and comprehensive conception of the good for citizens. It therefore amounts to an exceptionalism in regards to the family and children that is not in fact in breach of liberalism's core commitment to neutrality.

Notes

I extend my grateful thanks to all participants of the From Procreative Ethics To Procreative Rights workshops for their many insightful comments and discussions from which this paper has greatly benefitted. Special thanks to Anca Gheaus and Marc Ramsay for particularly extensive feedback; to Jaime Ahlberg and Michael Cholbi for organizing the events and inviting me to participate; and to the Spencer Foundation for their generous financial support of this project.

1 Importantly, although I refer throughout this discussion to 'family' making, this paper does not seek to provide a defense of the family itself, either as the best arrangement for the rearing of children or on any other grounds. Questions concerning the justification and structure of the family, and the family's role within liberal society, are thus here left unaddressed. I take it that the fact that it is currently predominantly within families that children are cared for—rather than within collective rearing institutions of some kind—is a contingent matter. My goal here is purely to consider whether the prevailing orientation of liberal states towards the bearing and rearing of children—in terms of the allocation and distribution of resources—presents a genuine problem of internal tension or incoherence for political liberalism. Thanks to Colin Macleod for prompting this clarification.

2 As will become clear I regard this tension to be merely apparent rather than real, deep, or insurmountable, since I regard the special allocation of resources to the family to be ultimately justifiable within liberalism.

3 Perhaps it may be queried whether, rather than prioritizing parenting or the parent–child relationship, the liberal state is not instead simply attending to the welfare of a vulnerable group of its own citizens—namely its children. Such an analysis does not confront any problem of an apparent internal tension within liberalism. However, for that to be a plausible analysis it would need to be explained why the state allocates its welfare provisions to families and parents, rather than utilizing purely direct means of distribution or service provision for children. I follow other analysts in maintaining that whatever the ultimate distributive goals and assumptions, families and parents *are* accorded special treatment by the liberal state (and indeed I will suggest that that is ultimately justifiable). Thanks to an anonymous reviewer for raising this possible query.

4 Of course not all liberal states offer all of these provisions, or offer them to equal extent. However all Western liberal democratic nations currently do offer a high majority of these forms of special allocations for families.

5 Serena Olsaretti, "Children as Public Goods?" 226–58. I here refer only to the care-related costs. Olsaretti points out that in thinking about the cost of children for a society, we can distinguish between costs of care and costs of added adult members. The cost of added adult members are "the costs involved in meeting whatever claims children will make as adults," such as a fair share of access to natural and social resources (Olsaretti, 230). Importantly, however, considered from a societal perspective, the real costs of children in society extend beyond necessary financial and material resources to include also the cost of the time involved for parents (and other carers) in looking after them and meeting their needs (229). It is not easy to accurately estimate the cost of a child for a society, but if we consider solely the cost to families of providing for a child within the parameters of the above state provisions the estimates are already considerable: recent research

in Australia estimates the cost of raising a child to age 21 (average age of leaving home) to be $AU450, 000. That figure falls well below the cost to society overall. See http://www.natsem.canberra.edu.au/storage/AMP_NATSEM_33.pdf

6 Of course, within progressively taxed liberal societies, those taxation burdens are not shared equally but vary according to individual or family income. But this does little to mitigate the concern, since income-earning individuals without children will not receive the tax credits or exemptions that families benefit from.

7 Olsaretti, "Children as Public Goods?" 226–7 and note 2.

8 As is often acknowledged, however, Mill's commitment to the development of individuality may more plausibly amount to a form of liberal perfectionism rather than a purely political non-substantive liberalism.

9 Taylor, "Children as Projects and Persons: A Liberal Antinomy," 557.

10 Ibid., 561.

11 There is more to his argument than indicated here, but for my purposes the details need not concern us.

12 Bernard Williams refers to 'ground projects' as the concerns, commitments, relationships, etc. that are fundamental for a person's life having meaning and worth for them. See Bernard Williams, "Persons, Character, and Identity," in *Moral Luck: Philosophical Papers 1973–1980*, ed. Bernard Williams (New York: Cambridge University Press, 1981): 1–20.

13 Parent-centered accounts are typically presented alongside child-centered ones. However, in the context of the present discussion, child-centered accounts are not relevant, since we are discussing family making as a project, and it could only be considered a 'project' (if it can be considered that at all) for parents, not for children.

14 I draw here on the analysis of Harry Brighouse and Adam Swift though they do not ultimately endorse a parent-focused account but rather a 'dual-interests' one. Harry Brighouse and Adam Swift, "Parents' Rights and the Value of the Family," *Ethics* 117 (2006): 80–108.

15 See for example Ferdinand Shoeman, "Rights of Children, Rights of Parents, and the Moral Basis of the Family," *Ethics* 91 (1980): 6–19; Colin Macleod, "Liberal Equality and the Affective Family," in *The Moral and Political Status of Children*, eds. David Archard and Colin M. Macleod (Oxford: Oxford University Press, 2002): 215.

16 See for example James Rachels, *Can Ethics Provide Answers?* (Lanham, MD: Rowman & Littlefield, 1997): 223.

17 Harry Brighouse and Adam Swift, "Parents' Rights and the Value of the Family," *Ethics* 117 (2006): 80–108.

18 William Galston, *Liberal Pluralism: The Implications of Value Pluralism for Political Theory and Practice* (New York: Cambridge University Press, 2002): 97–8 and 102.

19 Charles Fried, *Right and Wrong* (Cambridge, MA: Harvard University Press, 1978): 152.

20 Will Kymlicka, *Multicultural Citizenship: A Liberal Theory of Minority Rights* (Oxford: Clarendon Press, 1995): 82–5.

21 This is certainly not a view shared by all, but for reasons of space I will not attempt to justify it here.

22 Gerald Gaus, Shane D. Courtland, and David Schmidtz, "Liberalism," in *The Stanford Encyclopedia of Philosophy*, ed. Edward N. Zalta (Spring 2015 Edition). Accessed May 27, 2016. http://plato.stanford.edu/archives/spr2015/entries/liberalism/. Emphasis added.

23 Thanks to Colin Macleod for this observation.

24 Taylor, "Children as Projects and Persons: A Liberal Antinomy," 555.

25 For an excellent discussion of the personally transformative experience of parenting see Laurie A. Paul's recent book, *Transformative Experience* (Oxford: Oxford University Press, 2014).

26 My sympathies lie closer to conceptions that construe parenting as a 'guardianship' or 'stewardship' role, rather than in the terms of ownership connoted by the term 'project.' But I cannot defend that claim here.

27 Olsaretti, "Children as Public Goods?" 250.

28 David Archard, *The Family: A Liberal Defence*. (New York, NY: Palgrave Macmillan, 2010): 80.

29 Olsaretti, "Children as Public Goods?" 250.

30 Rolf George, "Who Should Bear the Cost of Children?" *Public Affairs Quarterly* 1, no. 1 (1987): 1–42, 31.

31 Olsaretti, "Children as Public Goods?" 239.

32 Ibid., 228–9.

33 John Rawls, *A Theory of Justice* (Cambridge: Mass: Belknap Press, 1999): 235.

34 Olsaretti, "Children as Public Goods?" 248.

35 Ibid., 247.

36 Ibid., 245–6.

37 For example, I may buy a cake from the local patisserie, with the intention of benefitting my daughter and her friends at her birthday party; and in buying that cake I knowingly produce third-party benefits for a business in my local community. However, the fact that those third-party benefits are realized, and that I am aware that they will be, is not sufficient for a claim that by my action I intended to and was motivated by an intention to produce third-party benefits to my local business community. My support for my local community may be genuine but it cannot be assumed that the desire to provide that support was at all operative in my intention or motivation to buy a cake for my daughter (though of course it could have been). Likewise, I do not find it persuasive to suggest (as I think Olsaretti can be interpreted to do) that parents have children (even inter alia) in order to benefit third parties. And the fact that the outcome—an economically active and productive citizen—is beneficial to society, is certainly not sufficient to establish intention or motivation.

38 Paula Casal, "Environmentalism, Procreation, and the Principle of Fairness", 367.

39 Rolf George, "On the External Benefits of Children," 209.

40 Serena Olsaretti, "Children as Public Goods?" 250. Olsaretti actually refers to three distinct grounds, but as far as I can see her first and third grounds amount to the same point, so I will not represent all three here.

41 Olsaretti, "Children as Public Goods?" 251.

42 Ibid., 248.

43 Ibid., 252.

44 Ibid., 256.

45 Ibid., 252.

46 Ibid., 255.

47 Casal, "Environmentalism, Procreation, and the Principle of Fairness", 365, citing Rawls, *A Theory of Justice*, 111.

48 Casal, "Environmentalism, Procreation, and the Principle of Fairness," 367.

49 Ibid., 368.

50 Thanks to Anca Gheaus for reminding me of this example.

51 Casal "Environmentalism, Procreation, and the Principle of Fairness," 365.

52 It should be noted that the question of whether or not we can appropriately *conceive* of children as goods is of course entirely separate from the question

of whether or not we should communicate to children that that is our view and valuation of them.

53 If it is on pure quantitative grounds that families are thought to be distinguishable (i.e. in virtue of the fact that families produce more of the relevant good than non-families) then we have still not excluded groupings of multiple individuals of taxpayers from being equal collective candidates for the purposes of determining cost sharing obligations. Again the key point is that the implications of the public goods and socialized goods arguments for sharing the costs of children, extend a lot further than their liberal proponents are likely to have intended.

54 I set aside here the potential objection that it is surely contestable that reproduction and parenting are always good or beneficial, given alleged overpopulation (or at least, depletion of existing natural resources) and the extra cost to society that results from neglect and inadequate parenting. I likewise set aside the objection (put to me by Michael Cholbi) that one implication of a public or social goods account of children is that procreation might justifiably be limited to those cases most likely to actually produce the good. My reason for setting these aside is that it need not be the case that every instance of reproduction and parenting be a good in order for it to be recognized that in general terms, the existence of some future citizens who have been adequately parented, is beneficial for the maintenance of liberal society. Relatedly, my task here is not to defend reproduction or parenting *per se*, but rather to give an account of how liberalism's orientation towards reproduction and family making is able to be justified as compatible with its core commitments.

55 It might be countered (as Marc Ramsay has pointed out to me) that it is surely not inappropriate to propose an economic solution (namely of the value of children as public/social goods) to meet an economic complaint (that those without children should not be forced to subsidize the cost of them). I accept that the proposal that we conceive of children as public or social goods is intended solely as an economic justification for economic cost sharing, and not as a comprehensive account of the value and good of having children. My point is, however, that the question of the sharing of the costs of children is not a purely economic question, and therefore discussion of it ought therefore not be limited to economic justification.

56 The role of families in reproduction is of course not incontrovertible, and children are regularly born outside of the confines of a nuclear family unit. However, while I take there to be no consensus that the nuclear family unit offers the best possible social arrangement for bringing children into existence, it is nevertheless the case that within liberal democratic societies, the family is the social arrangement within which most children are born; and in spite of its non-necessity that is surely likely to remain the case for the foreseeable future.

57 Archard and Macleod, *The Moral and Political Status of Children*, 14.

58 Indeed these interests may themselves be political, or perhaps pre-political, but I will not assert either of those claims here.

59 Albeit more clearly in Rawls, *Justice as Fairness: A Restatement* (Cambridge: MA: Belknap Press, 2001) and *Political Liberalism* (New York: Columbia University Press, 2005) than in *A Theory of Justice* (1999).

60 Archard, *The Family: A Liberal Defence*, 84–8.

61 Taylor, "Children as Projects and Persons: A Liberal Antinomy," 563.

62 Veronique Munoz-Darde, "Is the Family to Be Abolished Then?" *Proceedings of the Aristotelian Society* 99 (1999): 37–56.

63 A point that she attributes to Bertrand Russell. Munoz-Darde, "Is the family to be abolished then?" 49.

64 Munoz-Darde, "Is the Family to Be Abolished Then?" 49.

65 Harry Brighouse and Adam Swift, "The Goods of Parenting", in *Family-Making: Contemporary Ethical Challenges*, eds. Francoise Baylis and Carolyn McLeod (Oxford: Oxford University Press, 2014): 11–28.

66 Mianna Lotz, "Rethinking Procreation: Why It Matters Why We Have Children," *Journal of Applied Philosophy* 28, no. 2 (2011): 105–119.
67 These conclusions bring into sharp relief the question, amongst others, of whether a liberal state must tolerate non-liberal private educational arrangements, and whether any share of state resources could legitimately be allocated for a private education sector. It seems to me that unless the existence of such alternative non-public schooling opportunities is clearly necessary or beneficial for liberal society and liberalism itself, parents' own alleged interests, and their alleged children's interests, must figure as just two of the three relevant sets of interests to be given weight in decisions regarding resource distribution, and cannot readily trump the state's own interests without jeopardizing the liberal state's adherence to its own core political principles. But I shall refrain from entering fully into that discussion here.

Bibliography

Archard, David. *The Family: A Liberal Defence*. New York, NY: Palgrave Macmillan, 2010.
Brighouse, Harry and Adam Swift. "Parents' Rights and the Value of the Family." *Ethics* 117 (2006): 80–108.
Brighouse, Harry and Adam Swift. "The Goods of Parenting," in *Family-Making: Contemporary Ethical Challenges*, edited by Francoise Baylis and Carolyn McLeod, 11–28. Oxford: Oxford University Press, 2014.
Casal, Paula. "Environmentalism, Procreation, and the Principle of Fairness." *Public Affairs Quarterly* 13, no. 4 (1999): 363–376.
Fried, Charles. *Right and Wrong*. Cambridge, MA: Harvard University Press, 1978.
Galston, William. *Liberal Pluralism: The Implications of Value Pluralism for Political Theory and Practice*. New York: Cambridge University Press, 2002.
Gaus, Gerald, Shane D. Courtland and David Schmidtz. "Liberalism," in *The Stanford Encyclopedia of Philosophy* edited by Edward N. Zalta, Spring 2015. Accessed May 27, 2016. http://plato.stanford.edu/archives/spr2015/entries/liberalism/.
George, Rolf. "Who Should Bear the Cost of Children?" *Public Affairs Quarterly* 1, no. 1 (1987): 1–42.
George, Rolf. "On the External Benefits of Children," in *Kindred Matters*, edited by Diana T. Meyers, Kenneth Kipnis and Cornelius F. Murphy, 209–217. Ithaca, NY: Cornell University Press, 1993.
Kymlicka, Will. *Multicultural Citizenship: A Liberal Theory of Minority Rights*. Oxford: Clarendon Press, 1995.
Lotz, Mianna. "Rethinking Procreation: Why It Matters Why We Have Children." *Journal of Applied Philosophy* 28, no. 2 (2011): 105–119.
Macleod, Colin M. "Liberal Equality and the Affective Family," in *The Moral and Political Status of Children*, edited by David Archard and Colin Macleod, 212–230. Oxford: Oxford University Press, 2002.
Munoz-Darde, Veronique. "Is the Family to Be Abolished Then?" *Proceedings of the Aristotelian Society* 99 (1999): 37–56.
Olsaretti, Serena. "Children as Public Goods?" *Philosophy and Public Affairs* 41, no. 3 (2013): 226–258.
Paul, Laurie A. *Transformative Experience*. Oxford: Oxford University Press, 2014.
Rachels, James. *Can Ethics Provide Answers?* Lanham, MD: Rowman & Littlefield, 1997.

Rawls, John. *Justice as Fairness: A Restatement*. Edited by Erin Kelly. Cambridge: MA: Belknap Press, 2001.

Rawls, John. *Political Liberalism*. New York: Columbia University Press, 2005.

Rawls, John. *A Theory of Justice*. Cambridge, MA: Belknap Press, 1999.

Shoeman, Ferdinand. "Rights of Children, Rights of Parents, and the Moral Basis of the Family." *Ethics* 91 (1980): 6–19.

Taylor, Robert. "Children as Projects and Persons: A Liberal Antinomy." *Social Theory and Practice* 35, no. 4 (2009): 555–576.

Williams, Bernard. *Moral Luck: Philosophical Papers 1973–1980*. 1–20. New York: Cambridge University Press, 1981.

7 Parents' Rights and the Control of Children's Education

Roger Marples

I

Introduction

The interest shared by so many people in having children is so funda-mental as to warrant the imposition of duties on others not to prevent prospective parents from either conceiving or adopting, short of providing very good reasons as to why any specific attempt to parent is incompatible with the interests of other people, including both the children for whom the parents will assume custodial responsibility and those of the wider community of which they are a part. In other words, if one's interest in parenthood is sufficient to render it a right, then it is not an unconditional right.

There are numerous conditions by reference to which the right of anyone to become a parent may be restricted. Consider the case of a fertile woman who is so mentally retarded that becoming a mother would be incompat-ible with both her own welfare and that of her child. It may well be a moral requirement for a court to insist on either a termination or sterilization, or both. A woman with the mental age of a three-year-old should not become a mother; and in view of her disability, it is incumbent upon others to rule on the matter. Again, a woman may find herself living in abject poverty such that she is unable to provide the basic requirements of childcare. While it may well be stretching the arm of the law too far in forcibly preventing her from giving birth, it is far from clear that her interest in the matter is suf-ficient to accord her the moral right to procreate. The one child policy of the People's Republic of China may well appear draconian, but within the context of the daunting task of accommodating one and a quarter billion people, it may well have a measure of justifiability. Again, the ecological consequences of having one child, let alone five children in a wealthy coun-try such as the UK, are far more serious than those resulting from those of a Bihari peasant farmer's decision to become a parent, in that the child born in the west, according to some calculations, is likely to consume forty times more of the earth's resources than the Bihari child. In the first example, the interests of the mother and her children are relevant considerations; the sec-ond is largely child-centered in focus while the third acknowledges the social consequences of unsustainable population increase. The so-called right to parent is thus hedged in with considerations relating to parental interests, children's interests, and the interests of the national and global community. These, however, are but only some of the limiting conditions.

The above-mentioned circumstances, in which the right to parent is problematic, lends support to the idea that the right to parent is, at most, nothing more than *prima facie*. Someone who is incapable of showing affection, or conceives of her parental obligations as involving little more than engaging the right nanny in order to be able to pursue an active social life, may well forfeit the right to parent on the grounds that she is simply unsuited to carrying out the role to the minimal degree of adequacy required. If Hugh LaFollette goes too far in insisting that a licensing process should be enacted in order to ensure that potential parents possess the requisite "knowledge, abilities, judgment and dispositions to competently discharge their tasks" (2010: 332), he is right in maintaining that a parent is unlikely to be 'good enough' unless she possesses the rudimentary knowledge of what children need, together with a whole range of abilities and dispositions without which her children's interests are likely to be adversely affected. This is not to say that children, once born, have the right to the best possible custodian; to suggest as much could result in the alarming prospect of children being removed from those biological parents whose parenting skills, while far from inadequate, are of average standard or below on any scale envisaged by LaFollette.[1] So much for the right to parent; what has proven to be more contentious is whether or not one's interest in having children provides sufficient grounds for child-rearing rights. After a critical evaluation of arguments designed to justify the notion of parental rights on the basis of parental interests, the first part of this chapter will conclude by considering the respects in which the interests of both children and those of the wider society of which they are members, are sufficient to establish limitations on child-rearing procedures. The limitations in relation to educational provision are considered in part II.

1.1 *Parents' Interests and Parents' Rights*

One familiar argument for the justification of parents' rights is that advocated by Ferdinand Schoeman, and stems from a parent's interest in forming intimate relationships with his children. According to Schoeman, it is in virtue of the extent to which intimate relationships between parent and child contribute to a meaningful life that the state should withhold from interference in such relationships, subject to a minimum threshold of treatment not being met, and conditions relating to what he calls a 'clear-and-present-danger' criterion, before coercive state intervention should be allowed (1980: 10). Apart from the fact that the clear-and-present-danger criterion, if taken literally, would endanger the lives of many children, it is far from self-evident as to what exactly constitutes intimacy or what its appropriate boundaries might be; whatever importance a parent might attach to an intimate relationship with his child, it would require considerably more argument than that provided by Schoeman in order to establish the fact that he had a *right* to such a relationship. As Harry Brighouse and Adam Swift ask, "How might an argument appealing to the value of intimate relationships succeed in vindicating parental rights as fundamental?" (2006: 91). For it is manifestly the case that adults are perfectly able to engage in intimate relationships with one another in order to provide their lives with some kind of meaning without necessarily having relationships with children. While they are right to point out that a parent–child relationship is not interchangeable with other relationships—and for that reason provides a unique and distinct contribution to a parent's well-being, any such relationship is a relationship between people with unequal 'power or standing'; unlike intimate relationships between adults, children have no choice as to whether or not to enter the relationship in the first place, resulting in the fact that the powers of exit from such relationships are unequally distributed—they are too ready to concede that it is in virtue of the "very important contribution to [parents'] well-being" afforded by an intimate relationship with one's children, that lends support to the idea of parents' rights.[2]

In their more recent *Family Values: The Ethics of Parent Child Relationships*, Brighouse and Swift attempt to account for parental rights by reference to values and goods that are distinctive of familial relationships. Both children and adults, they maintain, "have an interest in engaging in familial, parent–child, relationships that is important enough to imply duties for others, and thus allows us to think of those interests as grounding their *prima facie* rights [it being in] the interest of those relationship goods that ground the rights. . . . [Parental rights] are justified only insofar as they are required for protecting that relationship" (2014: 118–119). The rights to which parents are entitled, they argue, are the "activities internal to the valuable relationship" (*Ibid.*), which is an important consideration in determining the extent to which parents may justifiably shape their children's values or confer advantage upon them (*Ibid.* Chs. 5 and 6). Nevertheless, in spite of their conviction that parents' rights (and duties) are "entirely fiduciary" and that it is children's interests which determine parental rights—even though they wish to deny that a child's interests should necessarily trump those of her parents—they remain committed to the idea that parents *qua* parents have rights, without which the familial interests and goods they celebrate and seek to protect would be threatened. The fact remains, however, that it is unclear what it is about intimate familial relationships and their flourishing that is supposed to provide plausible grounds for the existence of such rights.

Appealing to the value of intimate familial relationships is one way of trying to establish the existence of parental rights; appeals to the respects in which children are relevantly different from most adults in terms of their knowledge and understanding of the world and their place within it, is

another. Although the correlation between age and maturity is far from perfect, there are many respects in which people below a certain age must, for
practical purposes, be regarded as immature. Although not in itself sufficient
to distinguish children from adults, it is indubitably the case that children
are, for the most part, less intellectually, emotionally, and sexually mature
than adults. In order to clarify the significance of this, it is helpful to invoke
the more determinate and objective notion of 'competence.' With regard to
a decision of a particular kind, a person may be incompetent, according to
Jeffrey Murphy, in three important respects; she may be ignorant, compul-
sive, or lacking in rationality. (1974: 482ff). Children in general not only
know less than most adults but they lack the emotional maturity associated
with adulthood in the sense that they lack the wherewithal to understand
and control their emotions, the result of which is that they are all too often
driven by them. If the relationship between the aging process and intellectual and emotional competence is not readily specifiable, that between
physical growth and sexual maturity is obvious. In spite of this however, a
sexually mature adolescent may justifiably be deemed sufficiently incompetent in order to render paternalistic restrictions on her legal right to sexual
intercourse permissible. Insofar as children have a limited understanding
of the ways of the world and are lacking in rationality in relation to their
decision-making, their relative incompetence in these respects justifies certain paternalistic restrictions on their liberty providing they are controlled,
limited, and specifically designed to protect them from harm.[3]

The respects in which children may be deemed incompetent justifies Shelley Burtt's claim that it is mistaken to focus on a child's rational capacity as
the distinguishing criterion of childhood to the exclusion of its developmental needs, if we are to have a justifiable case for the proper scope of parental
authority (2002). She is rightly critical of those who wish to constrain it by
reference to the principles of liberal neutrality, and is equally correct in her
condemnation of those who would argue that parental authority is justified only if children subsequently consent to their parents' interventions, on
the grounds that such a restriction would prevent one from being able to
determine the justice of parental intervention before a child reached the age
at which she could provide any meaningful consent.[4] While undoubtedly
correct in suggesting that children are 'comprehensively needy,' which has
a significant bearing on the scope and purpose of parental authority, her
conclusion to the effect that this is sufficient to justify the parental right to
deny their children an 'open future,' or that "parental authority grounded
in developmental needs sets appropriate and effective limits on the abuse
of parental power . . . without short-changing children's interest in a just
upbringing" (*Ibid*: 263–265), is unwarranted. Such a conclusion would
result in excessive parental latitude in the shaping of children's values. As
far as Burtt is concerned, the meeting of a child's developmental needs is the
sole criterion; as long as these are met, "keeping children out of the public
school system so as to give a fundamentalist education the best possible

chance of succeeding, is a legitimate exercise of parental authority" (*Ibid*: 266). The reasons as to why this is unacceptable will be made explicit in what follows.

William Galston has attempted to defend the notion of parents' rights by reference to what he calls the 'expressive interests' of parents in "raising their children in a manner consistent with their understanding of what gives meaning and value to life" (2003: 212). He believes that laws against abuse and neglect notwithstanding, parents should be permitted sufficient *expressive liberty* to "raise their children in a manner consistent with their deepest commitments" (*Ibid*: 225), as long as they do not result in the disempowerment of people "intellectually, emotionally or practically, from living successfully outside their bounds" (*Ibid*: 227), which would be incompatible with the fiduciary obligations of parenthood. Galston bases this claim on the not unreasonable assumption that parents know their children better than any state-approved agency. The fact remains however, that parents qua parents are in no more an epistemically privileged position than anyone else when it comes to determining a child's educational requirements. Apart from any reservations we might have about his faith in parents' ability to determine what is in a child's educational interests, his commitment to parental choice in education is almost certainly, according to Martha Fineman, likely to derail the balancing process of accommodating the legitimate interests of children, parents, and the state in the education system, in allowing parents' interests to take precedence over those of their children. As she rightly observes: "The big question is not whether the state must recognise parents' expressive interests in their children's education, but where we draw the line separating that expressive interest from the child's interest in the diversity and independence-conferring potential of a secular and public education" (2002: 240).

In acknowledging that parenting is a fundamental interest, affording as it does opportunities for intimate and loving relationships, it remains to be seen why such perfectly respectable concerns fail to provide sufficient ground for the right to control either the kind of education children receive or the values in accordance with which a young person tries to provide her life with purpose and meaning. To suggest otherwise would, as Philip Montague says, be to conceive of children as little more than personal property.[5] He defends this conclusion in the context of an attempted denial of the supposition that parents have even "*presumptive* moral rights to influence the courses of their children's lives in significant ways" (2000: 52–53), maintaining instead that a parental interest in a child's welfare "is worth protecting because the welfare of children is worth protecting" (*Ibid*: 55). As John Dwyer points out, there is a distinct oddity involved in linking a person's rights to another's interests. While "all of the important interests one might attribute to children can give rise to a right of one kind or another residing in the child . . . a world without parents' rights but with an appropriate set of children's rights [is perfectly compatible with] the necessary institutional mechanisms when actions by third parties threaten the child's interests" (1994: 1429). The privileges associated with the role of parent are sufficient, he maintains, to render it "nonsensical to assert that parents need rights against the State . . . in order to carry out their legal responsibilities" (*Ibid*: 1437). Disputes arising between parents and the state over child-rearing practices should be settled by reference to the importance of balancing a child's interests against those of her parents because, Dwyer insists, parents have no such rights *qua* parents. Instead, he argues, it would be incumbent upon the courts to impute to the child the hypothetical preference that she be appropriately cared for and given an education whereby she might develop the wherewithal for independent thought.

It is the parents on whom these obligations or duties may be said to rest—at least in the first instance—in spite of the fact that talk of 'duties' and 'rights' in a familial context may, according to some, be thought inappropriate in the context of family life.[6] No doubt something of undoubted value would be missing if personal relationships were conducted entirely by reference to rights and duties, but without reference to notions such as these, the illegality of rape within marriage would probably not have been established; the fact that it is not illegal to humiliate one's partner in public does nothing to support the view that the offended party has no rights in this context, or that a spouse has no duty of forbearance in this regard. As Brighouse and Swift say, "framing familial obligations and expectations in terms of rights and duties clarifies the proper role of the State [and to] suggest that rights discourse has no place in the heads of family members is dangerously to romanticize and idealize the family" (2014: 19–20).

Not the least demanding feature of parenthood is the recognition of the moral imperatives with which it is associated. Hannan and Vernon are quite right in their insistence that any exclusionary rights to which parents may be said to have a claim—exclusionary in the sense that others should be excluded from the parental decision-making process—cannot be grounded in the parents' own interests' (2008: 186–187). "Those who bear the rights," they claim, "may do so by way of a mediated relation to the interests of others. [Parental rights] are mediated by the notion of a role that parents have an interest in occupying, but which, once occupied, engages the occupier in another's interest" (*Ibid*). The legitimate authority attaching to the role of parent, grounded as it is in the duty to "protect children from irreversible deprivations," leads them to conclude that this "gives parents all that they can reasonably ask for" (*Ibid*: 189). Dispensing with the whole idea of parental rights and replacing it with parental privilege neither undermines the importance of legitimate parental authority nor underestimates the extent to which parents should be allowed considerable discretion as to *how* they carry out their duties. Parental discretion ends, however, at the point where a child is in danger of being either harmed, through not having her fundamental needs properly catered for or when deprived of the minimum conditions necessary for normal functioning, below which she has a right to be prevented from falling. Society as a whole has an interest in the way children are raised and the kind of education they receive, and for this reason it is necessary to look a little more closely at both the interests of children themselves as well as those of the wider community, with the intention of determining the extent to which parental autonomy might justifiably be constrained.

1.2 Children's Interests and Parental Obligations

Unlike most adults, children have little or no conception of what is in their interests or where their well-being might lie. As Robert Noggle points out: "Their preference structures are in a state of flux and they have not yet developed an evaluative compass and internalised the moral norms necessary for harmonious action with other moral agents" (2002: 100). Having little or no conception of the good, or the capacity for what Charles Taylor refers to as 'strong evaluation' (1985: 30ff), they lack 'moral agency.' Children, according to John Rawls, need to acquire the moral powers of a sense of justice and the capacity "to decide upon, revise, and rationally pursue" a sense of the good (1993a: 19–21) and for which, in the first instance, parents have to a duty to try to ensure. That such a task is beyond the capabilities of many parents is beside the point; what matters is that parents should not frustrate their children's opportunities to develop such powers by failing to ensure that their children receive an appropriate civic and moral education in an environment other than a replication of their own. If children are to be liberated from the present and particular (the here and now), they need to experience a wider range of alternative possibilities than life at home affords, which means that it is a parent's duty to see to it that the array of options, such as with whom to live, what career to pursue, one's sexuality or religion—significant options, in short, from amongst which someone approaching adulthood should be in a position to choose—should not, either intentionally or otherwise, be foreclosed. This right to self-determination is, as Joel Feinberg memorably puts it, "the child's right to an open future," albeit a "right in trust" (1980). A child is a potential adult and it is that adult's autonomy that must be safeguarded.[7]

The truth of the claim that children have an interest in becoming autonomous is not self-evident; its justification depends on the value of that state. Unlike being six feet tall, autonomy is a matter of degree; the transition from heteronomy to autonomy is neither smooth nor something corresponding straightforwardly with age. What is undoubtedly the case, however, is that the lives of very young children are more episodic than their adolescent counterparts insofar as they lack much in the way of self-direction. An autonomous life requires much in terms of knowledge and understanding of the respects in which the agencies of socialization have contributed towards the shaping of one's beliefs, attitudes, and convictions. Autonomous agency presupposes the ability to give some kind of direction to one's life in spite of the fact that the values by reference to which such self-determination takes place do not themselves arise *ex nihilo*.[8] Where our projects and goals are incompatible, our autonomy is diminished accordingly; thereby providing credence to the idea that a reasonably coherent belief system is also an essential component of an autonomous life–although to focus exclusively on the coherence of a system of *beliefs* is, as Diana Meyers indicates, to ignore the importance of a coherent *personality*, including one's emotional responses and commitments (1989: Part 2, Sec. 1).[9]

An autonomous agent possesses a whole repertoire of mental capacities including the ability to think for herself and to assess the merits of competing alternatives in accordance with her own convictions, as well as the courage and determination to resist pressure to conform to the mindset of other people. Such conditions have both objective (or external), and subjective (or internal) dimensions.[10] The fact that personal autonomy is not a necessary condition of well-being in any social context whatever, in a rapidly changing society such as that of a modern industrial democracy, it is inconceivable that someone so inured by convention that she is unable to respond to changing circumstances would find it possible to flourish.

Autonomy's undoubted instrumental value in enabling one to pursue a life worth living is employed by Brighouse in order to demonstrate the necessity of our obligation to provide children with what he calls an "autonomy-facilitating education," as opposed to an "autonomy-promoting education" (2000: Ch. 4). The justificatory strategy of the former "does not appeal to the civic responsibilities of future citizens or to the intrinsically superior value of autonomous living over non-autonomous living [resting in an] education that is purportedly 'character neutral' in that it seeks to provide certain critical skills without aiming to inculcate the inclination to use them" (*Ibid*: 80–81). As long as the skills associated with autonomy are taught, children should not be encouraged to live autonomous lives "any more than children taught to speak French are encouraged to live French-speaking lives" (*Ibid*: 94–95).[11] Civic education beyond equipping children with the moral and political virtues associated with a sense of justice and a commitment to the ideals of equality and freedom would, according to Brighouse, violate the requirements of liberal legitimacy insofar as such legitimacy requires the free consent of those who are subject to liberal governance. However, it is the very fact of confining an education to one that merely *facilitates* autonomy—equipping children with little more than knowledge and skills (but not the habits) required for its exercise, that leads Callan to justifiably complain that it "casts a distorting light" on autonomy's value in that it reduces the significance of the cultivation of an autonomous personality or character to nothing more than a matter of personal choice, having no intrinsic value whatever (*Ibid*: 144). Failure to acknowledge the importance of an autonomy-promoting education, at the expense of an exclusive reliance on knowledge and skills associated with an autonomy-facilitating education is, Callan insists, to ignore the respects in which non-autonomous preference-formation may leave people vulnerable to abuse. "Teaching character-neutral skills of autonomy to those who are already thoroughly close-minded or predisposed to disregard their own interests"—(he cites the example of a housewife who has been manipulated into accepting a servile role with equanimity, where reasons to do with the unacceptability of such a state have no bearing on her perception of the invidious situation with which she identifies)— "will do nothing to shake her sense of domestic destiny" (*Ibid.*: 146–147). In order to combat the likelihood of such non-autonomous belief and preference-formation, "an education for legitimacy will require autonomy promotion instead of mere autonomy facilitation" (*Ibid.*).[12] It is for reasons such as these that education's concern with character-formation should not be an optional extra.

1.3 Societal Interests and Parental Obligations

Were children to grow up without the knowledge and skills required for independent functioning and a willingness to respect the rights of others, social life would be intolerable. In addition to the duties associated with its role as *parens patriae* where, in the event of parental failure to provide a satisfactory level of care, the state must assume an appropriate custodial responsibility, a liberal state has a legitimate interest in trying to ensure that children are equipped with the wherewithal required for both independent living and the assumption of those responsibilities associated with democratic citizenship. A Liberal state could not function without a literate and numerate citizenry capable of formulating and evaluating the values underpinning the political system. For this reason it is within its right, through a publicly funded system of schooling, to ensure that children are equipped with the requisite knowledge and skills essential to its effective functioning. The quality of social life is diminished if people are not committed to the values of equality, freedom, and justice and it is equally diminished if citizens are not committed to the value of autonomy and the importance of an autonomy-promoting education; for it is difficult to *live* an autonomous life if one is surrounded by others who attach little or no significance to its promotion and preservation, or who (albeit autonomously) renounce it altogether.

In one of the few places where Rawls mentions education, he says that it is one of the aims of political liberalism to require of children that they learn "such things as knowledge of their constitutional and civic rights . . . [in order to] prepare them to become fully cooperating members of society [and to become] self-supporting." If, as a result of which, children should acquire a *comprehensive* liberal conception, then this "may have to be accepted *often with regret*" (1993a: 199–200, emphasis added). This is an unsettling passage in many respects. First, it is an essential part of liberal education's concern with civic education that the autonomy it seeks to develop cannot be restricted to the political in the way Rawls would have us believe. Second, why should we accept the consequences of such an education with regret—even though it has the unavoidable feature of favoring a particular view of the good, namely that which accords special importance to personal autonomy in citizens' private lives? For this reason Galston is wrong to assume that the state's interest in education extends no further than the cultivation of those virtues required for diversity, while having no truck with the Socratic ideal of the examined life (1991: 253, 1995: 529).[13] According to Rawls, comprehensive liberalism's concern with autonomy beyond the confines of the political, will result in the failure to obtain the consent and support of all reasonable citizens, and he sees it as oppressive and in danger of rendering liberalism "but another sectarian doctrine" (1985: 246, 1988: 267–268).

Although he is correct in attaching central importance to the idea of citizens possessing the "moral powers of being able to form, revise and pursue a conception of the good as well as a sense of justice," Rawls is wrong in sharply distinguishing between a (reasonable) person's political views on the one hand and her comprehensive views on the other (1993a: 140), on the questionable grounds that citizens' convictions and attachments are part of their "non-public identity" (1985: 241), and thus an inappropriate norm upon which to rely in formulating a theory of justice in that it would favor certain conceptions of the good above others and even prevent some people from pursuing their chosen conception. His position presupposes an untenable distinction between the public and the private, resulting in the counterintuitive requirement that moral convictions should be excluded from the (purely) political.[14]

The concepts and dispositions required of the anemic civic education envisaged by people such as Rawls and Galston, amounts to little more than the essentials required of citizens *qua* citizens. A civic, and indeed a moral education designed with the intention of transforming a student's *character*, such that amongst other things she is disposed towards self-examination, should be welcomed as perfectly compatible with liberalism. One of the implications of a Rawlsian civic education would, as Tim Fowler notes, result in a lower threshold for what would count as full and cooperating members of society, thereby allowing a free hand to those parents who wish to prevent their children (all too frequently their daughters) from receiving further education, as long as in so doing they pose no threat to the stability of liberal institutions (2011). Society not only has an interest in the cultivation of people with the character traits associated with autonomy *and* compassion, it has an equal stake in ensuring that as a result of a publicly funded system of schooling, people are disposed to actively and ungrudgingly engage in the democratic process with a determination to promote social justice and human rights. For these reasons the state needs to ensure that the parochial interests of parents, especially where these are incompatible with a child's right to an open future or society's need for a politically and morally literate citizenry, should not be the determining factor in child-rearing or the educational provision a child receives. The respects in which societal and children's interests impose limiting conditions on the autonomy of parents to confer advantage upon their children, or to shape their values in accordance with their own view of the good life, are addressed in what follows.

II

2.1 Parents' Rights to Shape Their Children's Values

It is part of the very idea of healthy familial relationships that activities and enthusiasms are shared, without which it is difficult to see what value might be attributed to the institution. A parent who shares his interests and enthusiasms with his children is, for the most part, acting in accordance with his role requirements.[15] The implicit qualification is important in view of the fact that certain enthusiasms are such that it would be inappropriate or wrong for a parent to try and infect his children with everything about which he is enthusiastic. A parent who is passionate about cookery, cigars, and Catholicism, for example, would be perfectly within the bounds of moral acceptability if he were to involve his children in the preparation of appetizing family meals—although even here, much depends on the degree of pressure exercised, the age of the child, and such like; there being no right to compel. Were he to introduce his children to cigar-smoking, on the other hand, he would be completely out of order in view of its harmful effects. If these are fairly clear-cut examples of what is acceptable or not within a child-rearing context, it is far from certain that sharing one's enthusiasm for Catholicism is something in which the good parent should engage, for one's religious beliefs and commitments are replete with values that serve to underpin one's whole outlook on life, which raises the difficult question of the extent to which a parent is morally entitled to shape a child's values, either intentionally or unintentionally.

A parent would be well within his rights, according to David Archard, in encouraging his children to participate in common activities "including religious observance and practice," the uncritical acceptance of which may well result in their subscribing to the beliefs and values associated with such practices, while having no right "to insist that the child be educated outside the family home in just those values that the family shares" (2002: 151). As long as a child's future autonomy is not endangered as a consequence of sharing her parent's religious values, Archard would appear to accept such a practice with equanimity.[16] What he is strongly opposed to however, is the idea of a parent directly aiming at the inculcation of such values.

In his critique of Archard's position, Jeffrey Morgan points to the undeniable fact that the distinction between church attendance as part of a shared family life and the inculcation of religious values is not always possible in practice "because many religious groups insist that the children of members be subject to religious instruction within the community . . .

and it is hard to see how a family could share religious worship without at least some acceptance of the doctrines by the children" (2006: 11).[17] The point of this criticism is to question the coherence of allowing parents to take their children to church as part of shared family activity on the one hand, and disallowing the inculcation of religious beliefs and values on the other. What requires emphasis, however, is that much depends on the kind of sharing that is taking place when a child accompanies her parents to church. If it were *accompanying* in the way a child might accompany her parent to the supermarket, with no particular enthusiasm for, or interest in the purpose of the expedition, or if once in church she were left free to observe the proceedings, it is difficult to see what is wrong with anything so innocuous. What is unacceptable, however, is the practice of *initiating* children into the beliefs and practices associated with religious or political creeds; something altogether different from teaching *about* them.[18] (Most people would think it quite inappropriate for a committed communist to require his children to accompany him to party meetings as part of a healthy familial relationship, especially if such attendance necessitated a full-throated rendition of the *Internationale*). Morgan, however, is adamant: "if the initiation is permissible as an unintended by-product of some other legitimate activity, then it is unclear why it could not be directly intended" (2005: 375), and he is at pains to argue that "there are always ways in which religious initiation can be carried out that do not violate a child's right to an open future" (*Ibid.*).[19]

The conclusion so far, is that parents do not have the right to initiate their children into the values and beliefs associated with an organized religion if there is the least likelihood, irrespective of intent, of their coming to accept them for no other reason than that they are those of their parents and/or the consequence of which being that they find it difficult to renounce them if and when they appear to be no longer tenable. Discussions of the respects in which religious upbringing might fail to accommodate the present or future autonomy of children frequently ignore the ways in which a person's emotional autonomy may be undermined as a result of a particular upbringing. Someone may experience an overwhelming sense of guilt when acting in accordance with convictions at variance with those of her parents, resulting in a lack of nerve or courage to act in the light of those of her own. Parents are not only duty-bound to be mindful of their children's burgeoning cognitive autonomy, the principal concern of which is the process by which they decide what to *believe*, they should also be sensitive to the ways in which children are rendered *emotionally* dependent by being initiated into those religious beliefs and values to which their parents adhere. Where a child finds it painfully difficult to reject the religious values of her parents, in spite of the 'pull' of contrary points of view, it is fair to say that not only is she the victim of indoctrination, but the parent stands accused of dereliction of duty and responsibility.[20]

When it comes to providing one's children with a set of moral values on the other hand, the situation is more straightforward. As far as Noggle is concerned, "there seems nothing intrinsically immoral or illiberal about giving the parent at least prima facie permission to instil her own value system and the world-view on which it rests as an initial 'default' position," subject to the requirement that the belief system instilled is not unreasonable, intolerant, or morally indecent (2002: 113–114), on the grounds that without at least *some* evaluative criteria by reference to which a child may formulate a value system, she would be deprived of meaningful choice.[21] As has already been suggested, without the vocabulary of contrastive evaluation whereby things are seen as right or wrong, cruel or compassionate, cowardly or courageous, and so on, a child would have no moral compass with which to navigate, and her criteria of significance would be subjective and desire-dependent. Giving shape to *some* values is therefore an appropriate part of the parental role. As long as a parent does not frustrate his children's capacity for autonomous deliberation about moral issues, he is not open to the charge of indoctrination, and to the extent that he tries to convey the importance of values such as justice, compassion, and respect for persons, it is wrong to suggest that he is instilling one set of controversial values amongst many. The fact that value pluralism entails the near impossibility of rendering values consistent with one another (as is the case with justice and compassion, the demands of which all too frequently conflict), does nothing to imply that they are 'morally controversial.' In spite of the fact that there is widespread disagreement about their significance or applicability, or that some people do not give a fig for social justice or personal liberty, there is no reason to conclude that are controversial; issues should be counted as controversial, according to Michael Hand, "when opposing values on them are rationally defensible" (2007: 76).[22]

The remainder of this section will be devoted to showing what is problematic with the claim made in Article 26 of the United Nations Universal Declaration of Human Rights, insofar as it grants the parental right "to choose the kind of education that shall be given to their children," with specific reference to faith-schooling, home-schooling, and private schooling.

2.2 *Parents' Rights and Educational Provision*

(a) *Faith Schools*

As far as Brighouse and Swift are concerned, some forms of religious upbringing are perfectly compatible with a due concern for a child's autonomy. They cite the case of an Anglican churchgoer who "*can* raise her child within the practices of her religious community, *can* teach him her faith, and *can* expose him to a whole range of influences some of which may lead him to break with that faith" (2014: 171, emphases added).[23] Well, of course she can; the question is the extent to which she actually does any such things. It is all too easy to adopt a rose-tinted view of the Church of England and its mission, especially in relation to its schools (of which there are 2,500 in the UK and to which so many English children, especially in rural areas, have no alternative). It is too easy to slough off the charge that the products of faith schools are as capable as other school leavers of subjecting the claims of religion to rational scrutiny when faith schools actively foster religious commitment through their assemblies, religious education lessons, and selection of teachers. In the light of avowals by the Church of England to the effect that the Church's mission is "to bring others into the faith" (2001: 3.11), that the Church school "*promotes Christian values* through the experience it offers all its pupils" (3.24, emphasis added), values that will "run through every area of school life as the writing runs through a stick of rock" (3.25), it is easy to see why there are reasons to be skeptical of the idea that its prime concern is with the child's anticipatory autonomy rights whereby she is able to reject the whole package if and when she thinks fit. If faith schools were serious about such a laudable goal, they would find themselves operating with double standards insofar as they would be required to provide some kind of education that ran counter to what they are explicitly attempting to achieve. No doubt there are faith schools that operate with a genuine concern for the autonomy of their students, but there remains sufficient warrant to suppose that where children are surrounded by devout teachers and students, the *likelihood* of their developing the courage and convictions to argue against such an all pervasive *Weltanschauung* may be so reduced as to merit the charge of indoctrination, however unintentional.

The potential threat to a child's autonomy is not the only reason for doubting the legitimacy of the so-called parental right to faith-schooling; their very existence poses a serious threat to social cohesion. One has only to look at the recent history of Northern Ireland—where very few children have had the opportunity to relate to their peers from different religious backgrounds—in order to appreciate how difficult it is to achieve the cross-cultural understanding about which Mark Halstead (1995), for example, is rightly concerned. Unfortunately, not only does he appear blind to the difficulties confronting so many young (and not so young) people, in their attempts to break from their primary culture, his attempted compromise between a religious minority's demand for faith schools as part of its concern relating to the preservation a cultural identity on the one hand, and a society's legitimate concern about a future generation's capacity for autonomous decision-making, is unpersuasive. It is all very well for him to talk about the necessity for an "education for cross-cultural understanding [designed to provide] tolerance and respect and the ability to live alongside groups with different cultural values" (*Ibid*: 269), but on the assumption that this is indeed a vital part of a liberal education, it seems willfully perverse to hive children off from one another on the basis of their *parents'* religion.[24] Our fears in relation to the socially divisive consequences of faith schools would be no less misplaced were we to rely on a curriculum that merely teaches *about* other cultures and religions, with actual contact with children from different religious backgrounds having no bearing on the matter.[25] A parent's faith, therefore, is no justification whatsoever for his claim-right to send his children to a faith school, and in view of the potentially adverse consequences for children themselves and wider community relations, the case for their abolition is overwhelmingly strong.

(b) The Curriculum

There are numerous other ways in which parents seek to shape the values of their children by fair means or foul. One such is a concerted attempt to restrict the areas of the curriculum to which their children are exposed, and the other is to educate them at home.[26] The motivating reasons as to why parents seek recourse to such measures are numerous and varied, but it is all too frequently religious considerations that are the decisive factor. Since 1944, when religious instruction and the daily act of corporate worship became a statutory requirement for maintained schools in England and Wales, parents have had the legal right to withdraw their children from such activities. However, there are reasons as to why they have no moral right to withdraw their children from subjects of which they disapprove, unless there is reason to believe that indoctrination is taking place. Since 1996 parents in England and Wales have had the right to remove their children from sex education, except to the extent that the subject is covered in science lessons as required by the National Curriculum. Teaching about homosexuality, for example, as part of sex education is anathema as far as some parents are concerned, but as Patricia White points out, while we have no *choice* about our sexual orientation, we have a great deal of choice when it comes to sexual *activity*, and that if sex education "is partly concerned with helping people make wise choices in this area of their lives, both for their own sakes and others' sakes, there is no good reason to restrict it exclusively to a consideration of heterosexual behaviour; to do so disadvantages us all, irrespective of our sexual orientation" (1991: 401–402). Of course there are many other reasons for teaching about homosexuality, many of which have been rehearsed by Michael Reiss, and include the fact that its absence is hurtful to homosexuals, many teenagers have homosexual tendencies, and as citizens we need to know whether homosexuals should be allowed to marry, adopt, teach, join the military, etc., not to mention the fact that such teaching may well contribute to the prevention of homophobia (1997: 344–345). Fundamental to democracy, according to John Petrovic, are the virtues of recognition and the principle of non-oppression, from which it follows that "allowing damaging arguments to be placed before children struggling with their present and future sexual identities, predisposing them to buy into the heterosexist presumption of abnormality and sin" should be firmly rejected (2002: 150–151). An education that denies a child's right to information about anything (sex included) that is likely to assist her in the making of rational choices between significant competing options, conspires to frustrate her autonomy; as such, it cannot be a parental right and there is no reason to pander to those parents who believe that it can.

Religious reasons provided the basis for a group of fundamentalist Christians in the American State of Tennessee, who sought the right to prevent their children from being subject to a reading scheme that was in direct violation of their faith in its apparent presentation of diverse ethical viewpoints such as those associated with women in roles other than that of the domestic.[27] If it were the case that the reading materials were taught in a way designed to malign Christian fundamentalism, the parents may well have a duty to protest, but as Callan points out: "If students were permitted and encouraged to draw on their own beliefs in interpreting the reading material, and the religious views they expressed were treated with due respect, then the charge of bias would be weak" (1997: 238, n. 10). Clearly, bias in school textbooks, especially in matters relating to politics and religion or anything involving racial or sex stereotypification should be avoided, but, as he rightly adds: "even if the parents in *Mozert* were right that the prescribed reading series was biased against their way of life, then that is just what we should expect from schools that purport to serve everyone equally well. Any attempt to correct that bias will come at the price of bias against some other group" (*Ibid*: 161). A parental claim to actually prevent children from being exposed to values and beliefs other than those of their own, is unjustified if it is demonstrably the case that children and/or the wider community of which they are soon to be fully-fledged citizens, will benefit from exposure to value diversity in non-indoctrinatory ways, together with being afforded sufficient opportunity for critical evaluation of the values conveyed by any subject or text.[28]

While the Supreme Court's ruling *in favor* of the Old Order Amish desire to withdraw their children from compulsory schooling after the age of 16—in order that further attendance would not only pose a threat to their way of life but would compromise their religious freedom to raise their children in accordance with their values and traditions—invoked the Free Exercise Choice in support of the parents,[29] the Appeal Court's ruling against *Mozert* was based on the view that a State's demand that children should be required to attend the classes it deems appropriate, was in violation of neither the Free Exercise nor Establishment Clauses of the First Amendment to the American Constitution. Nevertheless, the Amish claim is similar in at least one respect to that of *Mozert*, as well as to those who demand the right to home-school their children, in that they all presume not only the right of parents to shape their children's view of the world in ways that are incompatible with any interests the state might have in a civic education or an education with the explicit intention of furthering children's autonomy, but also the view that parents' interests should trump those of their children.

However, there are strict limits to what a liberal society should be prepared to tolerate. It is simply nonsense to pretend that a child belongs to a social group or to her parents in such a way that she may be insulated from the wider societal values, because the rights of individuals should never be subordinate to those of groups. This is no less true when it comes to an individual parent's right to 'protect' his child from interacting with her peers from different religious or cultural backgrounds, because she is not (in the proprietarian sense) 'his' to protect.

(c) Home-Schooling

Whatever the merits of the arguments advanced in support of *Mozert* or *Yoder*, the resulting verdicts provided a green light to the home-schooling brigade.[30] As with the so-called parental right to determine curriculum content, there are a number of objections to the parental claim-right to withdraw one's children from school altogether, unless what is being provided is the very antithesis of 'education,' or that a child's special needs are not being met, or bullying is rife and unaddressed. Even in such dire circumstances, however, a parent should voice his concerns and not invoke his legal right to withdraw his child as the first move in what may be a complex strategy to improve an unacceptable state of affairs. Having done so to no avail, the case for withdrawal may be sufficiently strong as to render it a parental duty, albeit on a temporary basis—difficulties of specifying what exactly counts as 'bad' or 'inadequate' notwithstanding.[31]

It would be absurd to deny that a child whose education is controlled exclusively by her parents will necessarily be restricted in terms of a limited potential for autonomous decision-making, but there is every reason to believe that exposure to beliefs and values afforded by school attendance—values that would almost certainly differ from those of her parents in view of the number and variety of students and teachers with whom she would be in daily contact—would go some way towards introducing her to perspectives very different from those resulting from home-schooling. Reich is correct in maintaining that if "minimalist autonomy requires that a child be able to examine his own political values and beliefs, and those of others, with a sympathetic and critical eye [as well as being able] to think independently and subject his ends to critical scrutiny [then] at a bare minimum schooling cannot replicate in every particularity the values and beliefs of a child's home" (2002: 162). If home-schooling were a parental right, then highly illiberal parents who took exception to their children being capable of any such thing, would be in the unacceptable position of being able to deny their children access to anything like the open future to which they are morally entitled. It would be equally foolish to suggest that every parent who decides to home-school his children operates with an illiberal agenda, but there are grave dangers in refusing to protect children from those parents who wish to prevent them from being exposed to beliefs and values that differ from their own. Exposure to a wide range of worldviews may, as Randall Curren and Jason Blokhuis say, "reduce the likelihood that they will demonize others on doctrinaire grounds, and it may enrich the array of realistic life choices available to them, enhancing the likelihood that they will go on to lead flourishing and happy lives of their own choosing" (2011: 5). These and other dangers associated with home-schooling, such as the fact that parents may not be 'qualified,' or sufficiently impartial, as well as the inevitable distractions associated with domestic life in general, provide reasons for a strong *prima facie* case against their right to home-school.

(d) Private Schooling

In his *How Not to be a Hypocrite: School Choice for the Morally Perplexed Parent*, Adam Swift defends the decision to opt for private education *even if* the educational opportunities for those left in the mainstream sector are fewer than they would have been if their wealthier peers remained alongside them, on the grounds that "parents are justified in helping their children avoid inadequacy," with the caveat that its acceptability is premised on the assumption that "the cost to others of that micro choice is minimal" (2003: 135). However, withdrawing one's child from school in circumstances where the threshold of adequacy is not only below a minimum standard of acceptability, and where in the foreseeable future there is little or no prospect of approaching such a threshold, is altogether different from withdrawing her from a perfectly adequate school in order to provide her with the competitive advantages associated with fee-paying schools. In removing a child from a totally inadequate school (criteria of adequacy having been specified), a parent is not exercising his right; he is exercising his custodial duties stemming from his fiduciary obligations as someone charged with the responsibility of ensuring that his child's present or long-term interests are secured. When it comes to the decision to 'go private,' however, it is undoubtedly the case that many parents who avail themselves of this option do so for reasons other than the fact that the local schools are *totally* inadequate. Their reasons are more likely to be related to the competitive advantages that such schools are able to bestow.

The question to which this gives rise, is whether or not parents who can afford it have a *right* to private schools. In view of the obvious need for moral constraints on what a loving and concerned parent may do in order to benefit his child, the problem lies with specifying the limits in accordance with which legitimate parental partiality is permissible. Brighouse and Swift, as part of their defense of parental rights, usefully distinguish between benefiting one's children and conferring upon them a competitive advantage over other people's (2014: 127–128). They suggest several paradigm cases essential to the flourishing of familial relationships, including bedtime stories, accompanying parents to religious ceremonies, and the enrollment in sports clubs, even if it results in a child finding herself in a competitively advantageous position *vis-à-vis* other people. In sharing his religious and sporting enthusiasms with his child, or spending intimate time together reading stories, a parent is engaged in something utterly different and, they believe, more readily justifiable than signing a school-fee check payable to Eton College. What is protected in the former activities is the parent–child interaction, not the advantage-conferral associated with private schooling. Given the principle of fair equality of opportunity, they maintain that parents do not have the right to favor their own children in violation of this principle, but "it could still be that, all things considered, governments would be justified in letting them do just that [because] parents' rights and fair equality of opportunity do not exhaust the set of relevant considerations . . . *equality* [not being] the most important deliberative goal" (*Ibid*: 130). Parents, in other words, should be permitted to do things for their children over and above whatever it is they have a (supposed) right to do. Were the state to attempt to interfere with those domestic activities essential to family life having any value whatever, with the sole interest of securing equality of opportunity, it would itself be in violation of legitimate parental partiality.[32]

The fact remains, however, that education is a public good of inestimable value in which society as a whole has a legitimate interest. In addition to its concern with the quality of the civic education to which children are exposed, given its potential for the shaping of character, it is well within the purview of a democratic state to legislate in favor of fair equality of opportunity and the elimination of class barriers, as Rawls himself recognized (1971: 63), because the costs to the children of those who are least privileged and least able to rectify their disadvantageous circumstances are such as to warrant a redistribution of resources (such as teachers and learning materials) in order to alleviate the invidious circumstances in which so many families unjustly find themselves. Injustice is compounded when parents opt for private education, the existence of which contributes not one jot to the enhancement of a parent–child relationship.[33] Apart from the intrinsic injustice associated with a system of schooling whereby the wealthier members of society are allowed to purchase an education that is better resourced, with the inevitable consequences of being more favorably placed in terms of admission to elite universities and the life prospects they afford, no society with a concern for democratic equality and the importance of mutual respect, should remain sanguine about the unacceptable consequences of a wealth-based educational apartheid. It is not only the children left behind in the maintained sector who are likely to suffer as a result of being denied the opportunity of social and working relationships with their more affluent and (all too frequently) their more able and highly motivated peers, but many privately educated students emerge with an erroneous belief in their own superiority that is altogether incompatible with the aims and purposes of civic (and moral) education in a democracy. The implications for social solidarity and social cohesion are serious and incalculable. In order to combat the socially divisive consequences of private schooling, the state has a whole raft of compensatory strategies at its disposal through its powers of taxation, or by severing in some way or other the connection between a child's competitive advantages resulting from parental partiality, and what Macleod refers to as partially constituted goods (or "activities and relationships which contribute to well-being and flourishing and which exist in virtue of strong partiality," 2004: 313).

To those who would argue that education is a purely private good and is infinitely sharable, such that my knowing all there is to know about the First World War in no way prevents you from knowing as much, with the implication that the existence of private schools does not necessarily result in a diminution of the quality of education on offer within the state sector, it is important to point out, as does Swift, that education is also a *positional good* in that its value depends "not only on how good it is in absolute terms, but on how good it is compared to that of other people. . . . What matters is not so much how much education one gets, or how good that education is . . . but one's position in the distribution of things" (2003: 23). If true, the implications are profound; for as Ruth Jonathan argues, "If the exchange value of education in combination with the stratified nature of society in which it is embedded, make the relative advantage of one child in part a *necessary* function of the relative advantage of other children, then the parent cannot seek to promote the interests of his own child without indirectly damaging the interests of children with a less effective agent" (1989: 334). Moreover, even on the assumption that the criteria for what is to count as an 'adequate' provision of schooling are clearly specifiable, references to such should not remain indifferent to inequalities in educational provision above an identified threshold. As William Koski and Rob Reich point out, once the positional advantage of education is recognized, "the adequacy paradigm not only tolerates but provides new incentives for the well-off to maintain and increase their positional advantage. . . . If the state settles for adequacy in the orientation of educational policy, it effectively cements the advantages of the well-off; it confers on them the state's imprimatur in using public (state) schools to entrench advantages that they are already securing at home, in private"; something they rightly regard as indefensible (2007: 612).

It would be pushing the boundaries too far in order to explore the extent to which Clayton and Stevens are right to insist that parents ought to accept a measure of inadequate education as part of a fair contribution towards ending social justice, or what precise policies are necessary in order to guarantee fair equality of (educational) opportunity, but they are indisputably correct in their assertion that "if someone's situation is worsened by your appropriation, then you must either compensate them or renounce your claim to the resources you have taken" (2004: 117). If there is any truth in the claim that the position of children who are already in a disadvantageous position in relation to educational opportunities is significantly worsened, or if the consequences for social cohesion and solidarity are significantly damaged by the continued existence of fee-paying schools, then where there is a choice between public and private educational provision, it is far from self-evident that conflicts of interest should always be resolved in favor of one's own children by reference to the myth of parental rights when, in the interests of social justice, the case for their abolition is as equally strong as it is in the context of faith or home-schooling.

Notes

1 For a persuasive argument designed to show that "adequate parents have a moral right to keep and raise their babies," see Anna Gheaus (2012), who justifies her position by reference to a combination of the interests parents have in this task and the undoubted threat to the parent–baby relationship resulting from baby redistribution. Difficulties of specifying the threshold at which parental adequacy should be determined notwithstanding, the 'best custodian condition' is too demanding.

2 According to Sarah Hannan and Richard Vernon "a parental right to unmonitored intimacy could indirectly undercut children's autonomy in the very same way that a right to intentionally shape children's values would" (2008: 180).

3 Questions relating to whether or not harm-avoidance is a *sufficient* condition for paternalistic intervention in the lives of children are ignored here, as are questions relating to the appropriate stage in a child's development at which paternalism ceases to be morally acceptable. There are numerous objections to 'maturity' being the appropriate criterion, not least of which concerns the design and execution of maturity tests. Suffice it to say that the only plausible alternative, in spite of its apparent arbitrariness, is to adopt an age criterion, albeit one that may vary in accordance with activities as different as voting and flying a fighter plane; there being no *a priori* reason why one age in particular should be all-embracing.

4 In determining the ways in which children should be treated, reference to that about which a child is likely to consent is remarkably unhelpful. A person is likely to consent only to what she believes is a *reasonable* curtailment of her liberty, and that is a separate issue for which the argument from subsequent consent is unable to provide any guidance. If a child were to grow up refusing to concede that her parents were justified in their treatment of her, it in no way follows that the parents behaved unreasonably. Moreover, given certain child-rearing practices, there is a racing certainty that the requisite consent to almost anything will be forthcoming. Appeals to subsequent consent are therefore useless as a means of distinguishing between justified and unjustified paternalism, and where such consent is not forthcoming, our conviction as to the appropriateness of paternalism in a specific context is not necessarily dented. Paternalism is acceptable only in those circumstances when it is *reasonable* to believe that a rational agent would lend her consent, which means, as Jack Lively says, "the legitimating consent necessarily follows from the *rationality* of the intervention and the burden of justification for intervention rests on the claim that it will prevent self-harm. It is difficult to see what force the secondary appeal to consent adds to the justification" (1983: 156, emphasis added).

5 Although Locke did not view children as the literal property of their parents, such a view has its roots in Lockean philosophy, according to which one is the rightful owner of the product of one's labor. See his *Two Treatises on Government*. For a clear exposition of Locke's defense of private property, and the respects in which it is unconvincing, see David Archard (2003: 87ff).

6 Harry Brighouse and Adam Swift are correct in maintaining that it is "essential to intimate and loving relationships that participants are not acting *out of duty* [and] that they do not claim the right to be to be treated in particular ways" on the grounds that to do so would "fail to capture what is special about the family" (2014: 17), but they may well be too hasty in denying that children have a right to be loved on the grounds of the supposed incoherence in the idea of a duty to love. In support of this they quote Kant according to whom: "Love is a matter of feeling, not of willing, and I cannot love because I will to, still less because I ought to; so a duty to love is an absurdity." (Immanuel Kant, *The Metaphysics of Morals*, trans. Mary Gregor (Cambridge: Cambridge University Press, 1976): 161). However, this is to assume too much, and is only one conception of love amongst many. Not only is love incapable of being identified as such by reference to any particular 'feeling' it is not certain that a feeling of any kind is one of its necessary conditions. If so, it is doubtful that love is necessarily an *emotion*—at least in any conventional interpretation of that term. If X loves Y then she must, at the very least, do her best to imagine how Y sees the world and how she feels about it and as a result come to *care* about that. On the assumption that love and non-feigned affection is something a child needs, it may well be a parental duty to care in the way suggested. For an excellent debate on the question of a child's right to be loved, see Matthew Liao (2006), and Mhairi Cowden (2012).

7 Not least of what is wrong with Charles Fried's claim that "the right to form one's child's values . . . and the right to lavish attention on the child are *extensions* of the basic right not to be interfered with in doing those things for oneself" (1978: 152, emphasis added), is that it rides roughshod over the fact that a child is a person in her own right.

8 See Robert Brandon (1979: 193–194). As Feinberg reminds us, it is an exaggeration to suggest that there can be no self-determination unless the self that does the determining is already fully formed (1977: 290).

9 Meyers is critical of Harry Frankfurt's claim (1976) that an autonomous person can be identified by the extent to which she is able to identify with her motivational set. Difficulties in specifying what is involved in acts of identification apart, she draws attention to the fact that an agent whose identification proved ephemeral or fleeting would lack a sufficiently distinctive personality in order to count as autonomous (1989: 263).

10 To the internal constraint of ignorance may be added external constraints such as the coercion resulting from manipulation and physical constraint. Feinberg provides a systematic classification of constraints by reference to the following four-fold distinctions: external positive, external negative, internal positive, and internal negative constraints (1973). While useful as a reminder that the very idea of constraint need not be restricted to external factors, it remains to be seen whether such a neat distinction can be consistently upheld; emphasis will vary between circumstances, rendering the distinction between 'internal' and 'external' rather more arbitrary than it might first appear.

11 For an account of the instrumental benefits of an autonomy-facilitating education, see Eamon Callan (2000: 119–20), where he clearly demonstrates the ways in which the capacity for critical rationality helps in: (i) overcoming the "fallibility of our ethical understanding and the need to adjust our ends to changing circumstances"; (ii) being able to change our beliefs and conduct as and

when required; and (iii) because it is "a normative requirement of good lives that [we should accept] a strongly privileged epistemic perspective in determining whether our lives are going well or badly."

12 He continues: "And since autonomous character operates as a powerful and pervasive constraint on belief and preference-formation, its inclusion within the scope of education for legitimacy cannot be a small tactical retreat from the idea of character neutrality. Its inclusion must signal instead the wholesale rejection of character neutrality" (2000: 147). In fairness to Brighouse, he not only admits to the practical difficulties of distinguishing between autonomy-facilitating and autonomy-promoting education, but concedes that if it is the case that many deeply religious parents, in deciding to send their children to faith schools or to home-school them in accordance with their religious convictions, will almost certainly favor an autonomy-facilitating education at the expense of an autonomy-promoting education, which means that the "pragmatic advantage of [Brighouse's] position would have to be sacrificed" (*Ibid.*). In demonstrating how the form of Socratic nurturing he wishes to develop parallels and compliments Brighouse's defense of autonomy, Colin Macleod argues that it is not possible to "extol the value of having the capacities constitutive of autonomy without also accepting that the children we seek to equip with these capacities should understand their value and hence be favourably disposed to exercising them" (2003: 328, n. 6).

13 The civic virtues identified by Galston include general virtues such as law-abidingness, social virtues such as independence, economic virtues such as acknowledging the importance of work, and political virtues such as the respect for the rights of others (1991: 221–4).

14 The coherence of the distinction is questioned by Will Kymlicka. If justice requires the capacity to evaluate public policies and institutions, then how can the capacity for critical evaluation not impinge upon our private identity? Since the capacity involved just is the capacity to form and revise our comprehensive ends, it would seem that any exercise of it involves our private identity (1995: 232, n. 9). As he notes elsewhere: "accepting responsibility even as a purely political conception has inevitable 'spillover' effects on private lives" (2002: 236); a point recognized by Rawls himself when he says that "requiring children to understand the political conception . . . is in effect, though not in intention, to educate them to a comprehensive liberal conception" (1993a: 199). Such a recognition notwithstanding, however, Rawls is wrong to insist that it is none of the state's business to concern itself with domestic affairs or the practices internal to a religious group (1993b), given the liberal commitment to not frustrating individuals in their determination to question and revise such practices. As Penny Enslin and Patricia White say: "to . . . treat the private as beyond the legitimate scope of legitimate educational intervention is to ignore a major obstacle to the acquisition of equal citizenship" (2003: 122). Rawls's distinction between political and moral autonomy fails, according to Rob Reich, in that it is "less a capacity that we switch on and off at will, than a sort of character that colors our life as a whole" (2002: 49).

15 According to Hannan and Vernon (2008: 184), while it is appropriate to speak of parental roles, we should not think of the family exclusively in terms of the roles of its members. Cf. Gerry Cohen's claim to the effect that the citation of a role is never a *sufficient* reason to φ; for "when roles are conceived as persons, the social *status quo* is then protected: when roles constitute selfhood, to change society is to mangle human beings" (1976: 66).

16 Cf. Brighouse and Swift: "The idea that parents should constantly monitor themselves in their relations with their children in order to screen out anything that might have any influence in their children's emerging values is ludicrous . . .

the spontaneous sharing with their children of at least some of who parents really are is crucial to healthy family life; that sharing is bound to result in some shaping of values" (2014: 154).

17 In an earlier paper he says that "a full sharing of family activities will require that the members of the family, to some extent at least, share one's underlying values. . . . If family activities are to be shared, then parents must be granted some authority to initiate their children into the respective traditions" (2005: 374).

18 The Humanist Philosopher's Group, as part of its case against faith schools, relies on an account of 'religious education' as nothing more than "teaching *about* religion" (2001: 14, their emphasis). While there is no obvious reason *not* to teach one's children about one's own religion or that of other people, as part of their social or anthropological education, initiating them into a religion is a very different matter. I have elsewhere argued that in order to understand a religion, one needs to understand religious concepts (such as 'God'), which entails that one is, to some extent—the extent depending on the depth of the understanding—on the 'inside' of it. If one had no idea as to the appropriate deployment of such concepts, how could one possibly understand in anything other than a superficial sense. To understand anything at all about the nature of God is to believe that there is something that counts *as* God—which is another way of saying that understanding presupposes belief. If true, and if it is not the business of a publicly funded system of schooling to get children to believe in the truth of highly disputable propositions, then it is difficult to see how there could be a place for religious education of this kind. Indeed, it is difficult to see how it could be distinguished from indoctrination (1978).

19 In this respect he is sympathetic to Terry McLaughlin's attempt to ensure 'autonomy via faith' whereby only subsequent to the instilling of an initial faith, should the child be "encouraged to put his or her faith into critical perspective" (1990: 118). McLaughlin believes that it is a parent's responsibility to ensure that his child emerges [from her "primary culture"] with fixed beliefs "as are necessary for the provision of such a primary culture; such beliefs being 'stable' in the sense that they are open to subsequent challenge and development" (1984: 80). The questionable sustainability of the distinction between beliefs that are fixed in the 'stable' sense but not in the unshakable sense notwithstanding—it being far from clear what parents would have to do in order to succeed in instilling one but not the other—McLaughlin is as wrong to assume that requiring a family to "excise the religious element from its culture for the purpose of child upbringing" would be tantamount to the infringement of the liberal principle of freedom of religion, as he would were he to suggest that a parent's political freedom would be infringed by requiring him to leave his children at home while attending a political rally. As Callan says: "parents can enjoy the life of political activism while eschewing any attempt to rear their daughter as a socialist, [so too may they] enjoy extensive opportunities for religious self-determination while forgoing any claim to rear their children as members of their own faith" (1985: 113).

20 'Indoctrination' is a deeply contested concept, the complexities of which cannot be pursued here. The present argument is in contradistinction to the stance adopted by, for example, John White (1967) and Ivan Snook (1972), both of whom defend the *intention* requirement. Indoctrinating (and teaching for that matter) may be undertaken in both a task (intentional) and achievement (unintentional) sense. In this respect they are unlike (purely) 'task' and 'achievement' verbs, such as 'searching,' and 'finding.' See Gilbert Ryle (1949).

21 Cf. Taylor (1985: 124), who clearly demonstrates that the 'radical chooser'—one whose actions are determined by reference to mere preference satisfaction—would "at the moment of choice have *ex hypothesi* no horizon of evaluation." It is thus perfectly acceptable, as Colin Macleod argues, to allow parents the prerogative

of *provisionally privileging* their favored conception of the good—with the proviso that they "not seek to exempt the ends they wish their children to adopt from rational scrutiny [nor] undertake to foreclose the possibility of deliberation about such matters by tightly insulating children from exposure to access to the social conditions of deliberation" (1997: 130).

22 The extent to which parents are morally entitled to transmit their 'comprehensive conceptions' in relation to the good life, is a matter of deep and ongoing controversy. A particularly noteworthy, albeit unpersuasive, attempt to deny the right of a parent to transmit any of his (non-political) comprehensive doctrines to his children (with the exception of justice), has recently been made by Matthew Clayton. His reasoning is complex, but turns on his reliance on a belief in the 'parallel' between those features of a political relationship and those of a parent–child relationship in being non-voluntary, coercive, as well as having a profound effect on the lives of individuals. If Rawls invokes such features in order to justify the ideal of liberal legitimacy, Clayton believes that the very same legitimacy "insists that parental conduct should be guided by ideals and principles that do not rest on the validity of any reasonable comprehensive doctrine. The ideals that guide parents must not . . . be secular or religious [as they are disputed] by reasonable persons" (2006: 95). His principal objection to the right of parents to pass on any comprehensive doctrine whatever to their children lies in his idiosyncratic and highly demanding 'precondition view' of autonomy; the view that "individuals may not be legitimately enrolled into comprehensive practices, without their informed consent, and individuals may not seek to impart controversial beliefs before [their children] possess the capacities for autonomous deliberation" (*Ibid*: 93, emphasis added). It would require a digression of inordinate length to explain why he adopts this view, as opposed to the more conventional 'end-state view' of autonomy according to which X is autonomous if at some stage subsequent to acquiring beliefs as a result of parental influence, she ends up with a set of beliefs that are authentically hers. However, according to Clayton, unless a child's beliefs have "the right kind of history," then the beliefs she acquires prior to becoming autonomous undermine her prospects of ever becoming so. He attempts to justify his precondition view on both instrumental grounds—in that it not only "enables individuals to revise their conception of the good," but would "help in preventing the emotional costs associated with renouncing the values of one's parents in later life" (*Ibid*: 106–109)—and intrinsic grounds "because it ensures that each individual is self-determining and the central features of her life are the product of her autonomously held convictions [which] render it impermissible to steer a person into a particular lifestyle without her consent" (*Ibid*: 104). Justification apart, Clayton's precondition view requires the acceptance of much that is counterintuitive. First, why is it the case that one's deeply held convictions should have the right sort of history when the end-state view itself provides reason enough for not inducting children into a whole range of comprehensive views? As Brighouse says: "whether a belief or preference is held autonomously is not just a matter of its genesis. . . . Commitments generated by non-autonomous processes become autonomous when the agent reflects upon them with an appropriate degree of critical reflection" (2000: 67). It is important to emphasize the fact that what really matters in the debate about children's autonomy is the extent to which the influence of others is likely to impinge on a child's subsequent capacity for autonomous decision-making. Second, even if there is a 'parallel argument' between the features governing a state–citizen relationship and a parent–child relationship, children are different from adults in not being as free and equal in the relevant respects; they simply lack the wherewithal to formulate a set of convictions that possess the requisite moral relevance, which casts doubt on the view

that their autonomy is necessarily violated as a result of their being initiated into a comprehensive doctrine not of their choosing. Third, and crucially, Clayton's position ignores the respects in which comprehensive doctrines differ; not every doctrine has the indoctrinatory potential of religion. While a religious upbringing may well result in indoctrination, thereby providing Clayton's thesis with a measure of justificatory force, others are much less costly to reject (in relation to parental disapproval, for example), but may well be considered essential to any meaningful interpretation of the good life. In order to avoid a wholesale ban on the comprehensive enrollment of children into all and every doctrine, each requires evaluation on its merits. For an excellent critical appraisal of Clayton's overall thesis, see Morgan (2009), to which Clayton (2009) provides a detailed response. For a critique of his parallel case argument, see Christina Cameron (2012) to which Clayton provides a not entirely convincing reply (2012).

23 Mere exposure, however, is neither sufficient nor, as Mill says, is it enough "that he should hear the arguments of adversaries from his own teachers, presented as they state them and accompanied by what they offer as refutations. That is not the way to do justice to the arguments. . . . He must be able to hear them from persons who actually believe them; who defend them in earnest and do their very utmost for them" (1975: 36).

24 As Susan Moller Okin says, "individuals must not only be formally free but substantially and more or less equally free to leave their culture of origin; they must have a *realistic right of exit*" (2002: 206).

25 Neil Burtonwood cites the extraordinary comments made by the governors of the Torah Maczikei Hadass school in London who, when criticized by the inspectors for failing to prepare their pupils for the wider society, "simply declared no interest in this particular educational purpose" (2003: 424).

26 It is matter of dispute as to who should control a child's curriculum. In view of the fact that the educational diet she receives has a major impact on the lives of everyone, it should ideally be determined democratically; although it is unclear how this might be cashed out with any degree of specificity. In view of the fact that neither parents nor teachers have been elected to the task, the broad outlines of the aims and purposes of schooling and the appropriate content by which such aims might be realized, should be left to the agencies set up by central government designed for the purpose, on which there might be representatives from universities, business, ethnic minorities, the teaching profession, parent–teacher associations, and such like, in order to widen the democratic mandate. The resulting curriculum should not be so rigid as to prevent teachers from being able to modify the details in accordance with the needs and interests of their students.

27 See *Mozert v. Hawkins County Board of Education* 827 F2d 1058 (1987).

28 The *Mozert* claim to have their religious convictions take precedence over an appropriate civic education is vigorously attacked in many places. Stephen Macedo, for example, argues that "children must be exposed to the religious diversity that constitutes our polity for the sake of learning to respect as fellow citizens those who differ from them in matters of religion" (1995: 226). As such, he is right to suggest that "a liberal order does not and should not guarantee a level playing field for all the religions and ways of life that people might adopt. . . . We have no reason to be equally fair to those prepared to accept, and those who refuse to accept, the political authority of public reasons that fellow citizens share" (*Ibid*: 227). According to Amy Gutmann, a well-considered democracy "expects us to exercise critical judgment in our willingness to take unpopular political decisions, respect reasonable points of view that we reject, and respect public policies from which we dissent. A civic education that satisfies the *Mozert*

parents' objections . . . would interfere with teaching the virtues and skills of liberal democracy such as the teaching of toleration, mutual respect, racial and sexual non-discrimination, and deliberation" (1995: 563).

29 See *Wisconsin v. Yoder*, 406 US 205 (1972).
30 According to the National Center for Education Statistics, Institute of Education Studies (2013), approximately 1.7 million (or 3%) of the country's children are home-schooled in the USA, with about 60,000 (or 0.6%) of the nation's children being home-schooled in the UK, according to Home Education UK (2012). Parents in the UK also enjoy the right to withdraw their children from a school altogether, and for any reason, unless a child attends a special needs school where permission from the Local Education Authority is required. Home-schooled children are not constrained by the requirements of the National Curriculum and are not required to complete any examinations or, what are referred to in the English and Welsh context, Standard Attainment Targets. Moreover, there is no statutory requirement by reference to which representatives from the local authority may gain access to a home or child, although the Education Welfare Service will, in all probability, endeavor to ensure that parents are meeting their duty to promote an education. If the local authority is unsatisfied with the provision made, it can issue a School Attendance Order requiring a parent to either provide further evidence of education or to enroll a child in a school named in the order, within 15 days.
31 For a useful attempt to explicate the kinds of inadequacy that would justify withdrawing children from school, see Swift (2003, Chapter 8).
32 The value of parental partiality and the issues surrounding the extent to which it might be constrained are clearly rehearsed by Macleod (2004), and in addition to the chapter on 'Conferring Advantage' in their Family Values, Brighouse and Swift provide a judicious account of the complexities associated with the notion in their 'Legitimate Parental Partiality' (2009). For an alternative stance, see Paul Bou-Habibs's contribution to the debate (2014).
33 The liberal fears of an over-intrusive state are familiar enough, but while a softly softly approach to state intervention in the lives of families may be both morally and prudentially appropriate, there are occasions, such as those posing threats to equality of opportunity, when the state has a moral obligation to intervene against practices premised on such things as sexist or homophobic prejudices, especially, according to Clare Chambers, where such norms are expected to apply to a group "into which children are born and to which their attachments are not chosen" (2002: 165).

Bibliography

Archard, David. "Children, Multiculturalism and Education," in *The Moral and Political Status of Children*, edited by David Archard and Colin Macleod, 142–159. Oxford: Oxford University Press, 2002.
Archard, David. *Children, Family and the State*. Aldershot: Ashgate, 2003.
Archbishop's Council. *The Way Ahead: Church of England Schools in the New Millennium*. London: Church House Publishing, 2001.
Bou-Habib, Paul. "The Moralized View of Parental Partiality." *The Journal of Political Philosophy* 22, no. 1 (2014): 66–83.
Brandon, Robert. "Freedom and Constraint by Norms." *American Philosophical Quarterly* 16 (1979): 187–196.

Brighouse, Harry. *School Choice and Social Justice*. Oxford: Oxford University Press, 2000.

Brighouse, Harry and Adam Swift. "Parents' Rights and the Value of the Family." *Ethics* 117, no. 1 (2006): 80–108.

Brighouse, Harry and Adam Swift. "Legitimate Parental Partiality." *Philosophy and Public Affairs* 37, no. 1 (2009): 43–80.

Brighouse, Harry and Adam Swift. *Family Values: The Ethics of Parent-Child Relationships*. Princeton, NJ: Princeton University Press, 2014.

Burtonwood, Neil. "Social Cohesion, Autonomy and the Liberal Defence of Faith Schools." *Journal of Philosophy of Education* 18, no. 1 (2003): 55–61.

Burtt, Shelley. "The Proper Scope of Parental Authority: Why We Don't Owe Children an 'Open Future'," in *Child, Family and State*, edited by Stephen Macedo and Iris M. Young, 243–272. New York: New York University Press, 2002.

Callan, Eamon. "McLaughlin on Parental Rights." *Journal of Philosophy of Education* 19, no. 1 (1985): 111–118.

Callan, Eamon. *Creating Citizens: Political Education and Liberal Democracy*. Oxford: Oxford University Press, 1997.

Callan, Eamon. "Liberal Legitimacy, Justice and Civic Education." *Ethics* 111 (2000): 141–155.

Cameron, Christina. "Debate: Clayton on Comprehensive Enrolment." *The Journal of Political Philosophy* 20, no. 3 (2012): 341–352.

Chambers, Clare. "All Must Have Prizes: The Liberal Case for Interference in Cultural Practices," in *Multiculturalism Reconsidered*, edited by Paul Kelly, 457–477. Cambridge: Polity Press, 2002.

Clayton, Matthew. *Justice, Legitimacy and Upbringing*. Oxford: Oxford University Press, 2006.

Clayton, Matthew. "Reply to Morgan." *Studies in Philosophy and Education* 28 (2009): 91–100.

Clayton, Matthew. "Debate: The Case Against the Comprehensive Enrolment of Children." *Journal of Political Philosophy* 20, no. 3 (2012): 353–364.

Clayton, Matthew and David D. Stevens. "School Choice and Burdens of Justice." *Theory and Research in Education* 2, no. 2 (2004): 111–126.

Cohen, Gerry. "Beliefs and Roles," in *The Philosophy of Mind*, edited by Jonathan Glover, 53–66. Oxford: Oxford University Press, 1976.

Cowden, Mhairi. "What's Love Got to Do with It? Why a Child Does Not Have a Right to Be Loved." *Critical Review of International Social and Political Philosophy* 15, no. 3 (2012): 325–345.

Curren, Randall and Jason Blokhuis. "The *PRIMA FACIE* Case Against Homeschooling." *Public Affairs Quarterly* 25, no. 1 (2011): 1–19.

Dwyer, John. "Parents' Religion and Children's Welfare: Debunking the Doctrine of Parents' Rights." *California Law Review* 82 (1994): 1371–1447.

Enslin, Penny and Patricia White. "Democratic Citizenship," in *The Blackwell Guide to Philosophy of Education*, Nigel Blake, et al., 110–125. Oxford: Blackwell, 2003.

Feinberg, Joel. *Social Philosophy*. New Jersey: Englewood Cliffs, 1973.

Feinberg, Joel. "Harm and Self Interest," in *Law, Morality and Society: Essays in Honour of H.L.A. Hart*, edited by P.M.S. Hacker and J. Raz, 285–308. Oxford: Oxford University Press, 1977.

Feinberg, Joel. "The Child's Right to an Open Future," in *Whose Child? Parental Rights, Parental Authority and State Power*, edited by William Aiken and Hugh LaFollette, 124–153. Totowa, NJ: Rowman & Littlefield, 1980.

Fineman, Martha. "Taking Children's Interests Seriously," in *Child, Family and State*, edited by Stephen Macedo and Iris M. Young, 234–242. New York: New York University Press, 2002.

Fowler, Tim. "The Limits of Civic Education: The Divergent Implications of Political and Comprehensive Liberalism." *Theory and Research in Education* 9, no. 1 (2011): 87–100.

Frankfurt, Harry. "Identification and Externality," in *The Identities of Persons*, edited by A. O. Rorty, 239–251. Berkeley: University of California Press, 1976.

Fried, Charles. *Right and Wrong*. Cambridge, MA: Harvard University Press, 1978.

Galston, W. William. *Liberal Purposes: Goods, Virtues and Diversity in the Liberal State*. New York: Cambridge University Press, 1991.

Galston, W. William. "Two Concepts of Liberalism." *Ethics* 105, no. 3 (1995): 516–534.

Galston, W. William. "Parents; Government and Children: Authority Over Education in the Liberal Democratic State," in *NOMOS XLIV: Child, Family and the State*, edited by Stephen Macedo and Iris M. Young, 211–233. New York: New York University Press, 2003.

Gheaus, Anna. "The Right to Parent One's Biological Baby." *The Journal of Political Philosophy* 20, no. 4 (2012): 432–455.

Gutmann, Amy. "Civic Education and Social Diversity." *Ethics* 105 (1995): 557–579.

Hand, Michael. "Should We Teach Homosexuality as a Controversial Issue?" *Theory and Research in Education* 5, no. 1 (2007): 69–86.

Hannan, Sarah and Richard Vernon. "Parental Rights: A Role-Based Approach." *Theory and Research in Education* 6, no. 2 (2008): 173–189.

Halstead, Mark. "Voluntary Apartheid? Problems of Schooling for Religious and Other Minorities in Democratic Societies." *Journal of Philosophy of Education* 29, no. 2 (1995): 257–284.

Humanist Philosophers' Group. *Religious Schools: The Case Against*. London: British Humanist Association, 2001.

Jonathan, Ruth. "Choice and Control in Education: Parental Rights, Individual Liberties and Social Justice." *British Journal of Educational Studies* XXXVII, no. 4 (1989): 321–338.

Koski, William and Rob Reich. "Why Adequacy Isn't: The Retreat from Equality in Educational Law and Policy and Why It Matters." *Emory Law Review* 56 (2007): 545–617.

Kymlicka, W. Will. *Multicultural Citizenship: A Liberal Theory of Minority Rights*. Oxford: Oxford University Press, 1995.

Kymlicka, W. Will. *Contemporary Political Philosophy: An Introduction*, 2nd edition. Oxford: Oxford University Press, 2002.

LaFollette, Hugh. "Licensing Parents Revisited." *Journal of Applied Philosophy* 27 (2010): 327–343.

Liao, Matthew. "The Right of Children to Be Loved." *The Journal of Political Philosophy* 14, no. 4 (2006): 420–440.

Lively, Jack. "Paternalism," in *Of Liberty*, edited by A. P. Griffiths, 147–165. Cambridge: Cambridge University Press, 1983.

Macedo, Stephen. "Multiculturalism for the Religious Right? Defending Liberal Civic Education." *Journal of Philosophy of Education* 29, no. 2 (1995): 223–238.

Macleod, Colin M. "Conceptions of Parental Autonomy." *Politics & Society* 25, no. 1 (1997): 117–140.

Macleod, Colin M. "Shaping Children's Convictions." *Theory and Research in Education* 1, no. 3 (2003): 315–330.

Macleod, Colin M. "The Puzzle of Parental Authority: Reflections on How Not to Be a Hypocrite: School Choice for the Morally Perplexed Parent." *Theory and Research in Education* 2, no. 3 (2004): 309–321.

Marples, Roger. "Is Religious Education Possible?" *Journal of Philosophy of Education* 12 (1978): 81–91.

McLaughlin, Terence "Parental Rights and the Religious Upbringing of Children." *Journal of Philosophy of Education* 18, no. 1 (1984): 75–83.

McLaughlin, Terence. "Peter Gardner on Religious Upbringing and the Liberal Ideal of Religious Autonomy." *Journal of Philosophy of Education* 24, no. 1 (1990): 107–126.

Meyers, Diana T. *Self, Society and Personal Choice*. New York: Oxford University Press, 1989.

Mill, John Stuart. *On Liberty* (1859). New York: Norton, 1975.

Montague, Philip. "The Myth of Parental Rights." *Social Theory and Practice* 26, no. 1 (2000): 47–68.

Morgan, Jeffrey. "Religious Upbringing: Religious Diversity and the Child's Right to an Open Future." *Studies in Philosophy and Education* 24 (2005): 367–387.

Morgan, Jeffrey. "Children's Rights and the Parental Authority to Instil a Specific Value System." *Essays in Philosophy* 7, no. 1 (2006): Article 10.

Morgan, Jeffrey. "A Critical Review of Matthew Clayton: Justice and Legitimacy in Upbringing." *Studies in Philosophy and Education* 28 (2009): 79–89.

Murphy, Jeffrey. "Incompetence and Paternalism." *Archiv fur Rechts und Sozialphilosophie* 60 (1974): 465–486.

Noggle, Robert. "Special Agents: Children's Autonomy and Parental Authority," in *The Moral and Political Status of Children*, edited by David Archard and Colin M. Macleod, C. M., 97–117. Oxford: Oxford University Press, 2002.

Okin, Susan Moller. " 'Mistresses of Their Own Destiny': Group Rights, Gender and Realistic Rights of Exit." *Ethics* 112 (2002): 205–230.

Petrovic, John. "Promoting Democracy and Overcoming Heterosexism: And Never the Twain Shall Meet?" *Sex Education* 2, no. 2 (2002): 147–156.

Rawls, John. *A Theory of Justice*. Oxford: Oxford University Press, 1971.

Rawls, John. "Justice as Fairness: Political Not Metaphysical." *Philosophy and Public Affairs* 14 (1985): 223–251.

Rawls, John. "The Priority of Right and Ideas of the Good." *Philosophy and Public Affairs* 17, no. 4 (1988): 251–276.

Rawls, John. *Political Liberalism*. Cambridge, MA: Harvard University Press, 1993a.

Rawls, John. "The Idea of Public Reason Revisited," in edited by S. Shute and S. Hurley, *Philosophy, Politics and Society* 5 (1993b): 6–20.

Reich, Rob. *Bridging Liberalism and Multiculturalism in American Education*. Chicago: Chicago University Press, 2002.

Reiss, Michael. "Teaching about homosexuality and heterosexuality." *Journal of Moral Education* 26, no. 2 (1997): 343–352.

Ryle, Gilbert. *The Concept of Mind*. London: Hutchinson, 1949.

Schoeman, Ferdinand. "Rights of Families, Rights of Parents and the Moral Basis of the Family." *Ethics* 91 (1980): 6–19.

Snook, Ivan. *Indoctrination and Education*. London: Routledge & Kegan Paul, 1972.

Swift, Adam. *How Not to Be a Hypocrite: School Choice for the Morally Perplexed Parent*. London: Routledge, 2003.

Taylor, Charles. "What is Human Agency?" in his *Human Agency and Language*, 15–44. Cambridge: Cambridge University Press, 1985.

White, John. "Indoctrination," in *The Concept of Education*, edited by R. S. Peters, 123–133. London: Routledge & Kegan Paul 1967.

White, Patricia. "Parents, Rights, Homosexuality and Education." *British Journal of Educational Studies* 39, no. 4 (1991): 398–408.

8 Liberalism, Parental Rights, and Moral Education

Yet Another Reflection on *Mozert v. Hawkins*[1]

Marc Ramsay

I am a secular, atheist, liberal. I support the rights of homosexual and transgender persons, including recognition of same-sex marriages. My wife is a liberal of the same stripe. We are academics by trade, and we find ourselves accepting positions at a private religious college nestled within an affluent, but deeply conservative community. We enroll our nine-year-old son in a well-regarded local public school. After a few weeks, we encounter a disturbing element in the local school board's mandatory curriculum, a critical reading program, which uses the same required "reader" series for all elementary-level students. The idea of such a program does not strike us as problematic, but we are shocked by the actual curricular content. One story concerns the seemingly happy lives of children in a close-knit Christian community that shuns those who engage in either homosexual behavior or sex outside of marriage. Another reading concerns a rather frank depiction of Hell by an adolescent character who warns her friends that unorthodox belief in God may not save them from eternal punishment.

We bring our concerns to the local school board. We are told that our conception of diversity is defective—it is constrained by a commitment to value pluralism, which fails to recognize the reasonableness of monist religious commitments. One board member explains that exposing children to stronger religious views serves a legitimate purpose in a liberal society. It reminds children that the range of moral diversity may be wider than what their parents depict. Likewise, it shows children that such ways of life are objects of choice for them, even if these ways of life conflict with their parents' moral conceptions. "Exposure," the board member says, "is not indoctrination, and exposure does not become indoctrination just because some parents oppose the ways of life presented in the curriculum. You do not have a right to ensure that your children adopt your particular form of secular morality, and your children must be taught political respect for rival conceptions. If you disagree, you can always run for board membership in the next election."

Flabbergasted, my wife and I float the idea of some alterative reading assignments for our son. We do not have the time to be active in local politics, and we feel that attempting to revise what appears to be a popular curriculum would not endear us to our new community. But the board does not permit individual schools or teachers to provide such accommodations.

Those familiar with the case will recognize my "inverted" version of *Mozert v. Hawkins*.[2] As the "inverted example" suggests, I have some sympathy for the *Mozert* parents. The board member's defense of mere "exposure" would ring hollow for me, so I can understand how it rang hollow for Vicki Frost.[3]

My sympathy for the *Mozert* parents guides me to a tentative case for some modest accommodation of parents' moral and religious sensitivities, specifically exemptions from what they regard as controversial assignments in elementary-level education. But rethinking *Mozert* does not support a general parental override on educational content. The claim to parental accommodation is weakened, if not eliminated, where educational programs aim to secure respect for gender equality and tolerance for specific vulnerable groups.[4]

Section 1 explains *Mozert* and provides a brief account of two more recent cases from the Supreme Court of Canada. Section 2 explains the dispute between political liberalism and autonomy (or comprehensive) liberalism and the role this dispute plays in framing cases such as *Mozert*.

Section 3 examines both the idea of parents' political authority over children's education and the notion of parents' substantive right to control their children's education. I argue that parental authority over education must be seen as pragmatic (or derivative); it cannot ground the claims made in *Mozert*. Parental rights (or interests) are also insufficient, by themselves, to ground such exemptions. However, the relevant parental interests are important enough to prompt serious reflection on the alleged benefits of contested civic education programs.

Section 4 deals with personal autonomy. I argue that autonomy liberals should accept a somewhat deflated concept of personal autonomy. In particular, liberals should deemphasize the general importance of critical reflection on one's standing conception of the good life. However, this move does not reinforce parental objections to educational policies that promote gender equality and the protection of vulnerable groups such as homosexual youth. And it does not legitimate parental objections to sex education programs.

Section 5 examines the argument that diversity-oriented civic education is required for the teaching of tolerance or political respect. Here I suggest that extensive engagement with moral and religious difference, through reading or course content, is not necessary at the elementary school level. Moreover, enforcing the demand for such engagement may have harmful effects on some children, particularly those with fundamentalist religious commitments.[5]

1 Cases

1.1 Mozert

References to *Mozert* are almost obligatory for authors who discuss the tension between parental rights and public education. But while references to the case are still ubiquitous, recent discussions of *Mozert* provide little depth about its background. With the help of Stephen Bates's excellent account of its history, I aim to breathe some narrative life back into the discussion of *Mozert*.[6]

In 1983, the Hawkins County school board adopted the Holt series reading textbooks for elementary students in grades one through eight. The Holt series was intended to develop "higher order cognitive skills that enable students to evaluate the material they read, to contrast the ideas presented, and to understand complex characters that appear in reading material."[7] The dispute began when Vicki Frost discovered the science fiction story "A Visit to Mars" in her daughter's sixth-grade Holt reader. Frost was disturbed by the story's positive portrayal of telepathy. Reading further she found another story that denigrated the differences between the sexes and yet another that endorsed Catholicism.[8]

Frost and her friend Jennie Wilson were deeply concerned with the steady advance of "Humanism," an atheistic philosophy dedicated to the destruction of Christianity and traditional American values. For Frost, the appearance of the Holt readers marked the first serious intrusion of the secular humanist movement into the previously safe Christian stronghold of her rural Tennessee community. Frost and Wilson organized community meetings to discuss the threat, and they, along with a handful of other families, attempted to convince the school board to replace the Holt readers.[9]

Frost and her allies were rebuffed at a September board meeting. From the outset, many if not all members of the board found the parents' complaints pointless and irksome. From the board's perspective, replacing the already purchased texts was a non-option for the cash-strapped county. And Frost's complaints about an anti-Christian agenda also seem to have struck a nerve with the board. Church was a central feature of life in Hawkins County, and the label "fundamentalist" Christian was worn proudly by many of its residents.[10] The board, along with many teachers and principals, saw themselves as working hard to improve the county's poor performance in reading assessment. Frost and the other complaining parents didn't seem to show much appreciation for the hard work. Indeed, they seemed to be labeling that work as anti-Christian.[11]

Frost and Wilson, along with Bob Mozert, continued to campaign against the Holt readers, and they also pressed a variety of other concerns about the state of public education in Hawkins County. At the same time, Frost and other concerned parents approached individual schools, seeking special accommodations for their own children. One school refused such accommodations, but others excused children from the Holt curriculum. Instead, during the relevant class times, the children worked in the library or other alternative rooms using older readers acceptable to their parents.[12]

At a November board meeting, Frost, Wilson, and Mozert pressed additional complaints, including requests for the removal of some books from Hawkins County school libraries. The meeting also brought the various individual accommodations to the board's attention (it appears that at least some board members were not aware of the accommodations prior to the meeting). Without warning, the board voted to ban all such accommodations, insisting that all county students use the Holt reader prescribed for their grade level. Perhaps this was a hasty and overly punitive response. It seems likely that many of the other parents involved in the subsequent suit would have been content with their individual accommodations. And it is clear that the board made no effort to determine how well the scheme of individual accommodations was functioning. It is fair to say, however, that Frost and her closest allies maintained a more ambitious agenda, one that they did not abandon until they turned to litigation.[13]

With Mozert as the lead plaintiff, Frost and a handful of other parents launched a constitutional challenge, claiming that the mandatory Holt readers violated their freedom of religion. With Frost presenting the bulk of their testimony, the plaintiffs set out several more specific complaints:

- by forcing them to read the Holt Series, the school board forced the children to act against their religious convictions.
- reading the Holt series threatened the children with eternal damnation.
- the curriculum denigrated the children's religion, subjecting them to shame and embarrassment.
- forcing children to read the Holt materials against their parents' expressed wishes disrupted the parent/child relationship.
- the materials encouraged children to question authority relationships, thereby disrupting parental control over home life.
- the readings promoted particular ways of life incompatible with the plaintiffs' religious beliefs.
- the readings promoted a general moral relativism, which holds that all ways of life are equally true or morally valid.[14]

The plaintiffs proposed that the previous individual accommodations be restored and that their children work from an alternative set of readers published by Open Court. Their lawyer attempted to maintain a narrow focus, avoiding questions of how the plaintiffs' religious views might affect other areas of the curriculum such as history and science. The board's lawyer, on the other hand, pressed hard on this issue; he insisted that the plaintiffs' arguments, if accepted, would establish a dangerously wide-ranging right to individual accommodations. Likewise, he argued that Frost was unable to explain the alleged difference between the offensive Holt readers and the acceptable Open Court alternative. School boards, he maintained, would face pervasive requests for accommodation with no clear sense of how to distinguish legitimate claims from arbitrary demands.[15]

Judge Thomas Hull affirmed the parents' constitutional complaint, but, mindful of the board lawyer's second line of argument, crafted his own remedy. The plaintiffs would have the option of home-schooling their children for reading classes; the children's performance would be assessed through standardized testing.[16]

However, the board's hardline position was validated on appeal by the United States Court of Appeals, 6th Circuit. Chief Judge Pierce Lively found no evidence that children were compelled to make critical judgments about their religious beliefs. While he admitted that exposure to the Holt readings encouraged such a critical stance, he also noted that children were free to comment on the readings from their own "value base."[17]

Judge Cornelia Kennedy agreed, but also maintained that even if such compulsion had been established, the state's interest in public education should prevail. Kennedy saw the individual parental right to "opt out" of required assignments as both undermining the board's ability to establish a common curriculum and unduly burdensome to teachers. She also maintained that excusing students from contentious assignments on religious grounds would only exacerbate existing problems of divisiveness. Finally, she found that the state's interest in promoting civic respect for different religions and ways of life overrides freedom of religion in this context.[18]

Judge Danny Boggs felt forced to concur with his colleagues, noting that the Supreme Court would be unlikely to side with the parents. He regretted that agreements between individual schools and parents were set aside for the sake of establishing the school board's legal authority.[19] Judge Boggs' prediction proved accurate. The Supreme Court refused to hear the plaintiffs' appeal of the 6th Circuit decision.[20]

Most of the plaintiff children had already been removed to religious schools or home-schooling after the board's cancelation of individual accommodations. Few returned after the legal challenge failed.[21] Thus, on purely pragmatic grounds, there is a strong case for some accommodation of parents' religious sensitivities. Unless the option of home-schooling is removed, civic education is easily frustrated by the parents who exercise that option. The pragmatic argument accepts that parental objections are irrational, but maintains that accommodating their irrationality may be a regrettable necessity.

As I indicate in my introduction, I think there are non-pragmatic moral reasons for accommodating parents such as Frost.[22] At the same time, however, I am wary of who I am defending.[23] In constructing a moral case for accommodating the *Mozert* parents we should accept that we are, to some degree, constructing a case on their behalf. And that is fine. As Bates notes, the real question is whether the complainants have a legitimate claim to accommodation—they may have such a claim even if they do not understand or endorse its proper basis. But we should not pretend that we are merely polishing up poorly articulated but otherwise reasonable demands. In defending the *Mozert* parents we must be mindful of the risk that we are supporting partial satisfaction of objectionable parental goals.[24]

1.2 More Recent Cases

I would like to update the controversy with a brief discussion of two Canadian cases, *Chamberlain v. Surrey School District No. 36* and *S.L. v. Commission scolaire des Chênes*.[25] In *Chamberlain*, a British Columbia school board refused a K-1 teacher's request for approval of supplementary materials, three books with stories that presented children with same-sex parents.[26] The board cited sensitivity to some parents' religious beliefs and respect for parental discretion concerning the age at which children are exposed to controversial ideas (including those related to sexuality).

In a 2002 majority decision, the Supreme Court of Canada rejected the board's decision, ordering a new appraisal of the teacher's application.[27] According to Chief Justice McLachlin,

> Children encounter it [cognitive dissonance] every day in the public school system as members of a diverse student body. They see their classmates, and perhaps also their teachers, eating foods at lunch that they themselves are not permitted to eat, whether because of their parents' religious strictures or because of other moral beliefs . . .
>
> Exposure to some cognitive dissonance is arguably necessary if children are to be taught what tolerance itself involves. . . . When we ask people to be tolerant of others, we do not ask them to abandon their personal convictions. . . . The belief that others are entitled to equal respect depends, not on the belief that their values are right, but on the belief that they have a claim to equal respect regardless of whether they are right.[28]

According to the Chief Justice, the readings did not pursue difficult issues of biology or sexuality; they simply encouraged students to accept that children within same-sex parent families are cared for by loving, thoughtful persons. Since children are likely to be exposed to the existence of same-sex parents by social life or media, "[t]he only *additional* message of the materials appears to be the message of tolerance. Tolerance is always age-appropriate."[29] That sounds right. But how many of the school board members who scoffed at Vicki Frost would have rethought their position if the Holt readers had included brief but positive portrayals of same-sex parents?

The 2012 SCC decision in *S.L. v. Commission scolaire des Chênes* provides an even closer analog of the 6th Circuit decision in *Mozert*. The case concerned a constitutional challenge to Quebec's mandatory Ethics and Religious Culture program (ERC). The ERC, which became mandatory in 2008, replaced the previous models of Catholic and Protestant religious and moral instruction. The complainants, a pair of Catholic parents, argued that the ERC promotes a kind of moral relativism and that its promotion of diversity would be confusing for their children. They claimed that their freedom of religion entitled them to exempt their children from the program.[30]

The ERC is not one specific text or course. Rather, it is a description of general goals, desired competencies for different academic levels, and recommendations for implementation. All provincial schools are required by law to implement the program, but the legislation does not demand that schools use specific texts or educational materials. General outlines are provided for both the elementary and secondary levels, and each outline is supported by the same preamble.

> For the purposes of this program, instruction in ethics is aimed at developing an understanding of ethical questions that allows students to make judicious choices based on knowledge of the values and references present in society. The objective is not to propose or impose moral rules, nor to study philosophical doctrines and systems in an exhaustive manner.
>
> Instruction in religious culture, for its part, is aimed at fostering an understanding of several religious traditions whose influence has been felt and is still felt in our society today. In this regard, emphasis will be placed on Québec's religious heritage. The historical and cultural importance of Catholicism and Protestantism will be given particular prominence. The goal is neither to accompany students in a spiritual quest, nor to present the history of doctrines and religions, nor to promote some new common religious doctrine aimed at replacing specific beliefs.[31]

Writing for the majority, Justice Deschamps recognized parents' constitutional right to transmit their religion to their children. However, she held that the complainants' subjective perception of interference with this transmission could not, by itself, establish an infringement of their rights. Justice Deschamps denied that a respectful or neutral presentation of various religious traditions constitutes the promotion of relativism, and she maintained that exposing children to religious diversity does not constitute a form of indoctrination. Citing the Court's earlier decision in *Chamberlain*, she also rejected the idea that exposure to religious diversity would confuse children in a harmful way.[32]

The majority insisted that the formal purposes of the ERC could not be impugned. Moreover, because the complainants' children never actually took the ERC courses, there was no evidence to support a problem with the program's implementation. In a concurring opinion, Justices Lebel and Fish emphasized that the state of the record allowed for the possibility that the ERC's implementation might, at some point, infringe the rights of similarly situated persons.[33]

The claim that exposure to diversity does not constitute indoctrination is a common theme in *Mozert*, *Chamberlain*, and *S.L.*, and SCC insists that a respectful presentation of various views need not promote relativism. All three decisions push the idea that exposure to diversity serves a legitimate state goal, the teaching of mutual tolerance. I do not dispute any of these general claims, but we should recognize that exposure to diversity in the classroom is different from "fact of life" exposure. The latter may be difficult to ignore, but the former comes with a formal demand for attention. Even if this demand falls short of outright indoctrination, the "inverted example" shows that it is easy to imagine circumstances in which liberal parents might feel that "exposure" is more than mere exposure.

2 Autonomy Liberalism and Political Liberalism

Clarifying what is at stake in cases such as *Mozert* highlights tensions within liberalism. Moreover, the dispute over civic education often serves to illustrate the dispute between political liberalism and autonomy (or comprehensive) liberalism.

Autonomy liberals hold that the state's commitment to political principles such as individual liberty must be explained and clarified by appeal to deeper moral commitments. Not surprisingly, autonomy liberals maintain that the value of personal autonomy, properly understood, is the grounding value of the political commitment to individual liberty. On this account, personal autonomy is a crucial moral value, one that routinely, but not always, overrides other moral considerations (at least in questions concerning enforceable moral principles). It does not follow that the ideal of personal autonomy dictates all answers to questions about the good life. However, as Joseph Raz suggests, autonomy liberalism, while it does not provide a full account of the good life, does take a position about good lives that precludes the truth of some comprehensive conceptions.[34]

Autonomous choice may be considered partial self-creation, a matter of choosing self-defining commitments from a range of equally valuable (or objectively incommensurable) ways of life.[35] Because it is based in value pluralism, such an account precludes the truth of monist conceptions of the good, ones that claim their own account of the good as superior to others (the one truth). To make room for monist conceptions, some autonomy liberals appeal to fallibilism about the good. There may be one singular moral truth, but the possibility that our current conception is in error (value pluralism or some rival monist conception may be the real truth) entails an overriding interest in maintaining the ability to reflect upon and revise our plan of life.[36] Autonomy liberals who defend the *Mozert* decision stress that children's personal autonomy cannot be secured without some level of cognitive dissonance with their parents' beliefs.[37]

Political liberalism, however, attempts to avoid grounding political principles in controversial moral ideals such as personal autonomy. For the political liberal, what matters is that respect for individual liberty and distributive justice are supported by an overlapping consensus of diverse, reasonable, "comprehensive" moral doctrines. Whether citizens regard their own moral/religious doctrines as exclusively true is irrelevant if they accept liberalism as their political doctrine. Likewise, citizens need not consider whether their own commitments are mistaken, as long as they are committed to respect for other persons' liberties.

Some authors argue that political liberalism's ambitions are untenable and that defending liberal principles requires us to address deeper moral questions including the value of personal autonomy. Some allege that Rawls himself recognized this problem, and that this led him to incorporate "the burdens of judgment" into his later turn to political liberalism. The burdens of judgment are a list of factors that explain the difficulties and complications of deliberation about the good life. Rawls may not intend the burdens of judgment to prompt critical reflection on our own commitments, but he does see them as supporting respect for other persons. The burdens allow us to see persons with rival conceptions of the good as reasonable persons who can be trusted in social cooperation (and not as heathens who are either unable or unwilling to accept obvious moral truths). Of course, while accepting the burdens of judgment may not demand that we reexamine the value of our own commitments, it is likely to encourage such reflection. Thus, the distinction between Rawls's political liberalism and autonomy liberalism (especially fallibilist versions) seems to collapse.[38]

Sensitive to this issue, some political liberals insist on a moral, as opposed to an epistemic, conception of political liberalism.[39] They deny or downplay the role of the burdens of judgment in securing respect and trust between citizens. On this account, reasonable citizens simply need to affirm their commitment to the political ideal of persons as self-directing agents with their own conceptions of the good.

All political liberals recognize the importance of encouraging political tolerance within children's education, but the epistemic and moral conceptions yield different approaches to this goal. Following the epistemic conception, Stephen Macedo maintains that the purpose of materials such as the Holt readers is to instill the distinctively political virtues of tolerance and civic respect. Following Chief Judge Lively, Macedo maintains that the burden on the plaintiffs' religious freedom was minimal. Students were not forced to endorse any particular view. They were not required to criticize their own views, and they were free to speak from their own value base.[40] Autonomy liberals may see the cognitive dissonance fostered by the Holt readers as early ignition for children's personal autonomy. For fallibilists, exposure to diverse perspectives and ideas is likely to ready the ground for critical reflection on the moral and religious beliefs that children receive from their parents. Value pluralists, on the other hand, may see such early exposure as opening children's minds to a diverse range of valuable but incommensurable life choices. Macedo does not deny the likelihood of such effects, but he insists that political liberalism does not aim to produce them. For him, students should undergo an experience of cognitive dissonance with their received beliefs, but the aim of this experience is to foster a sense of respect for different beliefs and traditions.

According to Macedo, parents cannot require the state to forgo otherwise justifiable policies just because those policies have non-neutral consequences.

The political liberal state does not aim to promote deeper ideals of personal autonomy and it does not judge parents' religious beliefs. Parents, on the other hand, must be prepared to "bracket" their beliefs where the state offers a sound public justification for its policies.[41]

Macedo's conception of neutrality does not satisfy political liberals who follow the moral conception, and these authors call for greater trust in parents' teaching of tolerance. On this view, each reasonable moral tradition has its own reasons for valuing liberty, so parents and churches can be trusted to handle this aspect of children's education. According to Kyla Ebels-Duggan, reasonable citizens should not be expected to "bracket" their deeper moral beliefs—instead, sound policies must be justifiable to all reasonable citizens. And, because she endorses the moral conception of political liberalism, Ebels-Duggan disputes the claim that mandatory exposure to diversity (through readers such as the Holt series) is needed to teach children the virtue of tolerance. For her, if parents have genuine moral or religious objections to aspects of curricular content, then that content cannot be justified to all reasonable persons and parental discretion should be respected.

Moral conception political liberals such as Ebbels-Duggan also place a great deal of weight on the traditional (or consensus-based) authority of parents. Few dispute that parents should enjoy substantial control over their children's day-to-day lives and educations, but it does not follow that one must accept parental authority as a tie-breaker in every controversy. All political liberals recognize that children have independent moral status (children are not property). Of course, this abstract truth does not refute the *Mozert* parents' claim to accommodation, but it does problematize sweeping appeals to parental authority or rights. As Matthew Clayton points out, children are governed by, but cannot contribute to, the overlapping consensus that underwrites political liberalism.[42]

Parents may eschew a comprehensive commitment to personal autonomy, while maintaining a sense of political respect for the liberty of other adults. Whether they have a right to refuse personal autonomy on behalf of their children is another question. One response is that securing children's right to choose their own moral conception requires only that they be apprised of their political rights; sufficient cognitive dissonance is already provided, in abundance, by the background culture and social media.[43] But it is clear that the authors who offer these responses also place great value on the alleged parental right to transmit values to children.[44] Moral conception political liberals may wish to avoid controversial theorizing about moral values, but they cannot avoid dealing with the tension between parental authority/rights and children's own claims.

3 Parental Rights, Interests, and Authority

Are parents wronged if, against their expressed wishes, the state exposes their children to alternative moral views? There are two basic ways of establishing a parental claim to non-interference here. First, one might argue that parents have political authority over children's education and that the state is simply non entitled to second-guess parental judgments (even if parents are sometimes mistaken). Second, parents have a substantive right to transfer their religion to their children—this right is either consistent with or superior to children's own interests.

3.1 Authority

The authority approach stands or falls with the substantive approach unless we adopt a very controversial account of parental authority's source. Accepting that A rather than B should have authority over C within a certain domain does not imply that A is always right about what is best for C. A may make some incorrect decisions, but, over the long term, A's decisions are more likely to serve C's interests than B's decisions. In other language, A's authority is a derivative right, afforded because it is thought to serve C's long-term interests. But this kind of analysis makes sense only if we accept that, in general, children are well served by an education controlled by their parents' religious sensibilities (or that full control over a child's religious beliefs cannot be severed from other beneficial aspects of parental authority). If this is true, then occasional errors in judgment about how religious control is exercised are possible, but respect for parental judgment should remain. However, if children do not have a strong interest in the transmission of their parents' religious or moral views, the appeal to parental authority cannot, by itself, settle *Mozert*-type disputes. If the state has plausible reasons for holding that unfettered parental efforts to transmit religion to children often impede children's development, the parental authority argument cannot be invoked against the state's corrective efforts.[45]

I think that support for a deeper notion of familial authority is rooted in a broadly Lockean framework. On this view, the authority of the state is conventional (as all liberals accept), but families (not individuals) are the underlying fundamental units that ratify the state's authority. Families provide the natural mechanisms of social reproduction that could, in principle, operate in the absence of a state. Thus, family units carry a kind of natural authority, and the state's legitimacy depends on a limited transfer of authority from familial units.[46]

A similar account of familial authority can be found in the conservative literature opposing legal recognition of same-sex marriage. Some conservative scholars argue that the naturalness of the nuclear heterosexual family places it beyond state authority and that the state is precluded from recognizing alternative non-natural family units.[47] Obviously, this view also has strong historical connections to patriarchal authority within the family unit. But even if the natural model of authority can be disentangled from its patriarchal and homophobic connections, it still valorizes procreation as an intrinsic source of authority over children. The intrinsic importance of procreation is contested, and its support is drawn from religious and teleological doctrines that do not command universal assent. So the political liberal who endorses a strong or deep conception of parental authority is taking sides in debates about comprehensive moral issues. Only the derivative or pragmatic account of authority is uncontested.

3.2 Substantive Rights and Interests

Do parents have a substantive right to transfer their religious commitments to their children? To challenge *Mozert*, such a right must either override or be consistent with the rights of children themselves.

Galston maintains that parents' interests have intrinsic weight; children's interests should not trump parents' rights in all cases.[48] To be sure, parenthood should not be servitude.[49] However, any discussion of the balancing of parents' interests with children's interests still requires us to recognize the basic separateness of persons. In becoming a parent one does not abandon her own freedom of religion—if moving to a better school district would preclude worshiping at a church of her own faith, then, perhaps, her freedom of religion should prevail. But transferring her beliefs to her child is not a pre-existing interest that can be balanced against the child's interests. The interest cannot be pursued in the absence of the child—the parent needs (to use uncharitable language) to *use* the child. So unless the child's own interests are served, or at least not harmed, by the transmission of religion, successful transmission is not a basic right.

Harry Brighouse and Adam Swift defend the idea that parents have an important interest in an intimate relationship with their children.[50] Intimacy is possible only if parents are permitted to share many of their beliefs and preferences with their children, and Brighouse and Swift maintain that children have a corresponding interest in this intimacy. Of course, parents must accept that as children develop their own preferences and goals, the maintenance of intimacy becomes a two-way street. A parent can maintain intimacy by developing an appreciation of the child's pursuits, even if the parent does not share the child's enthusiasm for those activities (the same point applies in reverse as children distance themselves from their parents' goals and interests). No doubt, the task of maintaining intimacy is easier for parents who accept a fairly strong form of value pluralism.[51] However, intimacy alone cannot ground the *Mozert* parents' claims to accommodation. Parents must accept that their children may, at some point, develop beliefs that conflict with their own. It is hard to believe that the Holt series would generate any immediate break with intimacy, unless parents insist on treating any and all questions about their religion as an immediate threat.

Ebels-Duggan's criticism of *Mozert* emphasizes that parents often view the transfer of religious beliefs as a matter of duty, not a self-interested exercise of right.[52] The concern with failing in one's duty is, I think, distinct from the concern with loss of intimacy. A parent might regret a loss of intimacy with his child, but still feel that he has succeeded in teaching the child sound values (the adult child might agree with this assessment). Likewise, a parent might, to some degree, preserve intimacy but feel that he has failed with respect to values. So the concern with failure of duty can be a distinct source of anxiety and emotional loss for parents.

However, a subjective sense of duty cannot be a decisive consideration here. Consider Vicki Frost's duty to protect her daughter from eternal damnation. Perhaps the *Mozert* parents truly believed that their children were threatened with damnation by reading the Holt series. If so, then moral conception political liberals might advance the following line of argument. A liberal state's policies must be justifiable to all reasonable persons (justifiable from the perspective of all reasonable comprehensive doctrines). Deeply held religious beliefs, including beliefs in afterlife concepts such as Hell are reasonable beliefs (situated within reasonable comprehensive doctrines). Therefore, the liberal state must respect parental concerns about damnation in the formation of educational policy; it cannot justify an educational policy that conflicts with parental concerns about damnation. More specifically, the goal of promoting personal autonomy (as it is understood within autonomy liberalism) cannot trump the relevant parental concerns, because reasonable persons need not accept the moral priority of personal autonomy.

The problem with this line of argument is that it proves too much. If subjective beliefs about damnation were accepted at face value (infinite disutility) then they would trump any public rationale for contested educational policies. From the perspective of the believer, the partisan value of personal autonomy cannot justify the risk of sending one's child to Hell.[53] But if Hell is understood as infinite disutility, no public policy, no matter how strong its justification in terms of well-being promotion or harm prevention, can justify that risk. A liberal state must develop some conception of the interests (children's interests and state societal interests) that can override parental discretion. Where that conception applies, subjective beliefs about damnation cannot be allowed to trump otherwise justifiable policies. For example, if a girl's right to information about the prevention of pregnancy and sexually transmitted diseases turns on her parents' subjective beliefs about her damnation, then she has no right to such information. Allowing free play to the damnation concern would be functionally equivalent to affording religious parents an absolute property right in their children.

As Macedo recognizes, a liberal state must sometimes act in a way that implicitly rejects certain beliefs. It need not claim that Hell does not exist, but it may need to act as if particular views about the activating conditions for damnation are false (or that certain views about when one may intervene to prevent damnation are false).[54]

The same point applies to any "overriding" sense of duty that parents feel regarding their children—the state can be sensitive to the relevant parental anxieties, but it cannot accept these anxieties as trump cards. Some level of sensitivity is appropriate, however. Most parents accept that they have a duty to raise autonomous children (in some sense of autonomy), but their sense of good autonomy is bound to be conditioned by their own comprehensive commitments.[55] This is hard for some autonomy liberals to see, because their value pluralism allows them to see virtue even in monist commitments that they regard (in the strict sense) as mistaken. In one way, we are all value pluralists—even fundamentalist Christians may think that some important life choices (the particulars of one's career for example) are not objectively determined. The dispute over value pluralism concerns its scope—like many if not most autonomy liberals, I think that value incommensurability pervades questions of the good. I also think that some false beliefs, especially ones in the areas of meta-ethical and theological questions do not prevent people from living objectively valuable lives. So my son might travel rather far from my beliefs and commitments before I find either our intimacy or my sense of duty threatened. But I still have limits.

In the "inverted example," I worry that my son may be gay or transgender. But my resistance to the inverted Holt program is not contingent on this concern. There may be such a thing as a fundamentalist Christian who respects full political equality for homosexual and transgender persons (I am not entirely sure that this is even possible), but I don't want my heterosexual son to be one. I do not want his personal relationships with gay and lesbian family members to be hampered by deluded views about natural design and human sexuality. I want to control his early exposure to these views, to the extent possible, because this exposure threatens an important kind of experience—unhampered emotional relationships with the people who are denigrated by bad ideologies. Ultimately, my son may choose a cold form of political respect over deeper acceptance; other aspects of his education will provide him with the critical skills needed to evaluate the opposing side's arguments. But facing these arguments too early, in an unstructured way, hampers what I see as a kind of knowledge (what-it-is-like knowledge) that should be weighed against them in deliberation.

Liberals who are dubious of purely political respect for homosexuals may endorse my objections to the "inverted" Holt series, but remain hostile to the *Mozert* parents' claims. The matter is not so easy for political liberals who claim that purely political respect is both possible and normatively sufficient for reasonable citizens. If moral conception political liberals such as Ebels-Duggan accept my story, then they have good reason to think that the *Mozert* parents can tell a parallel story that they must also accept. Such a story would deny the objective value of homosexual relationships (a story that would be emphasized early in children's introduction to sexuality), but still insist on political respect for homosexual lifestyles.

All liberals should pause here to consider what kind of space they intend to preserve for religious commitments that are in tension with liberalism's political commitments. In different ways, both Ebels-Duggan and Macedo act as if the tension did not exist—Ebels-Duggan refuses to see any threat to liberal principles while Macedo downplays the potential cost to religious commitments. Others, such as Eamonn Callan, Harry Brighouse, and Adam Swift are more frank in recognizing the tension but also seem more comfortable with the demise of such commitments.[56] I find myself in a somewhat different position. I think of myself as an autonomy liberal and a value pluralist, but I also feel the pull of political liberalism's core ambition—making the liberal tent as wide as possible.

I also accept that parental rights are largely derivative ones, but that is an easy thing to say for someone who does not anticipate any real challenge to his parental decisions. In the "inverted example," I would end up saying something philosophically unsophisticated like, "But this is my kid!" And I would hope for this claim to ring in the board members' ears in spite of our other intractable disagreements. The pragmatic argument holds that we should accommodate some irrational demands in order to keep children within the public school system. But suppose that Vicki Frost was unable to remove her children from public school.[57] Despite our differences, I have real sympathy for the *Mozert* parents' position, their feeling of anxiety. I am not sure that Frost ever became a reasonable fundamentalist—and I am not sure whether it is even possible for believers such as Frost to become reasonable political liberals without serious costs to their core beliefs. But we should not impose anxiety such as Frost's without compelling reasons, even if we find the anxiety, to some degree, irrational. And we should consider whether commitments such as personal autonomy can be understood in way that allows us to see some of Frost's complaints as reasonable.

4 Children's Autonomy

Authors sympathetic to the *Mozert* parents may opt for a fairly weak sense of autonomy. Autonomy liberals, of course, are apt to complain that autonomy should not be weakened just to make room for a dubious parental right.

However, as Gerald Dworkin points out, few of us engage in much critical reflection on our conceptions of the good (autonomy liberals included, I think). For this reason, Dworkin settles for a fairly weak requirement—persons are autonomous if their first-order desires are consistent with their second-order desires.[58] He does not demand much in the way of critical reflection on the rationality of second-order desires—too many of us would be non-autonomous. I hesitate to go as far as Dworkin on the matter, but I do think that the importance of critical reflection has been overstated in recent liberal theory. The question of whether commitments that one finds deeply satisfying (at both the first- and second-order levels) merit serious critical reflection is one that different persons may answer differently.

Moreover, the character of critical reflection is itself a matter of controversy. As I noted earlier, virtually everyone is some kind of value pluralist. But the scope of our value pluralism varies; we disagree about how many questions of the good admit of rational or objective resolution. We may agree that children should be open, in some way, to different possibilities, or that they should feel entitled to explore different possibilities as adults, but this provides little concrete guidance for public education.

4.1 Cognitive Dissonance

The primary value of the Holt readers seems to be the cognitive dissonance provided by the readings and classroom discussions. In *Chamberlain*, Chief Justice McLachlin argued that such cognitive dissonance is a pervasive "fact of life" in pluralistic societies; parents should not feel threatened by a bit more cognitive dissonance in the classroom. But this brings us to William Galston's response. If cognitive dissonance is already provided in abundance by the background culture, what need is there for additional cognitive dissonance in the classroom?[59]

The answer, I presume, is that courses based on material such as the Holt readers both legitimate critical reflection and provide a safe space in which such reflection can occur. It should be clear, however, that there is room for reasonable disagreement about how and when parental values should be subjected to critical reflection.

The case for enforced critical reflection seems contingent on pockets of complete resistance to critical reflection among parents who are, at least provisionally, willing to place their children in public schools. Moreover, we have to think that these parents are well positioned to affect their agenda unless we impose mandatory critical reading programs for elementary students. Here, Shelley Burtt insists that autonomy liberals who support the *Mozert* decision underestimate the level of discursive engagement within Christian fundamentalist communities. She pushes for a charitable interpretation of Frost's concerns about the stories from the Holt reader, insisting that critics should try to see those stories from the perspective of Frost's concern with "secular humanism."[60] And while I find Frost's hostility to science fiction tales rather disturbing, I'm not sure that her children's future autonomy was threatened by the absence of these readings. Like Burtt, I am not convinced that Frost's children's future autonomy was compromised just because Frost sought to delay their imaginative engagement with alternative ways of life.

As Burtt points out, "[t]he children at issue in *Mozert v. Hawkins* . . . were only in the sixth grade. Liberal theory needs to be clearer about the stage at which exposure to alternative understandings of the good life is appropriate, linking this claim to a better understanding of what we now know about children's psychological and cognitive development."[61] It is fair to say that autonomy liberals have not risen to this challenge. On the other hand, authors such as Burtt and Ebels-Duggan have not shown that the research on children's development supports parental discretion in this context. Burtt regards 16 as a more plausible age for exposure to alternative understandings of the good. However, she simply asserts that children past this age have developed the capacities for evaluating their parents' conception of the good in light of other values.[62] Burtt seems to underestimate the cognitive capacities of pre-adolescent children, but this does not establish that younger children require imaginative engagement with alternative conceptions of the good.[63] If children learn a variety of skills through the course of their earlier education, I see no reason why they cannot begin autonomous exploration of alternative moral conceptions around the age that Burtt stipulates.

4.2 Constitution Pluralism

Autonomy liberals who support *Mozert* must explain why this process must be engaged at an earlier age, and I doubt that any such explanation will emerge. However, as Brighouse argues, matters are different where an individual's personal dispositions conflict with her received moral and religious views (her standing second order views). Persons who experience this conflict need to consider whether their second order views are impeding more authentic aspects of their characters. Brighouse calls this the problem of "constitution pluralism."[64] Perhaps persons with strong individual dispositions would benefit from the cognitive dissonance provided by a diversity oriented curriculum. David McCabe, on the other hand, argues that protecting the interests of these individuals comes at the expense of another group, those who would feel left adrift by the choice promoted in diversity oriented education. McCabe thinks that the two sets of interests cancel each other out, and he concludes that respecting parental discretion is the appropriate default.[65]

Some people encouraged to engage in critical reflection on their parents' beliefs may, in later life, report that the experience was burdensome and unhelpful. Moreover, many people who abandon their parents' beliefs may report that their value-laden education was, nonetheless, crucial to their successful development. Finally, there is something to the idea that robust critical reflection and dialogue about life requires the participation of adults who have been thoroughly immersed in very different moral conceptions. So, at a high level of abstraction, McCabe's reply appears sound.

However, as McCabe recognizes, Brighouse's argument invokes a concrete example, homosexuality.[66] Homosexuality is not an abstract possibility; it is a well-known disposition that a fairly predictable number of persons will display. Similar considerations apply to the protection of girls' autonomy. We must be concerned with the deliberative process of women who settle for traditional subordinate social roles. We should ask whether they have engaged in general critical reflection, but a more crucial concern is whether they have internalized mistaken beliefs about their own capacities or disparaging stereotypes about the motivations of women who pursue careers outside the home.[67]

McCabe acknowledges the problem, but still rejects robust educational measures:

> . . . merely being informed that the state protects one's right to homo-sexual relationships, absent a more imaginatively compelling depic-tion of such a choice, may leave gays and lesbians facing problems that would be lessened under RLE [robust liberal education]. Or again, RLE may increase the chance that some women will depart from gendered norms and pursue options more suited to their character and abilities. It is, however, no fatal objection that a political arrangement permits some harms that would be better controlled under different arrange-ments . . . Where one's choices demonstrably and seriously harm others (theft, assault, physical coercion, and so on), liberty is properly con-strained. But the cases we are considering here do not rise to that level: they involve parents trying to pass on to their children ideals that, while perhaps mistaken, are not harmful in this way (e.g. that God intends sexual intimacy to occur between men and women, that women are especially well-suited to be caregivers for young children). To permit expressive liberty concerning such ideals is *pro tanto* to permit parents to shape their children in various ways.[68]

If the state addresses children about its reasons for supporting gender equal-ity and homosexual rights, it speaks to the good, parental territory. This concern with transgression on matters of the good is reinforced by more general concerns about "robust liberal education." Religious parents worry that extensive exposure to diversity encourages their children to adopt a consumerist model of moral deliberation, one that undermines the teaching of values such as community, discipline, and piety.[69]

McCabe considers no compromise here. We accept either an unfettered parental right of transmission or a regime of education that completely undermines the teaching of conservative religious views about gender roles and sexual orientation. Moreover, his sanitized presentation of the relevant religious reasoning trivializes the difficulties faced by girls and adolescent homosexuals.

Historically, opponents of gender equality and homosexual rights have helped themselves to disparaging empirical claims about homosexuals, women's capacities, and women's motivations for seeking political equality. If the state can only report on current political rights, it is precluded from contesting these stereotypes. I don't want to endorse a naïve view about the easy separation of normative and empirical claims within moral and religious conceptions. But an analogy with fraud and false advertising is not out of place here. Consent is vitiated by fraud, and the right to free-dom of speech does not protect false advertising. Likewise, parents have no right to secure their children's assent through demeaning stereotypes about the homosexuals and women who exercise their political rights. Moreover, false advertising is itself a rather mild way of describing the difficulties that homosexual and transgender youth may face in fundamentalist families.[70] And girls' later adolescent pursuit of personal autonomy is compromised if they internalize views that inhibit the development of the skills and capacities that are deemed normal or natural for boys.

I have put myself in a difficult position. I claim to support accommodations for religious parents, but I am also set to deny them what are probably their "big ticket" items, exemptions for materials related to sexual orientation and gender equality.[71] Authors such as McCabe may complain that vigorous attempts to combat "homophobia" will undermine any effort to teach accounts of sexual morality that privilege heterosexuality. Similar complaints apply to gender equality and teaching of "traditional" gender roles. As I noted earlier, political liberals (moral conception ones especially) seem committed to the idea that fundamentalist Christians can retain their deeper moral objections to homosexuality as long as they commit themselves to political respect for homosexual persons' rights. Should we worry that a message of unconditional support for homosexual and transgender youth violates political neutrality by dis-privileging fundamentalist views? I think not. Instead, such a message simply informs fundamentalist parents that they should treat their homosexual and transgender adolescent children with an area-specific form of respect similar to the more general respect they show to adults with rival religious commitments.

Critical reading programs such as the Holt series are not the obvious mechanisms for delivery of the relevant messages, and the same point holds for survey courses in religion and ethics. Support for gender equality and vulnerable youth should stand out clearly; it should stand out from ideas and concepts that we defend with the rhetoric of mere exposure and open deliberation.

4.3 Sex Education

Clearly, some of the relevant work can be handled by sex education courses. Moreover, consideration of the general merits of sex education courses provides a useful contrast with both the Holt readers and Quebec's ERC program. The evidence that comprehensive sex education programs for teens diminish the rate of sexually transmitted diseases and teen pregnancy, while also raising the initial age of sexual activity, is mounting.[72] Likewise, recent research supports comparable sex education programs for older pre-adolescent children.[73] By contrast, so-called "abstinence only" programs are failing along the same measures.[74] The relevance of these measures does not require one to accept a controversial account of personal autonomy or critical reflection.[75] Moreover, there are sound strategic reasons for attempting to provide older pre-adolescent children with basic information about sexual practices and their risks. These children are about to enter a life phase in which uniformed sexual experimentation poses a serious risk to their well-being. Here the argument that there are no pressing reasons for overriding parental discretion concerning the timing and content of curriculum simply fails. The serious risks faced by children entering adolescence gives the liberal state a reason to experiment with different educational strategies, and the evidence from such experimentation supports comprehensive programs.

Respect for children's autonomy and well-being requires support for gender equality and identifiable vulnerable groups, and this comes at this expense of respect for parental discretion. However, autonomy liberals lack a compelling case for more general promotion of personal autonomy in elementary-level education. This leaves some room for accommodating parental objections to reading programs such as the Holt series and courses such as Quebec's ERC program. But we still need to consider whether such programs can be defended in terms of tolerance and political respect.

5 Diversity Education, Political Respect, and Value Bias

According to Macedo's epistemic conception political liberalism, political respect requires imaginative and sympathetic engagement with different moral conceptions and religious views. Burtt denies this claim, and her denial has some plausibility.[76] In *Chamberlain*, Chief Justice McLachlin insists that "[t]he belief that others are entitled to equal respect depends, not on the belief that their values are right, but on the belief that they have a claim to equal respect regardless of whether they are right."[77] If this is true, then why does tolerance require detailed engagement with other people's beliefs and values?

The epistemic conception political liberal's answer, I think, is that we have a difficult time trusting people who can turn a blind eye to obvious truths about value. So even if we remain convinced that our own views are correct, we need to see how reasonable people can come to very different values and beliefs. There is something to this idea, but perhaps Macedo overplays its significance in elementary education. Of course, even moral conception political liberals such as Ebels-Duggan concede that imaginative engagement with other reasonable doctrines becomes important later in life. Because her political liberalism demands that social policies and laws be justified to all reasonable citizens, Ebels-Duggan concedes that citizens should, at some stage, become attentive to the particular features of rival comprehensive views.[78] To my mind, this entails that high school students, who are approaching the stage of voting citizenship, can be expected to engage with alternative worldviews.

Whether such engagement should be required at the elementary level is another question. Let us consider two of the major lines of argument invoked on behalf of the *Mozert* parents.

5.1 Balance of Presentation

Vicki Frost was appalled by the lack of representation of traditional Protestant Christians as characters within the Holt readers, and she objected to an overemphasis on exotic themes and religions. Likewise, she would later explain that her objection to the presentation of women in non-traditional roles would have been mitigated if the reader had contained positive portrayals of women as homemakers.

Emphasizing concerns with balance of presentation provides a more reasonable-sounding formulation with the *Mozert* parents' concerns. On the other hand, pressing this aspect of their complaints problematizes both their appeal to freedom of religion and the selection of an appropriate remedy. If the parents had selected a few specific readings that violated their religious sensibilities, then the path to a stable remedy would have been clearer (however objectionable accommodating their complaints about mere exposure might be). But their complaints about the Holt reader's overall balance of presentation were, it seems, baffling even for the trial judge who sympathized with them. They were denied their preferred remedy, alternative assignments with the Open Court series, because they could not provide an adequate explanation of its satisfactory balance.

In the strictest sense, balance of presentation must be impossible to achieve. No matter how extensive a text writer's efforts, there may always be some person who finds that their own traditions or views are not given equal representation. As Eamonn Callan points out, some authors appear to treat this as a reductio of public schooling itself—since perfect balance is not possible, parents should be subsidized to pursue their own private educational options.[79] But parents may find their sense of balance thwarted even within private schools that are sympathetic to their general outlook. More importantly, Frost's concerns about balance probably placed too much emphasis on the content of the Holt readers. Presumably, the teachers and board members who supported the Holt readers felt that traditional Protestant Christianity, including fundamentalist versions, was already well represented in the local culture. Likewise, the board members argued that the county's Christian schoolroom teachers had no interest in pressing children to favor the exotic religions portrayed in the Holt readers over Protestant Christianity. More generally, as Callan argues, students' classroom experience cannot be reduced to reading content—good teachers fill gaps in content and address the shortcomings of textbooks by attending to the needs of their particular students.[80]

The background to *Mozert* also makes it clear that parents' sense of balance can be influenced by factors related to, but distinct from, their basic religious or moral beliefs. Frost's sense of balance appears to have been dictated by a combination of personal Biblical interpretation and conspiracy theories about the plans and methods of nefarious secular humanists. At some points, Frost seemed willing to accept some exposure to what she regarded as dangerous ideas, but her threshold was, I think, rather low. Part of what kept it low was her sense of the way in which secular humanists intended to use the seductiveness of exotic ideas to undermine Christian faith and commitment.

We should also note that the balance argument was not available (at least not obviously) to the Catholic parents in *S.L.* with respect to the ERC's religious component. The ERC's religious survey courses are to include a robust presentation of Catholicism. With respect to the ERC, the balance argument would need to target the more secular orientation of the ethics courses. Here, the balance argument retains some force. We should not pretend that omission of moral and religious perspectives such as Frost's is accidental or just an instance of the *you can't include everything* rule. If such perspectives are not included, it is probably because they are deemed either intolerant or too parochial for general discussion. So I can understand why parents in Frost's position do not expect teachers to "fill the gap" in a sympathetic fashion. That task is likely to be left to fundamentalist children themselves. I'll return to this issue shortly.

5.2 *Relativism/Value Pluralism*

According to Ebels-Duggan, the *Mozert* parents' main concern was that teaching from the Holt readers would encourage students to adopt the view that all ways of life (all the ones presented in the reader, at least) are equally true or equally valuable. This normative message violates the requirements of political liberalism, which requires that the state treat all reasonable comprehensive moral conceptions with the same neutral respect. Monist or exclusivist comprehensive moral conceptions are reasonable as long as their adherents accept political respect for other reasonable doctrines.

According to Ebels-Duggan, the "non-neutrality objection" presents

> [a] second-order challenge with implications well beyond the case at hand: In teaching the material in these readers, an instructor must either present the various views and lives represented there as on a evaluative par with one another or present some as superior to others. But neither option can be justified to all reasonable citizens.[81]

Ebels-Duggan recognizes that this claim seems to conflate two distinct forms of neutrality, *neutral presentation* and *substantive neutrality*. Substantive neutrality is the position that all ways of life presented are equally valuable, but neutral presentation need not imply substantive neutrality.[82] However,

> in practice disagreements concerning [the two forms of neutrality] will tend to arise together for good reason: in formative educational contexts, it is extremely difficult to present normative positions without explicitly or implicitly taking *some* position on their permissibility, value or truth. . . . The parents object that presenting a variety of normative outlooks in a way that aims to be neutral among them will tend to communicate substantive neutrality with respect to these views.[83]

Ebels-Duggan maintains that avoiding the conflation of a teacher's even-handed presentation of different views with the idea that all views presented are equally valuable is a "demanding cognitive task," and "children who lack well-formed conceptions of the good cannot reasonably be expected to perform it."[84]

Ebels-Duggan does not deny that, at some point, it is important for citizens to engage sympathetically with rival comprehensive moral conceptions. But she maintains that early attempts at neutral exposure to rival moral conceptions are likely to frustrate political liberalism's ends. She suggests that early teaching of intellectual charity is best handled from an opinionated perspective (where students are taught that one particular moral conception is best). This helps students to distinguish between a principle of charity and the idea that all views presented are equally valuable. She also suggests that students who are unable to distinguish between *neutral presentation* and *substantive neutrality* may end up associating political respect with a deeper form of relativism or value pluralism that they find abhorrent. This may lead them to reject a commitment to political respect.[85]

Some may complain that focusing on *Mozert* distorts our thinking, because the defects of the Holt readers need not carry over to other, better designed, courses. But if Ebels-Duggan is correct, the practical problem of non-neutrality (conflation on the two senses of neutrality) will plague implementation of all diversity-oriented civic education. A weaker version of her non-neutrality objection appears to motivate Justice Lebel and Justice Fish's claim that the implementation of Quebec's ERC Program could, conceivably, violate freedom of religion. To be sure, the ERC's preamble makes it clear that the program is not intended to encourage students to abandon their received beliefs, and suitable textbooks and course introductions would repeat this message. But there is a long distance between formal statements and the day-to-day reality of students' classroom experience.

5.3 The Risks of Discursive Courses

I am somewhat skeptical of Ebels-Duggan's claims about children's abilities. Like Burtt, she probably underestimates elementary-level children's cognitive capacities, and the claim that pre-adolescent children need to remain wholly within the direction of their parents' comprehensive moral conceptions is doubtful. Research shows that pre-adolescent children can and do reason about moral problems without reference to religious or scriptural teachings.[86] Likewise, delaying children's experience with neutral presentation of opposing views may carry its own problems. Readers who have taught introduction to philosophy at the undergraduate level likely understand just how easily young adults can conflate *neutral presentation* with *substantive neutrality*. That anecdote might be read as supporting Ebels-Duggan's view, but it can also be read as supporting the need for an earlier introduction to courses that require students to deal with *neutral presentation* of opposing moral views. However, it does not follow that this earlier introduction must occur at the elementary level. And while elementary-level children may have a somewhat greater capacity to distinguish *neutral presentation* from *substantive neutrality* than Ebels-Duggan believes, there are other practical problems.

I am not entirely sure that the distinction between value pluralism about religion/moral commitments and political respect for rival religious/moral commitments is fully grasped or accepted at the adult level. The distinction seems to enjoy lip service in the relevant SCC decisions, but I often find that other philosophers have a rather ambiguous commitment to it. Fundamentalist parents are, I think, attentive to this issue, so I can understand why critical reading courses and programs such as the ERC would trouble them.

Of course, Brighouse and Swift claim that the home-schooling of religious children deprives the children remaining within public schools of additional exposure to diversity.[87] But we need to ask ourselves whether fundamentalist children will be welcomed *as they are* in discursive courses. I am not saying that elementary students' developmental stage precludes the possibility of fruitful exchanges between fundamentalist students and their classmates. Given the right conditions, some remarkable discussions might emerge. However, the risk that these students will be marginalized—sometimes by other students and sometimes by their teachers—for expressing seemingly intolerant views is quite real. I would not want my son to be tasked with filling the "liberal gap" in the "inverted example."[88]

And it is naïve to think that Vicki Frost's children would have been well-placed to speak from their own "value base." Frost probably had a coherent (if rather paranoid) rationale for her objection to elementary students reading science fiction stories. Whether Frost's daughter should be expected to provide an accurate presentation of that rationale is another issue. Likewise, we cannot assume that classmates who are perfectly accustomed to reading such stories are disposed to provide a charitable hearing for this rationale. Frost was right to worry that her daughter would find this exercise combative, frustrating, and demeaning.[89] There is also good reason to think that in articulating her mother's concerns, Frost's daughter would have been perceived as denying the Christian credentials of the other children. Elementary-level children with a strong sense of fidelity to their parents' religious commitments could, I think, face similar problems in ERC mandated discussions of "balanced relations within a group or society, the distribution of wealth among peoples or protection of the environment."[90]

However, these concerns may not apply to the particulars of the *Chamberlain* case. I presume that K-1 students are not expected to engage in too much discursive reflection on their readings. Realistically, the presence of same-sex parents in their readers is simply meant to accustom them to the presence of same-sex parent families—to instill the belief that same-sex parents have the same love for their children as other parents. Ebels-Duggan may object that the early teaching of tolerance is best left to parents themselves. Chief Justice

McLachlin, however, seems content to leave the particulars of this teaching to parents. Of course, the message conveyed to children interferes, potentially, with parents' teaching of their moral conceptions. Parents may teach their children that heterosexual families are morally superior social units, but the readings would sound against certain reasons for this view—reasons based on invidious stereotypes about same-sex parents. By including same-sex parents within K-1 readers, the state sends parents an additional message of tolerance along the following lines: "Presumably, you have a way of explaining the importance of tolerance for other religions and customs to your children. Those methods of explanation should also be deployed to explain the importance of tolerance for same-sex parent families."

We have plausible reasons for allowing parents to exempt their elementary-level children from courses that require imaginative engagement with alternative ways of life and deliberation about controversial social issues. I am not arguing that the state should abandon such programs, and there is nothing wrong with encouraging participation in them. Schools might use "nudge" tactics to ensure that parental concerns about programs such the ERC are well-informed. Parents might be required to attend informational meetings or provide a written account of their concerns before being permitted to exercise their exemption options.

Even where these options are exercised, schools and teachers still have a variety of options for promoting tolerance and civic respect. As Alisa Kessel points out, civic respect can be taught through "embodied" difference and shared tasks. Critical reading programs aspire to teach tolerance by humanizing people with different moral and religious commitments. Reading about people with different beliefs is supposed to help students see these people in a sympathetic light, as fellow citizens who can be trusted in social cooperation. But strong trust develops because of interactions with real people, not stories, and elementary students discussing their (often confused) understandings of their differences may not be an optimal strategy for promoting trust and cooperation. Children should understand that their various differences need not impede mutually beneficial cooperation—in other words, they need to learn that their differences are often irrelevant. Children from different cultures and religions already have some sense of their differences—elementary school can be a good place to distract them from these differences, to engage them in cooperative tasks. As Kessel points out, even menial shared tasks can teach early versions of the skills and virtues needed for more sophisticated projects. Students should enjoy a secure sense of belonging before they engage in critical discussion of their deeper differences. Forcing such discussion too early in public education may actually impede the development of mutual trust.[91]

6.0 Conclusion

I reject many of the simpler rationales for accommodating the *Mozert* parents, but there is a plausible case for some for accommodations at the elementary level, including individual exemptions from courses that require imaginative engagement with alternative worldviews or religions or discursive discussion of controversial subjects. However, the rationale for such exemptions does not legitimate parental objections to the promotion of gender equality, the protection of vulnerable youth, or even sex education programs.

Notes

1 I thank the workshop participants, especially Mianna Lotz, for their feedback on an earlier version of the paper. I would also like to thank the audience from my public talk version of the paper at Saint Mary's University in Halifax (Jan 22nd 2015).

2 *Mozert v. Hawkins County Board of Education* 827 F.2d 1058 (6th Cir. 1987), cert, denied, 484 U.S. 1066 (1988).

3 Here, I am engaging in an act of sympathetic imagination along the lines requested by William Galston. See William Galston, *Liberal Pluralism: The Implications of Value Pluralism for Political Theory and Practice* (Cambridge: Cambridge University Press, 2002): 117.

4 I am not sure that parents have a constitutional right to opt their children out of reading assignments on moral or religious grounds. Constitutional rights must be supervised by the judiciary, and I do not think that judicial supervision is feasible in this context. It does not follow, however, that all remaining parental complaints should be treated as irrational. Rights protectable by the judiciary do not exhaust the realm of important moral rights; public institutions should not use their constitutional discretion as a carte blanche to ignore residual moral rights. See John Tomasi, *Liberalism Beyond Justice: Citizens, Society, and the Boundaries of Political Theory* (Princeton, NJ: Princeton University Press, 2001): 102–5.

5 My discussion focuses on Christian fundamentalists, but the arguments for exemptions (and their exceptions) also apply to other fundamentalist commitments, including Islamic ones.

6 Stephen Bates, *Battleground: One Mother's Crusade, the Religious Right, and the Struggle for Control of our Classrooms* (New York: Poseidon Press, 1993).

7 *Mozert*, 1060.

8 Ibid., 1062; Bates, *Battleground*, 16–22.

9 Bates, *Battleground*, 12–39. Wilson was not a plaintiff in the case, as her own children were adults by the time of the dispute. However, along with Frost and Mozert, she was a driving force behind the complaints against the Holt readers.

10 Ibid., 31–32.

11 Ibid., 34–39. Perhaps Frost was not entitled to the sense of anxiety I experience in the "inverted example." There it seems as if an already dominant local community perspective is being reinforced through public education under the thin rationale of exposure to diversity. Frost, however, saw matters from a larger perspective—she already struggled against the anti-Christian atheist mindset that pervaded the national media. The board's terse response revealed that Frost was more of an alien within her local community than she had realized both in terms of media concerns and the particulars of scriptural interpretation. Even if she should have felt relatively safe within her strongly Christian community, not all fundamentalist Christians live in such communities.

12 Ibid., 66–78.

13 Ibid., 84–92. The political agitation of Frost, Mozert, and Wilson is conveniently ignored in William Galston's brief account of the dispute that led to the *Mozert* litigation. Galston refutes the concern that accommodating the *Mozert* parents would generate a "slippery slope of endless claims" by emphasizing what he

regards as the targeted and specific nature of the parents' request for accommodation. "If this accommodation had been accepted by all schools in Hawkins County, that would have been the end of the matter." According to Galston, it was only when the board terminated the individual accommodations that "the parents felt compelled to escalate a limited policy dispute into a broader legal controversy." The parents did not initiate legal proceedings until the individual accommodations were canceled, but there was a broader policy dispute (as far as Frost, Mozert, and Wilson were concerned) that preceded the litigation. Galston must be aware of this fact, as he notes that his "history" of the case is drawn from Bates's *Battleground*. See Galston, *Liberal Pluralism*, 120–121 & 121, note 16.

Of course, it is possible that Frost and Mozert might have abandoned their more ambitious agenda in exchange for maintenance of the individual accommodations. Moreover, while Frost's initial goals were less modest than some of her academic apologists suggest, the subsequent media coverage of her complaints was also uncharitable. She was ridiculed for objecting to her children reading the diary of Anne Frank. In fact, the relevant Holt reader provided only a brief selection from a dramatization of the diary, a selection in which characters suggest that unorthodox belief in God is better than no belief in God. The *Mozert* parents never raised a complaint about reading the diary of Anne Frank (before or during litigation); they felt that the specific section of the dramatization pushed the idea of relativism about religious truth. See Bates, *Battleground*, 250–251.

14 For a more extensive summary, see Nomi Maya Stolzenberg, " 'He Drew a Circle That Shut Me Out': Assimilation, Indoctrination, and the Paradox of a Liberal Education," *Harvard Law Review* 106 (1993): 596–97.

15 Bates, *Battleground*, 233–67. For their legal case, the plaintiff parents dropped their complaints about the first- and second-grade Holt readers, focusing their demands on the readings for the higher grade levels.

16 Ibid., 273–77.

17 *Mozert*, 1069.

18 Ibid., 1070–73.

19 Ibid., 1073–78. Judge Boggs, however, notes that many religions, including Catholicism, have treated the reading of "objectionable" materials as a prohibited action. In his view, Chief Judge Lively and Judge Kennedy unfairly ignore parental concerns about mortal sin. Boggs also found Judge Kennedy's claims about both the divisiveness of exemptions and the Holt curriculum's role in promoting civic respect overly speculative.

20 *Mozert*, 1080; Bates, *Battleground*, 301–2.

21 Indeed, the acrimonious nature of the dispute seems to have convinced some parents to keep their children out of public school regardless of whether legal proceedings concluded in their favor. See Bates, *Battleground*, 279.

22 Affording school boards more or less final authority over these matters allows them to limit or refuse individual accommodations where such measures strain either resources or the maintenance of common curriculum. With this authority in hand, school boards may still owe parents a good faith duty to consider at least some reasonable requests to respect parents' religious sensitivities. Tomasi, *Liberalism*, 102–5.

23 Some of the *Mozert* parents' academic apologists offer overly sanitized versions of the parents' actual motivations. These authors deemphasize or reinterpret the parents' objections to "mere exposure." Some suggest that the parents evolved towards a more reasonable and sophisticated concern with balance of presentation; others insist that this theme was always the dominant feature of the parents' concern with the Holt readers. These descriptions are dubious. Even in litigation, complaints about exposure to objectionable materials were

side-by-side with complaints about balance of presentation. Kyla Ebels-Duggan, "Moral Education in the Liberal State," *Journal of Practical Ethics* 1 (2013): 43–45; Tomasi, *Liberalism*, 91–100.

24 Bates, *Battleground*, 306–7.

25 [2002] 4 S.C.R. 710, 2002 SCC 86; 2012 SCC 7, [2012] 1 S.C.R. 235.

26 Approval of the books would have allowed individual teachers to use them as supplementary reading materials, but approval would not have resulted in any required usage (by individual teachers or schools). *Chamberlain*, para 34–35.

27 My presentation of this case is somewhat oversimplified. The claimants argued both that the board exceeded its authority under the relevant legislation and that the board's decision violated the Charter of Rights and Freedoms. The majority decided the case on the former basis, but its interpretation of the board's obligations (and legitimate discretion) under administrative law was influenced by Charter values. *Chamberlain*, para 1–74.

28 *Chamberlain*, para 65–66.

29 Ibid., para 69.

30 *S.L.*, para 3–4.

31 Ibid., 34.

32 Ibid., para 39–43.

33 Ibid., para 58.

34 Joseph Raz, "Facing Diversity: The Case of Epistemic Abstinence," *Philosophy and Public Affairs* 19 (1990): 24–7.

35 Joseph Raz, *The Morality of Freedom* (Oxford: Oxford University Press, 1986): 369–99.

36 Will Kymlicka, *Liberalism, Community and Culture* (Oxford: Oxford University Press, 1989): 9–13. See also Marc Ramsay, "The Burdens of Judgment and Fallibilism," *Contemporary Political Theory* 6 (2007): 150–174. The latter construal of personal autonomy might mollify some fundamentalist parents' concerns about the endorsement of relativism, but emphasis on critical reflection raises its own problems. The *Mozert* parents alleged that early emphasis on critical thinking may lead to a kind of confusing instability in children's commitments, one that pushes them towards relativism (or value pluralism). Likewise, it is not clear whether a parent with deep religious commitments can, on their own terms, treat the possibility of error (in their own beliefs) as a crucial reason for endorsing individual liberty.

37 For an extended discussion of the relation between autonomy liberalism and political liberalism in relation to *Mozert*, see Marc Ramsay, "Political Liberalism and Moral Education: Reflections on *Mozert v. Hawkins*" in *Responsibility for Children*, ed. Samantha Brennan and Robert Noggle (Waterloo: Wilfrid Laurier University Press, 2007): 118–28.

38 Eamonn Callan, *Creating Citizens: Political Education and Liberal Democracy* (Oxford: Oxford University Press, 1997): Chapter 2; John Rawls, *Political Liberalism* (New York: Columbia, 1993): 55–62; Brian Barry, "Review: John Rawls and the Search for Stability," *Ethics* 105 (1995): 874–915; Ramsay, "The Burdens of Judgment."

39 Leif Wenar, "Political Liberalism: An Internal Critique," *Ethics* 106 (1995): 32–62; Ebels-Duggan, "Moral Education," 36 & 36, note 7. Ebels-Duggan draws a distinction between moral and epistemic conceptions of reasonableness, and her work is the source of my terminology here. She seems to construe Rawls as following the moral conception, but I think this is inconsistent with his appeals to the burdens of judgment.

40 Stephen Macedo, "Liberal Civic Education and Religious Fundamentalism: The Case of God v. John Rawls?" *Ethics* 105 (1995): 475.

41 Ibid., 478–80.

42   Matthew Clayton, *Justice and Legitimacy in Upbringing* (Oxford: Oxford University Press, 2006): Chapter 3.
43   William Galston, *Liberal Purposes*: *Goods, Virtues, and Diversity in the Liberal State* (Cambridge: Cambridge University Press, 1991): 248–56.
44   Galston, *Liberal Pluralism*, 101–4.
45   Of course, if the impediments were relatively trivial and the required interventions threatened other highly beneficial elements of parental authority, state interference would not be justified. But it's hard to see how the denial of exemptions for school reading assignments would fit this description.
46   Opponents of *Mozert* require a stronger and less pragmatic account of parental authority, one that treats interference in parental control over education more like interference with another sovereign state. Amy Gutmann maintains considerations of this sort explain the discrepancy between cases such as *Mozert* and *Wisconsin v. Yoder* 406 U.S. 205 (1972). Because the Amish are, to some degree, a separate self-sustaining community (they have long been only "partial" citizens), they have a special claim of communal authority. That argument falls short when applied to *Mozert*, because the plaintiffs could not claim that the children were being prepared for life in a separate political community. See Amy Gutmann, "Civic Education and Social Diversity," *Ethics* 105 (1995): 568–69.
47   For example, see Daniel Cere and Douglas Farrow, eds., *Divorcing Marriage: Unveiling the Dangers in Canada's New Social Experiment* (Montreal: McGill-Queen's University Press, 2004).
48   Galston, *Liberal Pluralism*, 93–6.
49   David McCabe, *Modus Vivendi Liberalism: Theory and Practice* (Cambridge: Cambridge University Press, 2010): 203–4.
50   Harry Brighouse and Adam Swift, "Parents' Rights and the Value of the Family," *Ethics* 117 (2006): 80–108; Harry Brighouse and Adam Swift, *Family Values: The Ethics of Parent-Child Relationships* (Princeton: Princeton University Press, 2014): 85–93.
51   Appreciating a child's attachment to a new sport is one thing—appreciating her attachment to a new religion is quite another (if the parent believes in the exclusive truth of her own religion). Brighouse and Swift's standard examples reveal an insensitivity to religious belief. It is hard for me to see how a religious parent can see the sharing of favorite bedtime stories as comparable to the sharing of a place of worship. Harry Brighouse and Adam Swift, "Family Values and School Policy," in *Education, Justice and Democracy*, eds. Danielle Allen and Robert Reich (Chicago: University of Chicago Press, 2013): 206–7; Harry Brighouse and Adam Swift, *Family Values: The Ethics of Parent-Child Relationships* (Princeton, NJ: Princeton University Press, 2014): 155–7.
52   Ebels-Duggan, "Moral Education," 42. Authors on the other side of the debate do not miss this point. But they maintain that the parental feeling of duty cannot have decisive weight in the state's deliberations about intervention.
53   The same kind of argument can be made without reference to Hell. In a religious view, where there is Heaven (infinite positive utility) but no Hell, deeply religious parents could always claim that they are protecting their children from infinite loss (in terms of possible gains). Engaging with parental beliefs about the afterlife seems to invite a discussion of both Pascal's Wager and its criticisms. See, Alan Hájek, "Pascal's Wager," in *The Stanford Encyclopedia of Philosophy*, ed. Edward N. Zalta (Stanford: The Metaphysics Research Lab, Summer 2011 Edition). URL = <http://plato.stanford.edu/archives/win2012/entries/pascal-wager/>.
54   Macedo, "Liberal Civic Education," 492. Ebels-Duggan resists this implication: "This strikes me as a problem, given the values that political liberalism purports to serve. Consider a policy that could be justified only by appeal to a

general theism. The justification would not depend on any particular theological doctrine—Lutheran Christianity, Sunni Islam, or the like. But clearly it would still fail to be a justification that all reasonable people could accept. This, rather than lack of dependence on any particular doctrine, seems to me to be the most relevant feature of the policy for our purposes." This demand for perfect justification to all reasonable doctrines cannot be satisfied unless one narrows the range of reasonable doctrines, an approach that Ebels-Duggan also resists. The liberal state need not deny the existence of Hell, but it must act if as children do not end up there just because it has made them do things such as read books. See Ebels-Duggan, "Moral Education," 39, note 14.

55 If my son comes to lead what I regard as a base or mistaken life, I will deem myself to have failed as a parent even if there is some more neutral or detached sense in which I can regard his choices as autonomous.

56 Brighouse and Swift, *Family Values*, 170–2. Callan, *Creating Citizens*, 37–9.

57 Several of the plaintiff children remained in public school. Presumably, financial considerations played a role in this decision. Funding private religious schooling for their children was difficult for the Frost family. Bates, *Battleground*, 176–81.

58 Gerald Dworkin, *The Theory and Practice of Autonomy* (Cambridge: Cambridge University Press, 1988): Chapters 1–2. This is something of an oversimplification of Dworkin's view, but it is sufficient for my purposes.

59 Galston, *Liberal Purposes*, 248–56.

60 Shelly Burtt, "Religious Parents, Secular Schools: A Liberal Defense of an Illiberal Education," *Review of Politics* 56 (1994): 62–4.

61 Shelley Burtt, "Comprehensive Educations and the Liberal Understanding of Autonomy," in *Education and Citizenship in Liberal Democratic Societies: Teaching for Cosmopolitan Values and Collectives Identities*, eds. Kevin McDonough and Walter Feinberg (Oxford: Oxford University Press, 2003): 202–3.

62 Ibid., 202.

63 For a survey of some relevant research, see Larry Nucci and Deborah W. Powers, "Social and Cognitive Domain Theory and Moral Education," in *Handbook of Moral and Character Education 2nd edition*, eds. Larry Nucci, Darcia Narvaez and Tobias Krettenauer (New York: Routledge, 2014): 121–39.

64 Harry Brighouse, *School Choice and Social Justice* (Oxford: Oxford, 2000): 73.

65 McCabe, *Modus Vivendi Liberalism*, 212–13.

66 Brighouse, *School Choice*, 73.

67 This is similar to Callan's concern with servility. But I am more sympathetic than Callan to the *Mozert* parents' complaints. Callan, *Creating Citizens*, 152–9.

68 McCabe, *Modus Vivendi Liberalism*, 215.

69 Ibid., 216–17.

70 See Samantha Brennan and Colin Macleod, "Fundamentally Incompetent: Homophobia, Religion, and the Right to Parent" (this volume).

71 Likewise, I seem to show the defects in my own "inverted" example, because I have flagged sexual orientation as a special case.

72 Pamela K. Kohler, Lisa E. Manhart and William E. Lafferty, "Abstinence-Only and Comprehensive Sex Education and the Initiation of Sexual Activity and Teen Pregnancy," *Journal of Adolescent Health* 42 (2008): 344–351.

73 Susan M. Igrasa et al., "Investing in Very Young Adolescents' Sexual and Reproductive Health," *Global Public Health: An International Journal for Research, Policy and Practice Global Public Health* 9 (2014): 555–569.

74 Hannah Brückner and Peter Bearman, "After the Promise: The STD Consequences of Adolescent Virginity Pledges," *Journal of Adolescent Health* 36 (2005): 271–278; Peter Bearman and Hannah Brückner, "Promising the Future: Virginity Pledges and First Intercourse," *American Journal of Sociology* 106 (2001): 859–912.

75 Perhaps some fundamentalist parents would prefer that their teenage daughter bear the "natural" risk of her sexual activity, pregnancy. They might then prefer that she not receive information about contraceptive options. However, they do not have the right to deprive their daughter of this information, unless they have a right to put her at high risk of serious and long-lasting consequences. This kind of right to control her future is, I think, rather close to a property right in her person, something that political liberals such as Ebels-Duggan claim to deny.
76 Burtt, "Comprehensive Educations," 194–5.
77 *Chamberlain*, para 66.
78 "In order to enact political liberalism so conceived, we need to attend to what our fellow citizens actually think, and what they can actually endorse from their own point of view. We need to do the hard work of conversation and co-deliberation. We cannot generate the content of public reason in our offices in the philosophy department. We can only generate it together." Ebels-Duggan, "Moral Education," 41.
79 Callan, *Creating Citizens*, 158–61. Callan sees this argument in the work of Paul Vitz. See Paul Vitz, *Censorship: Evidence of Bias in Our Children's Textbooks* (Ann Arbor: Servant Books, 1986).
80 Callan, *Creating Citizens*, 238, note 10.
81 Ebels-Duggan, "Moral Education," 48.
82 Ibid., 49.
83 Ibid., 49–50.
84 Ibid., 50.
85 Ibid., 50 and 54.
86 Nucci and Powers, "Social and Cognitive Domain Theory," 122–6.
87 Brighouse and Swift, *Family Values*, 210. They do not say that the relevant children should carry the full load of representing their religion or culture.
88 Mitja Sardoc, "Citizenship, Diversity and Education: An Egalitarian Pluralist Approach." Ph.D. dissertation, University of London, 2012): 123–6.
89 Ibid.
90 "Program—Elementary Level: Focus of the Competency," accessed May 25, 2016, http://www.education.gouv.qc.ca/en/programme-ethique-et-culture-religieuse/program-elementary-level/competency-1-reflects-on-ethical-questions/
91 Alisa Kessel, "Moving beyond *Mozert*: Toward a Theory of Democratic Education," *Educational Philosophy and Theory* 47 (2015): 1419–1434.

Bibliography

Barry, Brian. "Review: John Rawls and the Search for Stability." Ethics 105 (1995): 874–915.
Bates, Stephen. *Battleground: One Mother's Crusade, The Religious Right, and the Struggle for Control of our Classrooms*. New York: Poseidon Press, 1993.
Bearman, Peter and Hannah Brückner. "Promising the Future: Virginity Pledges and First Intercourse." *American Journal of Sociology* 106 (2001): 859–912.
Brennan, Samantha and Colin Macleod. "Fundamentally Incompetent: Homophobia, Religion, and the Right to Parent" (this volume).
Brighouse, Harry. *School Choice and Social Justice*. Oxford: Oxford University Press, 2000.
Brighouse, Harry and Adam Swift. "Family Values and School Policy," in *Education, Justice and Democracy*, edited by Danielle Allen and Robert Reich, 199–220. Chicago: University of Chicago Press, 2013.
Brighouse, Harry and Adam Swift. *Family Values: The Ethics of Parent-Child Relationships*. Princeton: Princeton University Press, 2014.

Brückner, Hannah and Peter Bearman. "After the Promise: The STD Consequences of Adolescent Virginity Pledges." *Journal of Adolescent Health* 36 (2005): 271–278.

Burtt, Shelly. "Religious Parents, Secular Schools: A Liberal Defense of an Illiberal Education." *Review of Politics* 56 (1994): 51–70.

———. "Comprehensive Educations and the Liberal Understanding of Autonomy," in *Education and Citizenship in Liberal Democratic Societies: Teaching for Cosmopolitan Values and Collectives Identities*, edited by Kevin McDonough and Walter Feinberg, 202–203. Oxford, 2003.

Callan, Eamonn. *Creating Citizens: Political Education and Liberal Democracy.* Oxford: Oxford University Press, 1997.

Cere, Daniel and Douglas Farrow (eds). *Divorcing Marriage: Unveiling the Dangers in Canada's New Social Experiment.* Montreal and Kingston: McGill-Queen's University Press, 2004.

Chamberlain v. Surrey School District No. 36 [2002] 4 S.C.R. 710, 2002 SCC 86 (Can.).

Clayton, Matthew. *Justice and Legitimacy in Upbringing.* Oxford: Oxford University Press, 2006.

Dworkin, Gerald. *The Theory and Practice of Autonomy.* Cambridge: Cambridge University Press, 1988.

Ebels-Duggan, Kyla. "Moral Education in the Liberal State." *Journal of Practical Ethics* 1 (2013): 34–63.

Ethics and Religious Culture Program. "Program—Elementary Level: Focus of the Competency." Accessed May 25, 2016. http://www.education.gouv.qc.ca/en/ programme- ethique-et-culture-religieuse/program-elementary-level/competency-1-reflects-on-ethical- questions/

Galston, William. *Liberal Purposes: Goods, Virtues, and Diversity in the Liberal State.* Cambridge: Cambridge University Press, 1991.

———. *Liberal Pluralism: The Implications of Value Pluralism for Political Theory and Practice.* Cambridge: Cambridge University Press, 2002.

Gutmann, Amy. "Civic Education and Social Diversity." *Ethics* 105 (1995): 557–579.

Hájek, Alan. "Pascal's Wager," in *The Stanford Encyclopedia of Philosophy*, edited by Edward N. Zalta. Stanford: The Metaphysics Research Lab, Summer 2011 Edition. URL = <http://plato.stanford.edu/archives/win2012/entries/pascal-wager/>.

Igrasa, Susan M., M. Marjorie Macieirab, Elaine Murphy and Rebecka Lundgren. "Investing in Very Young Adolescents' Sexual and Reproductive Health." *Global Public Health: An International Journal for Research, Policy and Practice Global Public Health* 9 (2014): 555–569.

Kessel, Alisa. "Moving Beyond *Mozert*: Toward a Theory of Democratic Education." *Educational Philosophy and Theory* 47 (2015): 1419–1434.

Kohler, Pamela K., E. Manhart Lisa and William E. Lafferty. "Abstinence-Only and Comprehensive Sex Education and the Initiation of Sexual Activity and Teen Pregnancy." *Journal of Adolescent Health* 42 (2008): 344–351.

Kymlicka, Will. *Liberalism, Community and Culture.* Oxford: Oxford University Press, 1989.

Macedo, Stephen. "Liberal Civic Education and Religious Fundamentalism: The Case of God v. John Rawls?" *Ethics* 105 (1995): 468–496.

McCabe, David. *Modus Vivendi Liberalism: Theory and Practice.* Cambridge: Cambridge University Press, 2010.

Mozert v. Hawkins County Board of Education 827 F.2d 1058 (6th Cir. 1987), cert. denied, 484 U.S. 1066 (1988).

Nucci, Larry and Deborah W. Powers. "Social and Cognitive Domain Theory and Moral Education," in *Handbook of Moral and Character Education 2nd edition*, edited by Larry Nucci, Darcia Narvaez and Tobias Krettenauer, 121–139. New York: Routledge, 2014.

"Program—Elementary Level: Focus of the Competency," Accessed May 25, 2016, http://www.education.gouv.qc.ca/en/programme-ethique-et-culture-religieuse/program- elementary-level/competency-1-reflects-on-ethical-questions/

Ramsay, Marc. "The Burdens of Judgment and Fallibilism." *Contemporary Political Theory* 6 (2007): 150–174.

———. "Political Liberalism and Moral Education: Reflections on *Mozert v. Hawkins*," in *Taking Responsibility for Children*, edited by Samantha Brennan and Robert Noggle, 113–138. Waterloo: Wilfrid Laurier University Press, 2007.

Rawls, John. *Political Liberalism*. New York: Columbia University Press, 1993.

Raz, Joseph. *The Morality of Freedom*. Oxford: Oxford University Press, 1986.

Raz, Joseph. "Facing Diversity: The Case of Epistemic Abstinence." *Philosophy and Public Affairs* 19 (1990): 3–46.

Sardoc, Mitja. "Citizenship, Diversity and Education: An Egalitarian Pluralist Approach." Ph.D. dissertation, University of London, 2012.

S.L. v. Commission scolaire des Chênes 2012 SCC 7, [2012] 1 S.C.R. 235 (Can.).

Stolzenberg, Nomi Maya. " 'He Drew a Circle That Shut Me Out': Assimilation, Indoctrination, and the Paradox of a Liberal Education." *Harvard Law Review* 106 (1993): 581–667.

Swift, Adam. *Family Values: The Ethics of Parent-Child* Relationships. Princeton: Princeton University Press, 2014.

Tomasi, John. *Liberalism Beyond Justice: Citizens, Society, and the Boundaries of Political Theory*. Princeton: Princeton University Press, 2001.

Vitz, Paul. *Censorship: Evidence of Bias in Our Children's Textbooks*. Ann Arbor: Servant Books, 1986.

Wenar, Leif. "Political Liberalism: An Internal Critique." *Ethics* 106 (1995): 32–62.

Wisconsin v. Yoder 406 U.S. 205 (1972).

9 An Interest, Not a Project

Hegel on Ethical Love and Procreation[*]

Ashli Anda

Contemporary philosophical discussions of procreation and the family rarely mention Hegel or Hegelian thought. This is surprising, inasmuch as in his *Philosophy of Right*, Hegel develops a comprehensive position on what continue to be fundamental issues regarding the family, e.g. why we should have children, what we owe them, and what children are entitled to.[1] However, because Hegel's position is situated within his larger, and somewhat obscure, political philosophy, how (if at all) his position intersects with contemporary philosophical discussions of procreation and the family proves difficult to decipher.

The purposes of this article are to situate Hegel's thought in relation to contemporary philosophical discussions of procreation and the family and to argue that Hegel offers an intriguing resolution to a conflict between the interests of parents and children regarding procreation. On the one hand, contemporary liberal thought often represents procreation and parenthood as discretionary personal projects oriented around such goals as creating and maintaining special loving relationships between parents and children.[2] Conversely, family units are made up of future societal and political participants whom (it is hoped) will become autonomous, law-abiding, politically involved members of society. Hence, while parents aim to create a special love between themselves and their children, they also have this incredibly weighty responsibility of preparing them for a life independent of them. These two aims are not in tension at a practical level, since there is no obvious reason why children cannot be raised to be autonomous, etc., in the context of a special loving relationship with their parents. However, these aims suggest contrasting ethical rationales for procreation and parenthood. The former suggest that procreation and parenthood are justified in a parent-centered way, in terms of their individual projects or commitments. The latter suggest that procreation and parenthood derive their justification from the needs of children (and perhaps from the needs of the communities of which children will eventually be members).

Hegel's positions on procreation and the family imply a novel way to synthesize these two justifications. The key to this synthesis is Hegel's thesis that children have a crucial role in love and marriage precisely because they come into being as the object of their parents' love. Parents can only fully objectify their love, and attain a more substantial existence as a family unit, through procreation. However, this objectification can only be achieved if parents recognize that children have a right to have their needs fulfilled. Hence, parents have a right for their love to be objectified, and an ensuing right to procreate and establish a family, if and only if the rights of their children are maintained and their interests fulfilled. According to Hegel then, we are expected to raise children to become autonomous, law-abiding, politically involved members of society, and we err if that is not the aim of our procreating and parenting. Hegel's model of the family is such that parents fulfill their ethical interest through love and specifically through loving their children. This model acknowledges a special intimacy between parent and child but denies that this interest grounds either their right to procreate or their obligations *qua* parents. So by identifying a *particular sort* of parental interest in procreation that does not undermine or neglect the rights and interests of children, Hegel contributes to our understanding of what parents owe their children and how that responsibility is not incompatible or in tension with children's rights to being brought up properly.

In the first section, I discuss Hegel's account of love and marriage, showing that the interest to procreate is an ethically substantial interest to create an object of love rather than an interest in child-rearing as a way to form a special relationship. In the second section, I map out Hegel's comments on the role of children and their right to be brought up in a certain way that proves they are more than just mere means to fulfilling their parents' interest. I argue that, according to Hegel, parents' ethical interest in procreation is only justified if the right of children to have their needs fulfilled is realized. I conclude by articulating some of the advantages of the Hegelian model of the family and procreation, as well as answering several objections.

I. If we want to justify the creation of a family, then we first need to briefly identify how Hegel understands the family.

Hegel's account of the family is that it is an ethically substantial unity rather than a personal project for the satisfaction of its members' needs or desires. What makes it ethically substantial is that its roles and responsibilities are precise and the family is motivated toward fulfilling an end that transcends the ends of the individual family members. When Hegel talks about *becoming ethical* or the *ethical life*, he is talking about the disappearance of the individual's will that strives to exist for itself and the new recognition that its existence is continued and actualized by the universal (PR § 152). An extremely simplified example that approximates what he is talking about is found in child development. Children go through a destructive phase to test their boundaries, how much control they have over their belongings and relationship with their caretakers, and essentially test whether the world bends according to their will. However, part of the maturational process requires a healthy detachment by the caretakers to promote independence in the child and also experiences of compromising with others to transition him out of the belief that he is leader of the world and into the understanding that he is one member of a norm-guided community.[3] So when we talk about an ethically substantial interest in forming the family—in procreation—we are talking about procreating for reasons beyond satisfying needs or desires restricted to particular individuals. An ethically substantial interest in procreation requires prospective parents to see themselves as part of a greater society; and our children must become proactive participants in that society or else our parenting fails. Last, this ethically substantial interest, as the previous claim already suggests, includes (and requires) both the parents' and the children's interests being fulfilled.

How is this ethically substantial interest in becoming a parent different from the view that treats procreation as a project adults carry out and invest in for various reasons? Procreation and the family viewed as a project generally has the good life, or happiness, as part of its goal (and in some cases, that may be the entire goal). One might believe that having a child and bonding with them will add significant meaning to their life. It is important to keep in mind that the project view makes procreation a *personal* project and as *my* project, I have a right to go about it in a way that I see fit. In some ways this liberty is unproblematic. Issues arise, however, if we think our rights over our children are thereby unlimited and unconditional. While I can definitely exercise a right to dress my newborn in cute, duck onesies every day until he is six months old, for example, I probably cannot make that same choice for him when he is 18 years old. At some point we have to question whether our methods for creating our own meaning and happiness are protecting and fulfilling our children's interests and rights. The project view, for Hegel, would not have a definite way of meeting the requirements for willing the universal because it seems that it could become too constrained by particular interests and affairs. To ground a Hegelian justification of procreation by appealing to an ethically substantial interest, we will instead turn to Hegel's discussion of marriage.

Once entered into, Hegel claims, marriage generates an ethical duty (PR § 162).[4] Marriage marks the end of individual existence because reconciliation with an other takes place. As an *ethical* relationship, Hegel understands marriage as a union of two people who bear legal rights and responsibilities as well as something that transcends individual, particular interests and goes on to contribute to a political community. Hegel says that it is unacceptable to talk about love as something that is temporary or fickle " . . . because love, as a feeling [*Empfindung*], is open in all respects to contingency, and this is a shape which the ethical may not assume. Marriage should therefore be defined more precisely as rightfully ethical [*rechtlich sittliche*] love . . ." (PR § 161a).

Hegel does not talk about the family primarily as a unit made up of individuals. Rather, it is a unit of members that have a substantial shared existence; the family is like one being rather than three, four, or five members. This is our first major clue about how Hegel can conceive of the interest in procreating; this interest must fulfill something for all members of the family unit without separating them! Here, Hegel subtly leads us toward the correct understanding of what an ethically substantial interest in procreation is: an interest that transcends individual desire and serves to promote unity and security.

In describing procreation as an ethically substantial interest, Hegel may seem to focus exclusively on one perspective in the parent–child relationship— the parents' perspective. It may seem like the child's interests and needs are secondary to his primary purpose, to unite the family into a single shared existence. When do his rights or interests kick in? This concern is less pressing if we understand that a prospective parent's ethical interest in procreation is not at odds with children's rights to be well-cared for because Hegel sees children as having at least one fundamental right.

II. Hegel insists that children have a right to a proper upbringing. In an early statement we can see Hegel highlighting the fairly obvious and uncontroversial idea that children are marked by their potential being and that in order to achieve fuller existence, they will have to progress in some way.

> The child is *in itself* a human being; it has reason only *in itself*, it is only the potentiality of reason and freedom, and is therefore free only in accordance with its concept. Now what exists as yet only in itself does not exist in its actuality. The human being who is rational *in himself* must work through the process of self-production both by going out of himself and by educating himself inwardly, in order that he may also become rational *for himself*.
>
> (PR § 10a)

With this, we see that while a child enters and completes a family unit that has substantial existence, the child starts the process all over again. They have a kind of independence that will be resolved once they have gone through training to become a rational, adult member of civil society. Before training or education, though, children have to rely on their parents. Hegel notes, ". . . children have no moral will and allow themselves to be determined by their parents; but the cultivated [*gebildete*] and inwardly developing human being wills that he should himself be present in everything he does" (PR § 107a). There is a point when children have a desire to develop.[5] It is a fairly typical yearning to grow up except for that 'growing up' in Hegel's world does not involve things like seeing a PG-13 movie or spending time with friends without a chaperone. The development in question is the improvement of the will that results in an individual becoming a participating member of a political, ethical society.

A child can reasonably expect that this improvement or growth will happen and they have an innate right to be brought up in this specific way. But Hegel observes that this improvement or growth is not natural or inevitable. "Human beings do not arrive by instinct at what they are destined to become; on the contrary, they must attain this by their own efforts. This is the basis of the child's rights to it upbringing" (PR § 174a). As children, we do not and cannot foresee what it is that we are supposed to become and the only way to find out is to work through our lives. However, we generally do not expect that a child will learn about who he is to become with no guidance; the child is entitled to the guidance that comes with being properly brought up to become full-fledged members of the ethical and political community. Simply put, what grounds a child's right to a certain upbringing is that they cannot raise themselves; they have no resources, but more importantly, a child will thrive when they are loved by their parents.

Parents must make it possible for children to thrive. Hegel makes clear what he thinks parents owe their children: "Children have a right to be *brought up* and *supported* at the expense of the family" (PR § 174). Financial resources are obviously important, but Hegel adds that the child ". . . must have lived with his parents in a circle of love and trust . . ." (PR § 175a). Hegel says that children must be loved and must trust their parents to care for and love them. I remember clearly that after being punished as a child, my mom would say something like, "I did this for your own good and I still love you." I imagine that this is exactly what parents should be doing on Hegel's account: lovingly enforcing rules. The point is for children to become independent, rational adults, and they are entitled to that because Hegel has attributed to them the innate right to be properly cared for.

In order to highlight more explicitly that children are not merely used for their parents' needs, I will briefly revisit two of the most important points of his discussion of children: 1) children are loved by their parents, and 2) children do not belong to their parents because their capacity to be rational individuals must come to fruition. It is telling that in the very first section of *The Upbringing of Children and the Dissolution of the Family*, Hegel mentions that the unity brought about by children is loved by the parents "as their love" (PR § 173). The child is the physical realization, or the object, of the love between his parents so he will naturally be the object that their love is constantly directed at. Even though the child becomes the realized object of his parents' love, he is not bound to them as a possession. This leads to the second point that children are free "*in themselves*" (PR § 175). If they are free in themselves even as children, and they must go on to become independent adults, then it is wrong to believe that they would be used solely to fulfill their parents' need for substantial unity. While they objectify their parents' love, they receive love and a good upbringing which results in their attainment of a fuller sense of existence. And in fact, they have a right to this.

Thus far, I have argued that a Hegelian justification of procreation is grounded in an ethically substantial interest, namely, the interest in a shared substantial existence that will contribute to the state or the community. It has also been established that children have an interest in and a right to a good upbringing, which includes the right to be loved; if children's needs are met by their parents, then they will benefit from that relationship and they do not have to be seen as merely satisfying their parents' interests. The benefit of interpreting Hegel in this way is significant. The ethical interest in parenting does not necessarily depend on a hypothetical relationship between the parent and their child. We can have many hopes and desires for what our relationship with our child might be like but it is difficult to ensure that the relationship will be positively fulfilling. An oversimplified, but not inaccurate, summary of Hegel's ideas on parenting and children is as follows: have children to create objects of love, take care of them, educate them, and love them, which, by doing so, will protect their right to become independent adults who will participate in society.

III. Hegel's model is not free of complications, especially if the working context is supposed to be contemporary, liberal society. Before addressing these complications, let us first describe some advantageous features of the Hegelian model.

The first advantage is that the parent interest–child interest conflict is subverted by the appeal to an ethical interest of procreation. Hegel says that children are not yet totally free because they need to be trained and educated to become independent and self-sufficient. Knowing that goal should promote the protection of the interests of children over granting unlimited rights to parents over their children. On the Hegelian account, parents do not have an unlimited right to raise their children in any way they please. They must do everything to ensure the child becomes a certain type of adult. Ultimately, the limitation of rights on the parent's part furthers the liberation of their children in the future. But what about parent's interest? Recall that the ethically substantial interest in procreating establishes that parental interests are satisfied. My interest in creating an object at which all of my love will be directed is automatically satisfied, as is my need for the greater, shared existence that is essential to familial love and unity.

The second advantage is that the Hegelian model acknowledges that procreation and the family are inherently social phenomena. The Hegelian model brings the community's interests in procreation and in how children are raised to the forefront of the procreative ethics conversation. One problem with treating the community as an afterthought when talking about family affairs is that the family can be mistakenly perceived as totally isolated from the larger community, which impairs our ability to analyze procreation and the family in relation to societal needs or interests. The isolated family is unproblematic if we live on an island—but a good many of us do not. Hegel sets up the family as a necessary contributor to social progress and that is also how contemporary liberals characterize the family. Presumably, these independent, self-sufficient people we raise have those qualities for specific reasons. For both Hegel and contemporary liberals, those qualities are conducive to a society made up of capable, active participants in the political, social, and religious aspects of life. However, if there is a systematic approach to create a society like this, then we must be able to address other social issues like education and justice (the tool used to create the society and the one used to maintain it), among others. Any account of the ethics of procreation and the family should address the community because we and our children make up the community and how we raise them will affect it.

A third advantage is that the Hegelian model elegantly links the ethics of procreation and the ethics of parenting. For the same ethical interest that justifies procreation provides a guide for how to parent. If my interest in procreation is only justified when I actually preserve and meet the interests and needs of my child, then my interest in parenting is only justified when I actually do a good job of parenting. This justification allows for and makes necessary the kind of independence that Hegel and now many contemporary liberals want for their children. We want to educate our children, provide for them, and love them but we want to do those things believing that they will in fact become independent adults. On Hegel's model, our goals for our children would likely be goals they would come to realize on their own and would be able to carry out after their successful upbringing. Hegel's explanation of how the family dissolves reveals something that further supports this interpretation. Hegel says, "The ethical dissolution of the family consists in the fact that the children are brought up to become free personalities . . ." (PR § 177). The family dissolves because children have been successfully raised to be independent and self-sufficient adults who will go on to create a society of even greater existence.

Now let us consider some worries about the Hegelian model, in particular, worries that are likely to be pressed by contemporary liberals.

One worry about justifying procreation by appealing to the notion of an ethically substantial interest is that other types of interests are excluded. What if I do want to benefit from a special relationship with a child or what if I have always imagined myself being a parent? The interest or motivation expressed by these questions shows that I—as an individual—have an interest in carrying out something because it matters to me. Because Hegel sets up the family (and then dissolves it) as just a necessary step in a political process, it sounds like I have to be willing to accept that my fulfillment, or private interests, will take a back seat to the successful operation of society. And if that is the case, can I be committed to procreating and being a *good* parent for reasons other than that as a member of the community I am obligated to be one?

Early on in *Philosophy of Right*, Hegel acknowledges particularity in a way that can be helpful in responding to the above-mentioned concern. "The right of individuals to their *particularity* is likewise contained in ethical substantiality, for particularity is the mode of outward appearance in which the ethical exists." (PR § 154) He later elaborates on this line of thought.

> Particular interests should certainly not be set aside, let alone suppressed; on the contrary, they should be harmonized with the universal,

so that both they themselves and the universals are preserved. The individual, whose duties give him the status of a subject [*Unertan*], finds that, in fulfilling his duties as a citizen, he gains protection for his person and property, consideration for his particular welfare, satisfaction of his substantial essence, and the consciousness and self-awareness of being a member of a whole.

(PR § 261)

In typical Hegelian fashion, it turns out that there is some sort of reciprocity taking place. When I am a member of the community and fulfill my duties, my private interests are secured. I very well could hold the beliefs that I want to be a parent because I have always desired to be one or that I think having children would make me happy. Hegel would not say that families should be joyless or loveless. Families should be loving and he says that an environment of love and trust will positively affect a child's development (PR § 175a). However, those desires and feelings cannot exist merely as individual desires—as if the family lives on a deserted island and affects no one else.

Prospective parents, and later the family, can have private interests. But the family unit cannot dismiss or ignore its place in society.

Individuals, as citizens of this state, are *private persons* who have their own interest as their end. Since this end is mediated through the universal, which thus appears to the individuals as a *means*, they can attain their end only in so far as they themselves determine their knowledge, volition, and action in a universal way and make themselves *links* in the chain of this *continuum* [*Zusammenhang*].

(PR § 187)

He goes on to explain that proper education or training will eliminate *natural simplicity*, which results in our liberation from immediacy and finally connects us with universality (PR § 187). It may continue to sound like private interests take a back seat to public ones. However, when we learn to universalize our thoughts and actions, we still end up getting what we want and need from society. We are liberated from self-interest and immediacy and finally begin to see what spiritual, universal life is like.

Another objection that contemporary liberals may have to the Hegelian model of procreation and the family is that Hegel does not place same-sex couples with children in his system.[6] He does not explicitly address who may or may not be parents but there are at least two measures by which we can address this as a deficiency of the view. First, we might offer a radical and charitable interpretation of Hegel's view of the partners in a relationship to better suit the variety of families that make up contemporary liberal society. He says that marriage is the union of two consenting individuals, who will be monogamous, and will accept self-limitation in exchange for a shared substantial existence. Those qualifications can certainly be (and often are) met by same-sex spouses.

A second option may be to use Hegel's own tools to transform his view such that it is appropriate for contemporary life: recognition and the importance of social integration. If we understand Hegel's theory of recognition as one that avoids alienation of self-consciousnesses, for example, then the exclusion of families that do not conform to heteronormative standards shows that recognition theory fails because not all people can achieve it. But Hegel does not want that and it is difficult to imagine how he could create a comprehensive system of deciding who deserves recognition and who does not even if he was inclined to limit recognition. This interpretation, like the one above, is quite charitable given Hegel's religious commitments. However, social change could very well bring about recognition for various family structures. Contemporary policy issues certainly reflect tensions between the political and religious spheres of life but despite that, it seems that the real foundation for recognition theory is personal identity and the need for it to be reconciled with others. If it is true that recognition theory is more about personal identity than biological sex differences, for example, then an LGBT person with an ethically substantial interest in family formation should receive recognition. Failure to recognize their identity as a self-consciousness would be a failure to meet Hegel's requirement for social life.

Finally, what are we supposed to say to the married couples who choose to be childless? Do they have a duty to procreate just because they are married? I think the answer must be no. They do not have a duty to procreate. First off, it is important to keep in mind the time in which Hegel wrote *Philosophy of Right* compared to contemporary life. One contemporary issue is whether we face an overpopulation crisis—an issue Hegel would not have had to address at the time. However, if it truly is the case that we have any obligations to our community, then perhaps some of us must refrain from having children because we need to preserve our resources. Subsequently, the very justification for procreation could present us with a reason not to procreate. Remember that the interest in procreation is only justified if the child is actually well taken care of and has all of his rights and interests secured. The flipside of that is that if I will not meet my child's interests or protect their rights, then I cannot and must not procreate.

IV. In conclusion, I have shown that Hegel's model of procreation and the family in *Philosophy of Right* deserves a greater place in contemporary ethical debates on those subjects. While his comments are few, what he does say is enough to ground a distinct account of interests in procreation that combines the preservation and fulfillment of both parents' individual interests and children's interests and rights. While his comments are few, what he does say is enough to ground a distinct account of interests in procreation that combines the preservation and fulfillment of both parents' individual interests and children's interests and rights. This interpretation of Hegel on the family not only alleviates possible tensions between interests of parents and children by requiring each of their fulfillment but also provides a robust justification for procreation that takes into account the community's interest in having its members be made up of well-raised citizens.

Notes

* I am indebted to my mentor, Michael Cholbi, not only for suggesting writing this piece but especially for his consistently patient and supportive presence during this writing process (and throughout my years as his student). I am also immensely grateful to him and to Jaime Ahlberg for their creation of a procreative ethics workshop that made this opportunity possible.
1 G.W.F. Hegel, *Elements of the Philosophy of Right*. Ed. Allen W. Wood. (Cambridge: Cambridge University Press, 1991).
2 Harry Brighouse, and Adam Swift, "Parents' Rights and the Value of the Family," *Ethics* 117 (2006): 80–108.
3 This is not a perfect example but it does highlight the transition from 'me'-based living to 'we'-based living that is what Hegel seems to be after.
4 This is not to be confused with the idea that marriage itself is an obligation, such that it would be forced if not entered into willingly. Hegel wants to preserve the idea that marriage is a union entered by two consenting people and says "there can be no compulsion to marry." (PR § 176)
5 Hegel says that the child will have a "desire to grow up" and they will develop through education (PR § 175).
6 These comments must be limited and brief not only due to the lack of focus on them by Hegel himself but also to avoid importing too much into Hegel's philosophy. However, they must be addressed in some capacity given that what we are dealing with is a contemporary application of Hegelian philosophy and ours is a society made up of families that defy the heteronormative standards of Hegel's day.

10 Parenthood and Personally Transformative Experiences

Michael W. Austin

Human beings face numerous potentially transformative experiences over the course of their lives. Decisions about education, moral values, religious belief and practice (or lack thereof), marriage, whether or not to have a child, and many other choices we face can be personally transformative as they lead us to undergo new experiences that have a deep impact on our preferences and identities. Other transformative experiences are not chosen, but happen to us, such as the death of a loved one or being diagnosed with a terminal disease. Personally transformative experiences (PTE's) are often among the most significant experiences that we have over the course of our lives, and the decisions we make related to such experiences are therefore also significant.

In light of this, in what follows I argue that parents have particular obligations to their children related to PTE's. I first provide a brief sketch of the conception of parenthood that I favor, which undergirds the responsibilities parents have to their children related to such experiences. I then consider the nature of PTE's, and distinguish several different types of such experiences. While parents have many obligations towards their children, in this paper I argue that there are important parental obligations related to PTE's and decisions that are connected to them. Good parents are obligated to prepare their children for the PTE's that they will face by seeking to cultivate their cognitive abilities, the virtue of open-mindedness, and the quality of resilience. Fulfilling these obligations not only prepares children for PTE's, but will benefit them in other aspects of life as well. Finally, I consider some implications of this for parental choice regarding youth sports and education.

This essay is motivated by my belief that some moral philosophy should be *intensely practical*, and it is in that spirit that the following is offered. Theory is important, and in this paper I assume a particular theoretical framework of parental rights and obligations. However, my primary aim is not to argue at a theoretical level about what justifies parental rights or obligations. My primary aim is to discuss a particular feature of human life—personally transformative experiences—that parents often do not attend to as parents, and consider some practical obligations they have related to the PTE's their children may face over the course of their lives.

212 Michael W. Austin

Parents as Stewards

While there are many ways of acquiring parental rights and obligations, in what follows I assume that parents should see themselves as stewards of their children.[1] A steward is a caretaker of something that she does not own. For example, I may care for my neighbor's dogs while she is out of town, acting as a steward on her behalf by making sure they have adequate food, water, shelter, and attention. There are many ways in which parents are stewards of their children. Parents *qua* stewards take the welfare and flourishing of their children to be one of their primary life aims. They make decisions that take the current and future interests of their children into account. While the interests of children need not always trump the interests of the parent, they will carry more *prima facie* weight on the stewardship conception of parenthood. Parents, as stewards, hold the child's life in trust, until they transfer responsibility and control of the child's life to the adult that the child becomes, though the process will ideally be gradual relative to the age and maturity of the child. Parents also act as stewards on behalf of society, which entrusts the care of particular children to them. Society has a clear interest in good parenting, insofar as children and the adults they become impact others both positively and negatively. As she makes parenting decisions, a parent acting as a steward will be mindful of the well-being of the child and of the adult the child will become. She will also be concerned with the child's potential impact on society as she makes such decisions. In light of these concerns, parents as stewards have good reason to prepare their child for the PTE's that they will likely undergo. In the next section, I consider the nature of PTE's.

The Nature of Personally Transformative Experiences

PTE's can change a person in a variety of ways. Such experiences may involve a radical change in one's perspective.[2] PTE's can impact a person's moral and intellectual character, including her beliefs, values, preferences, and dispositions. As Paul describes it, a PTE "changes you enough to substantially change your point of view, thus substantially revising your core preferences or revising how you experience being yourself."[3] This type of experience may change your personal preferences, aspects of your personality, character, and self-concept. When you undergo such an experience, you acquire new knowledge and you are changed. It seems to me that such experiences come in degrees. Some PTE's radically change our self-concept and worldview, while others impact us in less drastic but still transformative ways.

There are several important distinctions that can be made with respect to the different types of PTE's, as well as aspects of a particular PTE. Because of this, I develop a typology of PTE's before considering their relevance for the aims and practice of parenthood. The parent as a good steward ought to be sensitive to the type of PTE that her child is undergoing or will likely undergo, because she will then be better able to prepare the child for the PTE and its potential consequences. That is, she will be better able to fulfill the particular parental obligations that are in some way related to PTE's. This is one important reason that the following taxonomy of PTE's is relevant to being a good parent.

There are many different PTE's that one may encounter or choose to undergo. Consider one paradigm case of such an experience, the experience of becoming a parent:

> Parents . . . love to talk about how little they knew before becoming a parent. Perhaps they knew that they'd cradle their newborn in their arms, they'd feel her soft skin and smell a distinctive baby smell—and more generally, that they'd love her unselfishly, and that they'd have many sleepless nights with her—but they didn't know what it would be like to hold and love their very own baby, or to undergo these experiences as a parent, with all the love and concern the attachment to one's child brings, or how dramatically their preferences about their lives would change.[4]

Parenthood is a multifaceted and temporally extended PTE. When we consider this particular PTE, some distinctions emerge that are relevant to how we understand PTE's in general. Parenthood can be chosen or unchosen (though for those with the means and access to abortion services, it is ultimately chosen). A person can choose to undergo some PTE's, while some of these experiences happen to her. An *intentional PTE* is one that the agent chooses, via an exercise of the will. In addition to parenthood, the choice of a career, a spouse, a certain type of education, or a particular religious faith are potential examples of intentional PTE's.

An *unintentional PTE* is an experience that happens to one, in some sense. Some cases of parenthood may be unintentional. A woman may unintentionally conceive, and not have access to abortion services. Or a man's brother may die, and he feels it is his responsibility to be a parent to his brother's child. He does not intend to take on this role, but the contingencies of life in some sense throw him into it, via his relationship with his sibling. Other examples of unintentional PTE's include the death of a friend, having cancer, or winning the lottery.[5]

Parenthood can also be a *pleasant PTE* and an *unpleasant PTE* with respect to the emotions it produces. After a child is born, parents may enjoy the pleasant experiences alluded to above, and take great pleasure in "holding and loving their very own baby." There will also be unpleasant experiences, such as sleepless nights and the sometimes abrasive teenage quest for independence.

Parenthood can have a positive or negative in impact on the intellectual and moral virtue of parents, including their beliefs, desires, preferences, and dispositions. Parenthood can be an *areteic PTE*, but it can also be a *kakianic*

PTE. That is, it can be a virtue-producing or strengthening experience, or a vice-producing or strengthening experience.[6] It can, like at least some other PTE's, yield both virtue and vice, depending upon our experiences and choices. A parent may develop compassion via her relationship with her child, but at the same time she could develop the vice of impatience in certain situations that she finds especially trying. For example, when her child is injured she exemplifies the virtue of compassion, suffering with her child in some sense and helping to alleviate the pain. But when the child struggles against the restraints as she tries to secure her in a car seat, impatience may arise.

In summary, a particular PTE can be classified employing one or more of the following categories:

1   *Intentional*: directly and voluntarily chosen by the agent; it is something that she brings about.
2   *Unintentional*: not chosen by the agent; it is something that happens to her.
3   *Pleasant*: yields enjoyable mental states in the agent.
4   *Unpleasant*: yields painful mental states in the agent.
5   *Areteic*: produces or strengthens a particular moral virtue or set of virtues.
6   *Kakianic*: produces or strengthens a particular moral vice or set of vices.

The Problem of Transformative Experiences for Parenthood

The likelihood that children will have to make decisions concerning PTE's as well as undergo a variety of such experiences poses a problem for parents, namely, how to prepare them to do so in ways that will contribute to their flourishing. Camus describes how such an experience can have drastically negative effects on an individual. In *The Myth of Sisyphus*, Camus discusses suicide, and the fundamental question of whether or not life is worth living. He describes a man who managed an apartment building and committed suicide five years after losing his daughter. Camus states that he was told by others that this tragic experience "undermined" the man, and claims that "A more exact word cannot be imagined."[7] The relevance of this for my present purposes is that children may undergo experiences with the potential to undermine them in this manner. A PTE may be so unpleasant that it could contribute to suicide, but it might undermine one's flourishing in a variety of less severe but still significant ways. It might cause a form of moral despair, in which one gives up on the moral life. Or it could damage close personal relationships due to its psychological impact on one. Parents cannot prevent such tragedies. Such unintentional and unpleasant PTE's can have potentially deleterious consequences in one's life.

These realities are not pleasant for parents to consider. In the economically developed nations of the world we often seek to insulate ourselves and our children from such realities, but realities they are. And if we seek to be good stewards of our children, then we have good reasons for trying to prepare them for the different types of PTE's that they will face over the course of their lives. In light of this, parents have an obligation to prepare their children for these and other types of PTE's, if they are able to do so.

Next, then, I consider several moral obligations that are important for parents to try to fulfill in order to help their children deal with the different forms of PTE's that they may face. The particular obligations are in and of themselves fairly uncontroversial. In addition, there are other arguments and considerations that support the view that parents possess the particular obligations that I discuss. One of the primary aims of the next section, then, is to show how considerations related to PTE's provide further support for the claim that parents have the obligations detailed there. I take it that the content of the obligations I discuss in what follows is fairly uncontroversial. What is significant is that new arguments in support of those obligations emerge, resulting in additional reasons and a greater weight with respect to these obligations. Part of the value in this is that for someone who rejects any of the following responsibilities, there are now new arguments to consider. For the individual who already holds that parents have the following obligations *qua* parents, there are additional arguments in support of the existence of those obligations that can increase her justification for holding that parents have these obligations.

Solving the Problem

Given that human beings undergo a variety of PTE's over the course of their lives and also make decisions related to these experiences, as stewards of their children parents are obligated to prepare them for this. But what are the specific obligations of parents relative to PTE's?

First, it is worth noting that parents may be uniquely situated to help their children make good choices with respect to intentional PTE's. A parent may, in light of her own experiences and choices, qualify as a competent judge with respect to some PTE. Due to this she may have important information to share with her child that may be useful to the child as he considers a choice related to a PTE. Just as Mill's competent judges provide one with justification for believing that one pleasure is superior in quality relative to another pleasure,[8] a parent with the relevant background may provide a child with information that is relevant to choices connected to a PTE. In this way, some parents are uniquely situated to help their children by sharing insights, lessons, and other valuable information from their own experiences.

Second, it is important to note that I assume that the value of a PTE is dependent upon its content, including its *telos*. The mere experience itself does not necessarily have overall positive value. A child who becomes an active member of the Westboro Baptist Church or of the KKK will very likely be transformed by the experience. But this is a transformation that is intrinsically related to irrational and immoral perspectives and ways of life. As a kakianic PTE, it does not have positive value. I believe and here assume that the value of a PTE is connected with its correspondence to truth and morality.[9] The value is not in transformation as such, but in the content and *telos* of the PTE. If this assumption is true, then, parents should seek to equip their children with the skills needed for assessing such options according to reason, to consider, evaluate, and believe according to the evidence. This will rule out PTE's that involve racism, for example. Given that parents act as stewards on behalf of the society in which they live and rear their children, they have obligations to help their children avoid the choice of choosing to undergo a fatally flawed PTE, such as becoming an active member of the KKK.[10] And given that active membership in such a group is not conducive to individual human flourishing, parents as stewards of the adults their children will become have good reason to seek to fulfill this obligation.

Parents are obligated to some degree to help their children develop, physically, intellectually, and morally. This is an essential aspect of what it means for a parent to be a good steward. Given this, I now turn to a consideration of some particular obligations that parents have related to PTE's. After I discuss three such obligations, I will consider the practical implications of the foregoing discussion of PTE's and the following set of obligations in the areas of sport and education.

The first general moral responsibility that parents have in this context is

(R1): Parents are obligated to seek to cultivate the cognitive capacities that their children possess.

The common sense view is that intelligence—cognitive talents and giftedness—is a natural or innate trait. But there is research supporting the claim that gifted and talented students are actually such due to social and environmental factors.[11] In fact, according to Mark Vopat, there is an "overwhelming amount of research that shows that talent is not innate, but is a combination of *opportunity*, *encouragement*, and *deliberate practice*."[12] Even if this claim is too strong, and talent is innate to some degree, it is clear that this combination of opportunity, encouragement, and deliberate practice has a very significant impact on the cognitive development of children, and so still supports (R1).

But it appears that there is good evidence to support Vopat's claim. One study found that for individuals who were successful as adults in intellectually demanding fields such as mathematics and neurology, there was very little if any connection with their being identified at a young age as being someone with natural talent. Rather, their accomplishments were a result of environmental support, excellent teaching, and encouragement.[13] In fact, the absence of a correlation between identified natural talents and success in such fields has led many researchers to conclude that environmental factors explain this type of success, rather than the possession of innate talent. Training and practice are key factors, and these are often the result of the encouragement and support of parents. In addition, the support of parents (and teachers or coaches) can foster deliberate practice on the part of children. When children are encouraged to work hard in effective and sustained ways, this can lead to them achieving expertise and excellence. The explanation for such achievement, then, is not (primarily) natural or innate talent or genius, but other factors concerning which parents may play a key role in bringing about for their children.

The relevance of the foregoing with respect to parental stewardship and PTE's is that in order to equip children to avoid irrational and immoral PTE's, parents should focus on helping them develop their cognitive capacities and the intellectual virtues. This will make it more likely that they will not only reject such PTE's (e.g. the KKK), but also better deal with the difficult PTE's that they will encounter over the course of their lives (e.g. death of a loved one). That is, one set of reasons parents have for cultivating the cognitive capacities of their children is to help them avoid kakianic PTE's and deal with unpleasant PTE's in ways that support their flourishing. Parents should not simply assume that "my child is smart enough" or "strong enough" but rather they should help their child cultivate the capacities and character traits necessary for successfully navigating such experiences and decisions.

Development of these cognitive capacities can also help children capitalize on PTE's, both intentional and unintentional, for the sake of virtue formation. The intentions and responses of children can help a particular PTE or set of PTE's become areteic.[14]

Next, it will be useful to consider a particular intellectual virtue that is especially relevant for the avoidance of irrational and immoral PTE's, namely, open-mindedness. Parents, I argue, have a responsibility related to this trait.

(R2): Parents are obligated to seek to cultivate the intellectual virtue of open-mindedness in their children.

In their discussion of this trait, Christopher Peterson and Martin Seligman point out that what is referred to as open-mindedness (judgment, critical thinking) is present in nearly all virtue lists, both ancient and modern.[15] They are quick to clarify that open-mindedness is neither equivalent to nor does it entail indecisiveness, nihilism, or permissiveness. Rather, it is characterized by good thinking, arriving at conclusions thoughtfully, and examining and weighing the evidence for and against a belief. According to Peterson and Seligman, there are good reasons for considering this trait to be a virtue. First, it is fulfilling insofar as it yields feelings of satisfaction, leads to good decisions, and helps us develop a coherent worldview. It is also one important component of empathy, which is a significant and desirable trait. It does not diminish others, but rather it can elevate them if they are also sufficiently open-minded. It can undermine negative emotions that may arise when discussing controversial issues about which people are passionate. The opposites of open-mindedness—inflexibility, intolerance, prejudice, ethnocentrism, authoritarianism—are undesirable and such inflexible cognition is thought by many to lie behind many psychological disorders. More positively, open-mindedness is a distinct trait that is arguably an ingredient of other desirable traits like social intelligence, leadership, and prudence.

The intellectual virtue of open-mindedness will help its possessor resist the beliefs and practices intrinsic to and produced by immoral PTE's. Given the nature and functions of this trait as described above, it is clear that a child who develops it will be equipped to see the intellectual and moral flaws connected to such PTE's. With the foregoing in mind, there are good reasons for parents to seek to cultivate this trait in their children, and good reasons for thinking that they have a moral responsibility to do so.

Turning from immoral to traumatic PTE's, another character trait emerges as an important one for parents to seek to foster in their children. Marcus Arvan argues that one important implication of Paul's work on PTE's is that it is a corrective with respect to the moral education of children.[16] He argues, and in what follows I expand on his claim, that we should teach our children to become resilient. He also contends that resilience should be the focus of how we prepare our children to approach choices, rather than the dominant view of choosing based on one's personal preferences and values. Contemporary American culture does not value this trait, nor does it foster it in children during their formative years. Instead, according to Arvan, the focus has been on building self-esteem and insulating children from risk and failure. The results of these trends have been poor, and include narcissism, lower grades in school, decreased levels of empathy, and a lack of resilience, which is crucial given the difficulties that life can bring. Resilient people, however, are better able to dealt with PTE's.

In addition, resilience has been linked to several virtues, including open-mindedness.[17] Given this, parents who fulfill (R2) are also making progress in fulfilling another significant moral responsibility, to which we now turn.

(R3): Parents are obligated to seek to cultivate resilience in their children.

Resilience is an important trait for human beings to possess and exercise. It can be defined as "a relatively stable personality trait characterized by the ability to overcome, steer through, and bounce back from adversity."[18] This trait yields many positive benefits, including maintaining positive emotions when dealing with stress and experiencing positive outcomes when stressful events obtain. There is empirical support for (i) highly-resilient people more commonly have positive emotions; and (ii) people with low resilience have trouble regulating their negative emotions and are more reactive to daily stressful life events.[19]

A study that followed children in Minnesota over a 20-year period lends support to the claim that in children who face severe adversity, two predictors of resilience are cognitive skill and good parenting.[20] This reveals that parents who are successful in fulfilling (R1) and (R2)—both involve cognitive skills—are also well on their way to fulfilling (R3). Ann Masten claims that the research on resilience points to a variety of factors that appear to build this trait in children. These factors include having positive attachment bonds with caregivers, positive relationships with other adults who are competent and nurturing, intellectual skills, self-regulation skills, possession of faith/hope/sense of meaning in life, and positive cultural factors such as effective schools, social support for families, and cultural rituals and supports. Some of these factors are within the control of parents, and some are not (at least directly). Attachment relationships are crucial for fostering resilience, first with parents/caregivers, and then with teachers, coaches, friends, and mentors. Clearly parents can foster such relationships with their children, and then seek to facilitate them with others as their children grow and develop.

Another important element that supports resilience is the mastery motivation system, in which "we experience pleasure in agency, or being effective in the world."[21] As this system is engaged, it encourages children to develop competence, gain confidence, increases motivation to learn, and cultivates problem-solving abilities. This pleasure in mastery is important, and can be lost or undermined by trauma or neglect. Parents can encourage the development and strengthening of this system by giving their children opportunities that are appropriate for their level of development to act as agents and deal with the consequences of success or failure. This is yet another reason for refraining from authoritarian, insular, and helicopter parenting.

Cultural traditions, including religious traditions, also support resilience. According to Masten, not only do these types of belief systems offer a sense of meaning, they also can help individuals adapt when adversity is present. Religion offers much of value here, including "attachment relationships (spiritual and human), rituals of comfort and self-regulation (such as services for major life events, prayer, meditation), and many other kinds of emotional and physical assistance."[22] Parents who value particular religious beliefs and practices would do well to make use of the resources their faith offers related to resilience. Those who do not adhere to any form of religion will need to explore other ways that they can provide some of these benefits to their children.

One other crucial element for fostering resilience is optimism.[23] Resilient individuals are optimistic when setbacks occur, and take such setbacks to be temporary. They believe that setbacks can be overcome. This helps them to persevere through setbacks. One way of fostering resilience in children is to help them develop an optimistic outlook, to think in optimistic ways about setbacks, disappointments, and challenges. Parents ought to model this for their children, and discuss how one might take such a perspective when adversity is present. When they do so, they may be helping to build a character trait within their children that is relevant to PTE's as well as the rest of life.

How else can parents attempt to foster resilience in their children? Masten notes that there are several environmental factors, which, if reduced, can promote resilience. First, reduction in the level of exposure to violence, such as bullying at school or on the playground, is important. Preventing low birth weight is related to resilience as well. When there are such risks present, an increase in resources applied to counterbalance them can be effective in promoting resilience, such as schools providing meals, healthcare, and trained professionals who have competency in dealing with children who live in adverse conditions. Parents may need to take advantage of such services in order to foster resilience in their children. Finally, there are ways to intervene that can strengthen and develop (or restore) adaptive systems so that children can remain resilient (or recover the trait). For example, programs that contribute to the quality of the relationship that children have with their parents, mentors, and teachers can be effective. Programs that help young children (who are at high risk) to develop executive functions such as self-control, ability to direct their attention, and flexible thinking can also be helpful. Finally, there is a window of opportunity when adolescents transition to adulthood. During this period, parents and others have the chance to intervene at a time when cognitive capacities related to planning and decision-making are increasing, as are opportunities to employ these skills related to decisions about the future, including further education, military service, or some form of a career. Much of the above falls outside of the direct control of parents, but those who take (R3) seriously will seek to do what is under their control to help their children become resilient.

The attempt to inculcate resilience in one's children must be balanced by other considerations, however. An exclusive or excessive focus on cultivating resilience is problematic. The significance of resilience as a character trait does not justify a lack of kindness, compassion, or other forms of callous behavior and attitudes towards one's child engaged in for the sake of cultivating the trait. The parent who berates his child on the football field, or criticizes him for being soft when he expresses being hurt by the treatment of others at school, or justifies her lack of affection towards a child on the grounds that this will toughen her up for life in the real world makes a serious mistake. Resilience is important, but many other traits are as well, and in light of this good parenting requires practical wisdom in order to make judgments concerning what is called for given the particular personality and character of one's child and the relevant circumstances of life at any particular point in time. This is just one of the many reasons why parenthood is a demanding role and relationship.

One of the primary aims of this section is to show that considerations related to PTE's provide support for the claim that parents possess obligations (R1)—(R3). There are other arguments for this claim, but the focus here has been on the ways in which PTE's and decisions concerning them yield further support for it. One primary motivation for the foregoing and for what follows has to do with an Aristotelian concern for useful inquiry. In the *Nicomachean Ethics*, Aristotle states that "Our present discussion does not aim, as our others do, at study; for the purpose of our examination is not to know what virtue is, but to become good, since otherwise the inquiry would be of no benefit to us."[24] I am not interested in defending everything stated or implied by Aristotle here, except that at some point in our inquiry into moral issues, including and perhaps especially those related to parenthood, it is important to consider how one might apply the insights gained via moral philosophy to practical concerns. Attention to such practical concerns helps to clarify the implications of the stewardship conception of parenthood for particular cases, and underscores the importance of (R1)—(R3) for parents as they seek to fulfill these obligations in their particular context. With this in mind, in the remainder of the paper I consider the relevance of (R1)—(R3) for parental choices related to education and youth sports.

Implications for Youth Sports

Participation in one or more sports is common for children in the United States. Depending upon the data one accepts, at least somewhere between 21–28 million kids aged 6–17 are involved in organized youth sports of some form.[25] Some are skeptical that participation in sport could function as a PTE for a child. Participation in sport can be a PTE, and there is reason that this is especially the case for females. This is because while much progress has been made for girls and women in sport, there is still much resistance to the notion that girls and women are athletes in the same full-blooded sense as men. Many in society do not take women's elite sport as seriously as they do men's elite sport, and this is true at younger ages as well. With this in mind, how might participation in sport function as a PTE for a female? Consider a young girl who takes the opportunity to participate in a particular sport, such as soccer. She plays in a league where boys and girls play on the same team, and she excels. She is one of the best players on the field. In such a scenario, her self-concept may undergo a significant change. She may begin to see herself as an athlete. This can happen even if she fails to excel, of course, but the change in self-concept may be more likely or run deeper because of a discovery of such athletic excellence at a young age. Those who become athletes later in life may still experience such a transformation, but it may be connected more with what they do rather than how they perform.

Recall Paul's description of a PTE as something that "changes you enough to substantially change your point of view, thus substantially revising your core preferences or revising how you experience being yourself."[26] This aptly describes what happens to the young girl who begins to see herself as an athlete. Some of her core preferences are now different. She wants to excel in her sport, to learn more about it, and perhaps even try other sports to see if she enjoys them and to discover her potential in them. She experiences herself differently, because she now experiences herself as an athlete. She takes on a new aspect of identity, and it becomes a central part of how she experiences and sees herself. This does not always occur, but the point here is that it has the potential to do so in the lives of many individuals.

In the remainder of this section, the points I raised are intended to apply to all children, regardless of gender. I will assume that becoming an athlete can be intentional or unintentional (as in cases where the child is coerced by parents or someone else to participate). It can also be both a pleasant and at times unpleasant PTE. This much seems uncontroversial. Many, however, would accept that sport can and often does function as a PTE, but are concerned that it is kakianic rather than areteic. That is, they are concerned that it fosters moral and intellectual vice rather than virtue. However, there is great *potential* for participation in youth sports to be areteic. In what follows, I will briefly argue for two claims: (i) sport can be an areteic PTE; and (ii) this potentiality is more likely to occur if the child's cognitive capacities are more fully realized.

First, consider the claim that sport can be an areteic PTE for a child. The notion that sport can build character is not new. In Plato's *Republic*, there is an argument that physical training is potentially beneficial for the intellectual and moral development of individuals.[27] At present, I will focus on the latter. There are good philosophical and empirical reasons for thinking that sport can contribute to the formation of moral virtue in athletes.[28] If we approach sport in part as a moral practice, then we will take the cultivation and display of virtue to be two of its important functions. To be sure, it has other functions, including physical health, fun, and entertainment. But as a moral practice, it also can function as a means of character development. In a discussion of these issues, Carwyn Jones and Mike McNamee argue that

> the cultivation of certain virtues, such as trust, courage, and fairness, is paradoxically both a necessary condition and a consequence of proper engagement. In such an account we can think of sports in terms of a human, or moral, or character laboratory . . . where one tests oneself and one's competitors in order to find one's limitations in pursuit of the ends of the game.[29]

A level of trust is required to participate properly in a competitive sport. A player should trust her coach, as the coach seeks to help her become a better athlete (and is in fact trustworthy). Competitors need to trust each other in a variety of ways. They trust that they will not be intentionally injured by their opponents. Competitors also need to trust officials to fulfill their role in fairness, without favoritism. If sport is engaged in properly, such trust will not be misplaced. Courage can also be cultivated in sport. One aspect of courage is "standing firm against what is painful."[30] There is the physical pain associated with many sports that the athlete must struggle against to excel. There is also potential for psychological pain, as athletes risk public failure on the field or court when they choose to compete.

In connection with the claim that sport can be an areteic PTE, it is also the case that it can provide a setting in which parents can fulfill (R3). That is, sport provides opportunities to foster resilience in children, and in a setting where what is at stake is less significant than in other realms of life (it's better for a child to fail and learn resilience in soccer than to fail at gaining admission into college and learning resilience in that circumstance, for example). Sport can be a character laboratory for resilience, for learning how to overcome adversity. To see how this is so, consider again a daughter who plays soccer. She may be able to learn resilience as she struggles to earn playing time on her team. Rather than quitting, she could intensify her efforts related to her own development as a player, practicing on her own in order to earn more time on the field. If she is (or becomes) one of the better players on the team, there will be opportunities for growing in resilience as she deals with losses, inept officiating, difficult teammates and coaches, and even weather conditions that make playing difficult or very uncomfortable. These may be small instances of adversity, but taken together they have a significant potential for the development of resilience. Such a positive outcome from these experiences will depend in part upon how the parents capitalize on these opportunities. For example, when officials make a bad call, will the parents blame them for a loss as they discuss this with their daughter? Or will they agree that it was a mistaken call, but encourage her to learn to accept such mistakes as part of the game that is ultimately, like the weather, not under her control, and focus on playing the game rather than on the officials? If her parents opt for the latter approach, she is more likely to grow in resilience.

Sport can also provide opportunities for parents to fulfill (R2). How so may be less apparent initially, but sport can be a PTE that fosters open-mindedness in one's child. There are situations that can arise in sporting contexts that present opportunities to exercise the intellectual flexibility and concern for truth that are marks of open-mindedness. For example, returning to our young soccer player, she may need to develop open-mindedness as a coach instructs her in a different way to perform some skill, or in a different tactic to adopt during a portion of the game. She may need open-mindedness to respond appropriately to a coach who believes that she is better suited for a different position on the field, even if it is one that she has rarely or never played. Some of the opposites of open-mindedness, such as intolerance or prejudice, may be undermined by participation in sport. Being teammates with those of different ethnic or religious backgrounds can provide opportunities to grow in this virtue. For some children, sport may be one of the few contexts in which they can forge relationships with others who differ from them in these and other ways. Parents can help this to be a positive experience for their children.

If the foregoing is correct, then sport can build character, both intellectual and moral. But how does it connect with the cultivation of one's cognitive capacities as described by (R1), beyond the ways it may foster open-mindedness? This is perhaps less clear, and more controversial. Nevertheless, sport does have the potential to serve as a context in which such capacities can be cultivated and improved. Here I will merely sketch out some reasons that support this claim. If the claim is true, then it shows that sport provides an opportunity for intellectual development that is likely ignored or at least underappreciated in our contemporary context.

As I noted above, Plato held that sport can contribute to one's intellectual development. In her discussion of this claim, Heather Reid points out that in the *Republic*, athletics was to play a role in the education of future philosopher-rulers.[31] The traits that can be cultivated early in life through sport are also important for the practice of philosophy, understood as the pursuit of knowledge. Courage, the love of hard work, the capacity for strenuous pursuit, and the steadfastness in adversity that can be developed in sport can be transferred to the quest for knowledge and wisdom in more academic pursuits. As Reid observes, "In Plato's mind . . . the dedication, perseverance, focus, and self-sacrifice associated with athletics are exactly the kinds of qualities needed to succeed in finding truth."[32]

How can parents seek to foster this type of intellectual growth in their children via sport, as a way of fulfilling (R1)? While it is true that any kind of intellectual or moral growth that occurs in sport does not entail that such growth will occur in other realms of life, there is good reason to think that this expansion can occur.[33] One reason that this does not occur has to do with intention and the formation of character. Athletes who excel in their sports generally do so because they intentionally pursue excellence, displaying the virtues and traits emphasized by Plato. One plausible reason that these virtues are not exemplified in other areas of life is that these athletes do not intend this. An athlete may display great courage in the context of sport, but fail to take a stand related to some important issue concerning social justice or whatever moral convictions that she may hold. In the context of parenthood, there is good reason to think that if parents encourage their children to apply the lessons learned as athletes to other realms of life, their children will be able to do so. There is empirical evidence in support of the claim that if we form such intentions, including the means for implementing them, then then we will be successful.[34] Parents can help their children to do this.

The upshot of this section is that sport provides an indirect way for parents to fulfill (R1). As they help children employ sport not just for pleasure or physical health, but also for the sake of cultivating certain character traits, they are helping to build a foundation of virtue that can be transferred into the intellectual realm. Of course, one central realm of life that is often a deep concern for parents related to the intellect is the education of their children. In the next section, I consider how (R1)—(R3) are relevant to parental choices concerning the education of their children.

Implications for Education and Parental Choice

Education can be transformative. The educational process as well as the content can constitute PTE's. Education can awaken us to certain goods, and transform the intellectual, moral, and social dimensions of our lives. Great works of literature, philosophy, history, and scientific theory can have a transformative effect on human beings, as can our interactions with others related to such works. Many parents, however, fear that by allowing their child to be educated in particular ways, and in the process allowing them to be exposed to ways of thinking and living that conflict with their own, they are opening the child up to potential harm. They fear that if the child ultimately rejects their moral, political, or religious views, that this will be bad for her and perhaps for those in her sphere of influence. They may also feel that if this happens, they have failed as parents. Yet there are reasons that parents as stewards have for allowing their children to be educated in a way that exposes them to other belief systems, and to challenges to their own beliefs.

Not all forms of education are (potentially) transformative, of course. The type of education I have in mind can be described as a Socratic-Millian education (SME). My claim is that parents should seek such an education for their children based in part on the foregoing points related to PTE's and the importance of (R1), (R2), and (R3). The *form* of this type of education may be different—public, private, religious, homeschool—but the *function* is what I take to be crucial. SME allows children to undergo positive PTE's, and it further prepares them for such experiences in other realms of life. These are some of the reasons parents have, among others, for seeking such an education for their children.

The Socratic dimension of SME involves encouraging and developing within children the abilities relevant for informed and critical inquiry concerning questions that matter, especially those related to the ends or commitments that one may adopt.[35] It includes helping children develop the capacities required for leading an examined life, one in which investigating and evaluating potential goods and values related to one's life commitments is central. This type of education emphasizes the cultivation of the skills of reasoning, the application of those skills to evaluating different goods and comprehensive views, interaction with the relevant information and arguments, and a respect for the autonomy of individuals to arrive at and implement their hard-won views on such topics.

The Millian dimension of SME is closely related to the foregoing, but expands on it as well. In *On Liberty*, John Stuart Mill raises several points concerning freedom of thought and speech that are also relevant to SME.[36] The Millian dimension of SME focuses on the value of debate and discussion. As Mill points out, debate can supply the remainder of the truth. It is rare that anyone has the whole truth, and even wrong views can contain portions of truth that we lack. Free discussion and debate can uncover such truths. In addition, discussion and debate can also help us know why we believe what we do. If we do not have such knowledge, our belief may be mere prejudice or groundless opinion, and this is undesirable. As Mill argues, people should be able to defend their beliefs from the common objections that are lodged against them. Finally, an education that includes such discussion and debate also will help keep the truth alive; it will keep it from becoming a dead dogma. Frequent and full discussion of issues that matter encourages individuals to let the truth impact their character and conduct. One hoped-for result of SME is that children will develop "real and heartfelt conviction from reason [and] . . . personal experience."[37]

Consider a specific illustration of the requirements of SME. Christian parents, for example, should allow their children to learn about other comprehensive views and some of the standard objections to Christianity as is developmentally appropriate. Complete insulation and isolation from different or opposing views will likely prevent children from more fully developing their cognitive capacities. It also makes cultivating open-mindedness difficult, given a lack of exposure to views that oppose their own. And it can amount to a lost opportunity for the development of resilience, as I will argue below. Of course, the same points apply to parents in other religious traditions as well as secular parents who seek to insulate their children from exposure to different views.

Parents have reason to seek SME for their children, because it can help them to fulfill the obligations described above: cultivating the cognitive capacities of their children (R1), the intellectual virtue of open-mindedness (R2), and the trait of resilience (R3). The potentially transformative education I have briefly described would clearly help children cultivate some of their cognitive capacities. The type of cognitive activities involved in seeking to understand and evaluate the various life commitments that one and others have will require the development of cognitive capacities related to analysis, synthesis, and both comparative and critical thought. It will require that individuals seek to inhabit the perspective of others, and view things differently for at least the purpose of developing a greater understanding of other views.

SME would also enable children to cultivate the trait of open-mindedness as required by (R2). Once children realize that there are other ways of thinking about religious, moral, social, and political issues, and that some adherents to these views can provide reasons in support of them, this can be conducive to their own growth in open-mindedness. If children engage the process, and consider the arguments for and against a variety of positions related to such views, it is plausible to think they will grow in this intellectual virtue. A child from a Christian family, for example, who interacts with children from other religious or secular traditions in an educational setting stands to profit greatly from such interactions. Many of the ideas, values, and practices that she takes for granted may be uncovered as mere assumptions. Ideally, this will lead her to consider the relevant evidence, and the process itself will likely lead to growth in open-mindedness. Her parents, of course, will most likely want her to continue to believe and practice the Christian faith, but presumably they want her to do this in ways that are deep and meaningful to her, and for her faith to be something that she freely accepts and practices because she believes it to be true based on her assessment of the evidence. It is unclear how a religious faith or other comprehensive belief system is really *the child's* until she is able to sufficiently understand and embrace it for herself in an autonomous fashion, grounded in forms of evidence rather than mere assumption.

SME can also help foster forms of resilience. By being exposed to challenges to the deeply held beliefs of one's family, and either dealing with those challenges and strengthening those beliefs or changing some or all of them, it is plausible to think that resilience may be fostered. Consider again a child from a Christian family, examining challenges to her belief grounded in the problem of evil. For some, this is sufficient for rejecting or renouncing Christian belief and practice, though others will be satisfied with the responses on offer. It is plausible to think that a child who considers the nature of the problem of evil, feels its force, and then maintains her religious belief and practice after a consideration of the arguments given in response will grow in resilience. Some of the experiences that will be a part of this process will likely be stressful and constitute adversity for her, as she questions some of her foundational religious commitments, but by dealing with these honestly it seems that resilience will be fostered. This may serve her well in her spiritual life and in other domains of life when adverse circumstances obtain.

Parents have at least one more reason for exposing their children via SME to religious, moral, and political views that differ from their own. Parents, like all human knowers, are fallible. A child may end up with a different belief system than her parents, and it may be the case that she is correct and her parents mistaken. Providing SME to children allows for this possibility, and it also importantly communicates trust to the child that she is able to explore and answer such questions. This underscores the importance of her parents seeking to foster intellectual and moral formation throughout her childhood, so that she is equipped to make such judgments and implement them into her life as appropriate. Parents simply ought to allow for the possibility that a child will undergo a PTE via education or some other means that results in her departure from their favored views. But whether or not this occurs, as stewards, parents realize the importance of respecting her autonomy and continue to hope for and support her in her pursuit of a flourishing life. Their commitment to her is unconditional. It is not dependent upon her holding views of the good life that are identical to their own.[38]

Notes

1 See my Michael W. Austin, *Conceptions of Parenthood* (Burlington, VT: Ashgate, 2007). See also William B. Irvine, *Doing Right by Children* (St. Paul, MN: Paragon House, 2001).

2 L.A. Paul, *Transformative Experience* (New York: Oxford University Press, 2014): 15–16. Paul focuses on whether and how decisions related to these experiences can be rational, because she thinks we do not have sufficient epistemic access prior to having the experience to make sound judgments concerning it. I am less skeptical than she is about this, however, and assume without argument that we can make some sound judgments using a standard model of normative decision-making, where we make a decision based on our knowledge of the subjective values of the outcomes of our options and the relative probability of each outcome occurring.

3 Ibid., 16.

4 Ibid., 111.

5 Even if the lottery winner bought the winning ticket, it is a stretch to say that he brought about the state of affairs in which he won. He made winning *possible* by purchasing a ticket, but he did not *intend* it, in the sense in which I am using this term.

6 The Greek term for virtue, or moral excellence, is ἀρετή (arête). Κακία (kakía) is the term for moral viciousness.

7 Albert Camus, *The Myth of Sisyphus and Other Essays*, trans. Justin O'Brien (New York: Alfred E. Knopf, 1967): 4.

8 John Stuart Mill, *Utilitarianism*, ed. George Sher (Indianapolis: Hackett, 1979): 8.

9 I am not claiming that these are the only properties that matter relative to PTE's. Many other properties may be added to this list. Beauty comes to mind as one likely candidate.

10 The focus here is on the obligations of parents, rather than what the liberal state should tolerate.

11 See the research discussed in Mark Vopat, *Children's Rights and Moral Parenting* (Lanham, MD: Lexington Books, 2015): 107–123. Vopat focuses on the relevance of such facts to the justice of selective magnet schools.

12 Ibid., 109.

13 See Benjamin Bloom, "Generalizations about Talent Development," in *Developing Talent in Young People*, ed. Benjamin Bloom (New York: Ballantine Books, 1985): 507–49.

14 This will be discussed more fully in the context of youth sports later in this paper.

15 Christopher Peterson and Martin Seligman, *Character Strengths and Virtues* (New York: Oxford University Press, 2004): 100–103.

16 Marcus Arvan, "How to Rationally Approach Life's Transformative Experiences," *Philosophical Psychology* 28 (2015): 1199–218. Much of what I argue with respect to (R3) was inspired by this paper.

17 Peterson and Seligman, *Character Strengths and Virtues*, 79.

18 Anthony Ong, C.S. Bergeman and Toni Bisconti, "Psychological Resilience, Positive Emotions, and Successful Adaptation to Stress in Later Life," *Journal of Personality and Social Psychology* 91 (2006): 730–49, 731.

19 Positive emotions include the following: cheerful, peaceful, happy, excited, proud, strong, and determined. Negative emotions include such things as: anxious, worried, depressed, scared, hostile, and guilty.

20 Ann Masten, "Ordinary Magic: Lessons from Research on Resilience in Human Development," *Education Canada* 49 (2009): 28–32.

21 Ibid., 30.

22 Ibid., 30. I would add that the truth status of any particular religion is important to consider. The mere fact that religions are able to provide assistance in developing resilience is not sufficient for adopting one of them. Truth is important here as well.

23 Martin Seligman, "Building Resilience," *Harvard Business Review* (April 2011): 100–106.

24 Aristotle, *Nicomachean Ethics*, 2nd edition, trans. Terence Irwin (Indianapolis: Hackett Publishing, 1999): 1103b30.

25 http://espn.go.com/espn/story/_/id/9469252/hidden-demographics-youth-sports-espn-magazine accessed April 16, 2015. Some of the data does not include kids who start before age eight, while other data does not include those who start before age six.

26 Paul, *Transformative Experience*, 16.

27 Heather Reid, "Sport and Moral Education in Plato's *Republic*," *Journal of the Philosophy of Sport* 34 (2007): 160–75. See also Plato's *Republic*, 410bc, 411e.

28 See my "Sport as a Moral Practice: An Aristotelian Approach," in *Virtues in Action: New Essays in Applied Virtue Ethics*, ed. Michael W. Austin (New York: Palgrave Macmillan, 2013): 39–52. In this paper, I reply to several objections to the claim that sport can foster moral development, and offer a more complete defense of the claim. Most of what follows is based upon this essay.

29 Carwyn Jones and Mike McNamee, "Moral Development and Sport: Character and Cognitive Developmentalism Contrasted," in *Sports Ethics*, ed. Jan Boxill (Malden, MA: Blackwell): 42.

30 Aristotle, *Nicomachean Ethics*, 1117a30–35.

31 Reid, "Sport and Moral Education in Plato's *Republic*," 160–175.

32 Ibid., 171.

33 See my "Sport as a Moral Practice: An Aristotelian Approach," 47–50.

34 See Peter M. Gollwitzer, "Implementation Intentions: Strong Effects of Simple Plans," *American Psychologist* 54 (1999): 493–503.

35 The Socratic aspects of SME are drawn from a discussion by Colin Macleod, "Shaping Children's Convictions," *Theory and Research in Education* 1 (2003): 315–30.

36 See chapter 2, "Of the Liberty of Thought and Discussion." http://www.utilitarianism.com/ol/two.html

37 Ibid.

38 Thanks to Colin Macleod, Christine Overall, and others at the PEPR conference for their helpful criticisms and feedback.

11 Fundamentally Incompetent

Homophobia, Religion, and the Right to Parent

Samantha Brennan and Colin Macleod

Introduction: The Moral Right to Parent

It is widely assumed that adults who engage in procreation with a view having children that they intend to raise have a presumptive moral claim to serve as the custodial parents of the children they create. The moral right to parent grounded in 'ordinary' procreation of this sort in turn provides justification for legal rights of parents. Indeed, in most cases, legal guardianship of children by parents flows more or less directly from successful procreation by a couple.[1] Adults who become parents in this way typically acquire a special set of rights and responsibilities. Parents have responsibilities to protect and secure many important interests of their children but they also enjoy many special prerogatives to shape and control many facets of children's lives. The moral right to parent extends to parents a good deal of authority over children and affords parents protections from outside interference with respect to a wide range of matters that affect the upbringing of children. Thus parents have wide discretion to make decisions about their children's diet, education, cultural influences, language, and religious identity. The moral right to parent is not, of course, absolute. Parental authority must be exercised in ways that are compatible with the rights of children. Moreover, acquiring and maintaining the moral right to parent is conditional on satisfying a threshold of competency. Would-be parents need not be perfect but competent parents must be able to identify and promote at least their children's basic interests.[2] So the right to parent is jeopardized when parents violate or threaten to violate the basic welfare of children through various kinds of physical, sexual, or emotional abuse. Similarly, though somewhat more controversially, adults who seek to indoctrinate children with noxious ideologies or who deprive their children access to conditions hospitable to the development of normal moral capacities may be denied or may forfeit the right to parent.[3]

The precise contour of the right of parents to shape the values and commitments of children is the subject of considerable academic debate. Some theorists hold that children's right to an autonomy-facilitating upbringing imposes strict limitations parental efforts to influence children. Matthew

Clayton, for instance, opposes 'comprehensive enrolment' of children by parents.[4] He argues that parents not attempt to secure their children's allegiance to a conception of the good and may not require that children participate in distinctive religious or cultural practices of their parents. Macleod, by contrast, argues that parents may provisionally favor a particular conception of the good and may include children in religious and cultural practices deemed important by their parents.[5] But parents must favor their conceptions of the good in a way that is compatible with the facilitation of children's autonomy and they may not, consequently, attempt to authoritatively fix their children's views. More conservative theorists, such as William Galston,[6] contend that the limits on the authority of parents to shape their children's values are extremely limited. On his view, parents may go to great lengths to secure their children's allegiance to a conception of the good even at the expense of facilitating the autonomy of children. Our objective in this paper is not to resolve general issues about the extent of parental prerogatives to shape the views and attitudes of children. Indeed, for the purposes of our analysis, we shall assume that parental prerogatives in this domain are quite strong. That is, we assume that, to a significant degree, the right to parent allows parents to raise children in ways that express the religious and cultural values of parents. Similarly, we allow that parents may encourage children to adopt and share these views. The issue we wish to address, arises in cases in which the expression of parental values in child-rearing runs contrary to the claim of children to be loved and respected by parents. Our basic question is whether parents who hold, and seek to express, attitudes and beliefs that are contemptuous of sexual minorities are competent parents. We show that the expression of homophobic views and attitudes by parents poses a serious threat to the well-being and moral integrity of children. And we argue that adults who embrace and express extreme forms of homophobia fall below the threshold of competency requisite to acquiring and maintaining the moral right to parent. This paper explores this issue by considering whether conservative religious fundamentalists who hold and express strongly homophobic beliefs should be considered competent parents. We focus on the case of religious fundamentalists because some religious fundamentalists seem unwilling to love and respect children who are or might be gay. The systematic denial of love and respect to gay youth by homophobic parents causes a great deal of harm to children and arguably constitutes a form of abuse.

Denying religious fundamentalists the right to parent may seem, at first glance, illiberal and it also seems contrary to the widely accepted view that the decision of a couple to procreate normally gives rise to a right to parent. Liberalism traditionally endorses strong rights of religious liberty and such rights are usually understood as permitting religious people to hold and express controversial and illiberal views about sexuality. Fundamentalists, it would seem, have the right to criticize and even condemn sexual practices or relationships that they believe are morally objectionable or sinful.

But liberalism is also committed to safeguarding the welfare of children and to fostering the conditions in which all persons, including sexual minorities, are treated with respect. Rawls, for instance, argues that self-respect is the most important primary good and that a just society must ensure that all persons are provided with the social conditions of self-respect.[7] We consider whether the threat to the welfare and self-respect of children posed by homophobic parents is sufficiently grave to warrant state assessment of the suitability of religious fundamentalists to be parents. We do, of course, recognize that not all religious fundamentalists are homophobic and some religious people with who view homosexuality as sinful are able to love and nurture their children irrespective of whether they are gay or not. Similarly, we recognize that viscous forms of homophobia are sometimes held by non-religious people.[8] However, we focus on the case of religious homophobia because of its prevalence in contemporary North America and because homophobia rooted in religious belief is sometimes thought to be tolerable in virtue of its links to longstanding religious traditions. The theological, doctrinal, and cultural commitments of Christianity, Judaism, and Islam are, we realize, internally diverse and complex. Nonetheless, each of these faith traditions has strongly homophobic elements that are embraced by fundamentalist adherents to each of these faiths. From a liberal point of view, our suggestion that some religious fundamentalists—whether Christian, Jewish, or Moslem—may be denied the moral right to parent may seem especially contentious. It is important to emphasize that our argument focuses on the *moral* right to parent and not, in the first instance, on the legal right to parent. Our argument does have implications for laws and state policies and we will broach these later in the paper. We do not defend the view that homophobic fundamentalists can be legally prevented from procreating or from serving as the legal guardians of their children. Denying that homophobic fundamentalists have the moral right to parent need not entail denial a legal right to parent. After all, not all dimensions of morality are legally enforceable. Moreover, even in the realm of state policy, the best way to secure the protection of some important rights and interests of persons can be through non-coercive strategies. For the most part, we see our argument as offering a challenge to widely held views about the character and foundations of the moral right to parent. This argument is, however, relevant to state policy because, if sound, it establishes that state programs that encourage parents to love and respect their children, irrespective of their of sexual orientation, are not vulnerable to the objection that they violate the moral rights of religious parents.

Liberal Rights and Child-Rearing

Since we wish to develop our argument in a way that is congenial to a broadly liberal conception of justice, we begin by offering a simple characterization of a familiar variety of rights-based liberalism. We highlight four features of liberalism that frame issues about having and raising children. First, liberalism upholds strong rights of freedom of religion and conscience. Freedom of religion allows people to give expression to their religious convictions and to conduct their lives in accordance with their understanding of the values, traditions, and practices of their religion. It is only under exceptional circumstances that the state is warranted in limiting freedom of religion. Second, liberalism recognizes rights of freedom of association. Adults are entitled to determine for themselves the nature and character of their social, political, and intimate relationships with others. Among other things freedom of association permits individuals to form families for the purpose of having and raising children. Third, these first two rights provide the basis for recognition of extensive procreative rights. Individuals have very wide latitude to make procreative decisions (e.g., whether to have children, how many children to have).[9] Finally, there are rights of parental authority. Parents exercise a great deal of control over the rearing of their children; they are entitled make to decisions on behalf of their children in matters of health, education, culture, recreation, and religion. However, as we have already noted, parental authority is not legally or morally unlimited. In developing our argument, we emphasize some distinctive ways in which the scope and character of parental authority is constrained by the independent rights and interests of children.[10]

In practice, societies purporting to be liberal and democratic have frequently limited or violated these basic liberal rights in problematic ways. States have been hostile to certain religions or spiritual traditions (e.g., Indigenous religions and culture); they have restricted marriage to heterosexual couples and curtailed the procreation of disabled persons. States have also infringed the authority of some parents over their children in ways that generated grotesque harms. The Canadian government's policy of removing Indigenous children from their families and forcing them to attend Christian residential schools is but one appalling example of illiberal treatment of parents and children. Nonetheless, along many fronts there have been reforms in line with liberal values. For example, there has been increasing recognition of the right of gay and lesbian couples to form families through adoption and through the use of reproductive technology. Families with multiple parents (more than two) are also having some success securing legal parental rights for those adults who hold the moral status of parent. Recent political and cultural changes in liberal democracies concerning the status of sexual minorities have been quite dramatic and seem predicated, at least in part, in changes in moral attitudes concerning sexuality. Whereas homosexuality was once widely regarded as morally objectionable or as some form of psychiatric disorder, in most liberal communities there is now broad recognition that a person's sexual orientation is not properly characterized as either morally good or morally bad. Of course, the acceptance of homosexuality in liberal societies as entirely morally acceptable is far from complete. But it seems clear that moralized conceptions of sexual orientation have no place in a liberal theory of justice. So even if religious persons retain the right to hold and express homophobic views, those views are themselves in tension with the requirement of justice that respect be extended to all persons irrespective of their sexual orientation.

Liberalism and the Rights and Interests of Children

Liberal theory, until relatively recently, has given little systematic attention to how the character and content of the rights we have just identified should be influenced by recognition of children's rights and the importance of promoting their well-being and moral development. Similarly the issue of the scope and possible limits on procreative liberty has been largely neglected until recently. The research that is now being done in these areas by moral and political philosophers is diverse and complex. But some general and fairly obvious points about which there is broad consensus are worth noting. Parents clearly have an obligation to promote their children's welfare and a duty not to infringe their children's rights. They also have a duty to protect their children and see that others do not harm them. There are many ways in which the content of these duties can be further specified but, without providing a full elaboration, the following modest considerations seem relevant to understanding how attentiveness to the claims of children shape the contours of the rights of parents. In our view, children have a justice-based entitlement to an upbringing that: (a) prepares them for responsible citizenship as adults; (b) facilities their autonomy so that they are able to deliberate reflectively on their own conception of the good (including matters of religion); (c) secures their basic physical and psychological well-being as children; and (d) provides children secure access to the social conditions of self-respect. Parental authority must be exercised in ways that are compatible with respect for these claims of children. Competent would-be parents must be willing and able to play their role in securing their children's rights and promoting their welfare. Moreover, parental competency is relevant not just once people have become parents and are engaged in rearing them. It has a bearing on who can claim moral the right to parent. Voluntary procreation by adults is not sufficient to yield a right to parent because procreation itself does not guarantee that parents are willing and able to discharge their duties they owe to prospective children. The right to procreate (where this is understood as entailing a right rear one's offspring) is therefore limited.

   In light of these observations, a child-sensitive liberal theory arguably needs an account of *parental preparedness* that identifies the traits and capacities that would be parents must display in order to successfully claim and retain the right to parent. Different elements of an account parental preparedness can be identified. First, there is cost-bearing preparedness. This concerns the degree to which would-be parents must be able to secure their children's material needs (food, clothing, shelter, healthcare, educa-tion, recreation etc.) without state or community assistance. Persons who are unable or unwilling to devote adequate resources to meeting children's needs may not be suitable parents. Second, there is a dimension of mental and physical preparedness. This element concerns how physical and mental capacities of persons may affect their ability to discharge parental respon-sibilities. Some persons with severe cognitive or physical impairments may, even with the assistance of others, be unable to reliably attend the claims of children. Finally, there is affective and motivational preparedness. This element concerns the ability and willingness of parents to love their children as well as the motivation they have to monitor and respond appropriately to their needs. Competent parents must be able manifest respect for dignity for children and help to cultivate their sense of self-respect.

Developing and interpreting these elements of parental preparedness must be done in a way that is sensitive to the social division of moral labor. Secur-ing the justice-based entitlements of children does not fall only to parents. To take an obvious example the provision of basic education and health resources to children is arguably a societal responsibility. So the fact that a couple lacks the resources to fund a good education for a child need not disqualify them as suitable parents. If the project becoming a parent and raising children is especially important to a wide range of people then we have reason to ensure that social conditions are hospitable to most people becoming parents. Given suitable background social institutions that work in concert with parents to meet the needs of children then cost-bearing and mental and physical preparedness criteria need not significantly limit access-ing to parenting by those who are poor or mentally or physically disabled. However, there are limits to which clever design of the social division of labor can assist parents in meeting the claims of children. Some of the enti-tlements of children arguably cannot be reliably secured via institutional arrangements that distribute relevant moral labor between many people. Parents are especially, and perhaps uniquely, well-placed to secure some of the most important needs of children. This observation is particularly rel-evant to the affective and motivational dimension of parental preparedness. The provision of love and affection along with attentiveness to children of the sort that is integral to valuable relationships between children and adults falls and which contributes greatly to children's well-being and self-esteem can only be provided by a small group of adults with whom children have a close and ongoing relationship over the course of their childhood. Sustained affection of children of the sort that involves intimacy and close personal attention over a long period of time simply cannot be directly supplied by the state or social workers. (Of course, the state can still have a role in ensuring that background institutional arrangements are more or less hos-pitable to ensuring that children are loved and cherished by their parents.) This means that meeting some of the important entitlements of children will fall more or less directly to parents.[11] As a consequence would-be parents

who cannot reliably provide these entitlements will not be adequately prepared to be parents and thus may be unable to claim a right to parent.

Amongst the entitlements of children that are best secured by parents, our
argument places special emphasis on the entitlement of children to what we
label 'affective caring.'

Affective caring involves manifesting love, affection, and emotional support to children; being attentive to their emotions, concerns, and enthusiasms; and being moved and concerned by threats to their well-being in ways
that are transparent to children themselves. Expressed more succinctly, children have a right to be loved[12] and valued by their parents. In what follows,
we shall consider what role children's entitlement to affective caring has
in an account of parental preparedness and how this facet of parental preparedness generates limits on the moral right to parent.

Affective Care and the Right to Parent

What should an account of parental preparedness say about the capacity
for affective caring and the right to parent? Our answer has three elements.
First, as we have already noted, against the background of the family as the
major institution for rearing children, affective caring cannot be reliably
provided to children by non-parents. Second, a realized capacity for affective caring is a necessary condition to secure and retain the moral right to
rear children. Those who engage in procreation with a view to becoming
custodial parents must be able and willing to provide affective care to their
offspring in a reliable and ongoing fashion. Third, although affective caring
has core elements it is multiple realizable and hence compatible with diverse
family structures and parenting styles but not all. In particular, approaches
to parenting that embrace or reflect (extreme) homophobia are inconsistent
with the provision of affective care to gay children. This, in turn, raises
the issue of whether religious fundamentalists can meet the requirements
of parental preparedness. Does the affective caring dimension of parental
preparedness constrain the rights of religious fundamentalists who hold
strongly homophobic beliefs and attitudes to become parents? Our answer
is yes. Indeed we hold that because such would-be parents cannot reliably
meet acceptable standard of affective caring they are morally disqualified as
competent parents. Homophobic religious fundamentalists have no moral
right to parent.

In order to defend such a striking and controversial claim, we need to
consider the contribution of affective caring to children. Why does affective
caring matter so much? Our answer has three components. First, affective
caring contributes crucially to the current well-being and future well-being
of children. Children are emotionally fragile and the denial of love and
affection to them can create unhappiness and insecurity. Children who are
loved are happier and healthier than those who are not. Second, affective
caring is crucial to long-term healthy psychological and moral development.

By being valued and cherished by their parents, children learn how to esteem themselves and see themselves valuable and meriting respect. Affective caring is, in effect, one of the social bases on self-respect and thereby stands as an important precondition of children forming and pursuing meaningful life plans. Third, affective caring facilitates intrinsic goods of childhood—innocence, trust, and intimacy. These are goods that children can enjoy in childhood in especially valuable forms. Standing in a relationship of love to one's parents is, we suggest, intrinsically valuable. Children who are denied intimacy with their parents are denied access to an important good of childhood.[13] We think the interests of children at stake here are sufficiently weighty to warrant the conclusion that children have a right to affective caring. In reaching this conclusion, we implicitly appeal to a version of the interest theory of rights according to which moral rights function to protect especially important and fundamental interests of persons. But we view that commitment as entirely commensurate with contemporary liberalism since many familiar liberal rights, including most accounts of the right to parent, are grounded in an interest theory of rights.[14] We argue that liberal values condemn homophobic parenting and thereby severely limit the right to parent by homophobic fundamentalists.

We acknowledge that homophobia is a complex phenomenon that can be manifested in different ways. We deplore all forms of homophobia but our argument focuses on one especially noxious variety of homophobia that we call *strong homophobia*. What are the characteristics of 'strong homophobia'? It involves more than discomfort with or misunderstanding of gay sexuality and sexual identity. Rather strong homophobia consists in belief in the moral wickedness or depravity of gay sexuality and identity. The strong moral condemnation of homosexuality gives rise to attitudes of contempt, disgust, disrespect towards gay people. For the strong homophobe, homosexuality is viewed as deeply shameful and subject to strong moral disapprobation. Although there are both secular and non-Christian examples of strong homophobia, we focus on the variety present in North American fundamentalism. Some Christian fundamentalist Churches endorse strong homophobia and represent it as a matter of church doctrine and religious belief.

They encourage their fellow Christians to accept such views and they favor public culture in which homosexuality is demonized and discrimination on the basis of sexual orientation is legitimate. Of course, most adult fundamentalists are or expect to become parents. And most would, we suspect, endorse the idea that as parents they should love their children. But such fundamentalists do not typically think that their children are or could be gay. Yet this outcome is one over which they have no control. However, given their strong homophobia there is good reason to doubt that they can provide affective care to children who are gay.

Persons in the grip of such strong homophobia cannot be reliable affective carers to children since there is a non-trivial statistical possibility that their children will be gay. However, by the time the sexual identity/orientation of child of which the parent disapproves becomes evident it will be too late for other non-homophobic adults to become parents with healthy, supportive relationships with the children the homophobic parents have rejected. Children who turn out to be gay are especially vulnerable to harm from homophobic parents because by the time they come to terms with their sexuality they have already established close emotional and cultural ties with their parents. The withdrawal of parental love, affection, and concern and the substitution of parental disgust, hatred, and indifference is profoundly damaging to gay youth. It involves a cruel betrayal of a relationship that can instill shame and self-loathing in children. The loss of love and good relationships with parents is important as is disrespect manifested by parents to children.

It is easy to establish that gay and lesbian teens are at risk. The withdrawal of parental affection results in some very direct harms: non-completion of high school, homelessness, drug and alcohol abuse, and suicide. Here we is a brief overview of some of the evidence. The Lesbian, Gay, Bisexual, and Transgender (LGBT) Homeless Youth Provider Survey, a web-based survey conducted from October 2011 through March 2012, assessed the experiences of homeless youth organizations in providing services to LGBT youth. The analysis finds that 46% of LGBT youth are homeless or at-risk of becoming homeless because they "Ran away because of family rejection of sexual orientation or gender identity," and 43% were "Forced out by parents because of sexual orientation or gender identity."[15] Evidence of the uncontroversial harm wrought by strongly homophobic parents is alarming. Rates of homelessness and suicide amongst gay youth are extremely high and are closely correlated parental condemnation of their children's sexual identity. According to a recent study,[16] seven different forms of rejection toward sexual minorities in the home risk damaging their lives in various ways. Young people who reported regular, as opposed to little or no, family rejection as teens were 8.4 times more likely to attempt suicide, 5.9 times more likely to be prone to high levels of depression, 5.6 times more likely to engage in suicide ideation, 3.4 times more likely to use illegal drugs, and 3.4 times more likely to engage in unprotected sex, on the most recent occasion. The forms of rejection noted included (1) emotional distancing, (2) exclusion from family events, (3) trying to get a child to change her orientation, (4) refusing a child contact with peers of a similar orientation, (5) refusing a child access to information about her sexuality, and (6) making regular comments about the shamefulness and (7) general undesirability of a child's life on account of her sexuality.

In recent years concern for the lives of gay teenagers has made its way into mainstream media. For example, a recent issue of Rolling Stone magazine featured the article, "The Forsaken: A Rising Number of Homeless Gay Teens Are Being Cast Out by Religious Families"[17] "Research done by San Francisco State University's Family Acceptance Project, which studies and works to prevent health and mental-health risks facing LGBT youth, empirically confirms what common sense would imply to be true: Highly religious parents are significantly more likely than their less-religious counterparts to reject their children for being gay—a finding that social-service workers believe goes a long way toward explaining why LGBT people make up roughly five percent of the youth population overall, but an estimated 40 percent of the homeless-youth population. The Center for American Progress has reported that there are between 320,000 and 400,000 homeless LGBT youths in the United States." One might claim that these statistics of bad outcomes don't entirely establish that the fault lies with homophobic parents. Perhaps gay teens are particularly rebellious, develop drug and alcohol problems because they run with bad crowds, or have low self-esteem from living in a homophobic society.

To this we have two responses. First, the link between the withdrawal of parental affection and homelessness looks very direct. If parents have any responsibilities for children, the provision of food and shelter seems basic. Second, while the link between the withdrawal of affection from the closest of loved ones and suicide seems less direct, we believe our account of how this happens is plausible. Indeed, the very close bond between parents and children that develops in a society that has organized parenting the way that we have, namely in a way that encourages intimacy between parents and children, is only justified if parents do not abuse that intimacy.

Rights and Public Policy

What are the policy implications of recognizing limits on the rights of potential parents? While the first thought that comes to mind is parental licensing, here we intend to remain neutral on the question of the justification of parental licensing.[18] However, it is worth noting that licensing is not the only way in which the state can intervene to limit who gets to become a parent. In countries in which medically assisted reproduction is publically funded, there may be good reasons for putting limits on that assistance. Beyond procreation, adults also become parents through adoption and again, there is state involvement in deciding who gets to adopt. Should the standards be the same for adoption, access to IVF, and for the parental rights that follow from biological procreation? There are good reasons for thinking that we ought to treat all the ways of becoming a parent the same but again that's not something for which we argue here.[19] Our argument is not, and does not intend to be, by itself an argument for parental licensing. Instead, we think of it as an argument for paying attention to the ability of religious and strongly homophobic adults to competently parent gay children. If a scheme of licensing can be justified and feasibly implemented, then it might be reasonable to ask potential parents about their religious beliefs regarding sexual orientation. Similarly, it would be reasonable for parent education programs to address issues concerning the sexual orientation of children and the importance that parents love their children without regard to their sexual orientation. As well, government advertising schemes that promote good parenting might highlight the importance of loving one's children for the persons they are, no matter how difficult that might be for parents. The general point here is that from a public policy point of view, the most effective strategy for ensuring that parents respect the rights of children is not always one that involves coercive interference in the family.

Consider an analogy with parental smoking in the home. Exposure to secondhand smoke in the home jeopardizes the health of children. It is plausible to maintain both that children have a right to smoke-free homes and that parents do not have a moral right to expose their children to secondhand smoke. Since the state has a legitimate interest in safeguarding the rights of children, the issue arises as to how the state should respond to parental smoking at home. One route might be to legally prohibit all smoking in homes with children. (Since ex hypothesi parents have no moral right to expose their children to smoke such a legal prohibition would not violate a moral right.)[20] However, a different and perhaps more feasible and imaginative public policy response is to mount an advertising campaign that educates people about the dangers of secondhand smoke and praises parents for their "heroic" efforts in not smoking in the home. The province of Nova Scotia did just this in the early 2000s. The campaign, called "Everyday Heroes," featured parents who worked long days, for example, and came home and smoked on the snowy front step rather than in their own house. We can imagine a similar campaign featuring parents who have come to love and accept their gay children despite their religious beliefs and commitments. Such a campaign could be predicated on the claim that morally competent parents provide affective care to children irrespective of the sexual orientation of their children. So holding that homophobic parents lack the moral right to parent because they are not fully competent parents need not yield the conclusion that they should be denied a legal right to parent. We do not mean to suggest that there is an exact parallel between parental homophobia to secondhand smoke in the home. We merely note the comparison to show that there are a range of policy measures open to governments other than parental licensing or limiting access to IVF and adoption.

Objections

We anticipate a number of objections to our analysis. First, the reliable identification of strongly homophobic parents is problematic. Belonging to a religious group that endorses strong homophobia is compatible with rejecting it or subscribing to weak homophobia. It's also true that not everyone who starts out homophobic stays that way. Becoming a parent is a frequently transformational, parents with sympathies for strong homophobia may change their attitudes etc. via the process of becoming a parent and loving their child. Love can overcome strong homophobia. Indeed, becoming aware of a gay family member is frequently cited as a reason for widespread and relatively speedy changes in public opinion in the United States on the issue of same-sex marriage. There are sometimes very good outcomes when people who would have previously identified as endorsing strong homophobia come to parent and love their gay children.

We concede that prospective identification of people who are strongly homophobic and who bring their homophobia to bear on their parenting practices is imperfect. However, people who freely declare allegiances to religious doctrines and practices that are strongly homophobic or who evince sympathy for or acceptance of strong homophobia are at risk of being defective affective carers. Certainly self-declared strong homophobes—those who openly voice strongly homophobic views—are morally disqualified as adequately prepared prospective parents. Membership in a religious group that espouses strong homophobia should be considered a risk factor in assessing parental preparedness.

As well, the response that points to some examples of strongly homophobic parents changing and coming to love their gay child misses the mark. The good results that follow from this aren't enough to justify sacrificing the rights of gay children whose parents don't come around. This isn't an exercise in maximizing utility. Instead, we're interested in seeing how taking children seriously limits or constrains the right to procreate and parent.

Second, one might object to our view on the grounds of religious freedom. Does our view unduly limit religious freedom? We think it does not. Our view does not forbid people from holding or expressing religious doctrines that are strongly homophobic. However, it does constrain the domains in which it is permissible to act on strong homophobia. In general, one cannot exercise religious liberty in a way that jeopardizes the rights or basic well-being of others. Our analysis simply draws attention to the significance of the rights of children in the interpretation of the religious liberty. Structurally the argument is no different from a prohibition on religious indoctrination (even when well intentioned) that is grounded in children's rights to autonomy.

Third, some people object that the scope of our argument is too narrow. Why focus on strongly homophobic parents? Strongly homophobic parents aren't the only kinds of parents who fail to love their children because of the way that children turn out. If it turns out to be widely true that parents are at risk for failing to love their child, then perhaps we ought to be cautious about making this a requirement of parental preparedness. For example, consider a potential parent who is unable to love a child with a profound intellectual disability. While such a person may choose to undergo genetic testing to try to ensure that they don't end up with a disabled child, such testing is, at best, imperfect. As well, disabilities can happen later due to an accident or injury. Do we think that people who may be unable to love a disabled child shouldn't have children? To this worry, we have two responses. First, the wish not to have a child with a disability is usually described as a preference, rather than being based on the inability to love such a child. There isn't larger worldview, akin to a religious belief, that's connected to preference not to have a disabled child in the way that there is with sexual orientation. Second, suppose it were true that the potential parent was unable to love a disabled child, then it seems correct to us that such a person ought not to become a parent. Again, note that the age of the child matters. If a child is born disabled and others are able to parent and love the child, there may be no harm done. What's particularly worrying about sexual orientation is that by the time the parent becomes aware of the child's sexual orientation, the child has come to love the parent and the removal of that love is particularly devastating, especially in a culture with the strong parental rights we described early in the paper.

Conclusion

By way of conclusion, let us briefly recap the discussion. Although our argument yields a provocative conclusion, its basic structure is simple and relies on considerations internal to a liberal conception of justice. First, children have a right to affective caring that is grounded in their interests in basic welfare and developing self-respect. Second, competent prospective parents must be able to reliably provide affective caring to children. Third, strongly homophobic parents cannot reliably provide affective caring to children who are gay. The withdrawal of affection to gay children by homophobic parents along with the condemnation of their children's sexual orientation by parents imperils children's well-being and undermines their sense of self-respect. The evidence about the harm to gay youth caused by homophobic parents is strong and alarming. Fourth, since the moral right to parent is conditional on satisfying a threshold of competency and since strongly homophobic adults fall short of this standard, strongly homophobic adults should not be considered competent parents and do not have a moral right to parent. To the degree that religious fundamentalists embrace strong homophobia they place their moral right to parent in jeopardy.[21]

Notes

1 Of course, not all cases are typical. Technological developments in artificial reproduction technology and the associated advent of various kinds of surrogacy arrangements raise important moral and legal issues about the precise nature of biological procreation and the relationship, in more complex cases, between procreation and acquisition of the right to parent. Our analysis focuses on the 'ordinary' cases but would nonetheless have implications for the moral claim of persons to have parental rights in surrogacy cases.

2 Determining the precise dimensions of parental competency is a complex matter because it depends on (a) identifying the justice-based entitlements of children with respect to their upbringing and (b) determining how the social division of moral labor affects which agents are assigned which responsibilities for meeting children's claims. For instance, if we suppose that children have a right to healthcare then whether a parent is competent or not can depend whether the

state secures children's access healthcare. If the state does not provide healthcare to children and we assume that responsibility for meeting children's healthcare needs falls to parents, then parents who cannot provide healthcare to their children may, in that social context, fall below the threshold of competency. See Macleod 2015 for discussion of this point and facets of parental competency more generally.

3 In the Canadian case *Director of Child and Family Services v. D.M.P. et al., 2010 MBQB 32*, a white supremacist couple lost custody of their children on the grounds that efforts to inculcate their children with racist ideology made them unsuitable guardians of their two children.

4 M. Clayton, *Justice and Legitimacy in Upbringing* (Oxford: Oxford University Press, 2006).

5 C. Macleod,. 'Conceptions of Parental Autonomy,' *Politics and Society* 25, no. 1 (1997): 117–40.

6 Galston, W. (1991). *Liberal Purposes* (Cambridge: Cambridge University Press).

7 Rawls identifies two aspects of self-respect: "First of all, as we noted earlier, it includes a person's sense of their own value, his secure conviction that that his conception of the good, his plan of life, is worth carrying out. And second, self-respect implies confidence in one's abilities, so far as it is one's power, to fulfill one's intentions. When we feel our plans are of little value, we cannot pursue them with pleasure or take delight in their execution" (Rawls, 1999: 386).

8 We also recognize that there are other kinds of beliefs and attitudes of parents that can pose a parallel threat to the welfare and self-respect of children. For instance, some potential parents may harbor views about persons with disabilities that are harmful and demeaning to children with disabilities. If the general structure of our argument is sound then such would-be parents could also be deemed incompetent and would lack the moral right to parent.

9 We do not assume that procreative rights are unlimited but our characterization of liberalism does entail the rejection of strongly anti-natalist views that contend that procreation is wrong. See Benatar (2006).

10 The interests of other parties also impose limits on rights of parental authority. Some ways of parenting can generate needless social costs for society and these costs can provide an independent reason for limiting parental authority. We do not emphasize these costs in developing our critique of the rights of homophobic parents but it is worth noting that the damage done to gay youth by homophobic parents generates a need for social services to assist homeless young people who often struggle with drug and alcohol abuse.

11 We allow that the role of parents can be played by more than two adults and need not be performed by the mothers and fathers of children and there need be no biological relation between parents and children and parents can be of the same sex. See Brennan and Cameron (2014) for a discussion about the number of parents a child can have. Similarly, grandparents or other family members can serve as parents in the sense we have in mind. But for ease of exposition we shall generally assume that parents are usually the adults who are the legal guardians of children.

12 See Liao (2006) for examination and defense of the claim that children have a right to be loved.

13 The invocation of the intrinsic goods of childhood is an important but dispensable part of our argument (Brennan, 2014, Macleod, 2010). We think there are important goods of childhood and securing children's access to these goods is relevant from the point of view of justice, at least any account of justice that is concerned with human flourishing. We also think parents are especially well placed to help realize or to frustrate children's enjoyment of the intrinsic goods of childhood. But our argument challenging the right to parent by homophobic

fundamentalists does not turn on this. Less controversial considerations are sufficient to make the case. So even if one thinks that parents do not have an obligation to provide children with the intrinsic goods of childhood there is enough worry about ordinary facets of children's health, well-being, and self-respect that are jeopardized by homophobic parents to make our case.

14 See Brighouse and Swift (2006) and Macleod (2015) for discussion of so-called 'dual-interest' accounts of the right to parent.
15 Laura E. Durso and Gary J. Gates, "Serving Our Youth: Findings from a National Survey of Services Providers Working with Lesbian, Gay, Bisexual and Transgender Youth Who Are Homeless or at Risk of Becoming Homeless," 2012.
16 Caitlin Ryan et al., "Family Rejection as a Predictor of Negative Health Outcomes in White and Latino Lesbian, Gay, and Bisexual Young Adults," *Pediatrics* 123 (2009): 346–52.
17 Alex Morris, "The Forsaken: A Rising Number of Homeless Gay Teens Are Being Cast Out by Religious Families," 2014, accessed June 2016. http://www.rollingstone.com/culture/features/the-forsaken-a-rising-number-of-homeless-gay-teens-are-being-cast-out-by-religious-families-20140903.
18 See LaFollette (1980, 2010) for a defense of parental licensing and De Wispelaere and Weinstock (2012) for a sympathetic but critical assessment of the licensing proposal.
19 See Botterell and McLeod (2014).
20 Legal regulation of smoking in the home already has some traction: some Canadian provinces do consider smoking in home a relevant factor in the approval process for foster parenting and adoption.
21 Thanks to Tristan James for research assistance and to Eldon Soifer for helpful comments.

Bibliography

Benatar, David. *Better Never to Have Been: the Harm of Coming into Existence.* Oxford: Oxford University Press, 2006.
Botterell, Andrew and Carolyn McLeod. "Not for the Faint of Heart': Accessing the Status Quo on Adoption and Parental Licensing," in *Family-Making*, edited by F. Baylis and C. McLeod, 151–167. Oxford: Oxford University Press, 2014.
Brennan, S. "The Goods of Childhood, Children's Rights, and the Role of Parents as Advocates and Interpreters," in *Family-Making: Contemporary Ethical Challenges*, edited by F. Baylis and C. McLeod. Oxford: Oxford University Press, 2014.
Brennan, S and B. Cameron. "How Many Parents Can a Child Have? Philosophical Reflections on the 'Three Parent Case'," with Bill Cameron, *Dialogue*, available on CJO2014. DOI:10.1017/S0012217314000705.
Brighouse, Harry and Adam Swift. "Parents' Rights and the Value of the Family." *Ethics* 117, no. 1 (2006): 80–108.
Clayton, M. *Justice and Legitimacy in Upbringing.* Oxford: Oxford University Press, 2006).
De Wispelaere, Jurgen and Daniel Weinstock. "Licensing Parents to Protect Our Children?" *Ethics and Social Welfare* 6, no. 2 (2012): 195–205.
Durso, Laura E. and Gary J. Gates. "Serving Our Youth: Findings from a National Survey of Services Providers Working With Lesbian, Gay, Bisexual and Transgender Youth Who Are Homeless or At Risk of Becoming Homeless." *The Palette Fund, The True Colors Fund* and *The Williams Institute.* Accessed November 7. http://williaminstitute.law.ucla.edu/research/safe-schools-and-youth/serving-our-youth-july-2012/

Galston, W. *Liberal Purposes*. Cambridge: Cambridge University Press, 1991.

Liao, M. "The Right of Children to Be Loved." *The Journal of Political Philosophy* 14, no. 4 (2006): 420–440.

LaFollette, Hugh. "Licensing Parents." *Philosophy & Public Affairs* 9, no. 2 (1980): 183–197.

LaFollette, Hugh. "Licensing Parents Revisited." *Journal of Applied Philosophy* 27, no. 4 (2010): 327–343.

Macleod, C. "Conceptions of Parental Autonomy." *Politics and Society* 25, no. 1 (1997): 117–140.

Macleod, C. "Primary Goods, Capabilities and Children," in *Measuring Justice: Primary Goods and Capabilities*, edited by H. Brighouse and I. Robeyns, 174–192. Cambridge: Cambridge University Press, 2010.

Macleod, C. "Parental Competency and the Right to Parent," in *Permissible Progeny*, edited by R. Vernon, S. Hannan and S. Brennan, 227–245. New York: Oxford University Press, 2015.

Morris, Alex. "The Forsaken: A Rising Number of Homeless Gay Teens Are Being Cast Out by Religious Families," 2014. Accessed June 2016. http://www.rollingstone.com/culture/features/the-forsaken-a-rising-number-of-homeless-gay-teens-are-being-cast-out-by-religious-families-20140903.

Rawls, John. *A Theory of Justice*. Cambridge, MA: Harvard University Press, 1999.

Ryan, Caitlin et al. "Family Rejection as a Predictor of Negative Health Outcomes in White and Latino Lesbian, Gay, and Bisexual Young Adults." *Pediatrics* 123 (2009): 346–352.

12 Parental Licensing and Pregnancy as a Form of Education[1]

Christine Overall

A "Bizarro" comic from August, 2014, shows two infants facing each other from their strollers, each stroller gripped by a woman. One baby, with arms spread wide in disbelief, says to the other, "My life is in their hands & yet they've given me *no* references nor *any* evidence of their qualification to raise a child."

The right to parent a child is typically taken to include certain rights of authority and influence, including the right to rear the child and to shape the course of the child's education. One type of challenge to these apparently straightforward parental rights claim is implicitly cited in the "Bizarro" comic: the very real need for competence and preparation for assuming the parenting role. The cartoon baby raises a good point: What qualifies a person to raise a child?

In the case of adoption the answer seems clear: There is a formal preparation, screening, and licensing process[2] that certifies that an individual (or more usually a couple) is qualified for parenthood. The licensing of potential non-family member adoptive parents declares that they have been found competent to act as parents. Yet other parents never go through any formal process that evaluates and certifies their fitness to parent. These include not only those who raise their own "naturally conceived" biologically related children, but also the users of assisted reproduction technologies, the male partners of women who become pregnant through gamete or embryo donation, the commissioning parents in cases of contract pregnancy, step-parents, and family members such as grandparents who raise a grandchild.

This paper is not about the criteria for the acquisition of parental rights generally, but more specifically about the preparation and education that qualify individuals for the role of parent. If preparation and licensing are appropriate for adoptive parents who wish to raise a genetically unrelated child, why should they not also be appropriate for all other types of parents, including those who will raise their genetically related child?

The Case for Screening and Licensing (All) Prospective Parents

I will take for granted that the purpose of licensing potential parents is to evaluate and attest to their competence as parents, to indicate, that is, that they have at least some of the appropriate skills and preparation for child-rearing. Michael W. Austin suggests that there are two standards of parental screening: a "weak" standard, intended to "prohibit those individuals who would be very bad parents from raising children," and a "strong" standard, designed to "pick out those individuals who would be good (or good enough) parents" (Austin, 2007, 88). Austin argues that only the "weak" standard is justified (Austin, 2007, 90–92). I will not explore in detail the various arguments for each standard, but will simply assume that, where screening is justified, the use of the weak standard is at a minimum appropriate for assessing potential parents.[3]

Whatever the standards of parental screening, however, proponents of parental screening and licensing advocate that all prospective parents undergo it. In particular, it has been claimed that non-adoptive parents, like adoptive parents, should be denied the right to raise their biologically related children unless they comply with screening and licensing requirements that certify their (at least minimal) fitness to parent (LaFollette, 1980; LaFollette, 2010).

Hugh LaFollette argues that licensing serves the purpose of protecting vulnerable people from those with whom they have a special relationship (LaFollette, 2010, 143). Licensing is justified when individuals are engaged in an activity that may significantly harm those whom they are serving, when the activity can be safely performed only when the individuals are knowledgeable and competent, and when the benefits of licensing outweigh the reasons against it (LaFollette, 2010, 328). In such cases, licensing is justified even if some people will be deeply harmed if they fail to get a license, and even if the licensing procedures may sometimes fail to recognize competence, or may mistakenly license the incompetent (LaFollette, 1980, 183–4).

Parenting in general qualifies for licensing because, first, children are vulnerable and can be irrevocably harmed, and second, parenting requires appropriate knowledge, abilities, judgment, and dispositions (LaFollette, 2010, 329). Moreover, says, LaFollette, a putative right to have children does not defeat the need for parental licensing: it is similar to the right to become a physician, which is justifiably conditional on the possession of the appropriate qualifications (LaFollette, 2010, 335). One has a right to have children only if one is not going to abuse or neglect them, and the prevention of such abuse and neglect is precisely the purpose of parental licensing (LaFollette, 1980, 188).

Finally, LaFollette argues that it is possible to specify at least minimal criteria of parental competence (i.e., the avoidance of abuse and neglect), and to determine whether prospective parents meet those criteria. The practical challenges of implementing parental licensing are not insurmountable, he says: We should "set minimal requirements for a license, then reward those with licenses—say with special tax breaks" (LaFollette, 2010, 338). The minimal requirement would be the successful completion of a parenting course. In addition, a program to assist and monitor parents of young children could be established, along with "strengthening education, expanding healthcare, and bolstering children's services" (LaFollette, 2010, 339).

In a more recent paper, Carolyn McLeod and Andrew Botterell advance the potential case for licensing all parents by arguing that any reasons that support the routine and compulsory state screening and licensing of prospective adoptive parents also justify the state screening and licensing of some or possibly all biologically related parents. To put it another way, they argue that there is no justification for singling out non-family member adoptive parents for screening and licensing when other prospective parents are not compelled to undergo these procedures (McLeod and Botterell, 2014a).

First, the risks of harm to children are not demonstrably greater in the case of adoptive arrangements (McLeod and Botterell, 2014a, 158). Second, if the feasibility of licensing genetically related parents is a concern, it would at least also be possible to license individuals and couples who acquire children through the use of assisted reproduction (159). Third, if the transfer of responsibility for children provides a reason for licensing in non-family member adoptions, then it similarly provides a reason for licensing in cases of contract pregnancy. Moreover, arguably the *acquisition* of parental responsibility is just as morally significant as its transfer (161). Fourth, the claim that non-adoptive parents have a claim to a specific child (the one to whom they are genetically related), whereas adoptive parents do not, is not true in all cases of adoptive parents (and we could simply allow prospective adoptive parents to pick a child). And even where true, there is no argument, say McLeod and Botterell, to support licensing in the latter case but not in the former (164–65).

McLeod and Botterell are not willing to argue that *all* prospective parents *should* be licensed. But based on their own experiences, they say that parental screening and licensing can be expensive, time-consuming, intrusive, and frustrating. It is also unfair, because it is confined, without justification, not merely to prospective adoptive parents, but to prospective non-family member adoptive parents (166). For this reason, they suggest, it implicitly calls into question the value of non-family member adoption, and could thereby be harmful to adopted children and their families.

In other papers, McLeod and Botterell augment their case against special licensing only for prospective non-family member adoptive parents by arguing that there is no sound basis for appealing to a (negative) right to reproduce in order to excuse non-adoptive parents from undergoing just the sort of screening and licensing that adoptive parents do (McLeod and Botterell, 2014b, 229; McLeod and Botterell, 2015). They argue that there are no interests or choices that could ground such a right (including "an interest in reproducing genetically or biologically; an interest in parenting simpliciter or in parenting one's biological child; a right to autonomy; a right to procreative autonomy; and a right to beget equally").

Pregnancy as a Form of Education and Preparation

I agree with LaFollette that potential parents of all varieties should be *at least* minimally competent to raise their children. Indeed, I believe that preparation and education for parenthood, whether parenthood is achieved via adoption or via gestation, is both important and necessary.

And I agree with McLeod and Botterell that it is unfair to impose licensing requirements uniquely upon non-family member adoptive parents.

My view is that *anyone* to whom the responsibility for and authority over a child is transferred should be licensed to perform the role of parent. This process would apply not only to the typical non-family member adoptive parent or parents, but also to commissioning individuals or couples who pay a contract mother to gestate a baby; step-parents; and family members such as grandparents, if they have not previously been involved in rearing their grandchild. However, I believe that women who gestate with the intention of raising the child they gestated, along with their partners (of whatever sex) who are present throughout the pregnancy[4] (including cases where the pregnancy results from donated gametes or a donated embryo) ordinarily do not need and should not be required to undergo a formal licensing requirement.

The justification of this latter claim is not founded on claims about a right to reproduce[5] allegedly held only by people who are capable of biological procreation. Nor is it founded on the genetic connection, if any, to the future child (in fact, in some cases, one or both of the prospective birth parents may not be genetically connected to the child). Instead, the exemption from formal licensing, I shall argue, is founded on the prospective parent's[s'] experience of pregnancy.

Pregnancy is socially under-valued in some ways, and its significance is often not recognized. Because it is a commonplace phenomenon, its uniqueness is not recognized. But as Sara Ruddick remarks, "[n]either our own ambivalence to our women's bodies nor the bigoted, repressive uses which many men, colonizers, and racists have made of biology, should blind us to our body's possibilities" (Ruddick, 1980, 346).

Now, McLeod and Botterell write, "one would only be inclined to say that gestating and giving birth to a child is constitutive of adequate parenting if one already believed that biological parents have an entitlement to parent that adoptive parents lack" (McLeod and Botterell, 2015, fn 20). I will show that it is *not* a mere a priori and illegitimate preference for biological parenthood that grounds the value of pregnancy as a form of preparation for parenthood. They also write, "Do we really think that more thought and information should go into transferring or delegating responsibility for children than goes into acquiring that responsibility in the first place?" (McLeod and Botterell, 2014a, 161). The answer to their question is clearly no: It is important for all prospective parents to be ready for parenthood. But their question fails to recognize that biological parents, especially gestational mothers, engage in a process of thought, preparation, and the acquisition of information. My contention is that pregnancy provides the chance to undertake such a process, and that most pregnant women,[6] along with their partners, avail themselves of that opportunity. As a result, the default assumption should be that birth parents should not be required to undergo formal state screening and licensing.

As Hilde Lindemann Nelson says, "the purposeful, creative activity of mothering begins long before birth" (Lindemann Nelson, 1994, 263). Pregnancy is not a merely passive experience, a series of events that simply happen to women. Catriona Mackenzie writes,

> [P]regnancy cannot be thought of simply as a merely "natural" event which just *happens* to women and in relation to which they are passive. Although pregnancy certainly involves biological processes which are beyond the woman's control, these processes are always mediated by the cultural meanings of pregnancy, by the woman's personal and social context, and by the way she constitutes herself in response to these factors through the decisions she makes.
>
> (Mackenzie, 1992, 141, her emphasis)

Pregnancy is an active process of "work, both physical and mental, conscious and automatic" (Feldman, 1992, 99), in which most women deliberately participate in a thoughtful, engaged, and attentive manner. Indeed, to experience a pregnancy is, usually, to undergo a process of education, an education that is eminently appropriate as background for early parenting.

Now in ordinary cases of education, preparation does not, of itself, automatically yield an exemption from licensing. For example, one might learn a great deal about medicine, without thereby acquiring an exemption from the licensing process required for becoming a physician. But the education afforded by pregnancy is essentially different from most other forms of education, because it is founded, from the beginning, upon a *relationship* with the being whom the individual is learning to care for. In most cases, pregnant women develop an important and unique relationship with their fetus, which is the beginning of their relationship with their future child. Unlike cases of adoption, when a woman gives birth to her baby and raises it, with or without a partner who was present during the pregnancy, the child does not change hands and the responsibility for the child is not transferred. The relationship begun during gestation continues.

How is it possible to have a relationship with a fetus? It develops in many ways. For example, the woman may start to notice the fetus's presence, at least indirectly, early in pregnancy, as her biological condition changes to accommodate the growing being. Eventually she feels the fetus's movements and also notices when it is still. The fetus may push a tiny hand or foot into the wall of her abdomen, where she will notice a distinct bulge. It may roll from side to side. At a medical appointment the woman may hear the fetus's heartbeat, or see an ultrasound image. She may invite a family member to press his ear against her abdomen to listen for the sound, or to feel her abdomen to detect the fetus's movements.

As the woman becomes more aware of the presence and growth of her fetus, she may give it a name or nickname. She may attempt to interpret its patterns, noticing times of day or night when it is active and trying to understand its position in her uterus—head up, head down, or transverse. She may stroke her abdomen or press on a part of the fetus that is pushing against it. She may talk, read, or sing to it. She may describe her fetus to others as active or calm, and notice how it seems to react to her own activities and even to her food intake. She may think about the ways in which the fetus's size and activities are changing throughout the pregnancy, and speculate about what these changes may imply for its future after birth.

The fetus is not an inert or passive part of this relationship. The fetus also experiences and responds to the woman who is gestating it. In the sixth month of its development, it can hear her voice and the sounds of her heartbeat and digestion, as well as other noises in her vicinity, including the voices of family and friends (Eliot, 1999, 237–40). Its ability to hear also enables it to learn to recognize familiar sounds (Eliot, 1999, 240–241). In addition, the fetus can feel and respond to the woman's movements, changes of position, and patterns of exercise (Eliot, 1999, 90). It can even smell and taste odors and flavors of substances that are inhaled or consumed by the pregnant woman (Eliot, 1999, 163, 176).

What is important to notice is that the relationship between the pregnant woman and her fetus is interactive. Obviously the woman is engaged in a range of sensory, physical, intellectual, and emotional responses to her fetus, whereas the fetus's responses are straightforwardly sensory and physical. Nonetheless, because the pregnant woman and the fetus react to each other and change their behavior in response to each other, they are in a relationship that is not static but develops and changes. And this relationship, I argue, facilitates and enhances the learning that the pregnant woman undergoes.

The claim that the experience of pregnancy provides an important opportunity for education and preparation for parenthood, precluding the need for formal licensing, is in part an empirical claim and in part a normative claim. It is normative in that it is about the significance and value of pregnancy as more than a mere passive biological experience, but as an active, thoughtful process that serves as a *prima facie* qualification for parenthood. It is empirical insofar as it is about the facts of pregnancy as an experience in which genuine learning is possible. While I do not know of any formal scholarly studies of pregnancy as a site for parental learning and preparation,[7] in this section I present a description of seven kinds of learning and preparation that are attainable during gestation. I acknowledge from the outset that this description will seem notably Western in its content. But presumably, those who are proposing screening and licensing for birth parents primarily have in mind a Western context.

1) The pregnant woman is likely to be constantly **learning new information**—learning about the changes in her own body, but also about fetal development, how to cope with labor and delivery, how to care for her newborn, and how to breastfeed. In many cases she must also learn to understand and make choices about the use of prenatal technologies and the medicalization of pregnancy and birth. She may talk with other pregnant women and with mothers and grandmothers, consult with relatives, take prenatal classes, read books, blogs, and websites, watch relevant films, videos, and television programs, and observe others' children.

This acquisition of new information is obviously helpful not only for its immediate use, but also as an introduction to an ongoing process of self-education: A mother has to be constantly learning about her child's needs, physical and psychological condition, and developmental stages, whether she learns formally (by reading, by research on the internet, by taking classes in child development) or informally (by talking with family, friends, and neighbors, or simply interacting in a learning-positive way with the child herself). To be a competent parent requires being open to ongoing learning.

2) The pregnant woman **engages in self-care**, which is inevitably also care for her fetus, by seeking out good food, appropriate exercise, rest, and relevant healthcare (from midwives, physicians, nurses, perhaps physiotherapists or nutritionists). She avoids, where possible, exposing herself to illnesses; she refrains, if she can, from smoking, using recreational drugs, drinking alcohol, and engaging in other activities likely to be harmful to her fetus. She may take vitamins, give up caffeine, adjust her exercise habits, or make changes to her regular work routine, whether paid or unpaid.

Her engagement in self-care, animated at least in part by concern for the health of the fetus, helps to prepare the woman for many years of effort in caring for her child, including feeding him,[8] seeking healthcare for him, and attending to his other needs. The pregnant woman starts to accustom herself to thinking of, planning for, and acting on behalf of the well-being of another being, and treating that being as at least equal to herself. The woman may come to recognize that her own physical and psychological well-being cannot be paramount (if it ever was) once she is a mother, but must many times take second place to the psychological and physical well-being of the vulnerable child.

3) The pregnant woman **learns to adjust to constant change** in her body's shape, size, weight, balance, flexibility, skin texture, nutritional needs, and requirements for rest, sleep, and exercise. She learns to accept frequent interruptions in her routine and expectations, as she must respond to her

body's new needs to eat, to urinate, and to rest. She must adjust to the requirements of the healthcare system, with visits to a midwife or doctor and subjection to various kinds of medical examinations and prenatal tests. The pregnant woman learns to understand and accommodate to changing physical demands on herself—fatigue, her heavier body, greater hunger, and sometimes nausea.

Learning to adjust to these changes is appropriate preparation for handling the changing demands that child-rearing makes. This experience prepares the woman for the demands of breastfeeding a child, if she does; for carrying the child from place to place; for picking him up and putting him down; for getting up in the night repeatedly to feed or comfort a child; and for dealing with her own sleep deprivation. It's significant that pregnancy is spread over time and requires gradual adjustment. If people were to simply purchase children "at the local superstore" (LaFollette, 2010, 338), there would be serious justification for anxiety about their parental abilities, because (among other reasons) such a process would not allow the gradual adaptation and response to change that usually goes along with the process of gestating a fetus. One can never safely assume that a child's condition is static, or that one thoroughly understands the child, for the child will very soon go through another stage of growth and development. Some of the needs of children are predictable and some are not. The process of pregnancy is a preparation for adjusting to the constant changes that babies, toddlers, and children go through.

4) The pregnant woman learns to **make material adjustments** to her pregnancy and the upcoming birth: for example, in what she wears (especially in climates of extremes, she may need a variety of different clothes to get through her pregnancy); in her financial commitments (especially if she encounters health issues during her pregnancy or has to travel far to get healthcare tests, treatment, or support); and in preparing an environment for her future child (clothes for the baby, a place to sleep, diapers, and various kinds of equipment, depending on her financial means and the social environment). These material adjustments are a partial preparation for the material and financial costs of child-rearing: food, clothes, shelter, transportation, education, healthcare, and childcare will all demand material changes and financial outlay.

5) The pregnant woman prepares herself by **engaging in creative thinking and activity**.[9] "Giving birth may be closer to artistic expression than it is to the production of material objects; both can involve very hard work but the desire to express oneself in the activity may be paramount" (Held, 1989, 382). Pregnancy and birthing usually involve a series of choices: whether to become pregnant; whether to continue being pregnant; what to eat and

drink; where to live; how much domestic, unpaid, or paid work to do; what pastimes, hobbies, arts, or activities to engage in; whom to consult for pregnancy care; where to give birth; how to prepare for birth; and how to prepare for life with the child. And as Lindemann Nelson points out, the pregnant woman may have to exercise "considerable intelligence and imagination" to navigate pregnancy within demanding personal, social, work-related, or environmental conditions, including "not only obstacles of gender, but also those of class and perhaps race" (Lindemann Nelson, 1994, 266).

This engagement in creative thinking and activity helps prepare the pregnant woman for the creative nature of child-rearing, and the many kinds of choices that must be made in caring for the child, teaching the child, stimulating the child, and protecting the child. Pregnancy is a time when the future mother begins the process of engaging in what Ruddick calls "maternal thinking," "a 'thought' arising out of maternal practices organized by the interests of preservation, growth, and acceptability" of the child (Ruddick, 1980, 359).[10]

6) The pregnant woman may **experience tumultuous emotions, including hope for and worry and fear about the unknown.** No pregnancy's outcome is guaranteed. Sometimes pregnancy ends in miscarriage; sometimes an infant is born prematurely; sometimes the infant is born with illnesses or impairments; alternatively, sometimes the woman becomes ill for part or all of the pregnancy. Even in the developed world, some infants still die shortly after birth, and the maternal mortality rate is not zero. These experiences of hope, worry, and fear are appropriate preparation for parenting because caring for a baby and child will elicit many different emotions: positive ones, certainly (whose intensity may surprise her), but also worry and fear, because it is not possible to protect a child completely as he becomes more independent, or to control the social and physical environment in which he must live, and because the outcome of childrearing—who the child will become as a teenager and adult—is almost entirely unknown and can generate many surprises.

7) The pregnant woman **undergoes the experience of being *perceived* as pregnant,** and being conceptualized within her social environment as a person who will be a mother (or possibly even is already, depending on the attitudes around her toward the fetus). Those with whom she lives, works, and interacts are likely to regard her (whether justifiably or not) as being a different person than the one she was before becoming pregnant.

This experience helps the woman to know something about the scope and limits of likely social support for her role as a parent. That support may vary depending on whether she is considered to be the right sort of mother (not too old or young, not too poor, and not too eccentric, independent, or politically non-conformist). It also helps her to anticipate the ways in which she, and ultimately her child, will be subjected to social judgments and cultural pressures. The experience helps her to understand the extent of her ability to parent according to her own judgment, and to recognize that raising an "acceptable" child (in Ruddick's words) is, whether she likes it or not, part of the work of motherhood (Ruddick, 1980, 354–56).

Being perceived as a potential mother, or even as a mother already, also helps the pregnant woman to start seeing herself as a mother. That is, part of the process of preparation that she undergoes is the development of a new identity, one that may be quite distinct from her existing identities.

In summary, while her relationship with her fetus develops, the pregnant woman goes through a gradual education in some important facets of motherhood. She experiences firsthand an introduction to some of the challenges that parenthood brings. Therefore, it is simply a mistake to suppose that a woman who gives birth has no preparation for being a parent. Moreover, gestation is a learning process that is directly relevant to the specific future child whom she will parent.[11] Hence, women who gestate their infants should not be required to submit to formal state screening and licensing.[12]

The Partner of the Pregnant Woman

The foregoing argument should not be interpreted as saying that women who have gestated are necessarily better parents than men, because they cannot gestate, or than women who do not or cannot gestate. It is not intended to be a claim about social superiority derived from biological labor and experience. Instead it is intended to demonstrate the genuine value of pregnancy as a potential site for education, learning, and personal development.

But in addition, I suggest that the gestational woman's partner, if any (whether male or female is irrelevant), usually has a derivative entitlement not to be required to submit to formal licensing. The justification for the partner's exemption from formal licensing may less strong than that of the pregnant woman, but it is nonetheless significant. The reason is that many partners who are present during the pregnancy of a woman they love also go through a process of preparation and education for parenthood, while they also develop a connection to the baby from before his birth—albeit a connection that is, of course, mediated by the pregnant woman.

This preparation can take many forms. First and foremost, the partner may demonstrate commitment to the pregnant woman's physical and psychological health and well-being—perhaps by accompanying her to midwife/doctor visits and tests; by grocery shopping and cooking for her; by ensuring that she gets enough rest and sleep, especially if there are already other children in the family who need attention; by supporting the pregnant woman to acquire clothes that are comfortable and appropriate; and by providing psychological support if she is distressed. Second, the partner may learn, along with the pregnant woman, about her pregnancy, the development of the fetus, the upcoming delivery, and infant and child development and care. Third, the partner likely provides material and financial support, especially if the pregnant woman is unable, or no longer able, to do paid work and/ or domestic work. Fourth, the partner may work with the pregnant woman in preparing for the future child—planning where the child will sleep, making or buying clothes, buying or building furniture, perhaps acquiring toys and books, a stroller or carriage or baby carrier. Fifth, the partner may participate in rituals and social events related to the pregnancy—for example, announcing the pregnancy to family and friends, attending baby showers or "gender reveal"[13] parties, listening to the fetal heartbeat, talking or singing to the fetus, and taking photos of the pregnant woman throughout her pregnancy. And sixth, like the pregnant woman, the partner may experience emotions of hope, worry, and fear, which may be as powerful and instructive for the partner as they are for the pregnant woman herself. The partner has a mediated relationship with the fetus.

Some Qualifications

I have argued that the experience of pregnancy provides a form of preparation and education that makes formal licensing for parenthood unnecessary for birth mothers and the partners who accompany them through pregnancy. In order to forestall possible concerns about and objections to this claim, I want to add the qualifications that follow.

Qualification #1

As Caroline Lundquist points out, pregnancy experiences cannot "be captured in a single, totalizing account" (Lundquist, 2008, 137). I recognize that both the experience of pregnancy and the pregnancy itself are socially shaped, and that expectations of and provisions for pregnant women vary from society to society. Moreover, women's experience of pregnancy may be, in Ruddick's terms, "*aided or assaulted* by the help and advice of fathers, teachers, doctors, moralists, therapists, and others" (Ruddick, 1980, 348, my emphasis).[14]

So I am not claiming that all pregnancies are alike, or that all pregnant women do the same things, have the same resources, learn the same lessons, or react the same way to being pregnant. I am not claiming that every pregnant woman undergoes every one of the categories of learning experiences I have described.[15] Instead, I am trying to draw attention to the genuine psychological, intellectual, social, and physical work and resources of pregnancy. I simply claim that my characterization of the preparation that pregnancy can provide is accurate, to at least some degree and in most cases. I am pointing to evidence justifying the claim that birth parents should not automatically be subjected to formal licensing for parenthood.

I am also not claiming that all women choose to be pregnant, desire to be pregnant, or are unambiguously positive about their pregnancies. I recognize that for some women, pregnancy is unsought and unwanted, an intrusion or even an invasion. Some women are not remotely interested in becoming mothers or in undergoing any kind of preparation for motherhood. Thus, in some cases, pregnancy may not in any way provide an education and preparation for parenthood—for example, in instances of denied pregnancy (in which a pregnant woman does not recognize that she is pregnant) and rejected pregnancy (in which a pregnant woman, often one who is pregnant non-voluntarily or as a result of rape, rejects her fetus and experiences no connection to the experience of pregnancy or to the fetus itself) (Lundquist, 2008). I am not claiming that the experience of pregnancy inevitably or infallibly makes a woman (or her partner) a good parent.

Insofar as a complete lack of commitment to the pregnancy may mean a lack of commitment to the future child, a woman for whom the experience of pregnancy is quite alien may be thinking of giving up her child for adoption. But if, after a denied or rejected pregnancy, the woman nonetheless decides she wants to raise her child, it might be appropriate to evaluate her ability to do so and to ensure that she receives the further education and support she will need.

For I am *not* saying that no woman who gestates a child can ever legitimately be deprived of that child. Some women, or their partners, may not have benefited from what may be learned during pregnancy. If they are abusive, neglectful, or severely inadequate it is appropriate, for the child's sake, that they lose custody of their child.[16] While I believe that the rightful value of the experience of pregnancy should be acknowledged, I also recognize that the experience of pregnancy is not a guarantee of subsequent parental competence.

Qualification #2

Although I am saying that birth parents should not be formally screened and licensed for parenthood, I also believe in the value of parenting courses and other educational resources for all persons who raise children, including birth parents. I readily admit that the experience of gestation cannot possibly be a complete grounding, by itself, for the many and varied demands of years of child-rearing, including making difficult choices about the child's healthcare and education.[17]

Many prenatal courses are helpful to prospective birth parents, providing information about pregnancy, fetal development, birth, and early infant development. For the purpose of serving as pre-parenting education, however, prenatal courses have two limitations. First, they seldom provide information (presumably it is not possible for them to do so, given the temporal limitations) about child development beyond early infancy. Second, such courses are aimed only at people who become parents through gestation.

Therefore, I recommend that information about child development, child-care, and children's education be provided as a part (perhaps a mandatory part) of the curriculum in the first years of high school. Doing so could have several good features. First, it would be non-discriminatory, because it would educate all young people about caring for children, without necessarily assuming that they will procreate or be parents. Second, even though some people, probably a growing number, will not end up raising children, such courses would have a wider good: They would prepare students to interact with children in a knowledgeable, supportive way, for example if they coach a hockey or soccer team, lead a boy scout or girl guide/girl scout pack, become teachers, or simply have nieces, nephews, or young cousins. Third, such courses would be inherently multi-disciplinary, drawing upon such disciplines as biology, child psychology, the sociology of families, and educational theory, and hence they would be useful to the students' education by introducing them to a variety of interesting fields of study.

However they come to be parents, most people who are rearing children do not stop learning how to parent. Committed, devoted parents learn how to parent older children in part by parenting through each stage of their child's life. A mother learns how to parent a two-year-old by observing, interacting with, and guiding the child when he is one-year old, and by continuing that process as he gets older. She is in a close and loving relationship with the child in which she is constantly learning more about him and about herself as a parent. To support this process, courses about parenting and child development should be widely available (and inexpensive or free) to parents and prospective parents throughout the life course.

Qualification #3

According to McLeod and Botterell, "The current licensing regime serves to reinforce the belief that biological families are superior to (more natural, less likely to be dysfunctional, than) adoptive families" (McLeod and Botterell, 2014a, 166).

That's a worrisome suggestion. My argument is in no way an endorsement of the supposed biological superiority of birth parents. There is no reason whatever to believe that families with birth children are superior to other kinds of families (see Overall, 2014). Nonetheless, there is also no good reason to suppose that pregnancy is a purely biological process. Pregnancy has social, emotional, intellectual, and pragmatic value as preparation for parenting, and therefore it should be seen as being, most of the time, an effective preparation for parenthood.

Recall, also, that McLeod and Botterell argue that the fact that adoption involves a *transfer* of responsibility is not an adequate reason to uniquely require that only non-family member adoptive parents should be licensed; the *acquisition* of parental responsibility is also morally significant. In addition, they argue that the right to a specific child, which seems to be held by (most) biological parents, does not justify an exemption from licensing for such parents.

My response is that, through the relationship that is pregnancy, a birth mother, along with her partner (if any), provides (a) *continuity of care* to (b) *the specific child* who was gestated. The responsibility for the child is not transferred, and the connection to the child, along with the work involved in creating him, make the child uniquely the child of the gestational mother (and her partner, if any). The education and preparation afforded by the experience of pregnancy provides a *de facto* preparation for early parenting.[18] The fact that adoptive parents must be licensed does not mean they are not as good parents as those who do not adopt or that their families are not as valuable. It simply means, as Anca Gheaus suggests, that most adoptive parents have "a different, and in a way more difficult, starting point" (Gheaus, 2012, 453) for parenting, because they begin parenting a child whom they have not known since conception, who has lived some part of his life without them.

Implications for Other Kinds of Parents

At the beginning of this paper I pointed out that, under current practices, not only those who raise their own "naturally conceived" biologically related children, but also the users of assisted reproduction technologies, the male partners of women who become pregnant through gamete or embryo donation, the commissioning parents in cases of contract pregnancy, step-parents, and family members such as grandparents who raise a grandchild are not screened or licensed. I shall now briefly consider the question of licensing with respect to these other kinds of parents.

I have argued that the pregnancy experience of birth parents obviates any need for them to have formal licensing for parenthood. Is the situation any different for persons and their partners who make use of IVF, donor gametes or embryos, or other reproduction technologies in order to achieve a pregnancy? I think not. Formal licensing is not necessary for such persons because, however the pregnancy was achieved, they either go through pregnancy themselves, or share the experience of pregnancy with a woman who goes through it. In these cases there is continuity of care: The infant is not handed over to another person after birth, but is raised by the person who gestated him, along with her partner. The birth parents thus acquire the benefits of education and preparation that pregnancy offers.

The situation of individuals who use IVF and/or donor gametes or embryos to achieve a pregnancy is different from that of persons who commission and pay for a pregnancy by an unrelated woman. In a recent paper (Overall, 2015), I argue that the commissioning parents in contract pregnancy arrangements should be required to undergo a licensing process, just as non-family member adoptive parents are. The reason is that formal licensing is morally justified and necessary in all cases where a child changes hands and where the responsibility for the child is transferred from one person or persons to a different person or persons. That is, the licensing of prospective parents is warranted when there is an *interruption* in the care and responsibility for children. The mere fact that one or both of the commissioners may be genetically related to the child they have commissioned does not compensate for the discontinuity in the care and responsibility for the child that is enforced by the pregnancy contract. The commissioners do not experience the education and preparation for parenthood that individuals who closely accompany a pregnant woman receive;[19] hence, they should be required to undergo the type of preparation and licensing process used for prospective adoptive parents who are unrelated to their future children.[20]

Finally, whether or not step-parents and family members such as grandparents should be licensed before taking on the role of parent is a separate question from the one I have considered here. Its answer may well depend on the nature of their prior relationship, if any, with the child. Because of my focus on the unique and significant role of pregnancy, this paper has necessarily been concerned with parental roles in relation to infants. Obviously, children are not always adopted as infants, and step-parents and family members such as grandparents are likely to take on a parental role in relation to children who are no longer babies. These adults may not have been present for and in relationship with the birth mother during her pregnancy, and hence they did not receive the educational benefit that sharing a pregnancy offers. As a result, it may be appropriate for them to be licensed for parenthood. Nonetheless, if they already have an ongoing well-developed relationship with the child (as a grandparent might), then licensing seems less imperative.

Implications for Adoption Procedures

One argument used by LaFollette to support the screening and licensing of all parents draws upon the societal recognition and legitimacy of licensing procedures for adoptive parents:

> [T]here are striking parallels between the general licensing program I have advocated and our present adoption system. Both programs have the same aim—protecting children. Both have the same drawbacks and are subject to the same abuses. The only obvious dissimilarity is that the adoption requirements are *more* rigorous than those proposed for the general licensing program. Consequently, if we think it is so important to protect adopted children, even though people who want to adopt are less likely than biological parents to maltreat their children, then we should likewise afford the same protection to children reared by their biological parents.
>
> (LaFollette, 1980, 194–95, his emphasis)

In this section, because of my convictions about the importance of the experience of pregnancy, my strategy is the reverse of LaFollette's. In contrast to his argument that adoption sets a precedent for screening and licensing that should be applied to all potential parents, including those who become parents via gestation, I shall indicate some implications for the practice of adoption that can be gleaned from an examination of the preparation and education afforded by the experience of pregnancy. And I have in mind all cases of adoption—not only those involving non-family member adoptive parents, but also those involving the commissioning parent(s) in contract pregnancy cases, and step-parents and other family members, provided they do not have a previous relationship with the child—in short, anyone starting a parental relationship with a child who has not been in a gestational relationship with that child, either directly or via a relationship with the pregnant woman.

Andrew Botterell suggests that adoptive parents could be seen as engaging in a kind of gestational process: "[W]ith respect to thinking about parenting, preparing for parenthood, and acquiring information about becoming and being a parent, adoption affords (more or less) the same opportunities for knowledge, education, and insight as pregnancy." These opportunities include "researching adoption either domestically or internationally, privately or publicly, speaking with other adoptive parents, making material and financial sacrifices, thinking about education and schools, telling others about their prospective adoption, and so on" (Botterell, 2015, personal communication February 25). I find this idea plausible, and suggest that the best adoption practices—those that are good for children, are fair to prospective parents, and provide a good grounding for parenting—are likely to be those that help to make adoption preparation at least as useful as, and no more onerous than, the experience of accompanying a woman during pregnancy.

Parenthood via pregnancy, I have argued, is a process of preparation and education, via the development of a relationship. I therefore suggest that the adoption process should be focused not so much on screening[21] the potential adoptive parents as on helping them to be ready for parenthood. One important difference between the experience of pregnancy and the experience of preparing for adoption is that whereas the woman (along with her partner, if any) is in a relationship with her future child from the beginning of its existence, the adoptive parents do not have that advantage. The best adoption processes would therefore facilitate, as soon as feasible, the development of a relationship between the child and the prospective adoptive parents, to enable them to interact and get to know each other, as much as possible, before the adoption is finalized.[22] This process could at least include communications via the sending of photos, letters, and gifts, as well as (where accessible) electronic communication.

A course of preparation for adoption must both encourage thoughtful parenting decisions and enable the potential adopters to assume the identity of parent. The experience of pregnancy provides, certainly for the gestating woman herself, a kind of *compulsory* preparation. Unless she is extremely ill, seriously addicted, or badly mistreated, the pregnant woman is compelled by her condition to pay attention to what is happening to her. There is (in most cases) no such thing as sleeping through the class that pregnancy is. To make adoption preparation comparable, then, the process needs to be (to the extent possible) as interesting, absorbing, and compelling as the process of accompanying a woman through pregnancy, so that potential adoptive parents do not merely "go through the motions" and hence do not end up being unprepared.[23]

At the same time, I suggest that the best adoption processes would be no less demanding than the experience of accompanying a woman during pregnancy, and would take no less time. A preparation for adoption that is only minimal could lead to abuses. To say this is not to impugn the motives of potential adoptive parents; it is simply to recognize that child prostitution, child pornography, and trafficking in children persist throughout the world (see, e.g., Macias Konstantopoulos et al., 2013). Certainly in the past, when unrelated children were easily acquired, they were sometimes wanted mainly for the sake of their labor capacities (see, e.g., Bowcott, 2010). In order to forestall attempts by unscrupulous individuals who may want to acquire a child in order to exploit her labor or sexuality, it makes sense for the preparation for adoption to be rigorous, intensive, and capable of discouraging potential abusers. Clearly, LaFollette's scenario of merely picking up a child at the local superstore should not be possible (LaFollette, 2010, 338).

If the adoption process is (as I think it should be) intended to be at least as useful as the experience of accompanying a woman in pregnancy, and no more and no less onerous than that experience, then the licensing process in adoption would be primarily a certification that the adoptive parents have completed a process designed to educate and prepare them to be parents. As discussed earlier, McLeod and Botterell argue that it is unfair that only non-family member adoptive parents are required to be licensed. My response is that pregnancy is, in effect, the licensing process for the gestational woman and her partner. The birth of their baby is the signal that pregnancy—a nine-month process of education and preparation for early parenthood—has been completed.[24]

Thus, in comparing parenthood via adoption with parenthood via gestation, I reject the idea that it is mistaken or unfair to require preparation for adoptive parents when (supposedly) biological parents have none. Rather, the conclusion is that because the experience of pregnancy itself affords an important preparation for the woman and her partner, the process of preparation for potential adoptive parents should be comparable, in important respects, to the process of preparation that gestating women and their partners undergo. These practices would, ideally, place an emphasis not so much on screening and judging prospective parents, but rather on offering a useful education and helpful grounding for parenthood.

Conclusion

The experience of pregnancy, which affords a period of intensive parental preparation and education along with continuity of care and responsibility for the child, is a legitimate defense against the demand for formal screening and licensing of all birth parents. Because pregnancy is an active process involving real effort and genuine learning, it is unjust to fail to recognize the significance of what pregnant women do.

Moreover, recognizing the importance of pregnancy for continuity of care of the birth child and the education of both birth parents has desirable consequences for all members of the family. Imagine the possible negative outcomes of not recognizing pregnancy as a good preparation for parenthood. Requiring formal screening and licensing of birth parents would undermine women by making pregnancy and its related activities seem insignificant, indeed, personally and socially meaningless. It might also undermine the commitment pregnant women otherwise have to their own health and that of the fetus, and would lead to profound insecurity on the part of pregnant women, who would experience uncertainty, throughout gestation, about the possibility of not qualifying to be the mother of the fetus growing in their body.

I am not, of course, claiming that the experience of pregnancy is a universal panacea against child abuse and inadequate parenting. I acknowledge that in some cases people do not learn, or learn enough, from the experience of pregnancy, and sometimes children must be removed from their birth parents. But presumably, more formal types of parenting preparation are also not always successful. No human relationship or arrangement is ever 100% successful, and this will certainly be true if, contrary to my argument, formal screening and licensing are introduced for all biological parents.

Pregnancy provides a unique and usually helpful introduction to parenting, and there must be a very strong reason indeed to deprive a woman of a child whom she has gestated as a fetus. This claim also applies to so-called "surrogate" mothers who decide to keep their baby, even if they are not genetically related to the child they gestate. The experience of pregnancy is, in most cases, sufficiently significant as to provide a *prima facie* counter-argument to any requirement that women who gestate, and their partners, must be formally screened and licensed for parenthood. The burden should be on the state, in individual cases, to show that women who gestate and intend to raise the children, and their partners who are with them during pregnancy, are not adequately prepared to be parents.

Notes

1 I am grateful to Jaime Ahlberg and Michael Cholbi, and to all the participants in the Spencer Foundation project "From Procreative Acts to Parental Rights," for their feedback on an earlier version of this paper. Special thanks to Andrew Botterell for his extensive comments on my thoughts about adoption.
2 For a description of this process, see McLeod and Botterell (2014a). In this paper I am assuming neither that current adoption processes are perfect, nor that adoption preparation cannot be improved.

3   I am skeptical as to whether *good* parents can be identified prior to their becoming parents, but that skepticism in no way precludes an adherence to a weaker standard aimed at the prevention of harm to and abuse of children. In previous work I expressed the view that "there is no clear empirical method for predicting which individuals will be good parents and which will not" (Overall, 2012, 23). This claim was part of my argument that social screening (on the basis of sexual identity, gender identity, race, marital status, or parental fitness) of potential candidates for access to donor gametes or embryos, in vitro fertilization (IVF), or donor insemination is unjustified. The reasons are that physicians are not qualified to determine parental competency; social identity is irrelevant to parental success; and above all, individuals who procreate without using assisted reproduction technologies and processes are not screened. My main goal was to make the point that it is not appropriate to subject candidates for these reproductive technologies to special forms of screening that other biological parents are not required to undergo. This paper offers a justification for exempting women who gestate, and their partners (if any), from screening.

4   For convenience, I will call this child the "birth child," and the parents, the "birth parents."

5   I will not attempt here to summarize my views on the right to reproduce. See Overall (2012, chapter 2). But I believe that the right to reproduce (or more specifically, to engage in certain forms of reproductive behavior) is not the same as a right to a baby; nor is it the same as the right to be a parent.

6   There have been some cases of pregnant men. Since the vast majority of pregnant persons are women, I will use the term "pregnant women," and assume that whatever I say about the education and preparation of pregnant women also applies to pregnant men.

7   A search for relevant material instead turns up studies of ways in which pregnancy and mothering are shaped by the social environment, and advice manuals for pregnant women about preparing for infant care.

8   I use the masculine pronoun for the baby/child only for the sake of avoiding ambiguity in speaking about the pregnant woman and her offspring.

9   Hence the literal appropriateness of the word "procreation" rather than "reproduction."

10   "Although the form of preservation depends upon widely variant beliefs about the fragility and care of the fetus, women have always had a lore in which they recorded their concerns for the baby they 'carried'" (Ruddick, 1980, 348).

11   Colin Macleod raised the question whether a woman who gestates an infant who dies at birth could be automatically licensed to adopt a non-family member child, on the grounds that she has undergone preparation for parenthood. I'm inclined to skepticism about such a possibility, for the following reasons: a) Gestation involves a relationship to a particular child who is now dead. b) Adoption would involve a different child with whom she does not have a prior relationship (although she could develop one). c) In many cases, the adopted child is not an infant, and a child with post-uterine life experience is very different from an infant, so that preparation for parenting such a child would be different from preparation for parenting a child from infancy.

12   This claim is not without precedent in the philosophical literature. It is also made by Anca Gheaus, near the end of her excellent paper, "The Right to Parent One's Biological Baby" (2012, 453), which demonstrates that the forced redistribution of children is not justified: Parents have a *prima facie* entitlement not to have their birth children taken away to be raised by the state or by other parents who might, ostensibly, be superior. The reason is that "expectant parents form a poignantly embodied, but also emotional, intimate relationship with their fetus," which is also (presumably in part) fostered by their "willingness to

take on the costs of pregnancy and their experience of its burdens" (Gheaus, 2012, 446). Gheaus's paper is about justifying the right to parent the baby one gestated, whereas mine is more modest: It simply seeks to provide a bulwark against compulsory formal state screening and licensing of birth parents.

13 Of course, what is "revealed" at these parties is not the gender of the infant but its sex—although arguably the current social importance placed on these events contributes to entrenching the gendering of the future child.

14 Ruddick's observation indirectly draws attention to the fact that pregnant women (and their partners) sometimes fail to receive the psychological, medical, and material support and assistance they need. In order for the experience of pregnancy to serve as an adequate preparation and education for parenthood, sound social support for pregnant women and their partners is essential.

15 Nor am I saying that the experience of pregnancy automatically inoculates women against what might be called 21st-century parental vices—seeing children as vanity projects, as extensions of self, or even as pets.

16 But I am also not suggesting that a woman who does not go through much of this process of education afforded by her pregnancy must *automatically* lose her entitlement to raise her child. There may be reasons far beyond her control (such as wartime conditions, extreme scarcity and deprivation, or violence and abuse) that prevent her from engaging in parts of this process.

17 It is even possible that a very smooth and easy pregnancy and delivery could be misleading if, after such experiences, the parents have difficulty with rearing their child. They may then need further information and help to do a good, or at least adequate, job of caring for him.

18 My argument also has implications for men who seek custody of a child against the will of a birth mother who wants to put the child up for adoption. If such a man is genetically related to the child but was not present during the pregnancy (Shanley, 1995), then his situation is no different than that of any other prospective adoptive parents. He has not qualified for parenthood via a relationship with the woman when she was pregnant. Because he has not had the benefit of the preparation and education that sharing the pregnancy with the birth mother affords, he should be subjected to licensing to ensure his fitness to parent the child. The geneticist view of parental entitlements (according to which a child automatically belongs to a person merely by virtue of the person's genetic contribution to the child's existence) is unsuccessful as a defense against compulsory licensing.

19 Susan Feldman defends "the claims of the gestational mother over the claims of the genetic mother for custody of the child in a contest (*if there is no question of parental unfitness on either side*)" (Feldman, 1992, 98, my emphasis). My point, however, is precisely that the experience of pregnancy itself can provide some evidence of fitness to parent—evidence of a sort that an uninvolved genetic parent, of either sex, cannot provide.

20 The lack of pregnancy preparation on the part of commissioning individuals in contract pregnancy should not be dealt with merely by requiring the commissioners to stay in close connection with the contract mother during her pregnancy. Such persons are not in an intimate relationship with the woman, as a partner or relative would be. Instead, they are the woman's employers. As such, their close proximity to her would increase the likelihood that they would engage in surveillance of her behavior and enforcement or prohibition of certain kinds of activities. This monitoring of her pregnancy could result in serious problems for the contract mother herself, and could also be bad for the future child, since the commissioners may well urge certain treatments for or behaviors by the contract mother that are not necessarily good for the developing fetus (Overall, 2015).

21 Especially not on the basis of irrelevant characteristics of the prospective parents such as marital status, age, sexual identity, or gender identity.

22 Because adoption is a process of relationship development, I believe that, although the procedures could be expedited because the parents already know a lot about parenting, persons who seek to adopt a second or subsequent child would still need to go through the process of developing a relationship with their child before the adoption is finalized.

23 An important difference, in many cases, between becoming a parent via adoption and becoming a parent via pregnancy is that while the latter case always involves a child who is a newborn, the former case can involve a child of almost any age, up to late adolescence. Since a child who has post-uterine life experience (of whatever sort) is very different from an infant with none, it seems plausible that the adoptive parents of a child past infancy might need a distinct and perhaps additional preparation. This is an important way in which the experience of biological gestation and the experience of adoption gestation may be significantly different.

24 This thought suggests the possibility that when an infant is born very prematurely (let's say, more than a month early) there should be special attention to the parents as well as to the infant. Of course the infant will need particular medical care, but the parents may also need special support—not only because they will be worried about their baby's health and well-being, but also because they will have had less chance to undergo the full experience of pregnancy.

Bibliography

Austin, Michael W. *Conceptions of Parenthood: Ethics and the Family.* Aldershot, England: Ashgate, 2007.

Bowcott, Owen. "Brown Apologises for Britain's 'Shameful' Child Migrant Policy." *The Guardian* February 24, 2010. Accessed April 14, 2015. http://www.theguardian.com/society/2010/feb/24/british-children-sent-overseas-policy

Eliot, Lise. *What's Going on in There? How the Brain and Mind Develop in the First Five Years of Life.* New York: Bantam Books, 1999.

Feldman, Susan. "Multiple Biological Mothers: The Case for Gestation." *Journal of Social Philosophy* 23, no. 1 (1992): 98–104.

Gheaus, Anca. "The Right to Parent One's Biological Baby." *Journal of Political Philosophy* 20, no. 4 (2012): 432–455.

Held, Virginia. "Birth and Death." *Ethics: An International Journal of Social, Political, and Legal Philosophy* 99 (1989): 362–388.

LaFollette, Hugh. "Licensing Parents." *Philosophy and Public Affairs* 9 (1980): 182–197.

LaFollette, Hugh. "Licensing Parents Revisited." *Journal of Applied Philosophy* 27, no. 4 (2010): 327–343.

Lindemann Nelson, Hilde. "The Architect and the Bee: Some Reflections on Postmortem Pregnancy." *Bioethics* 8, no. 3 (1994): 247–267.

Lundquist, Caroline. "Being Torn: Toward a Phenomenology of Unwanted Pregnancy." *Hypatia: A Journal of Feminist Philosophy* 23 (2008): 136–155.

Macias Konstantopoulos, Wendy, Roy Ahn, Elaine J. Alpert, Elizabeth Cafferty, Anita McGahan, Timothy P. Williams, Judith Palmer Castor, Nadya Wolferstan, Genevieve Purcell and Thomas F. Burke. "An International Comparative Public Health Analysis of Sex Trafficking of Women and Girls in Eight Cities: Achieving a More Effective Health Sector Response." *Journal of Urban Health* 90, no. 6 (2013): 1194–1204. Accessed April 17, 2015. http://www.ncbi.nlm.nih.gov/pmc/articles/PMC3853176/

Mackenzie, Catriona. "Abortion and Embodiment." *Australian Journal of Philosophy* 70, no. 2 (1992): 136–155.

McLeod, Carolyn and Andrew Botterell. "'Not for the Faint of Heart': Assessing the Status Quo on Adoption and Parental Licensing," in *Family-Making: Contemporary Ethical Challenges*, edited by Françoise Baylis and Carolyn McLeod, 151–167. New York: Oxford University Press, 2014a.

McLeod, Carolyn and Andrew Botterell. "A Hague Convention on Contract Pregnancy (or 'Surrogacy'): Avoiding Ethical Inconsistencies with the Convention on Adoption." *International Journal of Feminist Approaches to Bioethics* 7, no. 2 (2014b): 219–235.

McLeod, Carolyn and Andrew Botterell. "Can a Right to Reproduce Justify the Status Quo on Parental Licensing?" in *Permissible Progeny*, edited by Richard Vernon, Sarah Hannon and Samantha Brennan, 184–207. Oxford: Oxford University Press, 2015.

Overall, Christine. "Reproductive 'Surrogacy' and Parental Licensing." *Bioethics* 29, no. 5 (2015): 353–361. DOI: 10.1111/bioe.12107.

Overall, Christine. "What Is the Value of Procreation?" in *Family-Making: Contemporary Ethical Challenges*, edited by Françoise Baylis and Carolyn McLeod, 89–108. Oxford: Oxford University Press, 2014a.

Overall, Christine. *Why Have Children? The Ethical Debate.* Cambridge, Mass: MIT Press, 2012.

Ruddick, Sara. "Maternal Thinking." *Feminist Studies* 6, no. 2 (1980): 342–367.

Shanley, Mary L. "Fathers' Rights, Mothers' Wrongs? Reflections on Unwed Fathers' Rights and Sex Equality." *Hypatia* 10, no. 1 (1995): 74–103.

Contributors

Jaime Ahlberg is an Assistant Professor of Philosophy at the University of Florida.

Ashli Anda is a Ph.D. Candidate at the University of Illinois.

Michael Austin is a Professor of Philosophy at Eastern Kentucky University.

Samantha Brennan is Professor in Women's Studies and Feminist Research at Western University.

Lindsey Chambers is an interdisciplinary postdoctoral fellow at Stanford University's McCoy Family Center for Ethics and Center for Biomedical Ethics.

Michael Chobli is Professor of Philosophy at California State Polytechnic University.

Russell DiSilvestro is Associate Professor and Chair of the Department of Philosophy at California State University, Sacramento.

Mianna Lotz is Associate Lecturer in Ethics and Applied Ethics at Macquarie University.

Roger Marples is Principal Lecturer in the School of Education at the University of Roehampton.

Colin Macleod is an Associate Professor in Law and the Department Chair of Philosophy at the University of Victoria.

Robert Noggle is Professor of Philosophy at Central Michigan University.

Christine Overall is Research Chair in Bioethics at Queen's University, Ontario.

Marc Ramsay is Associate Professor in Philosophy at Acadia University.

Index